The
Threat

The Threat

**Inside the Soviet
Military Machine**

Andrew
Cockburn

**Vintage Books
A Division of Random House
New York**

For Leslie and Chloe

*Grateful acknowledgment is given to the following for permission
to reprint previously published material:*

Battelle Memorial Institute: Excerpts from Interviews with the A-10 Armament Division, ASD WPAFB, Ohio. Published by Battelle Memorial Institute, Columbus, Ohio. Reprinted by permission.

CBS: Excerpts originally broadcast in the CBS News documentary *The Defense of the United States*. Copyright CBS News. All rights reserved.

Dow Jones & Company, Inc.: Excerpt from "U.S. Arms Used in Lebanon War Outstrip Soviets," August 5, 1982. Reprinted by permission of *The Wall Street Journal*. Copyright Dow Jones & Company, Inc. 1982. All rights reserved.

MIT Press: Excerpt from "Fallows Fallacies" by Dr. William Perry, published in *International Security*, Spring 1982. Copyright 1982 by the President and Fellows of Harvard College and the Massachusetts Institute of Technology.

The Nation: Excerpt from an article by Zhores and Roy Medvedev, January 16, 1982. Copyright 1982 *Nation* magazine, The Nation Associates, Inc.

W. W. Norton & Co., Inc., and Hamish Hamilton Limited (London): Excerpts from *The Liberators* by Viktor Suvorov. Copyright © 1981 by Viktor Suvorov. Reprinted by permission of the publishers.

Random House, Inc.: Excerpt from the introduction, by Bertram D. Wolfe, to *Ten Days That Shook the World* by John Reed. Copyright © 1960 by Random House, Inc.

Stockholm International Peace Research Institute: Excerpt from "Tactical Nuclear Weapons—European Perspectives." © 1978 by SIPRI, Bergshamra, S-17173 Solna, Sweden.

Time Inc.: Excerpt from *Reminiscences* by General of the Army Douglas MacArthur, McGraw-Hill Book Co., © 1964 by Time Inc. All rights reserved.

Excerpts from the PBS documentary *The Red Army*, broadcast on May 6, 1981: Reprinted with permission from "WORLD: *The Red Army*" © 1981, WGBH Educational Foundation, Boston; and Granada Television International Ltd. (London), by permission.

Library of Congress Cataloging in Publication Data
Cockburn, Andrew, 1947–
The threat: inside the Soviet military machine.
Includes bibliographical references and index.
1. Soviet Union—Armed Forces. I. Title.
[UA770.C63 1984] 355'.00947 83-40310
ISBN 0-394-72379-1 (pbk.)

Our government has kept us in a perpetual state of fear—
kept us in a continuous stampede of patriotic fervor—with the
cry of grave national emergency . . . Always there has been some
terrible evil to gobble us up if we did not blindly rally behind it by
furnishing the exorbitant sums demanded. Yet, in retrospect,
these disasters seem never to have happened, seem never
to have been quite real.
—**General of the Army Douglas MacArthur, 1957**

Welcome to the world of strategic analysis, where we program weapons that don't work to meet threats that don't exist.
—**Ivan Selin, Head of Strategic Forces Division
in the Office of the Assistant Secretary of Defense
(Systems Analysis), 1966**

Acknowledgments

In writing *The Threat*, I drew on the time and patience of many people. The debts incurred are more extensive and varied than can be detailed here, but certain salient contributions must be singled out.

I would first like to thank those former denizens of the Soviet military machine who gave hours of their time to recount their experiences in what had been for me, like for most people, a dark and hidden world.

On the American side, it would scarcely have been possible to write this book without the patient analysis, criticism, and instruction unstintingly donated, month after month, by Richard D. Anderson.

Steven Zaloga and David Isby were also more than generous with their time and knowledge. Valuable advice and assistance were similarly provided by Stan Norris, Tom Longstreth, David Holloway, Michael MccGwire, Mark Kushment, Jim Stevenson, Richard Kaufman, Richard Ward, Julian Perry-Robinson, Ulrich Albrecht, Matthew Meselson, Chris Payne, Tom Amlie, Jeff Frieden, Richard Barnard, John Sullivan, and Ron McRae.

There are many others whose assistance, however invaluable, must remain anonymous. They know who they are.

On a more general level I must pay tribute to Pierre Sprey for giving me an indispensable education on how to look at defense issues, and for making available many of his public briefings on modern weapons, east and west.

Since *The Threat* had its genesis as a documentary film, *The Red Army*, for WGBH-TV Boston, I also owe thanks to all who assisted and encouraged me in that endeavor, particularly David Fanning, my executive producer.

My agent, Andrew Wylie, originally persuaded me to think of writing this book and has remained a constant source of encouragement throughout.

Jason Epstein, my publisher and editor at Random House, never allowed criticism to outstrip encouragement, guiding me through the process with intelligence, insight, and care.

To be published by Random House meant that I was also the beneficiary of the conscientious labors of Beverly Haviland, who guided me through the tortuous transition from manuscript to printed page.

My copyeditor, Tatiana Ivanow, had a sharp eye for a solecism. Shirley Baker of Rat Race Typing performed valiantly, typing far into her evenings and weekends.

Fred Kaplan read the manuscript and thus sponsored numerous improvements and corrections.

Alexander, my brother, not only reviewed portions of the manuscript in successive stages of formulation but also allowed me to turn large areas of his apartment into a paper-strewn study for months at a time.

My wife, Leslie, read and criticized the book in all stages of production, encouraged me when all seemed dark, sustained me when the project seemed endless, and conducted on my behalf several interviews crucial to the enterprise.

Contents

x   **Contents**

Part I

Perceptions

One

The View from
Lenin's Tomb

A popular item for tourist shoppers in New York City is a poster originally designed as a cover for *The New Yorker* magazine by the artist Saul Steinberg. It depicts the world, or at least the West, as seen from the blinkered perspective of a Manhattanite. Most of the foreground is taken up by Ninth and Tenth Avenues, bordered by the Hudson River. New Jersey gets a good deal of space; but beyond that, the Middle West is vaguely defined, with obscure places such as Nebraska given uncertain location. The hump of California is depicted with more confidence, bounded on the other side by the Pacific Ocean, dotted with some nameless islands against a distant backdrop of China and Japan.

The same tricks of perspective might be usefully employed to show the Western perception of Soviet Russia as a military power. The foreground would be occupied by a jumble of enormous missiles, a great number of tanks, and rank upon rank of uniformed automata, marching in unbroken phalanxes past Lenin's tomb, on which are perched a row of stern-faced elderly men wearing medals and fur hats. In the background, interspersed with further acreage of missiles and tanks, might be rows of factory chimneys, which would denote the presence of industrial enterprises, churning out armaments at top speed and serviced by an underfed and gloomy population, whose needs are subsumed to the dictates of militarism. In the picture, the tanks, missiles, and guns, as well as the mighty fleets off the coast of this menacing land mass, would all be pointed our way.

At least for the foreground of this picture, little artistry would be necessary. Mere photography would suffice. On November 7 of every year, the Soviet government itself goes to great trouble to lay on a tableau of men, tanks, guns, and missiles and allocates exactly 45 minutes to march it through Red Square in the center of Moscow to give its own people and the rest of the world a vivid image of Soviet military power. "No matter how often one has seen this seasonal ritual," wrote Dusko Doder of the Washington *Post* after the 1981 display, "one cannot escape the feeling of awe."

Awesome it is, not just because of the size and quantity of the weaponry rolling across the cobblestones at 25 mph. As impressive are the sense of dedication and commitment conveyed by the impeccable drill and formation of the marching troops, drawn from every section of the armed forces; the evident pride of the tank commanders saluting from turrets of their tanks; and the ease with which enormous rockets, designed to travel thousands of miles through outer space, negotiate the downtown streets of a modern capital.

It is the threat represented by this parade which breathes life and energy into the five-sided headquarters of the

American armed forces across the Potomac from downtown Washington, which keeps busy the production lines in the aircraft plants of Texas, Long Island, and California, the tank factories of Ohio and the Ruhr, and which justifies the 42.6 percent of the American Federal budget that goes for defense.

The present leadership of the Soviet Union, which has diligently followed the custom of imparting a martial tone to the celebration of the state's most important anniversary—the October Revolution of 1917—knows about war in a way that most Western governmental leaders do not.

Egyptian President Gamal Abdul Nasser once advised Third World leaders headed for Moscow to get themselves briefed about the details of World War II on the Eastern Front, "You must resign yourself to hearing over and over again about the experiences of your interlocutors in the 'Great Patriotic War.'" The Soviet leadership appears to do its best not only to keep that memory fresh but to shade martial reminiscenses into the contemplation of another conflict. In the early seventies it began the practice of having small children stand guard at war memorials, holding real automatic rifles in their hands, schoolchildren who also participate in the nationwide series of Zarnitsa ("summer lightning") and Orlenok ("little eagle") military games, boy-scout-type exercises with weapons and real-life military tactics.

These little soldiers will be constantly reminded in the classroom and through media of the constant need for vigilance in the face of the military threats facing Soviet power, and sooner or later they will become aware of the extent to which Soviet society is itself organized on a warlike basis. If, for example, any of them should grow up to be a truck driver, he will know that his truck carries two sets of license plates, one civilian and one military, the latter for use in the event of mobilization, when the truck itself will be "called up" and sent to execute its allotted military task. If the children are destined to become factory workers in any one of the 3,500 defense-related plants in the USSR, they will know that it is officially forbidden to speak about their employment outside of work hours. In the city of Omsk, for example, workers at the enormous Factory 13, which employs 30,000 people in the manufacture of armored vehicles, are supposed to pretend, according to someone who once worked there, they they are engaged in making "cookware, toys, and other assorted household goods."

Whatever their future careers, the small boys stamping up and down in front of the war memorials will know that at the age of eighteen they will disappear into uniform for two or three years, to serve in one of the five branches of what in Russian is called in its totality *armiya* (or "armed forces"). The five branches are the ground forces, the strategic rocket forces, the troops of national air defense (or PVO as they are often called, after the Russian name *Protivovozdushnaya oborona*), the air force, and the navy. The eighteen-year-olds may even be drafted into one of the two other armies maintained by the Soviet Union: the troops of the State Security Committee (KGB), which guard the frontiers, and the internal security troops of the Ministry of Internal Affairs (MVD), which are responsible for putting down internal disorder.

Even after the draftee has served his time, he will still be part of the military, required to keep the new uniform issued to him just before his discharge ready at home against a call-up into his reserve unit, a call-up to which he is liable until the age of fifty.

The chances are that wherever our draftee has served, he will be ignorant of much basic information on the size and deployment of his country's armed forces; he will also be ignorant of the nature and even the name of any weapons system apart from the ones with which he has been directly concerned. Military secrecy is taken very seriously in the Soviet Union, and facts and figures available to any literate Westerner with access to a library are denied to all but a small circle within the Soviet military and civil leadership. It should not be surprising that in a country where travelers are admonished for taking pictures of railway stations, the weapons that are paraded with such pomp and publicity through Red Square are nameless as far as the native population is concerned.

Military attachés and observers—representatives of the U.S. armed forces and the armed forces of the NATO countries—watch keenly at the November 7 display for an innovation in the weaponry on show that the Soviets might have decided to let them see. Although they are incomparably better informed about Russian armaments than the Muscovites crowding Red Square, their knowledge is by no means complete, and what they do know is the result of an accumulation of data over many years by an enormous intelligence apparatus. Yet the picture they have built up and passed on to the public in their own countries, particularly in America, is frightening enough.

It is a picture of a country geared for war, with an army of 180 divisions, compared to a total of 19 in the U.S. Army and Marines combined; 1,398 land-based intercontinental missiles, compared to 1,040 in the United States; 50,000 tanks, or almost ten times as many as are in the U.S. arsenal; 350 submarines of all types, compared to 121 in the U.S. Navy; and a large civil defense establishment where the United States has next to none. Furthermore, while America gives the appearance of being merely the first among a group of contentious equals in the North Atlantic Treaty Organization, the Soviet Union can dispose of the 53 divisions manned by its Warsaw Pact allies, all of whom use standard Soviet equipment and are trained to fight according to Soviet tactical doctrine.

Reports from professional students of the Soviet military effort are no less gloomy about trends for the future. From sources as diverse as satellite photographs of the parking lots outside tank factories, published Soviet economic statistics, and assumptions about how hard a Soviet munitions worker might work, they have concluded that the Soviet Union spends more and builds more than America. As many as 2,500 tanks a year pour out of Soviet tank plants, along with 1,300 new fighter planes and 50,000 new antiaircraft missiles a year. All this at a steady rate, changing little except in a constant and upward direction. In military terms, it would seem, all the changes over the past generation have been in favor of the Soviet Union. Whereas twenty years ago the fledgling strategic rocket forces had only the most meager means of striking at the United States, they can now, as all agree, inflict crippling blows on their enemy. The Soviet navy, which twenty years ago was little more than a coastal patrol service of limited potential, can and does now cruise the oceans of the world.

The business of filling in the details of the Soviet threat, the existence of which has shaped American defense policy for thirty years, is a complex and exacting affair. This assessment has always proceeded with what might be considered a commendable sense of caution on a "worst-case basis." In other words, it is taken for granted that in the case of any doubt on the matter, "threat assessment" should always assume the worst.

The constant pessimism expounded by high U.S. and allied defense officials derives not only from this worst-case analysis but from facts on allied military preparedness readily to hand. Satellites and other such appurtenances of intelligence are not needed to reveal that Soviet factories turn out 2,500 tanks a year, while the U.S. tank program is producing only 700 tanks a year, and that the newest nuclear missile-firing submarine, the Trident, entered service almost three years late. It is a matter of record that the troops to man these weapons can be induced to serve only by the granting of massive pay raises or as an alternative to unemployment and that when they do serve, their educational attainments border on the illiterate and their bodies are polluted by drugs. More broadly, the NATO allies are loath to spend more on defense. Neutralism is growing in Western Europe. Grappling with these problems, U.S. policymakers could be excused for envying the men on Lenin's tomb gazing at the immaculate echelons pounding through Red Square.

There are many factors that affect the balance of power between the Soviet bloc and the West—economic, social, political, and military. But it is the *perception* of the military balance by Western analysts that shapes our own defenses and determines how much we spend and where and on what we spend it; it is the true shape and scope of Soviet military capability that concerns us here in this book. For the sake of argument, it might be useful to disregard the vexed matter of Soviet intentions and to assume, instead, that the Soviets are indeed bent on world domination through forcible means. Perhaps they would like to invade Europe in a blitzkrieg attack, to cripple the West by occupying the Middle East oil fields, and to knock out America's land-based missiles with a preemptive strike. The important question is perhaps not about their intentions but their capabilities. Could they do it?

As they survey the Taman and Kantimir Guards divisions parading through Red Square, do the Russian leaders feel the same confidence in their own military strength as hundreds of speeches and articles by American military leaders indicate they should? Generals look at their enemy's strengths and their own weaknesses, and these men are well aware of some of their country's own weaknesses and the strengths of the United States and its allies. They know, for example, that the immaculate troops beneath them in the square are from parade divisions, which spend much of the year practicing in their camp at Alabino, outside Moscow, and consequently receive very little battle training.

They must compute the numbers of their own forces conservatively, while erring on the side of caution in computing the numbers arrayed against them. The Soviet leadership is all too conscious of the fact that the United States and its allies face only one threat—the USSR—while the Soviet Union, on the other hand, must consider a series of threats. General Mikhail A. Milshtein was specifically authorized to tell the audience in a CBS-TV interview in June 1981 that the Soviet must "take into consideration the United States. We have to take, unfortunately, China's nuclear possibilities. We have to take French and British nuclear forces. We have to take into consideration NATO countries."

So, if we reverse the perspective of Saul Steinberg's poster and look at the world from the point of view of the Russian military leaders, we see the following picture. Immediately in front of them are the Eastern European allies: Poland, Czechoslovakia, the German Democratic Republic (East Germany), Hungary, Bulgaria, and Rumania, all linked by treaty in the Warsaw Pact alliance. But after thirty years, the gulf between the Soviet Union and its closest allies is very large. The Russians even write in a different script, which is why they face the problem of their troops getting lost in exercises on allied territory because they cannot read the road signs. Although linked to their allies by a land frontier, the Russians cannot even transport troops and supplies westward by train with any ease. This is because of the discontinuities of nineteenth-century railroad construction, which resulted in Russia laying its railroad tracks with a broader gauge than those in Europe. Trains must stop on the border to have their axles changed.

The Warsaw Pact allies are, of course, subservient to Moscow. The policies and even the personnel of their governments are ultimately subject to Soviet veto. But the Warsaw Pact is scarcely cohesive. In thirty years, the Soviet troops have had to intervene three times to keep an ally loyal: East Berlin in 1953, Budapest in 1956, and Prague in 1968. In 1981 the Polish armed forces had to take control of their government and declare martial law in order to forestall another exercise in alliance building on the Russians' part. The government of Rumania not only refuses to take part in joint exercises with other armies of the Warsaw Pact but has even allowed its Ministry of Defense to raise cash by selling weapons acquired from the Russians to American intelligence.

Even with the most compliant members of the Warsaw Pact, it is no easy matter to achieve a common stance on simple matters such as defense spending. Marshal Ustinov had to make a great many journeys to Budapest in 1977 and 1978 to get the Hungarians to make even a modest increase in their contribution to alliance costs.

The territory this unstable alliance must defend is vast. As the Russians tried to point out in *The Threat to Europe*, a pamphlet issued for Western European consumption in 1981:

The armies of the Warsaw Pact countries have a territory of 23,500,000 sq. km. to defend, out of which 22,500,000 sq. km. are Soviet territory. This is more than the area of the United States, Europe, and China combined; the Nato armies have only 2 million sq. km., or one eleventh of that area to defend.

The pamphlet went on to stress some other facts of life brought on in part by the circumstances of geography:

Faced in the west by the Nato bloc, which includes three nuclear powers, the Soviet Union is simultaneously exposed to danger in the east from two American Pacific nuclear fleets and from China with its growing nuclear potential and the world's most numerous army. Furthermore, the deployment of US naval nuclear forces in the northern sector of the Indian Ocean within reach of southern regions of the Soviet Union combines with the string of US military bases stretching from the Mediterranean across the Middle East to Pakistan and countries in Southeast Asia. In effect, the Soviet Union is compelled to reckon with the likelihood of a blockade being put up around it. This is being made increasingly apparent, among other things, by the growing political and military cooperation between the United States and China.

In authorizing the release of this statement, aimed at cultivating neutralist sentiment in Western Europe, the Kremlin leaders had no need to distort the realities of the world situation as they see it. In their Steinbergian view, the Soviets have every excuse for considering themselves beleaguered by a series of menacing concentric circles. On their immediate western national border, a number of subservient states are nominally under their control but wracked by internal dissent. Outside these states lies the ring of unfriendly powers armed with nuclear weapons. Not only do the British, French, and Chinese maintain bombers and missiles that can reach the territory of the USSR, but there are also American-made nuclear weapons under the partial control of Belgian, Dutch, West German, Italian, Greek, and Turkish forces.

Beyond this threat to the homeland from bordering states, the Russians contemplate four American fleets: one in the North Atlantic, one in the Mediterranean, and two in the

Pacific. Each fleet has aircraft carriers with nuclear bombers on board. The Russians also know there are 33 American nuclear submarines that patrol the Atlantic and the Pacific, each submarine carrying enough warheads to wipe out every Soviet city with a population of a million or more. They see an American buildup in the Indian Ocean. The island of Diego Garcia is prepared for a squadron of B-52 nuclear bombers, and already an American carrier task force with nuclear bombers capable of reaching the southern Soviet Union is permanently based in the Indian Ocean. The United States itself, isolated and protected by the oceans, contains the 1,020 intercontinental ballistic missiles (ICBMs) and the 331 intercontinental bombers under the Strategic Air Command, poised in their silos and on runways to send nuclear warheads and bombs to designated targets in the Soviet Union.

These are military problems, the immediate concern of the men charged with the defense of the Soviet Union. But there are other, less tangible, factors to be reckoned with when weighing the forces arrayed against them. The daily bread of the Soviet people must come, in part, from countries outside Soviet control. Despite the investment of billions of rubles, the country's agricultural sector still cannot deliver enough grain for the nation's needs, and year after year its leaders must turn to the capitalist West to make up the deficiency: Canada, Australia, Argentina, and the United States itself, their most powerful adversary. An increase in the number of rockets, planes, or tanks can make little difference when it comes to this strategic weakness.

More vague, and yet all pervasive, is the Soviets' sense of competing on unequal terms with the United States. In addition to the disadvantages imposed by history and geography—land frontiers with adversaries, the fact that all the major ports in the western Soviet Union are landlocked, the short growing season in the grainlands—the Soviet Union must struggle as a backward society against the world's most advanced economies.

The gross national product of the USSR is only two-thirds that of the United States, and yet the Soviet Union attempts to match American defense efforts. As the technology of weapons becomes increasingly complex and expensive, the Soviets try to match this too. Although they can point to an enormous investment in research and development, a program they have followed since the 1930s, the Soviets still cannot match the achievements of Western technology. It is true that the Americans looked on the success of the Sputnik in 1957 with foreboding and some envy, but the heyday of propaganda triumphs for Soviet science is more than twenty years in the past. If there is envy now, it is on the Soviet side. When in the early 1970s the Soviet computer engineers wanted to develop a new computer, the authorities felt it safer to order them to build an exact copy of the IBM 360, itself eight years old at the time. Nikita S. Khrushchev dictated his memoirs on a West German tape recorder. Brezhnev had a stable of expensive Western cars, including a Cadillac and a Lincoln Continental. It is Soviet power the Soviets celebrate on November 7, but after the parade the military elite goes home to apartments equipped with choice Western appliances, such as Japanese stereos or West German coffee makers, as indeed do their U.S. counterparts.

But Soviet leaders cannot equip their arsenal with American or West German weapons. They must develop their equivalents themselves, and thus far, it has been a struggle to catch up. The United States developed the atom bomb in 1945, while the Soviets achieved the same thing four years later. The United States had an intercontinental strategic bomber by 1948, while the Soviet version appeared in 1954. The Americans deployed their first nuclear-powered missile-firing submarine in 1960, eight years before the Russians could. Nine years elapsed between the time the first U.S. missile that could carry more than one warhead appeared and the year the Soviet Union achieved the same result.

Perception is something that cuts both ways. Our perception of the Soviets is of an aggressive military power, while our perception of ourselves is of a country and an alliance requiring military forces only to deter this aggression. Throughout the 1970s, American strategists' view of Soviet intentions became progressively gloomier. In July 1977, Richard Pipes, who was later appointed to President Reagan's National Security Council, published the article "Why the Soviet Union Thinks It Could Fight and Win a Nuclear War" in *Commentary* magazine. Pipes's conclusion was partly based on the assumption that Soviet losses in such a war might be perfectly acceptable: "as of today the USSR could absorb the loss of 30 million of its people and be no worse off, in terms of human casualties, than it had been at the conclusion of World War II." His view is by no means unique. Analyses of both Soviet military literature and intelligence data on the increasing accuracy of Soviet missiles have produced the widespread impression that the Soviets are indeed thinking of a preemptive first strike that could win a nuclear war.

The Russian perception may be different. The most comprehensive official presentation of their side of the story came in January 1982, when the Ministry of Defense in Moscow published a glossy booklet entitled *Whence the Threat to Peace*. In 78 pages the pamphlet details the size of the U.S. armed forces and their location, the number of U.S. bases overseas, the size of the U.S. military-industrial complex, and the planned expansion of U.S. forces. It emphatically declares, "The United States of

America is developing and widely advertising various military-strategic concepts of an undisguisedly aggressive nature . . . their main idea invariably centers on unrestricted use of the US strategic offensive forces in a pre-emptive strike against the USSR. The notion that a nuclear war is winnable recurs in all US strategic concepts ever since the 1950s."

Such a bleak view of U.S. intentions could easily be dismissed as Kremlin propaganda, except that it is supported by the evidence of handbooks issued by the Pentagon itself. U.S. Army Field Manual FM-287, *The Tank and Mechanized Infantry Company Team*, published in February 1980, baldly states, "The U.S. Army must be prepared to fight and win when nuclear weapons are used." Similar sentiments are to be found in many other military publications intended for perusal by the troops.

American ICBMs have, in theory at least, an accuracy far greater than is needed for any Soviet target save Soviet hardened ICBM missile silos. Such accuracy is unnecessary for any purpose but a preemptive first strike.

Constructing a Russian view of the world and the forces with which Soviet armed forces must contend requires no access to hitherto undisclosed information, merely a different perspective. Leaving aside the propagandistic aspects of the Russian summation of the military balance, the pamphlet *Whence the Threat to Peace* serves as a reminder that the United States is a formidable military power, amply underscored by the graphic illustrations depicting U.S. warplanes and ship flotillas pouring across the oceans from the eastern and western shores of the United States, American bases ringing the Soviet Union, and strategic missiles and bombers advancing on the USSR (pictured in a vivid chart entitled "Concept of Operations of U.S. Strategic Offensive Forces on the Basis of Major Military Exercises 1970–1980").

There is, however, a curious aspect to this pamphlet on the threat posed by the West. All of the illustrations are from either U.S. Department of Defense sources or the Western press. All the facts are taken from unclassified documents released as a matter of course by the Pentagon or through the Congress. This raises an important point: the Soviet picture of U.S. military power differs only in its conclusions from the picture the Pentagon likes to present of itself. U.S. military leaders would not agree with the Russian statement that "an approximate military balance has arisen, and is being steadily maintained, between the USSR and the USA." The justification for the current spurt in U.S. defense spending is predicated on the assumption that the United States is falling behind. Nor would American military planners agree that "for more than three decades the United States has been building up its war machine and initiating successive arms race spirals for anything but defensive purposes." The U.S. Army, on the other hand, would be more than happy to endorse the Soviet description of the new M-1 Abrams tank as having "almost twice the combat capabilities of the M-60 tanks now in service." The U.S. Air Force would be delighted to subscribe to the Soviet contention that "the C-5A Galaxy military transport plane ... [has a] range with full load of 100 tons, of over 6,000 kilometers." The U.S. Navy would be similarly pleased to hear that the F/A-18 Hornet fighter-bomber has an "action radius of 740 kilometers."

The only thing wrong with these descriptions is their inaccuracy. According to information unwillingly yielded by the U.S. services, the M-1 tank is almost certainly inferior in combat capability to the M-60 tanks it is replacing. It breaks down three times as often, and it requires twice as much gas. It has thinner armor in certain places and has exactly the same gun but carries less ammunition. The C-5A will not be able to carry a "full load of 100 tons" under any circumstances, until its wings have been strengthened at a cost of $2 billion, and even then, it cannot fly farther than 4,200 kilometers (2,604 miles), not 6,000 kilometers (3,720 miles) as alleged by the U.S. Air Force and reiterated by the Russian Ministry of Defense. Similarly, the Soviets have found it convenient to double the actual ComSat radius of the F-18, in reality not 740 kilometers but just over 380 kilometers.

In producing *Whence the Threat to Peace*, with its glossy rendition of U.S. military proficiency, the Russian military was merely returning a favor. In October 1981 the Pentagon had issued its own pamphlet, *Soviet Military Power*. This too was a glossy effort filled with richly colored illustrations. It depicted the global reach of the Soviet armed forces and the enormous size of their missiles, the proficiency of their most modern tanks, and the improvements in their navy.

Once again, the intention was to depict a military force of which its architects could feel proud. Unmentioned is the fact that the Soviet T-64 tank, which *Soviet Military Power* describes as "the most sophisticated of their modern family of battle tanks," has had to be taken out of production. There are severe problems with the track and engine, both of which continuously break down, and the automatic gun loader, which has a tendency to load the gunner, not the shell. The report indicates that "while small by comparison to the US Marine Corps, the Soviet Naval Infantry is the second largest marine force in the world." It does not mention that the Soviet marine force is one-fifteenth the size of the American equivalent. Moreover, the Soviet force is not the second largest marine force in the world but the fifth largest.

At first glance, the process by which both superpowers inflate the military threat posed by the other might seem to be an understandable, if dishonest, procedure. It does, after all, help generate funding and public support for the resources needed to fight each other. But there is another explanation for superpower behavior. It may be that the military on either side is engaged not so much in an arms race as in simply doing what it wants to do for its own institutional reasons. The other side is relevant only in that it serves as a convenient excuse for these unilateral activities.

Traditional rationales for the arms race present a more straightforward view of military buildups on either side. We are accustomed to the idea that one side develops a weapons system which is then countered by the other side, leading to a response and so on in an upward spiral of sophistication and cost. In fact, with some exceptions, the pattern of defense development for the past thirty years shows no particular connection of cause and effect between what the Russians do and what we do, or vice versa.

The main exception lies in the strategic area, and on the Russian side. Historically, the succeeding generations of Soviet jet fighters appear to have been designed as a response to the American strategic bomber threat. Thus, the MiG-15 subsonic fighter appears to have been built to shoot down the American B-29 and the MiG-17 to shoot down the B-36 nuclear bomber. The MiG-19 and MiG-21 came as a response to the faster and higher-flying B-47 and B-52. When the U.S. Strategic Air Command showed clearly that it would send the B-52 into Russia at a low rather than a high altitude, the Russians produced the low-level interceptor called the Su-15.

This sequence aside, there is very little actual evidence that either the Americans or the Russians have actually initiated research and development of a particular defense system in response to a move by the opposition. At its simplest, the process can be illustrated by the rates of production of weapons by either side over the past quarter century.

In the early 1950s, the Russians had a massive warship-building program, which fell away sharply in the middle of the decade and has remained at a relatively constant level ever since, apart from a small surge in the early 1960s. A line on a graph depicting U.S. naval construction activities over the same period appears to show a totally independent process. U.S. shipbuilding activities were down sharply in the early 1950s, up again in the late 1950s, and thereafter zigzagging up and down to the present day. If one looks at similar charts of production for aircraft and tanks, the same lack of correlation is also apparent.

Now we know that on the U.S. side at least, every increase in production was publicly justified by the proclaimed need to match an increase in Soviet efforts, an increase which on mature examination usually turned out not to have occurred. In the Pentagon publication *Soviet Military Power*, great play is made of the numbers of tanks produced by the Russians—3,000 a year. However, Soviet tank production has declined, overall, since 1970, when it was 4,500 a year. Since the U.S. Army is planning to increase its own tank production in supposed reaction to the Soviet efforts, it might be expected that the Soviets would in turn step up their own activities. But in fact, in recent years they have been diverting an increasing proportion of their tank production to the export market in order to generate hard currency. Almost half the combat aircraft produced in the Soviet Union between 1974 and 1982 were exported abroad (5,310 out of 11,430).

Almost invariably, the development of a new weapon or an expansion in production is justified as being simply a response to some initiative on the enemy's part. But the record indicates that the desire for the new weapon or a longer production line comes first; only afterward is the threat discovered that the weapon is supposed to meet.

This is by no means an unprecedented situation, peculiar to the Cold War. In the early 1920s, the British Royal Air Force wanted to proceed with an expansion of its airfields. Unfortunately, the only country that British planes had the range to reach at the time was France. The RAF accordingly postulated the strong possibility of a war with France and proceeded to construct a string of bases along the southern coast of England. As things turned out, this was a lucky move. When the Germans occupied France in 1940, a contingency in no way anticipated by the RAF, the British found they had a large number of airfields from which to fight the Battle of Britain. While the British were considering the French threat, the U.S. Navy, anxious to expand its fleet, postulated a maritime threat from Great Britain as an excuse for doing so.

A telling case of the same process in Soviet weapons development today lies in the story of the MiG-25. It began in the late 1950s, when the U.S. Air Force announced plans to develop a new strategic bomber that would be able to bomb Russia from a height of 70,000 feet at more than twice the speed of sound. The new bomber, called the B-70, failed its tests and was canceled by the Eisenhower Administration in 1960. But at the same time, the Soviet national air defense service and the Mikoyan-Gurevich Design Bureau (which develops MiG planes) wished to build a new interceptor that would fly higher and faster than any previously had been able to do. Using the threat of the B-70, they were able to get the authorization to proceed with this costly project. The cancellation of the American bomber in no way interfered with the Soviet endeavor, which emerged some years later as the MiG-25.

In the mid-1960s, the U.S. Air Force began planning

for a new fighter. Just as development was about to begin,
the Soviets unveiled the MiG-25, whose claimed performance in altitude and speed was used in Washington as a
justification for funding the proposed fighter, because,
Congress was told, the MiG-25 threat had to be confronted.
Thus, the MiG-25, code-named Foxbat, was the subject
of enthusiastic endorsements from U.S. defense officials.
The Secretary of the Air Force, Robert C. Seamans, called
it "the finest interceptor in the world today." The Secretary
of Defense, James R. Schlesinger, said that it represented
such a qualitative leap for the Soviets "that we might have
to reappraise our entire approach to the strategic technological balance." The F-15 got its appropriations from
Congress before reality intruded in 1976.

That year, a Soviet air defense force pilot, Lieutenant
Viktor I. Belenko, defected to Japan with a MiG-25. When
the plane was examined by American experts, it turned
out to be something less than the superweapon previously
depicted. It radius of action was one-third that which the
Americans had believed it to be. The top speed had been
described as Mach 3.3 (3⅓ times the speed of sound).
Belenko, however, reported that MiG-25 pilots were told
to fly no faster than Mach 2.5 for fear of melting the
turbines.

To complete the circle, it had become clear by the end
of 1981 that the F-15 developers, in their desire for Mach
2.5 speed, justified by the performance characteristics
falsely ascribed to the MiG-25, had built a fighter with
seriously compromised performance at Mach 1, the speed
at which actual flights take place. Designing an engine
that could operate at very high speeds, they ended up with
one that did not work very well at any speed. Thus, the
Air Force was forced to "detune" the engine so that it
could continue to operate, although it now makes only
two-thirds the speed originally envisaged.

This pattern of behavior was once summed up by Ivan Selin, who in the 1960s was head of the strategic division in the Pentagon's Office of Systems Analysis. Greeting members of other departments who came to hear him discuss his subject, he would say, "Welcome to the world of strategic analysis, where we program weapons that don't work against threats that don't exist."

The career of the Soviet Backfire bomber provides a particularly egregious example of a process by which assessments of enemy forces are tailored in order to provide justification for domestic weapons programs. This medium-range bomber was first unveiled by the Soviets in 1970. By the end of 1983, they had built fewer than 230 copies. But in spite of these modest numbers, the Backfire has been cited simultaneously by the U.S. Air Force, the U.S. Navy, and European NATO forces as a dangerous threat requiring increased funding for weapons to counter it. The U.S. Air Force has been looking for appropriations to refurbish and modernize the air defenses of the continental United States, a flagging industry since the 1960s. Although the Backfire does not have the intercontinental range to make a round trip to the United States, it has helped give the North American air defense branch a multibillion-dollar shot in the arm. The Backfire, the interested parties claim, could perform suicide missions.

Meanwhile, the U.S. Navy sees the Backfire in quite a different role. The Navy is anxious to maintain its own costly aviation program, including F-14 fighter planes at $35 million apiece, loaded with six $2 million Phoenix missiles. The Backfire, says the Navy, carries Kitchen missiles, which are designed to hit ships. Thus, the Backfire's "naval aviation" role justifies the high cost of the Navy's fleet of F-14s with the attached Phoenix missiles, both of which predate the Backfire.

Yet another role for the Backfire has been outlined by the NATO command and by the branch of the U.S. Air Force dedicated to moving the cruise missile into Europe. The Backfire, in this case, is a critical part of the Soviet tactical nuclear forces trained on Europe, which justifies the modernization of Europe's nuclear deterrent. The U.S. Army also takes great interest in the Backfire threat to Europe, as it makes a clear case for spending billions of dollars on the Army-run Pershing II nuclear missile to base it in Germany.

We know that the threat of the Backfire bomber is used by different branches of the U.S. military because the United States is a relatively open society. The Joint Chiefs of Staff and other national security officials are required to state periodically why they feel the need to build particular weapons systems or make particular dispositions with their forces. Thanks to an abundance of public record and an occasionally diligent press, as well as the accessibility of people with inside knowledge of Pentagon transactions, we can get some idea of what motivates our military apart from the desire to defend the nation.

For the same reason, we often know more about the efficiency of American weapons and forces than the Pentagon and weapons builders care to tell the public. We know that the F-18 range is only half of what it is officially meant to be; we know about the shortcomings of the M-1 tank; and we know that the C-5A cannot as yet carry its designated load. Although public knowledge may be hazy on details, the plethora of stories in the press and on television about shortcomings in our military has conveyed the impression that all is not well.

This impression promotes skepticism about the competence of our soldiery, which the military naturally does not appreciate. On the other hand, it helps reinforce the

message, endlessly repeated, that we are militarily outclassed by the Soviets. We know that the United States is
not as strong as it can be made to look on paper. But in
the case of the Soviet Union, the paper is all we normally
have to go on. In the words of Dr. Herbert York, former
director of Defense Research and Engineering at the Pentagon, "all our estimates of the military balance are based
on the assumption that Murphy's Law does not operate in
the USSR." It is not surprising that this should be so. As
Dr. York pointed out to me, "Generally speaking, the
people who have the most access to the data, who perform
most of the strategic and operations analysis which are
behind these exaggerated estimates, are people who in
some way benefit from a strong, vigorous, let's say over-
blown Western military research and development program."

It may be easy to suspect that official estimates of the
threat are determined by the straightforward greed of the
defense interests, but it is a far more difficult task to
challenge these estimates. We are conditioned to think of
the Soviet Union as, in Churchill's words, "a mystery
wrapped in a riddle inside an enigma." The Russians publish no Defense Posture Statements, issue no General Ac-
counting Office reports, and testify before no Congressional
Armed Services and Appropriations Committees. Information of the kind published in *Soviet Military Power*
supposedly has been collected only by employing thousands of agents and analysts, unimaginably sophisticated
photosatellites and electronic listening machines, and billions of dollars. It is the conclusions reached through this
process and selectively broadcast to the public that govern
all debate about the scope and price of U.S. defense, and
even if we suspect that the conclusions are being doctored
to fit the schemes and fiscal aspirations of the defense
community, there are no independent satellite reconnais-

sance services or electronic intercept facilities to draw on for an alternative conclusion.

The mystique of modern weaponry further compounds the problem. The pace of military technology is depicted as advancing so fast that yesterday's wonder weapon is supposed to be rendered obsolete by today's innovation. The process has become so refined that defense officials can and do claim without fear of incredulous contradiction the date on which a weapons system that has not yet been put into service will become obsolete.

Looking at Soviet defense, therefore, involves enlarging Churchill's aphorism: we confront a mystery wrapped in a riddle inside an enigma bound up in high technology. Unwrapping the mystery, however, is in many ways no different than discovering the reality behind Saul Steinberg's distorted vision of the view westward from midtown Manhattan. It is a matter of looking at some maps and talking to people who have been there.

Two

Looking at the Soviets

For half a lifetime, Cyrus R. Vance sat at the apex of the U.S. national security apparatus. As Secretary of the Army, Deputy Secretary of Defense, and Secretary of State, he was privileged with access to the innermost secrets of the vast American military intelligence-gathering apparatus. His "top secret" and higher clearances entitled him to hear and read the analyses of Soviet military power derived from such sources as spy satellites of the National Reconnaissance Office, the code-breaking and other communications interception facilities of the National Security Agency, and the espionage activities of the Central Intelligence Agency, as well as the similar efforts of the Defense Intelligence Agency and its related service offshoots. The conclusions of this omnivorous information-gathering machine remained basically unchanged over the decades: the military power of the USSR, to which all other activities of the Soviet state supposedly were subordinated, presented a clear and growing threat to the security of the United States.

The cost of accumulating, sifting, and refining all this disparate intelligence for the delectation of decision-makers like Vance has been and remains an official secret, but it is probably on the order of about $15 billion a year. In 1982, after he had retired from public office, Vance had occasion to take a $3 cab ride across midtown Manhattan. His driver was a recent Soviet émigré, one of the thousands of Soviet Jews who were allowed to emigrate and settle in the United States during the 1970s. Like most Soviet males, he had had to serve a two-year draft period in the armed forces between the ages of eighteen and twenty, and it was his experiences in a tank unit during that time that formed the burden of the conversation with his distinguished passenger. It was Vance's first opportunity to hear a description of the Soviet threat from the inside, and it was very different from what the secret intelligence briefings had been telling him all along. Vance was surprised to hear that the living conditions of the men were deplorable and that the training for the crews was exiguous at best. It sounded like a very different Soviet army from the one depicted by the intelligence briefers over the years.

On the face of it, the over-the-shoulder recollections of one cab driver should be of little weight compared to the product derived from America's multibillion-dollar intelligence investment. The sheer size of the effort is awesome. When a Soviet missile lifts off from the pad at Tyuratam in Central Asia on its 4,000-mile flight down the Siberian test range, the American listening posts in Turkey and China can monitor its progress almost as easily as the scientists who launched it. Through satellite photographs, U.S. Naval intelligence analysts can monitor the construction of a new cruiser at the Zhdanov Shipyard in

Leningrad almost rivet by rivet. Promotions, new postings, and retirements of all senior Soviet military officials are monitored and filed. Even the idle chitchat of Russia's ruling Politburo over car radiotelephones has been intercepted and recorded, as are the conversations of Soviet air force pilots on routine training flights far inside their country's borders.

Contemplating this impressive array of sophisticated and expensive information-gathering techniques, one finds it easy to believe not only that the assessments of U.S. national security policymakers about the Soviet threat are based on irrefutable evidence, but that it is impossible for the researcher unendowed with such facilities to pursue independent inquiries. The most that can be done is to sift through the information released by the agencies for facts that may amplify or possibly modify the official conclusions.

This mystique of high-technology intelligence-gathering needs to be put in context. Satellites can watch over enemy territory with an ease that would have been unimaginable before the Space Age, but they still cannot see through clouds. This is why, for example, the output from the tank factory at Kharkov in the Ukraine is regularly listed as 500 tanks a year in unclassified intelligence publications. Through a meteorological quirk, Kharkov is covered by clouds most of the time, rendering the specialists in watching Soviet tank production effectively blind as to the scale of the plant's operations. "That is why they give the figure of 500," one former intelligence official told me. "It's the number they use when they don't know if it is zero or 1,000."

Reliance on the wonders of high-technology intelligence techniques can be counterproductive in other ways. In the early 1970s, when it became known that the Soviets had developed a new tank, called the T-72, the U.S. Army "tasked" the intelligence agencies as a matter of the greatest urgency to find out the precise diameter (properly known as caliber) of its cannon. Was it 122 millimeters, which was already a standard caliber for large Soviet cannons, or 125 millimeters, which would mean it was an all-new gun firing an even heavier shell. At a reported cost of $18 million, satellites, radio-listening stations, and code-breaking computers were specially deployed in order to determine the vital question of the 3-millimeter difference. The limitless resources of U.S. technical ingenuity were to no avail, and it was only when America's British allies resorted to more old-fashioned espionage methods that the mystery was solved.

A British army team was reportedly able to infiltrate a Soviet tank-storage depot in East Germany, measure the gun, and depart with a copy of the tank's operating manual, which they discovered in the vehicle. The operation cost $400, the price of a replacement lock for the depot gate to keep the Soviets ignorant of the mission.

But even the $400 turned out to have been needlessly spent. A French military attaché stationed in Moscow mentioned to his Soviet liaison that he was particularly interested in the new T-72 and asked if it would be possible to have a look around. The Soviet officer was delighted to oblige, giving his friend a guided tour of the tank and its 125-millimeter gun, with a free dinner besides.

In the absence of help from guileful British officers or convivial Frenchmen, the intelligence agencies are frequently forced to resort to conjecture in the solution of high-priority questions. Conclusions arrived at by this method derive their authority from the accumulated mystique of the satellites and other mysteries of modern espionage. By 1982, for example, the imminent appearance of the new Soviet T-80 tank in operational service had been heavily advertised by U.S. military spokesmen. The

Pentagon's *Soviet Military Power* gave the following description, accompanied by an illustration: "The T-80 tank, now in experimental production, is the third, new class of tanks with markedly improved firepower, armor and mobility produced by the USSR in recent years, a weapons system underscoring the across-the-board Soviet quest for quantitative and qualitative weapons superiority." Yet in March 1982 a U.S. Army general revealed that such confident statements about the weapon's fearsome capabilities were derived from pure guesswork. The admission occurred during a Congressional hearing before the House Armed Services Committee in an exchange between Samuel S. Stratton, a veteran and somewhat cynical representative from New York, and Army Major General James P. Maloney.

Stratton: Let me ask you another question. Does Santa Claus really exist? Is this tank a real tank or is this a notional tank?

Maloney: The T-80, sir?

Stratton: Yes.

Maloney: The T-80 at this time is more than notional. We believe it is beginning to come off their production lines.

Stratton: But you haven't seen it and you don't have a picture of it?

Maloney: That is correct, sir.

Stratton: You don't know how it is configured [meaning what it looks like].

Maloney: We have indications generally of how it is configured, but we don't have any detail on it.

Stratton: It is kind of hard to figure on that basis.

Maloney: May I explain how we estimate what the tank is capable of doing. We get the best tank experts in four of the NATO countries, including our own, to independently come up with their estimate of what the T-80 is going to be like based on extrapolations of what we have seen the Soviets do in the past. We then merged these four studies together to come up with our composite estimate of what the T-80 will be. So, you know, it is not just based on whimsey.

It should perhaps be pointed out that the purpose of Maloney's testimony was to solicit funds for American tanks, the better to meet the threat of the T-80.

Pressed as they are by the military and other customers in the national security apparatus to come up with hard and fast answers to momentous questions, the intelligence agencies must use this kind of extrapolation in other areas. The CIA is unable to discover how many intercontinental ballistic missiles the Soviets are producing annually. Rather than confess their failure, the analysts have decided to extrapolate from what they do know, which is the number of missiles the Soviets have deployed in holes in the ground—information which satellites can supply. They then calculate the relationship between the number of *American* missiles deployed in silos and the number produced in the United States each year and proceed to apply the same ratio to arrive at a Soviet production figure. It is not quite pure whimsey but not exactly a hard and fast figure.

Even at the best of times, high-technology intelligence-gathering techniques cannot be expected to supply answers to many questions about the Soviet military machine. These intangibles include the preeminent subjects of Soviet strategy and tactics, morale and indiscipline within the forces, policy toward the Warsaw Pact allies, and a host of other factors which determine the effectiveness of a military force as much or more than the configuration of its weapons.

In the popular imagination, this kind of "human intelligence" is obtained from secret agents implanted in the heart of enemy territory; but over the years, the Soviets have shown that they are extremely good at defending themselves against this kind of penetration. In fact, much of the early emphasis on "scientific intelligence," such as the U-2 spy-plane program of the 1950s, grew out of frustration at the lack of alternative sources of information about what was going on behind the Iron Curtain. There have been occasional coups, such as the enlistment of the senior Soviet military intelligence officer Oleg Penkovsky in 1961 (the CIA actually rebuffed his first approach on the suspicion that he might be an *agent provocateur*), but Penkovsky was a rare exception. The CIA and other agencies have been able to garner a great deal of information from people who have left the Soviet Union forever, either illegally, like the fighter pilot Viktor Belenko, or legally, like Cyrus Vance's taxi driver and the thousands of other émigrés who came to United States in the 1970s. Defectors and émigrés, however, are obviously able to report only on what has happened in the past. For ongoing reports about the activities of the Soviet military, the intelligence agencies can turn to an invaluable but mundane source— literature in the form of books, newspapers, and magazines published by the Soviets themselves.

It may seem strange for supersecret espionage agencies to get their information from newspapers, but unglamorous though it may be, that is where much of their "secret" data are to be found. The former CIA employee Frank Snepp provides a revealing anecdote in his book *Decent Interval* about the fall of Saigon. As the North Vietnamese army tore southward in their spring 1975 offensive, the CIA was very much concerned about discovering the Communists' ultimate objective: were the North Vietnamese aiming merely to occupy a large portion of South Vietnam and then negotiate from strength, or were they actually trying to take Saigon and the rest of the country in one grand slam? Despite its enormous resources, the CIA experts were unable to solve the riddle until General Van Tien Dung did it for them by sending his tanks smashing into the capital of the defeated republic. But, as Snepp records, the answer had been available all along, since the North Vietnamese had spelled out their intentions in their Party newspaper before the invasion. Unfortunately, the CIA's copy had been held up in the mail until it was too late.

The Soviets publish a deluge of information about their own military affairs. There are 11 major military journals and newspapers, a host of minor and more specialized publications, and as many as 500 books on the subject issued every year. Certain subjects are usually taboo, particularly the physical characteristics and shortcomings of modern Soviet weapons, but in other ways the Soviets can be surprisingly frank about lapses in discipline, training, and petty corruption, as well as current and sometimes conflicting views on tactics and strategy. In addition, the newspapers provide the main source of information about promotions and postings in the upper ranks of the Soviet military.

Krasnaya zvezda (Red Star) is the largest and most important military newspaper. It is published daily by an institution called the Main Political Administration of the Armed Forces of the USSR. Unlike any Western defense organization, the Soviet Armed Forces include an entire branch—the Main Political Administration—which is devoted to ensuring the Marxist-Leninist ideological orthodoxy and education of the officers and men. Since its political officers have their own chain of command, they provide a separate channel of information for the supreme military and Communist Party leadership about what is going on down below. Thus, to a limited but important extent, *Krasnaya zvezda* is independent of the military structure about which it reports, which is why it is often so revealing about shortcomings.

All these disparate sources—satellites, spy planes, radio-listening posts, defectors, émigrés, books, and newspapers—provide a staggering amount of information. The National Security Agency alone has to burn 40 tons of excess material a day just to make room for more of the endless streams that continually flood in. The entire effort represents a triumph of human organization and ingenuity; the uses to which it is put are another matter.

Most intelligence "facts" about Russia, or anywhere else for that matter, are totally meaningless by themselves. Before they can be made to assume a coherent pattern, they must be analyzed and put in proper context, and such a process of analysis is not and cannot be objective. The teams of analysts who interpret the various facts must have some general idea of the conclusion they expect to reach before they start. In the intelligence business, while the raw data flow up from the bottom, the conclusions are sent down from the top. Inexorably, the data become adapted to gibe with preordained conclusions and assumptions.

This official overview has remained unchanged since the early Cold War era, when President Truman declared: "The Soviet Union and its colonial satellites are maintaining armed forces of great size and strength in both Europe and Asia. Their vast armies pose a constant threat to world peace."

Augmenting and complementing this attitude is the assumption that the Soviet military machine actually operates like a machine, with each and every one of its myriad parts deliberately designed to function the way it does, responding with perfect efficiency to the directions of the controllers. *Soviet Military Power*, published with the express purpose of alerting U.S. and Western European public opinion to the ominous extent of the threat, neatly summarizes this point of view in its section on Soviet military organization:

The key point to understand about the Soviet military control structure is that the reins of the instruments of state policy and power—not just the purely military—are in the hands of a tested political leadership supported by very experienced and long-established staffs. These men, aided by...lesser but equally experienced subchiefs of the military and industry, know how the Soviet military machine runs and what they want to achieve. They are able to marshal all available Soviet resources toward their strategic objective. They exercise absolute control of all instruments of Soviet power.

Richard D. Anderson, who has had plenty of time to contemplate the subject both as an analyst of Soviet military policy for the CIA and a staff assistant to the House Intelligence Committee, points out that this way of looking at the Soviets has far-reaching consequences for the way in which intelligence is collected and assessed:

If you believe that the Soviet Union, particularly the military, is a monolith comprised of millions of clones efficiently executing plans and orders sent down from the Kremlin, then details become less important. You don't have to be too interested in evidence of political conflict within and between the army high command and the Party leadership because you *know* that the Party is in total control, and that there are no politics in our sense of the word to be found in the Soviet Union. For example: If you find that they are building an anti-aircraft missile which appears on the face of it to be totally useless, you don't assume that someone over there has made a gigantic goof-up, you conclude that they are up to something particularly devilish and cunning.

If, on the other hand, you suspect that the Soviet military is like any other human organization in history, including our own defense department, with at least its fair share of screw-ups, inefficiency, cover-ups, waste, internal conflicts and rivalries, and all the rest of it, then details become very important because you know that what really goes on inside their military organization is probably different and more complicated than the public image it presents.

Details that illustrate the kind of malfunctions referred to by Anderson are collected by the intelligence apparatus as a matter of course, but they receive progressively less prominence in the summaries and analyses that work their way up the ladder to the decision-makers in the Pentagon and other high places. At the very top, things can become very simplified indeed.

According to the October 1981 edition of *Armed Forces Journal International*, Defense Secretary Caspar W. Weinberger had taken to briefing President Reagan on complex defense matters with the help of cartoons prepared by the Pentagon graphics department. Information about the differing sizes of various strategic nuclear forces, for example, was conveyed to the Commander in Chief by means of a chart showing different-sized mushroom clouds.

It is to the lower-level professionals in the intelligence community and the military services at large, men whose assessments of the enemy have not been clouded by political considerations, that one must turn for detailed insights. Men like Anderson, whose apartment is dominated by tottering piles of Soviet military newspapers and magazines, and who can discuss the most subtle shifts and turns of Soviet military politics with unbridled enthusiasm for hours on end. Even without access to data flow from billion-dollar listening posts, Anderson's $55-a-year subscription to *Pravda* and *Krasnaya zvezda*, supplemented by intuition and a prodigious memory, affords him the means to trace in startling detail what is going on inside the heavily guarded recesses of the Kremlin and General Staff headquarters. Such matters are not of course discussed by these papers in straightforward terms, but such obscure clues as the order of signatures under an obituary, a new face in a picture of a Kremlin reception, and a suggestive allusion in an article about a half-forgotten episode in Soviet military history enabled him, in the spring of 1981, to determine that Brezhnev had just concluded a thorough purge of the Soviet ground forces high command, including its commander in chief, an epochal event which had totally escaped the notice of the richly endowed Defense Intelligence Agency (see Chapter 4 for details).

There are many others who share Anderson's concern with the minutiae of the Soviet military apparatus, men like David Isby, a former war-game designer and Congressional aide, who is happy to dwell at length on the reasons why the Russians might have scaled down the production of a modern tank in favor of building more of an older model. There are enough examples of such people to make a rule: anyone with an open mind who has had occasion to pay close attention to the way the Soviet military goes about its business in any particular area will usually conclude that the threat in that instance is probably misinterpreted and inflated. Experts in fighter-plane design point out that the latest Soviet fighters are big (and therefore easily visible to an opponent), heavy, complex, hard to fly, and sluggish. U.S. Air Force and Navy instructors in fighter tactics remark on the apparently limited training and unimaginative tactics of their putative adversaries. Submarine commanders, who know from experience the preeminent importance of silence to a submarine's survival, question the effectiveness of the impressively big but noisy Soviet boats. An ordinary GI serving in an army unit that specializes in simulating Soviet tactics for exercise purposes, a man who will never be asked to testify before Congress or brief the President, sums up what one might call "the professionals' attitude": "A lot of people think that they all look like Hercules, y'know. They have just as many problems as we do with their army." A fellow soldier, standing beside him in equally grimy fatigues in the middle of the Fort Hood army base in Texas, chimes in: "Since I've joined the army, I've learned quite a bit about them and their capabilities and I don't see any problem with them at all."

The professionals with the most direct experience and insight of all are the officers and men of the Soviet armed forces. Western researchers are effectively discouraged from conducting on-the-job interviews, but as Cyrus Vance discovered, it is now possible to talk to men who have for a while been serving members of what military briefers like to call Threat Forces.

No one knows exactly how many Soviet veterans there are in the United States, but the number runs into the thousands. They have come here as part of what is called the Third Wave of emigration from Soviet Russia, the first having occurred after the 1917 October Revolution and the second after World War II. This latest wave started in the early 1970s and showed signs of tapering off by the end of the decade. It was prompted by a variety of factors, primarily détente and the worsening domestic situation of Soviet Jews following the 1967 Mideast war. As a result, tens of thousands of Jews, distinguished solely by race from their erstwhile fellow citizens (Jewish culture and Orthodox Jewish religious practices have all but disappeared in the USSR), crossed into the capitalist West. Most of them settled in Israel at first, but by 1975 emigrants were increasingly choosing the United States as their destination, a country offering them easy entry, working papers, and the prospect of prosperity. Some Jews were able to get their exit visas from the authorities only with great difficulty, and such cases received widespread and deserved publicity in the Western press; some were never allowed to leave. The vast majority of people who applied, however, were able to leave quite legally, with a minimum amount of fuss. These were ordinary working people who had never met a New York *Times* correspondent or attended an illegal demonstration.

Like most waves of immigrants from a particular country, the people of the Third Wave have tended to cluster together in communities in the major American cities—Los Angeles, Baltimore, and New York. The New York area has the main concentration, and within the city most of the émigrés have settled in a section of Brooklyn called Brighton Beach, just along the oceanfront from the roller coasters and amusement arcades of Coney Island. By 1982, the pervasive influence of 30,000 former Soviet citizens living in this area had earned it the local nickname of Little Odessa. Shop signs along Brighton Beach Avenue are often in Russian script, and the customers in them count their small change in kopeks, the Soviet equivalent of a cent. The restaurants serve delicious Russian dishes to customers drinking vodka in Russian quantities, and in winter the sidewalks are crowded with people wearing the distinctive fur hats of their homeland.

Contrary to widespread belief, Jews are not exempted from military service in the Soviet Union, nor, having served, are they precluded from emigrating for more than a few years at most. Like all other healthy eighteen-year-old males in the Soviet Union, they are liable for their obligations under the 1967 Law of Universal Military Service, and so they are involuntarily dispatched in varying numbers to one of the five Soviet military services—strategic rocket forces, troops of national air defense, air force, ground forces (army), or navy. They may even find their way into one of the two other Soviet armed forces that are manned by conscription: the KGB border guards or (though this would be unlikely for Jews) the MVD internal security troops. Even if a young man receives a deferment at eighteen because he is attending college, he will still be obliged to take an ROTC-type course and then possibly serve a two-year stretch as a junior officer after he graduates.

Before the days of large-scale Jewish emigration, witnesses to the inner workings of the Soviet military were rare, and the occasional defector was regarded as a prize catch for the intelligence agencies. The thousands of such people who started pouring through Rome, where would-be U.S. immigrants are processed, in the 1970s were obviously a windfall for the agencies, but they were also an embarrassment of riches. Émigrés who have occupied extremely interesting and sensitive posts during their service recall interrogators who hardly spoke Russian (at the time émigrés reach Rome, very few speak much English). Even when easy communication is possible, the questions tend to concentrate on such topics as the designation, physical description, and names of the commanding officers of the émigré's former unit. This reflects what one former U.S. Army intelligence officer calls "the military intelligence obsession with 'order of battle,' meaning what enemy units are where, and what weapons they have and where they are kept. Things that can be quantified. Less quantifiable stuff like training, unit morale, or race relations receive little if any attention."

A lot of the émigrés escape even this cursory examination. Enders Wimbush, who undertook his own survey of Soviet ex-servicemen for the Rand Corporation on a Defense Department contract, considers that "about 20 per cent of the relevant emigrés who pass through Rome are 'flagged' as deserving further attention, of which no more than 5 per cent are ever followed up."

Once they have settled in the United States, in Brighton Beach or elsewhere, these émigré veterans change addresses or jobs, just like most other American citizens and residents. There is no central file in the hands of the CIA or anyone else of where they are to be found. Hence, an ordinary unofficial researcher is not much worse off when it comes to tracing them than any government agency, however important. Locating them is simply a matter of patience, luck, and the benefits that accrue from being in touch with a close-knit and friendly community of people who are happy to pass along word of a researcher's interest. The inexpensive classified advertisement sections of the émigré Russian-language press are a quick way of gaining access to a world that most Americans imagine to be hidden deep behind the Iron Curtain, invisible to all but the probing cameras of the satellites circling far overhead, the world of the Soviet military.

No amount of study of intelligence assessments, classified or otherwise, can duplicate the insight that comes from talking to Sashas, Igors, Genadys, and Vladimirs about the lives they lived in bases and garrisons on the Chinese frontier, at antiaircraft missile sites on the coast of the Baltic Sea, or at an arctic radar station. Through their conversation, the mysterious entity against which the United States and its allies have been arming themselves on a scale unequaled in these countries' peacetime history suddenly comes alive, turning from an impersonal machine into an organization of good, bad, and indifferent human beings who behave in ways that are both familiar and unfamiliar to us all.

These young men—there are veterans of all ages to be found, but for a study of the modern Soviet forces, the ones who served during the 1970s are the most relevant—are not of course absolutely typical of their contemporaries back in Russia. They are Jews, one of the 90 or so minority nationalities to be found in the Soviet Union. They are privileged because by an accident of birth they were allowed to leave the USSR and have free and unrestricted entry into the United States. This does not mean that they carry with them a peculiar bias by virtue either of being Jewish or having fled from their homeland. The same themes recur so often in their accounts of their military experiences that it seems unlikely that there could be a Jewish bias, coloring and distorting the true picture of military life to a uniform degree. The young men exhibit no nostalgia for the military, although in some instances there is regret for the civilian life they have left forever. The émigrés come to the United States in the belief that a better life inevitably awaits them. However, some, particularly those who lack a marketable technical skill or who find it difficult to learn English, come to agree with what they used to read in the Soviet press about unemployment, insecurity, and crime being the dominant facts of life in America.

The former defenders of the USSR have little to say that is to the credit of Soviet military organization and efficiency, but their stories are rendered all the more believable because the raconteurs are unconscious of their effect. The Soviet military is the only one these men have ever experienced, and because they have no point of comparison beyond what they read in the newspapers and see on television, they assume that it is indeed as potent a threat to the security of the United States as the Pentagon asserts. They note that the United States has no draft; they see no men in uniform on the streets of American cities, unlike in the Soviet Union, where they are omnipresent. They hear constant statements from the nation's leaders that the United States is becoming inferior to the Soviet Union, and they believe it.

It is in this context that the former Soviet soldiers describe their personal experiences: how often they were allowed to practice with their weapons, the number of times their radar set broke down, how often they got punished for indiscipline, and how easy it was to get drunk. Introducing a survey based on such stories, Colonel Robert Bartos of U.S. Army intelligence wrote: "Despite the fact that the Soviet Army projects itself as the best equipped, largest tactical and strategic military force in the world . . . Western analysts can now speculate whether the man of steel has entrails of straw." It is, the colonel concludes, "a brutal insensitive world where the military ethos is still locked in the eighteenth and nineteenth centuries."

Part II

People

Three

The Unfortunates

Anyone traveling across the Soviet Union by train in early summer or late fall will see long trains full of young men passing up and down the lines. These youths are the product of the spring and fall roundups of fresh conscripts for the Soviet armed forces. All males are liable to service once they turn eighteen, but to simplify matters, the authorities simply draft men whose birthdays fall before July 1 in May and June and those born after that date in November.

In the course of a year, 1.8 million youths file onto those trains, because that is the amount of human raw material needed to keep the five services, as well as the KGB border troops and the MVD internal security forces, up to strength. The coordination of this gigantic twice-yearly migration involves a massive organization, which on paper at least is attuned to picking the right men for the right jobs. As we shall see, it does not always work that way.

Every district in the Soviet Union has a local office of the military commissariat, an institution akin to the old U.S. draft board. Each office holds dossiers on all the male teenagers in its area, providing details about each young man's ethnic, social, and political background, as well as details about his health, school record, and character references. When the time comes, the relevant youths will be herded together to wait for the arrival of what are called the *pokupateli*, or "buyers," officers from various units and branches of the services who travel around the districts accumulating their quota of fresh recruits. Theoretically, such officials should carefully examine the dossiers of the draftees and select the ones best suited to their unit—the intelligent youths with good political backgrounds for the air force and strategic rocket forces, the less intelligent but physically strong and healthy ones for the navy, and so on. But for a busy officer who is enjoying a rare chance to get away from his unit, which is most likely stationed well away from any civilian center, more rough-and-ready methods are often preferable.

Take the case of Genady, a smart and articulate thirty-year-old who now lives in an elegant apartment in Brooklyn. He was born and raised in a suburb of Leningrad and has the lofty attitude typical of the people of that city toward lesser breeds, such as Muscovites or Ukrainians. By date of birth he had been liable to the fall 1973 call-up, and he had heard a rumor that there was a strong chance that he might end up in the navy. The prime drawback to being selected for that service or for the coast-guard branch of the KGB border troops is that the term of service is not two years but three, and Genady had no desire to serve that long. Luckily for him, his mother worked at one of the big Leningrad hospitals and had

connections who could arrange a spurious medical certificate that earned him a six-month deferment.

The following May he was instructed by mail to report
on a particular day to the local commissariat, which was
on one side of a city square. When he got there, he found
several hundred young men milling about, while officers
in the uniforms of the various services circulated through
the crowd. The young men looked as nervous as he felt;
older brothers and friends who had already served their
time had graphically described the rigors of service life.
By and by, one of the officers approached Genady and
asked him if he had good school grades in technical subjects. When Genady replied that he did, he was brusquely
ordered to join a group of a dozen or so silent and appre-
hensive-looking youths standing in a corner of the square.
Similar groups were forming in other corners as the other
buyers made their selections. "It reminded me," says
Genady, "of a slave auction that I saw in a movie once.
Anyhow, that is how I became a member of the troops of
national air defense."

When Genady's buyer had collected about 60 recruits
in this fashion, he marched them off to the train station.
It was the last time Genady was to see his hometown for
two years, yet there was no opportunity to say goodbye
to parents or friends.

"The train was the worst kind, with hard wooden seats,
and there were armed guards on board to make sure we
didn't jump off. We were on it for two days, along with
a lot of other people they picked up in other parts of
Leningrad, and no one ever told us where we were going.
We got colder and colder, because it had been warm and
sunny in Leningrad and we were all wearing summer
clothes, but we were traveling very far north." Finally,
they pulled into Murmansk, the great port on the Barents
Sea well inside the arctic circle.

"We were ordered off the train and made to form into two lines. Then they told us to start running. After 2 or 3 miles we came to the barracks, where they sent us straightway to the bathhouse. Immediately after the steam bath, they gave us a haircut, in fact they pretty well shaved it. Then we had to hand over all our clothes, in fact, everything except for soap and toothpaste and shaving things. They even took my cologne to stop me drinking it, which I found is a pretty common thing. We were given uniforms, though of course they didn't bother with finding the proper size, just threw it at you, so mine was three sizes too big. Before we put it on, we had to sew a white strip of cloth inside the collar, so they could tell if your neck was clean. I had heard about this before and I had brought a strip of white plastic with me, so I didn't have to wash my collar all the time."

Other accounts of how the Soviet draft selects and divides its intake project the same impression of a haphazard process. Of course, some men escape the process altogether, either by faking a more permanent disability than Genady's putative ailment or resorting to bribery. A posting to the staff of a military commissariat is regarded as a highly desirable posting among regular officers, not just because it offers the chance of a reasonably relaxed life in a city or town, but also because there is a chance to make considerable sums of money. One veteran summed up the situation bluntly: "One can easily bribe people at the recruiting office. In the USSR, you can do anything with money. You can bribe to delay your service or to avoid it altogether. Doctors can be bribed to give a medical deferment. Everything connected with conscription can be bought and sold." Sometimes the bribe is in kind rather than in cash. An émigré told the Rand Corporation interviewers of a fellow recruit from Azerbaijan, in the far south of the USSR, who had entered the service at a later age than his comrades because he had bribed the military commissar of his district to avoid service. "The first time it cost him 12 sheep. The next time he came up to be drafted, the price was raised to 24 sheep, which he couldn't pay. So he was drafted."

All this sounds very different from the ruthlessly efficient military machine that threatens the security of the United States and the West. In fact, it sounds like an exaggerated version of the old U.S. draft system, in which youths could avoid the rigors of service and possible combat in Vietnam by faking medical disorders or making use of an affluent background as a means to a college deferment, which was more subtle than handing over a dozen sheep to the local draft board but had the same effect. On the other hand, the U.S. forces never attempted to deal with widespread draft evasion with a method reportedly used in some remote parts of the Soviet Union. One man, who served in a construction battalion, a unit given no combat training and simply used for unskilled building work, related the following bizarre story. "Sometimes they would simply fly a military helicopter around in the mountain regions. It would land in one place and they would look around, see a guy of approximately military age, and just take him. Because of this, one guy was brought to our construction battalion who was actually an Iranian citizen. He had crossed the border in the mountains— some of them don't even know that a border exists there— and they caught him and put him in service, although he had no passport and no papers. He served with us for a year and a half before they got it straightened out. It happened because one time when an officer was discussing something and using a map, the guy said, 'I think that is my region there. . . .' I think they sent him back."

Once a Soviet draftee has put on his uniform, willingly or unwillingly, he will spend the next two years (three years if the navy or the KGB coast guard has got him) shut off in a world that is remote and incomparably harsher than the life he has known at home. He has little or no official opportunities to see his family, meet women, go to a movie, visit a restaurant, or even leave the base. When Genady finally flew home at the end of his stint, he thought he had landed in the wrong city because they had built a new airport in Leningrad while he was away. He was unaware of this because during all that time he had never seen a hometown newspaper.

The regulations do indeed lay down that every soldier is entitled to ten days' leave during his two years of service, which is still exiguous compared to the Western practice of giving enlisted men about thirty days' leave in the course of a year. But very few Soviet soldiers actually get their ten days, except as a reward for outstanding service.

This policy of keeping the troops isolated is easier to enforce because most Soviet bases are well away from any city or even small town, but Genady's ultimate destination was the remotest of all. After six months of specialized training at a base several miles outside Murmansk, he was sent on to an early-warning radar station on the island of Novaya Zemlya, a region so remote that the Soviets use it for nuclear testing. There he spent the next 19 months, one more than he should have because the ship carrying his replacement was held up by bad weather. During all that time, he received mail from home precisely three times.

Genady could not go AWOL because if he had, he would have frozen to death. But for soldiers posted to less far-flung regions, any excuse or opportunity to leave the base is eagerly sought and exploited. Grigory, a burly cab-driver from Moscow, reminisced in his kitchen in Queens, New York, about the prolonged and intricate intrigue which ultimately secured him the job of camp projectionist for his army base in Estonia. This was a uniquely privileged position, since it allowed him to make the 30-mile journey into Tallinn, the capital of Estonia, in order to pick up new films and, more profitably, to carry on trade in food and alcohol on behalf of his comrades.

If a man lacks the guile or luck to get off base, not only does he see nothing of the outside world, he is never alone. Fifty years ago the American and other Western armies used to house their men in enormous dormitories, where they had no opportunity for privacy. Nowadays, an American enlisted man can expect to share a room with only one or two other men; but for the Russian, little has changed. In fact, we know exactly how much the personal space allotted to each man has been enlarged since 1905. That year, a Captain Falls of the U.S. Army visited a barracks outside Moscow and carefully noted that each man was allocated 1½ square meters of living space, an area slightly less than the size of a coffin. Nowadays, according to Dr. Richard Gabriel's exhaustive researches and calculations, the allocation stands at 2 square meters— only slightly more than an average-sized coffin.

The *kazarma*, as the Russians call it, is home, under-heated in winter and stifling in summer, with 50 to 100 men packed into tiered rows of bunks. The lavatories are likely to be outside, even in places where the temperature falls to 20 below in winter, and the hot-water supply in the washrooms is unreliable. Dr. Gabriel, who, as a former army officer himself, writes with feeling about the importance of adequate washing facilities for combat troops, goes so far as to declare that "there is a giant toilet shortage in the Soviet military that is shared by all soldiers."

Overcrowding is a way of life for most Soviet civilians, so the fact that émigrés remember the conditions of their military service as being especially confined indicates just how bad these conditions can be.

Crowded and confined at night, the soldiers are closely supervised during the day. Between reveille at 6:00 A.M. and lights out at 10:00 P.M., the day is given over to an unremitting program of training, physical exercise, and political indoctrination sessions. There is of course time out for meals, 30 minutes for breakfast and supper and 40 minutes for lunch, but these meals sound as if they provide only the barest sustenance and no gastronomic pleasure whatsoever. Everyone complains about the food, describing it as unappetizing, unvarying,' and inadequate. Very little of it is fresh, apart from potatoes, and the staples are *kasha*, a kind of porridge, and dried fish or salt pork. One survivor reported having been served dried fish for supper every night for *two years*.

Alex Rantinor did not have to eat the food. He was an officer, a short-term lieutenant drafted in August 1973 for two years after he had finished his college course, and so he could have enjoyed the somewhat more appetizing fare in the officers' mess. But in his unit there was a small charge for the officers' meals, and he was sending every kopek of his salary home to his wife and infant daughter, who was ill with a heart condition. So he sometimes ate with the men, and he remembers the experience with bitterness six years after he left the army and three years after he came to America in a vain effort to get treatment for his ailing child. "The whole year round they are fed on rotten potatoes, and even in summer they are not given fresh vegetables. Much of the food is canned, but the men don't even get the full amount because the soldiers who work in the kitchen steal it and pass it on to their friends. The quartermasters and supply officers steal as well. This is why you can sometimes see soldiers on the march stopping their tanks and scattering into the fields for vegetables or fruit in the gardens. I can remember them doing this when the fruit was unripe, so they all got quite ill."

Rantinor recalls a particularly vivid example of the inadequacy of the men's normal diet. At one point his platoon, a unit of about 30 men, got the regular assignment of going into town to fetch supplies from a depot. After a short period of access to the resources of the civilized world outside, the men grew plump and healthy-looking, distinguishable at a glance from their less fortunate brethren, who were still subsisting exclusively on army rations.

Sometimes the men rebel against their spartan diet. A veteran who served in the Soviet Far East as a communications specialist in 1969–70 described how soldiers would go on a food strike: "When we were given meat we would put it under the table, because of a very strong smell, which was impossible to stand. These cases [of food strikes] happened pretty often, both during training and in operational units. According to the regulations, such an incident is considered to be an emergency incident, and Moscow should know about it." In this particular unit, however, the commander would bring military police and threaten to open fire. Then he would threaten to convene a tribunal [a form of ad hoc court-martial empowered to issue draconian punishments on the spot]. Finally, he would give in and order a new meal to be cooked. "This happened maybe 15 times," according to this particular veteran, during the 18 months he served with the battalion.

Official Soviet statistics provide some interesting confirmation of the inadequacy of the military diet. Young men between the ages of eighteen and twenty are still growing fast. In the West the average male gains 12 pounds in this period, while his Soviet contemporary, who will be doing his military service during these particular years, gains only half that amount.

Army food does not have to be delicious, especially in

a conscript force, but soldiers do have to be strong and healthy enough to fight. The military authorities' disinterest in the Soviet soldiers' diet and the corruption of the kitchen and supply staffs may have a direct effect on the army's combat prowess. Dr. Gabriel made a special study of the various kinds of illnesses contracted by émigrés while in the service: 65 percent reported that they or someone in their unit had contracted running sores, acne, dental problems, night blindness, oversensitive eyes, or eye infections. All these are almost invariably linked to a vitamin-deficient diet, and none of them, particularly night blindness, could be welcome in a unit of fighting troops.

The soldiers who do manage to leave the base, like Grigory the projectionist or Rantinor's men, and thereby supplement their diet, do not buy the extra supplies out of their pay. A Soviet conscript is paid next to nothing—3.50 rubles a month, which is the rough equivalent of $6.50. A first-term volunteer in the U.S. Army, by contrast, gets paid $573 a month, plus allowances for housing and other expenses. Since a pack of cheap cigarettes can cost 50 kopeks (half a ruble) and the soldiers have to buy their own cleaning equipment, there is little or nothing to spare out of their meager stipend for luxuries like food. This is not to say that a Soviet soldier does not have extra cash, simply that whatever he has either comes in the mail from home or is obtained by stealing and selling state property.

Theft from the state is widespread in all areas of Soviet society. In 1973, Yekaterina Furtseva, the Minister of Culture and a member of the ruling Politburo, was discovered to have built an enormous country house for her daughters out of materials belonging to the state and with labor paid for by the state. The same year, *Izvestia*, one of the major newspapers, actually admitted that one-third of all the privately owned cars in the country were being driven on fuel pilfered from the state.

It is hard to find a former draftee prepared to reminisce about his own thefts of military equipment, but all can remember someone else in the unit who stole. "Fur-lined winter helmets for tank crews are in great demand among civilian motorcyclists, or anyone who has to work in the open," a former tank officer remembers, "so that the moment they were issued, any platoon commander who knew his business would take them and hide them under his mattress or in some such safe place. Otherwise they would quite certainly be stolen and sold by the men."

The consensus among former soldiers is that guns and ammunition are off limits for the most part, since these are closely guarded and stealing them is a capital offense. Otherwise, anything goes. The standard protective suits for use in case of attack by chemical weapons are made of rubber and command a high price from Soviet fishermen. Gasoline is ready to hand and always assured of a market; travelers in East Germany can sometimes see Soviet soldiers who have sneaked out of their barracks hawking a few cans from the side of the road. One man who served on the Chinese frontier recalled an indignant old woman who turned up at the camp one day. She was a dairy farmer, and an enterprising soldier had sold her a consignment of what he claimed was the very latest in automatic milking equipment. The farmer was now demanding her money back because the equipment had failed to extract any milk from the cows, which was not surprising, since they were gas masks.

Westerners, accustomed to thinking of the Soviet Union as a law-and-order state par excellence, may find it hard to accept that crime could be such a serious problem, especially where the country's defenses are concerned. Yet these not atypical comments by a former antiaircraft radar specialist indicate the contrary.

It's simply not true that the Soviet Army is powerful. It's all stupidity . . . if a soldier is supposed to guard the store and, since he's only human, he wants to sleep, he will go into his booth. At this someone who needs spare parts, tires for example, will go into the stores and steal what he needs. The crew of the vehicle will discover that they have no wheels. If war were to start now, such deficiencies would become apparent in the Soviet Army. In the unit where I served, for example, I had a radar. According to regulations I should have had two of them. But only one of them actually worked, and then only half the time. Why? Because the officers in my unit liked to drink, and to get extra money, and how are they going to get it? They would immediately think of selling spare parts. What kind of parts? Cables, various generators for the radar, various kinds of radio equipment which is in short supply in civilian stores, but which is available in the army. As a result the station would work only for a short time and then die out . . . my equipment was on its last legs. The second radar would not work because there was no generator—the officers sold it, and drank away the money.

The subject of drink dominates any and all reminiscences of life in the Soviet forces. Heavy drinking is a fact of all walks of Soviet life; alcohol is the one consumer article that is never in short supply, even in the most remote village store. Despite this general abundance, drink is illegal for the conscript rank and file, although officers are allowed to buy it. This attempt to keep the men sober does not meet with much success, judging by all personal accounts and even the occasional muffled reference in the press. In 1974 *Krasnaya zvezda*, the official newspaper of the Soviet armed forces, reported that one-third of all violations of the law by military personnel were committed "in a state of drunkenness."

Barred by law from possessing drink, the troops exhibit tremendous ingenuity in getting hold of it. There are three ways to solve the problem: having it sent from home through the mail, buying it off base with funds generated through the sale or barter of military equipment, or concocting various unappetizing and even lethal home brews.

Sergei, an erstwhile tank lieutenant, was frank in his admiration for some of the methods used to smuggle in liquor from the outside. Since he was a junior officer, his duties included inspecting the mail before it was distributed to the men. Once, a parcel arrived that contained an innocent-looking consignment of canned salt fish. Unfortunately, one of the cans had gotten damaged in transit and was dribbling vodka. "It was so ingenious really," he told me. "They had opened up the cans, taken out the fish, filled them up with vodka, and then sealed them up again perfectly. It was a shame to have to confiscate them."

"Drink, and how to get hold of it, was the dominant topic of conversation in the barracks. You could call it an obsession," a resourceful young man called Igor told me. He had been in a good position to profit by this obsession because he had been his unit's postman, a job that entailed picking up the mail for his unit from the main base post office and delivering it to an officer for inspection before it was distributed. "Men who were expecting booze in a parcel from home would tip me off, so I would take it out of the sack and hide it before the officer saw it. Of course, they had to give me something for doing this."

Usually, supplies from the local population are not actually vodka but less refined albeit equally potent liquors, such as *spiritus*, a powerful distillate that is legally on sale only in the colder northern parts of the Soviet Union.

When outside sources fail, the men fall back on ingenious means of intoxication. Viktor Belenko, who defected in his MiG-25 fighter to Japan, has given a vivid account of what went on at his Siberian air base:

Except for a televison set, no recreational facilities of any kind were available to the men (or the officers for that matter), and there was little they could do. There was much they were forbidden to do. They were forbidden to listen to a transistor radio, to draw pictures of women, to listen to records, to read fiction, to write letters about life in the service, to lie or sit on their bunks during their free time (there was no place else to sit), to watch television except when political or patriotic programs were shown, and to drink. But drink they did, in staggering quantities, for alcohol was the only commodity available in limitless quantities.

To fly seventy minutes, the maximum time it can stay aloft without refueling, a MiG-25 needs 14 tons of jet fuel and one half ton of alcohol for braking and electronic systems. So wherever MiG-25s were based, huge quantities of alcohol were stored, and in the Soviet Air Force the plane was popularly known as 'The Flying Restaurant.'

Other planes may not carry as much alcohol as the MiG-25, but they all carry tanks of alcohol deicing fluid for the cockpit canopy. A favored stratagem for pilots is to take off on a training mission and falsely report that they are encountering icing conditions and therefore activating their deicers. Then they land with a full tank of this alcohol, which has officially already been used, and take it home for a party.

Ordinary soldiers are sometimes reduced to spreading shoe polish on bread, leaving the bread out in the sun so that the alcohol content in the polish soaks into the bread, and then consuming it. Eau de Cologne, on the rare occasions that it goes on sale in some camp commissaries, is sold out within 15 minutes. Antifreeze for trucks, brake fluid from all kinds of vehicles—it seems there is nothing the Soviet soldier will disdain in his quest for oblivion.

Sometimes the consequences are lethal. Alex Rantinor remembers the day when eight men at his base went on a binge with the antifreeze used in their trucks. "All of them were badly poisoned. One soldier died, two went blind, the rest were in serious condition and had to be hospitalized."

The soldiers' relentless search for intoxicants may have an even more serious effect on their equipment. A modern military organization has an enormous number of machines that need constant cleaning. In the Soviet Union such cleaning is done with an alcohol-based fluid. Victor Sokolov, an émigré journalist, spent his military service as a member of a specialized construction crew working on the ring of air defense radars around Moscow. He remembers how the fluid issued for cleaning the moving parts in the big radars was regarded as being far too valuable for such purposes, so the men would substitute gasoline instead. When gasoline is wiped on metal, it makes a nice shiny gleam, but it also corrodes the metal.

Drunken troops are nothing new in the Russian army. They were present in tsarist times and at the dawn of the Soviet state. Vladimir A. Antonov-Ovseenko, who actually led the revolutionary troops in the attack on the Winter Palace in October 1917, the event which sparked the revolution and changed the history of the world, later recalled:

The Preobrazhensky regiment got completely drunk while guarding the wine cellars of the Palace. . . . The Pavlovsky regiment did not withstand the temptation either. . . . Mixed picked guards were sent; they too got drunk. Members of the regimental committees were assigned. . . . These succumbed too. Men of the armored brigades were ordered to disperse the crowds—they paraded up and down and then began to sway suspiciously. . . . An attempt was made to flood the cellars. The fire brigades got drunk. . . . The Council of People's Commissars appointed a special commissar with emergency powers. . . . But the commissar too proved unreliable.

Men who have seen at first hand the amount of drinking that goes on today in the Soviet forces and Western specialists who have studied the problem at a greater distance commonly use the word "epidemic." Enders Wimbush considers that "dependence on alcohol in the Soviet armed forces probably is at the epidemic level. We discovered looking at the American armed forces that there was, I believe, an alcohol dependence of about 18 percent. I would be very surprised if it were under one-third in the Soviet armed forces. Very surprised."

It should be noted that alcohol extracts a fearful toll on American servicemen as well, despite the fact that they drink less than their Soviet counterparts. For example, the U.S. Navy has conceded that as many as 22 of the Navy's 128 major aircraft crashes in 1979 had been caused, in part, by alcohol.

Nevertheless, it is drugs rather than drink that are popularly perceived as the major problem in the U.S. services, but this problem may be becoming more widespread in the Soviet forces. Just as the Vietnam War brought many American soldiers into contact with hard and soft drugs, so the war in Afghanistan is helping to popularize *anasha* (hashish) or *plan* (an opium derivative) among the soldiery. There have indeed been reports that servicemen are bartering ammunition for hashish. Even before the invasion, marijuana use was reportedly quite common among conscripts from the Moslem Central Asian republics, where supplies are abundant.

We can only guess at the precise effect of the epidemic of alcoholism on the Soviets' ability to fight. The men who fought their way across Europe, from the Volga to

Berlin, were accompanied not by field kitchens (soldiers were expected to look after their own cooking) but by field stills, and yet they won the war. On the other hand, German officers who fought against them have described occasions on which a Soviet unit was easily overcome because every man in it was drunk. Men who have experienced today's army often point out that drink does a lot of harm to the defenses of the Soviet Union. As a former lieutenant in the strategic rocket forces told Enders Wimbush, "the time for the Americans to attack would be New Year's Eve, because everybody was drunk and there was no one on duty." But then he paused and added, "New Year's Eve wasn't that much different from any other time."

Drink and lack of food can have a directly adverse effect on Soviet combat capability, but the miseries inflicted on conscripts have more subtle but far-reaching consequences for the defense of the USSR.

Western armies with or without the draft rely on a core of experienced "lifers," men who are not officers but who have chosen the service as a career. Such men become the sergeants and master sergeants. When only one-third of these men reenlist in the U.S. forces after completing their contracted tour of duty, it is considered cause for alarm. Such problems seem pale in comparison with the problems facing the Soviets. So unpopular is life in the ranks that only about 1 percent of the draftees reenlist at the end of their two years, despite considerable blandishments for them to do so in the form of pay and benefits.

There are professional noncommissioned officers in the Soviet services, but they are few in number and specialized in both their origins and occupations. They tend to be drawn from the Eastern Ukraine, where military service is popular among the peasantry. These Eastern Ukrainians are disparagingly referred to as *makaroniki*, or "macaronies," after their ubiquitous sergeants' stripes. They do not, it seems, serve as role models for the men. As one émigré reports: "About 75 percent of the noncommissioned officers are of Ukrainian origin. They all reenlist when their normal term expires. They were despicable people, much hated and feared by the soldiers." A former conscript in the troops of national air defense recalls: "You always find them running the stores and warehouses, because that way they can steal food and supplies and make a good living."

The lack of professional NCOs apart from this unpopular and specialized minority means that the Soviet forces have a rather different system of command at the lower levels from the systems of their potential adversaries in the West. The Soviet system of officer ranks corresponds closely to the Western model. They have professional career officers, who start off as junior lieutenants and then seek to advance through the ascending ranks of captain, major, colonel, lieutenant colonel, major general, lieutenant general, colonel general, general of the army, marshal of a combat arm, chief marshal of a combat arm, and marshal of the Soviet Union.

It is below the officer ranks that Soviet practice differs from the Western model. Officially it is the same: the line of authority descends through senior and junior sergeants, and first- and second-class private soldiers. The reality, however, is different. Authority in the ranks emanates not from a sergeant's stripes but from the oldest and strongest soldiers, regardless of their actual rank.

Because the authorities find it simpler to induct draftees only once every six months instead of calling them up as soon as they reach the requisite age, each unit is horizontally divided into four distinct strata, which are delineated by the number of six-month periods the men in them have served.

The social customs of this hierarchy have been vividly described by Kyril Podrabinek, a former draftee who served in a regiment stationed in the Central Asian republic of Turkmenistan between 1974 and 1976. Unusually, his account comes from inside the Soviet Union, where he is serving a prison term for dissident activities. Between leaving the army and his arrest, Podrabinek composed a memoir of his service life, *The Unfortunates*, which was smuggled to West Germany. This is how he describes the hierarchy of the Soviet barracks:

You and I, reader, are in Turkmenistan, in a Soviet Army barracks. Let's go straight to the heart of the matter.

In the barracks there is a strict hierarchy by years of service and date of conscription. Soldiers in their first year of service are deprived of any rights whatsoever; those in the second of their two-year term of conscription are the arbiters of the fates of the first. But besides the general demarcation between the mass and the oligarchy, there are also intermediate gradations.

The Soviet draft takes place every six months. The soldiers in their first six months of service are called the "youngsters." This is the lowest caste. Having served six months, the youngsters become "fishes," although, from the point of view of rights, the fishes have no advantage over the youngsters. The "regulations" for a fish are exactly the same as for a youngster. But he has served longer and gets a lesser share of washing the bosses' leggings and of scrubbing the barracks at night and so on.

Army customs have the force of law in the barracks. To work and to observe military regulations are customs only for the first year of service. For those who have served a year, the custom is to put everything off onto someone else. It's a metamorphosis to celebrate. A year goes by, and a fish has turned into a candidate. He is not a candidate for some office, but a candidate to become a boss. The functions of a candidate are basically repressive—police work. They persecute the youngsters and the fishes so the first-year soldiers don't get out of hand. Bluntly, they are responsible for "order." Having served another six months, the candidates become bosses, society's elders, so to say, the *crème de la crème*..

For bosses the custom is to relax. They do persecute the youngsters, but it's by way of private initiative or personal interest, and not for the sake of order, like the candidates. Then there's the highest rank of power, to be a "grandfather." Grandfathers are soldiers who have received their discharges but who have not yet left for home.

The degree to which the senior men abuse their authority varies in different units. In some, it is relatively mild; but in the majority of cases the hardships of army life fall far more heavily on the first-year men than on the candidates and bosses.

Rations, austere as they are, are shared unequally by the old men, as the senior conscripts are sometimes called, and the weaklings, with the former appropriating the lion's share of whatever is going. Podrabinek describes the scene at the dining table: "Not one weakling dares take bread, butter, sugar, the evening piece of fish, or anything until the older soldiers have served themselves. After that the youths pounce on the leavings. Those sitting near the bosses are in a more advantageous position for this than those sitting further away. Every seat around the table is strictly regulated; it corresponds to social standing, determined by strength, resourcefulness, submissiveness to the second year soldiers, chutzpah, and orneriness. And so, all the food is allocated."

The youngsters suffer the effects of the caste system in every aspect of their service lives. If they had not understood this as a fact of life before their induction, it is very soon pointed out to them, from the moment they are presented with their new uniform, which will most likely be appropriated by a boss in exchange for his old one. Soon afterward, they will start to learn the other unwritten but nonetheless rigid rules of barracks life. These consist principally of absorbing as much of the burden of conscript life as possible from the old men. They must clean their masters' uniforms and boots, as well as the barracks and lavatories. They frequently hand over the bulk of their slender salaries, as well as their food. Sometimes they even have to absorb punishments that higher authority has meted out to a boss. Igor, a New York taxi driver who had experienced both the degradations and the rewards of this caste system during his service in an infantry unit, told me how an officer had ordered him to clean the lavatories for some infraction. "I was an old man by that time, so I wasn't going to do it myself," he recalled in a matter-of-fact way, "so I ordered two youngsters to do it for me. The officer suspected that this had happened and asked the kids about it, but they knew better than to admit it."

All accounts of this phenomenon agree that the customs are enforced by physical force—ruthless beatings administered in the barracks after lights out when the men are alone.

Civilians to whom I have retailed these accounts of the vicious hazing system endemic in the lower ranks of the Soviet military sometimes flippantly suggest that it is of little significance, since it occurs in all armies. It is true that milder forms of the custom are not unique to the Soviet system. It is untrue to suggest that it is irrelevant to the combat capability of an army.

It is hard to find any military authority who will argue against the proposition that cohesion is the most important factor in creating a successful fighting force. This is defined as the bonds of trust and respect that link the fighting men to their officers and to each other, summed up in the aphorism that "you don't take a hill for your country but for your buddies." The basic strength of the German Wehrmacht, for example, is commonly held to have lain in the cohesion of the basic company unit of a 100 or so men. In *Crisis in Command*, Richard Gabriel and Paul Savage ascribe much of the blame for the collapse of the U.S. Army in Vietnam to the high command's failure to foster such cohesion. Yet another work on the Vietnam disaster, *Self-Destruction*, quotes one American officer's graphic description of what happened: "My God, [the army] was almost unusable because of the Vietnam experience. You had a fantastic breakdown in cohesion; discipline was absolutely shot; there were internal doubts, self-doubts, about those working and fighting beside you."

The unofficial organization of Soviet units, in which at any time half the strength is being brutalized and exploited by the other half, is hardly likely to foster the trust and mutual confidence that makes for cohesion. Podrabinek suggests that "if combat action began, one half of the company might shoot the other," and even if this is extreme, it is quite evident that a lot of the soldiers would have severe doubts about whether their "buddies" were worth taking a hill for.

There is another aspect to the caste system that bears the gravest implications for Soviet combat capability. The rigors of life in the ranks ensure that very few Soviets choose to reenlist. Thus, although the Soviet forces do have noncommissioned officers, these conscripts are just like the men they supposedly command. However, the authority bestowed by length of service carries more weight than that of official rank. Although a first-year man may have been given the rank of sergeant, he cannot, as a rule, command obedience from a boss. Most of the firsthand accounts agree on this. The former camp projectionist Grigory's voice was positively cracking with indignation when he described the effrontery of a first-year sergeant who had attempted to give orders to him, an old man. "I told him to fuck off or I would break his teeth," he declares emphatically.

This state of affairs may not matter so much in peacetime, but in the crisis of combat the higher command will be faced with the problem that the official chain of command in the lower ranks bears no relation to reality. Orders will be transmitted to sergeants who have had no experience in leading their elders. The bosses may be no more fitted to take on the task of leadership, since they have derived their authority not from any qualities of personality but simply through age.

It would be unfair to the Soviet military authorities to suggest that they are unaware of these morale problems in the ranks. The military press occasionally refers to "rudeness in relation to young soldiers having recently joined the military collective" and inveighs against "individual violators of discipline," who "sometimes treat the young recruits in an uncomradely manner." Unfortunately for the young soldiers, and perhaps the military prowess of the Soviet Union, the leadership has an unvarying answer to such problems: more political education. The late Marshal Andrei A. Grechko, Minister of Defense from 1967 to 1976, declared in his book *On Guard for Peace and the Building of Socialism* that "the ideological approach and political maturity are the foundation of all other traits which a true soldier requires."

The Soviet serviceman is subjected to a great deal of political education as a matter of routine. According to the official timetable, he receives three hours of such instruction on Mondays and Thursdays. These lectures consist of instruction by the unit's political officers on Marxist-Leninist precepts and the "leading role of the Party in the 'military collective,'" as well as question-and-answer sessions and occasional films. The ideological barrage can be intense. In a 1972 article on a submarine of the Baltic Fleet about to set out on patrol, *Krasnaya zvezda* listed the "spiritual fuel" being prepared by the ship's political officer for just one day: a political-information session on the theme "Sailor, protect and add to the heroic traditions of the Baltic submariners," radio newscasts on "Talks by advanced production workers in the socialist competition in honor of the Fiftieth Anniversary of the USSR," a seminar with warrant officers on how to "Help subordinates to fulfill socialist pledges," a radio meeting on a "Roll call of outstanding combat posts," an evening meeting on "Unabating hatred for the enemies of the socialist motherland," and at the evening's end, verses and songs about the motherland.

The indoctrination sessions are not entirely unwelcome to the servicemen, since they afford a release from work and an opportunity to relax. Their utility in making the conscripts into better soldiers or sailors is more questionable. Of course the émigrés, who after all decided to leave the Soviet Union, are unlikely to be ardent Communists. Still, it is worth taking note of their unanimous contention that the political indoctrination sessions were "boring" or "a good time to sleep," and "no one took them seriously."

Nevertheless, the leadership remains convinced that "the training process in our army is inseparably linked to the indoctrination process." Ineffective though this may be in producing cohesive units of men, the leadership is adamant that it is the only way.

While they struggle with problems of morale and motivation among the individual fighting units, the Soviet authorities have a larger problem on their hands—the cohesion of the entire country.

As its name suggests, the Union of Soviet Socialist

Republics is not a nation-state but a federation. At least 90 different ethnic groups live within its borders, speaking perhaps 130 different languages. This vast country is sometimes described, although never by the Soviets themselves, as the last empire. Only in the armed forces do the ordinary people of the state find themselves in a common institution with their alien, and in some cases unintelligible, compatriots.

For convenience' sake we use "Russia" and "Russians" interchangeably with "the Soviet Union" and "Soviets," but in reality, a Muscovite has as much in common with some of his fellow citizens from Soviet Central Asia or the Siberian Far East as a WASP American has with a native of Central America or Turkey. Russia and Russians dominate this vast and disparate collection of races and cultures, but Russians make up only slightly more than half the population, and the proportion is declining.

Over the centuries, the tsars extended Russian power from the original base around Moscow. They never made much pretense that they ruled anything other than a *Russian* empire. In particular, they were concerned to keep their army cohesive and homogeneous, so they excluded many of their subjects, especially Moslems from Central Asia, from military service. Writing to Tsar Alexander II in November 1870, the Minister of War, Dmitri Miliutin, advised that conscription should not be extended to the Caucasus or some of the eastern parts of the empire because the population there exhibited a "low level of civic development."

The terrible casualties of World War I forced the authorities to try and reverse this policy. In 1916 a government decree extended conscription to some of the Central Asians. This immediately resulted in a fierce rebellion, which took six months and the diversion of many troops from the German front to put down.

The Bolshevik regime that came to power in 1917 declared that the non-Russian nations of the old empire were free to choose their own paths. Thus, the Finns, the Poles, and the Baltic republics of Latvia, Lithuania, and Estonia were able to secure their independence (only temporarily in the case of the Balts) while the Bolsheviks were still fighting off the White counterrevolutionary armies, as well as the interventionist forces of the Americans, British, French, and Japanese. The Civil War was over by 1921, however, and the new regime then moved to reassert control over the remainder of the country. The Red Army was actively engaged against recalcitrant elements in Central Asia right through the 1920s.

Despite these rebellions, the official policy was that all races should have equal standing in the armed forces of the USSR. The 1938 law establishing a universal draft in the Soviet Union specified that military service must be performed in a multinational environment and that the language of the army must be Russian.

This policy did not survive the German invasion of 1941. The crisis was so sudden and severe that the government authorized the formation of national units from the minority nationalities, which could at least understand each other. While this expedient may have helped to make up for the enormous losses of the Red Army, the behavior of some of the non-Russian troops reinforced Moscow's doubts about their basic loyalties. There are reports that the Wehrmacht was able to recruit as many as 700,000 Soviet non-Russians to fight against their former fellow citizens.

After the war, the national units were gradually phased out of the army, and by the 1960s, the forces were once again fully integrated, at least in theory. Contemporary Soviet citizens are drafted under the 1967 Law of Universal Military Service, which stipulates clearly that the object of mass conscription is to fuse recruits into mixed units and to promote a cultural melting pot by the constant use of the Russian language. Leonid Brezhnev reaffirmed these intentions in 1972, declaring, "Our army is a special one. It is a school for internationalism, instilling sentiments of fraternity, solidarity and mutual respect for all the nations and nationalities of the Soviet Union."

Close observation of the trains carrying the raw conscripts about the USSR twice a year would reveal tangible evidence of this policy of fusing the peoples. The trains follow a curious pattern. They do not simply move their passengers to the depot nearest to their homes; they are carrying out a gigantic geographical reshuffle of the 900,000 eighteen-year-olds who are inducted every six months. Ukrainians are moved into northern Russia, Latvians and Estonians shifted east, Kalmyks and Kazakhs moved west, and so on. Whatever their nationality, conscripts have very little chance of serving in their home districts; the authorities do not like to encourage links between the military and the local population. Thus, the minority races are moved far from their native lands. In addition, the distribution of new conscripts among operational units is carefully arranged so that they find themselves mixed in with troops from other areas. Émigré reports suggest that the purpose of this massive dislocation may be less high-minded than that suggested by Brezhnev. One of them told the Rand Corporation interviewers that "there are several reasons the authorities send a minority soldier to serve as far away from his home as possible. First, the further away he is from home, the more difficult it will be for him to run away from his unit. Second, he will have less longing for his family. . . . Third, if you keep minorities away from their home areas, it will be easier to maintain control there in times of crisis. You have to keep minority soldiers from assisting their own people against the Russians."

Official distrust of the minorities goes further than simply removing them far from home. To a considerable extent these soldiers are kept away from any contact with weapons. The Rand Corporation émigré research project was specifically focused on the racial makeup of Soviet units. After interviewing 130 veterans in depth, the researchers concluded that 80 percent of the men in combat units, the units that actually fight, are Slavs. The Slavic races include the Russians themselves, the Byelorussians, and the Eastern Ukrainians. The other 20 percent are made up of a polyglot assembly of Asians, Western Ukrainians (who are racially akin to their Polish neighbors), Jews, Moldavians (who are Rumanian by race), and other representatives of peoples who are officially considered to be either backward or politically unreliable. For noncombat units, the racial proportions are reversed. Construction battalions, railroad troops, and elements of what the Soviets call the "tail," such as truck drivers or cooks, appear to draw 80 percent of their strength from the minority nationalities. The remaining 20 percent are Russians who have incurred official disfavor for showing signs of political unreliability.

The officer corps reflects this pro-Slav bias. Of the 42 generals mentioned by name in the Soviet press in 1975 and 1976, 40 were Slavs, one an Armenian, and one of German descent (there are about 1.8 million Germans in the Soviet Union).

There is a significant exception to the general principle of keeping weapons out of the hands of non-Slavs. The quarter of a million men of the MVD internal security forces, which form a separate army under the control of the Ministry of Internal Affairs, are drawn almost exclusively from the remoter parts of Central Asia. These security troops are exclusively concerned with controlling and suppressing outbreaks of popular disaffection, such as the bread riots in Novocherkassk in 1962, which were put down by Kazakh MVD troops. As one émigré put it, "A Russian soldier probably would not shoot at Russian women, but a Kazakh would. He would say, 'They are Russians. Let's get them.'" The same principle of control was used by the British in the days of their empire, when they used to employ Sikhs from India to control the Chinese population of Singapore.

The construction units, in which most of the non-Slavic conscripts serve their two years, constitute a huge proportion of the total Soviet forces. Together with the railroad troops, which are exclusively concerned with the construction and maintenance of railroads, they number about 920,000 men. They have the same internal structure as combat units—companies, battalions, and so forth—but they have little to do with soldiering as most people understand it. They do, however, play an important role in the Soviet economy; for example, the Siberian "science city" near Novosibirsk was built by them, as was Sheremetyevo Airport, outside Moscow.

Alex, a shy and slightly built engineer from Lvov, a city in the Western Ukraine, remembers with amusement that he actually made a special request to serve in a construction unit "since I had studied construction engineering and I thought I would be able to get some useful experience—at least that is what they told me at the military commissariat." He had been misled. In the two years he spent in uniform, he did the work of an unskilled building laborer, toiling on an extension to an officers' club in Moscow. The sum total of his military training consisted of three days' drill and half an hour on the firing range with a machine gun.

Sipping fruit juice in a Manhattan coffee shop, Alex recalls his fellow laborers. "We had 100 men in my company. Most of them were Moslems: Uzbeks, Kirghiz, Tadzhiks, Kazakhs, Tatars. The rest were Baptists, who refuse to carry weapons on religious grounds, and Volga Germans, in addition to myself and a few other Jews. Most of the Moslems could speak a little bit of Russian, but two of them went through their entire service without learning any at all except for a few swear words. I began by feeling sorry for the Asians, they got a very hard time from the officers. For example, there was a lot of pork in our diet, which they had to eat even though it was against their religion. That was a big trauma for them, and they used to worry in case their parents found out they had been eating it. After a while, though, I lost my sympathy, because they were mostly such crude and unpleasant people, stealing and picking quarrels all the time."

Repeated interviews bear out the point that a huge proportion of the Soviet population is considered fit only to be second-class soldiers or forced laborers. Many young men handle a weapon only when they take their obligatory military oath at the beginning of their service. This is traditionally administered while the new conscript holds a rifle, but in the *stroibaty*, as the construction units are called, the rifle is frequently a wooden dummy.

Just as the structure of the armed forces is based on racial discrimination, racism itself is endemic in the ranks. Soviet soldiers can draw on a rich and varied vocabulary of racial terms with which to insult each other. The Russians use a variety of epithets for the Central Asians: *churka*, literally "wood chip," which means that someone is dumb and worthless; *chernozhopyi*, literally "black ass," which has the same force as the English "nigger"; and *zhopomordyi*, literally "ass face," which is the most insulting of all. A Latvian calls a Russian *cuke*, meaning "pig." Anyone who wants to pick a fight with a Ukrainian calls him a *khokhol*, while a Jew in the army gets accustomed to being called *zhid*.

It is sometimes startling to hear otherwise civilized and well-educated émigrés express the most bigoted sentiments about the troops of different nationalities with which they served, although they are not always as blunt as the interviewee who declared: "From the beginning we, the white people, considered ourselves somewhat higher and with more privileges than the *Churkas*. . . . Words speak for themselves. That is why, when it is necessary to do some unpleasant work, say, clean a toilet, a Kazakh would be sent and the Russians would make him do it. . . . It was the same at all levels. At a table in the military dining room, Russians always take the first turn. Kazakhs and Uzbeks always the last. First *we* will eat and then they. The same holds true for who is going to sleep where. Kazakhs and Uzbeks will be sent to the most uncomfortable corner. . . . This is done by the soldiers themselves. It has always been this way in the army. If I worked with a screwdriver, the Central Asian worked with a shovel."

Alex Rantinor, otherwise a cultured and wryly humorous man, discusses the Central Asians he commanded in similarly prejudiced terms: "The soldiers who come from Asiatic Russia pretend that they do not understand the Russian language and therefore try to dodge their duties. They spend most of their time either asleep or trying to get first in line at the cookhouse. They are corrupt and steal from the supply stores, as well as try to bribe the officers. I personally was offered a bribe of 2,000 rubles by a raw recruit to fix the necessary documents to have him discharged."

Racial discord in the ranks goes well beyond insults. Violent and even homicidal incidents appear to be common. This report of what happened in a communications unit in the late 1960s is not untypical: "Ivashenko stole a Kazakh soldier's girlfriend. So the other Kazakhs took to beating up Ivashenko whenever they saw him. One day all the Russians were getting drunk because it was the anniversary of the October Revolution, when Ivashenko shouted that the Kazakhs were beating him up again. So they went over to the Kazakh barracks in a body and crippled 15 of them."

Firsthand accounts of life in the Soviet ranks describe an organization riven with hatred and strife to an extent that occasionally borders on anarchy. The older soldiers terrorize the younger ones and troops from different races despise and fight each other, while the command structure above them seems unable or unwilling to put a stop to it. Aleksandr Makushechev, a former sergeant, described in an interview how first-year soldiers were often denied cartridges on the rifle range for fear they might shoot their seniors. Veterans of the 1968 Czech invasion recall how afraid the officers were of the men once they were issued live ammunition before crossing the border. As one man put it: "One of my acquaintances slept with a pistol under his head and even then, only after having locked himself in the cab of his vehicle."

Defense observers who have become aware of the substance of these émigré accounts have been quick to draw an obvious conclusion. Congressman Les Aspin of Wisconsin, who is quite well known for his judicious criticisms of U.S. defense policy, states: "If Soviet officers can't trust their sentries not to shoot at them, if the Army is divided among hostile ethnic groups and between older soldiers and younger ones . . . and if the officers really are afraid of issuing weapons to their troops, then it would seem we have less to fear from the Russians than their numbers might make us think."

While this may be true, it leaves much unexplained. The Soviet soldier was the ultimate conqueror of Hitler's legions. The wartime Red Army could produce men who would call down Russian artillery fire on their own positions as they were being overrun by the enemy, or the fatally wounded tank crewman who stayed in his disabled tank amid the decaying bodies of his comrades for *a full week*, awaiting the opportunity to swing the cannon around onto a German target.

Those heroes were fighting against a barbaric horde which had invaded their country. Their sons and grandsons are pressed into a service which is supposedly intended to instill "sentiments of fraternity, solidarity, and mutural respect for all the nations and nationalities of the Soviet Union" and to defend the motherland against the threat of another invasion. The potential invaders—the United States and its allies—treat the present-day Soviet soldier as a potential attacker of *their* territories. Clearly, the conscript masses of today are ill-organized for any of these roles. How is it that this state of affairs is allowed to endure? For the answers we must examine another component of Soviet military society—the professional officer corps.

Four

Politics and the Professional Warriors

The gulf between Soviet conscripts and the officers who command them is wide and deep. The officers enjoy a standard of living that seems luxurious when contrasted with the squalid existence of the rank and file. They can have their wives and families with them, they are free to do what they like during off-duty hours, and they get extended periods of leave. They can drink as much as they can afford, and they get paid a living salary. The disparity between the military classes is far greater than in the U.S. Army. The most junior American officer will be paid about 4 times as much as a private soldier, while his Soviet equivalent receives 20 times as much as a conscript.

In the armies of the industrial West, the gulf between officers and men will to a certain extent be bridged by the career NCOs, but we have seen that this class of soldier hardly exists in the Soviet Union and why.

Thus, the Soviet forces lack any kind of catalyst between the career officers and their involuntary charges,

whose two-year term of service allows time for the acquisition of little more than the most basic military skills.
One consequence of this is that tasks which would be
routinely delegated to a master sergeant or a petty officer
in any Western force must in the Soviet Union be undertaken by an officer. The contrast was underlined by a
Soviet general visiting an American unit who was offered
a ride in a tank. He was reportedly astonished to hear that
his driver was to be a sergeant; in the USSR, a VIP would
automatically be driven by an officer.

This policy of playing safe by reserving any important
task for officers can be carried to extreme lengths. To
celebrate the coronation of Queen Elizabeth II in 1953,
the British arranged a naval parade of warships from many
nations. The Soviets dispatched the cruiser *Sverdlovsk*.
Western observers were most impressed by the skill and
smartness of the crew; what they did not know was that
every single one of the 900 men on board was an officer.

For Operation Dnieper, an enormous war game held in
1967 to celebrate the 50th anniversary of the Russian Revolution, the authorities extended this subterfuge of substituting officers for rank-and-file troops several stages
further. They decided that for an exercise of such importance and complexity, they should rely on officers dis-
guised as ordinary soldiers for all but the least important
roles. Viktor Suvorov, a former tank officer who defected
to the West, describes the scene in *The Liberators,* his
witty memoir of Army life:

"To build up only one division, over 10,000 officers
were required—because officers were cast in the role of
ordinary soldiers. And where can such a multitude be
gathered? Even every graduate from every military school
and academy would not have been sufficient. And, for
this reason, it was decided in addition to call upon the

majority of the officers of the Baltic, Byelorussian, Kiev, and Carpathian military districts . . . just imagine, four of the largest groups of armies, utterly devoid of officers."

To try to compensate for the shortage of skilled men among the rank and file, career officers are given very intensive training. There are at least 136 military schools in the Soviet Union offering four- and five-year courses, the equivalents of West Point or Annapolis.

Once he has been commissioned as a junior lieutenant, a Soviet officer can expect to stay in the service for at least twenty-five years. This does at least allow Russian officers to escape the ruthless pruning consequent on the American "up or out" system, but it also means that a lot of deadwood is left undisturbed. Khrushchev did retire thousands of officers prematurely in the late 1950s as part of his program of pruning the nonnuclear forces, but that initiative was abandoned in 1961 in response to the Berlin crisis of that year and the bellicose rhetoric of the incoming Kennedy Administration.

Since the armed forces are the repository of so much Soviet prestige and consume so much of the nation's resources, it is usually assumed in the West that the officer class enjoys a standard of living far more priveleged than that of most civilians. This is not necessarily the case.

It is true that an officer can expect to be paid about one-third more than a civilian with similar responsibilities. He may also have the opportunity to shop in special stores selling scarce consumer goods that are unobtainable by the general public. More importantly, he has guaranteed housing, itself a privilege in the USSR, although this may not be of a high standard.

The most senior officers, as we shall see, certainly enjoy a style of life that compares favorably with that of a Western millionaire, but the same does not apply for those lower down the totem pole. There is a scene in the Soviet romantic comedy *Moscow Does Not Believe in Tears* which points up this division: a maritally ambitious shop-girl is flirting with a general, only to be disappointed when the general's wife appears. A friend consoles her with the observation that "to get to be the wife of a general you first have to spend twenty years trailing round dreary army posts."

A Soviet survey carried out in 1969 on the relative prestige of various professions offers more empirical evidence that the military profession is not as highly regarded in the Soviet Union as is sometimes supposed. On a scale of 1 to 10, officers ranked 4.3, which placed them below scientists, doctors, university teachers, artists, and writers. Such an order of priorities clashes with the Western perception of Soviet military professionals as occupying an exalted position; their loyalty and dedication assured, as the hawkish scholar Harriet Fast Scott puts it, "by the perquisites, privileges, and status that they enjoy."

A Soviet officer will most likely be from a small town or village in Russia or the Ukraine, and will not be particularly gifted. A military career is one of the few avenues open to those without exceptional talents for getting off the farm or at least out of the backwoods. An officer candidate must be fluent in Russian, which would rule out many of the minority nationalities, particularly those from the Central Asian republics, whose greater prosperity tends to make a military career less attractive. Unlike entrance to the medical or scientific schools, entrance to the junior service academies is not notably rigorous, except perhaps for the navy and the rocket troops, and a secondary-school certificate and sound physique will usually suffice.

The émigré sources are almost unanimous in their low opinion of the career officers they met. "Boorish," "stupid," "drunken" are common epithets, which is an attitude that might be expected from a group of former conscripts who had spent two years in an extremely harsh environment under the control of these officers. The verdict is endorsed, however, by such men as Sasha Dorman or Alex Rantinor, who served alongside the career officers for two years as commissioned draftees, and by another source who enjoyed a fortuitous access to the middle and upper ranks of the officer corps for several years.

Edward Lozansky never served in the army, but he was in a position to observe a great deal about it. He now lives in Washington, D.C., and works as secretary of a human rights organization named for his hero Andrei Sakharov, the Soviet physicist and dissident. Before he was forced into exile for his own dissident activities, he was an associate professor of physics at the Military Academy of Armored forces, one of the many higher advanced military academies in Moscow. More commonly called the Malinovsky Tank Academy, after the former Minister of Defense, it is regarded as being second in prestige only to the Frunze Military Academy, which takes middle-grade officers from all branches of the ground forces, as well as the air force and air defense forces.

Despite the status of the Malinovsky Academy, the quality of the inmates is not high. The academic standard is mediocre; the physics course taught by Lozansky was the equivalent of a senior-high-school course in the United States. Even so, it was stiff enough for his students; Lozansky recalls the pressure put on him by the senior faculty to raise the average grade from a C or D, which would have been justified, to a more respectable B. Despite its prestige and the opportunities it offered for future promotion to ambitious officers, there was not a great deal of competition to get into the school during the time Lozansky taught there, which was from 1972 to 1975. Because of this, he was strongly discouraged from failing applicants on their entrance tests.

Lozansky's students were not candidate officers but captains and majors, who had already graduated from lower military schools and were destined for important commands or staff positions.

A sophisticated individual, Lozanky exhibits a characteristic Muscovite snobbery when he scorns the "boorish" accents of his erstwhile students. This does at least confirm the common report that Soviet officers tend to come from the backwoods.

Many of these officers are destined to spend their lives in the backwoods. Unless they are lucky enough to draw a semipermanent posting in a cosmopolitan center like Moscow or Leningrad, they will spend most of their twenty-five-year careers rotating around the garrison posts and bases of the Soviet Union. Most of these are in remote spots, where life can seem comfortable only by contrast with the hardships endured by the ordinary soldiers. Viktor Belenko, awarded an elite position as a pilot-instructor officer, found himself posted to Salsk, a city of 60,000 in the depths of southern Russia. He describes it as a drab, dingy, poor city, set on treeless flatlands over which stinging winds howled. Dust intruded everywhere except when rain turned it to mud. There were two movie houses, but they were small and going there usually entailed an hour's wait. There was also an hour's wait for service in the city's few restaurants, and "the fare was not worth the delay." Yet even Salsk seemed a glittering metropolis by contrast with Belenko's next posting, a base near a village called Chuguyevka in far eastern Siberia, where there was no movie theater or restaurant, or any paved streets or street lights either.

"Let's face it," says Edward Lozansky, sitting in his smart Northwest Washington apartment, "for anyone under the rank of general, life is pretty miserable. Even colonels lead a dog's life, since they are continually in terror of their superiors."

In view of all this, it is perhaps not surprising that the authorities do not always find it easy to recruit the requisite number of officers. One émigré recalled the desperate efforts of his local Komsomol (the Communist youth organization) to find the seven candidates for officer cadet school that were the quota of the district—"no one wanted to go to military school." *Krasnaya zvezda* has sometimes had to inveigh against the practice by which the faculty of these schools will grade indifferent students as "outstanding," just as Lozansky had to bump up the scores of his students at the advanced tank academy.

Another indication of the unpopularity of the military profession is the difficulty faced by officers who want to resign. The émigré journalist Victor Sokolov remembers an officer in his unit who had no desire whatsoever to stay in the service, so he resolved to drink his way out. Every time a senior officer appeared for inspection, this man took care to be as drunk as possible, but to no avail. His only punishment was to be called before an officers' "court of honor" and be demoted, "but they refused to kick him out, which was what he wanted."

Such an atmosphere is hardly conducive to the fostering of close ties between officers and men, bonds which students of American military shortcomings cite as the single most important factor in promoting military effectiveness. In *National Defense*, James Fallows quotes with approval the instructions of British Field Marshal William Slim to his officers: "I tell you, as officers, that you will not eat, sleep, smoke, sit down, or lie down until your soldiers have had a chance to do these things. If you will hold to this, they will follow you to the ends of the Earth. If you do not, I will break you in front of your regiments." Fallows contrasts this commendable attitude with what he found to be the current situation in the U.S. Army. He decries the emphasis in the American officer corps on management rather than leadership, careerism rather than a proper concentration on military skills at every level. Like several other military commentators, Fallows perceives these trends as a major cause of the disasters that befell the U.S. Army in Vietnam.

Though it is these trends that have led the U.S. Army into such trouble, American officers may be consoled by seeing their problems reflected in the Soviet forces. If a good officer puts his men's welfare before his own, as directed by Field Marshal Slim, he should also ensure that at the least they are not continually harassed by their conscript peers. Yet all the available evidence from inside the army suggests that the officers are as indifferent as they are remote from the conditions of the men. Kyril Podrabinek, the author of *The Unfortunates*, sums up the prevailing opinion of the men on what they feel are the officers' attitudes toward them: "Officers know perfectly well about the master system (by which the bosses rule the youngsters) but do not fight it. Why should they? It's easier the way it is. Outwardly things are as smooth as silk. None of the weaklings dares to complain openly, and it would be hard to root out the masters." Podrabinek goes on to put his finger on one of the central facts of life in the Soviet military, one which dominates the career of every officer and affects every aspect of the workings of their military system: "You would have to take drastic measures, and officers shun the light of day. Who wants to admit that such things go on in his battalion or company or platoon? You would be the first to be taken to task by your superiors, whos also do not want to incur the displeasure of their own bosses. Your whole career would go to hell."

Podrabinek is referring to the organizing principle of

the Soviet military command structure, known as unity of command. It means that the commander of a unit, whatever its size, bears total responsibility for its condition. On the surface this sounds sensible enough and not very different from the U.S. Army rule that a commander is responsible for everything his men do or fail to do. Yet in practice, the two systems work very differently. In the American forces it would be most unusual for a unit commander to be punished if one of his soldiers went absent without leave or got drunk on duty. But in the Soviet forces even the most minor transgressions by conscripts, if they are officially reported, can lead to reprimands and punishments right up the chain of command, a procedure known in the forces as the vertical stroke.

Even the official military press sometimes concedes that this draconian system may be a little unfair. An article published in *Krasnaya zvezda* in 1976 detailed the following incident:

"Major V. Bosoi found out about a severe violation of discipline by Sergeant A. Yantelskii. As required, the officer reported what had happened and what measures had been taken in connection with this. How did the officer's direct commander react to this report? Major Bosoi received a reprimand, his deputy for political affairs a strict reprimand, and the battalion chief of staff was warned about 'incomplete service correspondence'" (a very serious punishment for an officer).

Major Bosoi may have wished that he had kept quiet about whatever it was that Sergeant Yantelskii had done. His reprimand would now be entered on his service record and would affect his chances of future promotion. His superiors, who received more severe punishments, must have wished even more fervently that he had kept his mouth shut.

In the case of really serious offenses, the vertical stroke

can be applied all the way up to the top. In October 1981 a Soviet submarine of a type known as Whiskey class went aground in Swedish territorial waters, close to a secret naval base on which it obviously had been spying. The incident was very embarrassing, and poor Pyotr Gushin, the captain, knew what his fate would be. As the boat finally sailed away, he drew his finger across his throat in an expressive gesture. He was right, because as soon as he had returned to base, he was tried and sentenced to three years in a labor camp. But the vertical stroke did not stop there; it reached all the way to the deputy commander and chief of staff of the Soviet Navy, Admiral of the Fleet G. M. Yegorov, who was removed from his august position and demoted to be head of DOSAAF, the voluntary society that gives rudimentary military training to young Soviets before they get drafted.

The misadventures of Whiskey-137 were too well publicized for Admiral Yegorov to cover up, but Major Bosoi could have ignored Sergeant Yantelskii's dereliction and thereby kept himself and others out of trouble. This expedient appears to commend itself to Soviet officers on a large enough scale for wholesale violations of discipline and other bad news to be routinely covered up.

So widespread is this practice that the official press draws attention to it, although in bowdlerized reports as "rare incidents." Those with firsthand experience describe the situation in starker terms. Alex Rantinor displays a photograph of a smart-looking colonel who had commanded the division in which he had served. He recalls the eight really serious criminal offenses—"rapes and murders"—committed by men in his division in the course of 1974 which were all hushed up because "the commander was up for promotion to general, and because of this the regimental commanders stopped all proceedings in order to safeguard the good name and reputation of the division and to ensure that their man got his promotion."

Genady, the young man who was recruited into the troops of national air defense in his local town square and summarily packed off to Murmansk, retails a firsthand example of what the system does for discipline. At one point early on in his service, he got involved in such a fierce dispute with an officer that he struck him. Hitting an officer is a serious offense in any army, and his victim promptly put him under arrest. But Genady served only a few days in the brig. A more serious sentence, which his crime certainly merited, would have required a full report up the chain of command, and so the charges against him were reduced. Once again, his commanding officer did not want to incur a serious blot on his own record and thus spoil an impending promotion. As Genady laconically observes, "You can get away with a lot of bad stuff in the army."

The Dostoyevskian portrait of the Soviet forces which emerges from these personal accounts—an army in which drunkenness, theft, and indiscipline go unchecked because officers are unwilling to take action—calls some fundamental assumptions about Soviet military prowess into question. It clashes in particular with Western perceptions about the Soviet high command, those marshals and generals who gaze dourly out from their carefully airbrushed official portraits, uniforms resplendent with gold leaf. As the authors of *Soviet Military Power* respectfully observe: "These men . . . know how the Soviet military machine runs and what they want to achieve."

This specter of sage efficiency is rendered yet more formidable by a common assumption among Western observers that the Soviet military has no political role of its own but simply carries out the orders of the civilian Party bosses. General William Odom, who served as the military specialist on the staff of President Carter's National Security Council, is a prominent exponent of this view. According to him, "the military is an administrative arm of the Party, not something separate from and competing with it."

It is hard to find anything in the official Soviet publications on which the conclusions of commentators like General Odom are based to contradict this view. Officially, of course, the same holds true for the American military high command. In theory, the U.S. Joint Chiefs and their subordinates are also focused purely on "the military way," defined by the historian Alfred Vagts as the "primary concentration of men and materials on winning specific objectives of power with utmost efficiency . . . limited in scope, confined to one function, and scientific in its essential qualities." Yet we know that American military leaders are intimately involved in politicking, publicly lobbying, for example, against what they termed the "inadequate" 1981 defense budget proposed by the Carter Administration. We know that they do not necessarily construct forces with the single aim of achieving military objectives with the utmost efficiency, as when the U.S. Navy sought in 1982 to suppress information indicating that their favored large aircraft carriers were extremely vulnerable to Soviet submarines.

Our information on what goes on in the upper reaches of the Soviet military establishment is far more limited. The Russians have no open Congressional hearings, or a paper like the Washington *Post*. The official press publishes little information about individual generals and marshals, apart from bare details of their various postings. In contrast to specific censures directed at junior and middle-ranking officers, *Krasnaya zvezda* never criticizes the performance of high-ranking personnel.

Details on the personalities of the senior men are also hard to come by. American officers had no opportunity to observe their opposite numbers in the flesh between the visit of the Chairman of the Joint Chiefs of Staff, General Nathan Twining, to the Soviet Union in 1956 and the opening of the Strategic Arms Limitation Talks (SALT) in Helsinki in 1969. As a mark of the temporarily amicable relations between the superpowers engendered by these negotiations, some of the Soviet high command did occasionally turn up at diplomatic cocktail parties in Moscow during the early 1970s, sometimes even bringing their wives.

Some American defense attachés, given this unique chance to observe the men in charge of the Soviet military machine at close quarters, were not impressed. One such attaché decided that they were really "just a bunch of inward looking crustacean bureaucrats." As such, he observes, they were "not much different from most of the generals in the Pentagon."

We do not normally think of the men who directed the tanks into Budapest, Prague, and Kabul as crustacean bureaucrats; but that may be because we do not know very much about them.

That is why the testimony of Edward Lozansky, the former physics teacher at the Malinovsky Tank Academy, is so important and unique, not simply because of his recollections about teaching aspiring generals, but because of his involvement with some very senior generals. This involvement came about because in 1971 he met and married a girl named Tatyana Yershova. She was the daughter of Lieutenant General Ivan Dimitrivich Yershov, the chief of staff of the Kiev Military District and a rising star in the military hierarchy.

Yershov had been appointed to his post in Kiev in 1969. To understand how he achieved that position, an extremely important one, and where he hoped to go from there, it is worth reviewing his earlier career.

He was born in 1921, the son of peasants who lived in Ryazan Province in the depths of European Russia. Until he was twenty, there seemed no reason why he should not follow the same arduous but obscure career as tens of millions of other Russian peasants, or kolkhozniks, as they had been renamed under Bolshevik rule. The German invasion in June 1941 changed all that.

The government drafted 5 million men in the first eight days of the war. Yershov was one of them. He was lucky; he survived the disasters and retreats of the first two years and the long and bloody counterattack. He took part in the final victorious assault on Berlin, by which time he had been decorated for heroism and promoted to the rank of lieutenant.

The Red Army went through a crash demobilization after the German and Japanese surrenders, shrinking from a strength of 11 million men in 1945 to under 3 million by 1948. Lieutenant Yershov was one of the hundreds of thousands of young officers who suddenly found themselves back on the collective farm; but he had seen the world and had no desire to be buried alive again.

Abandoning the village girl whom he had married, he ran away to Ryazan, an industrial city of 400,000 people 130 miles southeast of Moscow. His aim was to get an education and make something of himself. The city was in the same state of chaos and ruin as the rest of Russia at that time, although it had escaped the most destructive effects of German occupation and Soviet liberation. There were thousands of young men like himself on the streets whose lives had been torn up by the war. Yershov was one of those who found that the only way to survive was by speculation and profiteering in a minor way on the black market.

Eventually, he was arrested and jailed. He might have disappeared into the Gulag, but he was lucky again. Somebody in authority took notice of his war record and decided to help him. Instead of being sent to a labor camp, he was released and enrolled into the local military cadet school for junior officers, where he was given a basic high-school education.

After he graduated, Yershov was sent to serve in a tank regiment for four years, but in 1951 he applied and was accepted for the prestigious Frunze Higher Military Academy in Moscow. While studying in the capital, Yershov took a decision that was to prove crucial in his career. He met and married Margarita, an intensely ambitious young Muscovite with a very different background from his own. She was educated and half Jewish, a fact that had proved fatal to her father. In the late 1940s Stalin's henchman Zhdanov had instigated an anti-Semitic campaign under the euphemism of "anticosmopolitanism." Margarita's father had been caught up in this purge and had died in prison. The newlywed couple had nowhere to go but up, and the only way open to them was through the ranks of the army.

For the time being, however, the Yershovs lacked the essential connections that seem to be the prerequisite for upward mobility in the Soviet forces, and for the next nine years they suffered the penalties. They moved from one garrison post to another, until in 1959 they were living in Kushka, a flyblown frontier post on the Afghan border.

This was long before the Afghan invasion, and Kushka was the end of the line so far as a military career was concerned. Yershov was a lieutenant colonel by now, and there seemed little prospect that he would go any further. Later on, Margarita spoke of that period as the low point in their lives. Ivan had more or less given up and was concentrating on bouts of heavy drinking that formed the chief recreation of the garrison's officers.

By 1960, Margarita had had enough. She left Turkmenistan and headed for Moscow, determined to cut her losses with Ivan and start again. But the Yershovs' luck was about to change. Soon after arriving back in the capital she befriended Galina Sokolova. She was the wife of General Sergei Sokolov, a wartime hero who was moving up fast through the ranks. At the time the two women met, Sokolov had just been appointed chief of staff of the Moscow Military District, an extremely influential post.

Galina explained to Margarita that Yershov was never going to get on without influential friends—that was the way things were done in the army. Her husband, the general, was now in a position to supply such help.

That was indeed all it took, although some of the Yershov family had their suspicions that Sokolov and Margarita were more than just friends. By late December 1960, Ivan Yershov had been abruptly summoned from his remote backwater and appointed to the Academy of the General Staff.

The academy is the most important and prestigious of all such institutions in the Soviet Union, where the students, all lieutenant colonels or higher, are trained for higher command. But it is more than just an educational institution. Whereas a great deal of U.S. military planning and analysis is farmed out to civilians, both inside and outside the government, the Soviet military prefers to keep such activities to itself. Many of these tasks are carried out by the Academy's faculty and students.

After graduating from the academy in 1962, Yershov was assigned to work at General Staff headquarters, a rambling nineteenth-century collection of buildings on Arbat Boulevard in the heart of Moscow. The Soviet General Staff is a far more powerful organization than its closest American counterpart, the Office of the Joint Chiefs of Staff. Officers assigned to the American institution serve only for a limited term. Thus, their career fortunes remain tied to their parent service, to which they will accordingly give their first loyalty, rather than to the overall planning body. The Soviet General Staff plans and directs the operations of all the individual Soviet services. It is divided into a number of different directorates, each of which is responsible for a specific area, such as intelligence, mobilization, communications, and operations. The officers who work there, the elite of the services, do so for an indefinite period.

Yershov served on the General Staff from 1962 to 1969, apparently with some distinction. By the time he left, he was a lieutenant general and in charge of Operations, the most important of all the directorates. He appears to have been capable in the execution of his duties; he boasted later that he had devised a key element of the plan to occupy Prague in August 1968. The problem had been to think of a way to land troops at the airport before the Czechs could realize what was happening and offer resistance. Yershov claimed to have suggested the eventual solution, which was to have a transport loaded with troops get permission to land under the guise of being a civilian airliner in distress.

His personal abilities were, however, no more important to his success than the escalating value of his connections. General Sokolov, his sponsor (or "daddy rabbit" in Pentagon vernacular), was moving steadily closer to the centers of military power and influence.

In 1967 the aged Defense Minister, Marshal Rodion Malinovsky, died suddenly. After prolonged debate, the Politburo appointed Marshal Andrei Grechko to the post, with consequent benefit to officers with connections to the new minister. Among them was a burly and energetic forty-six-year-old general, Viktor Kulikov, whose links to Grechko dated from the war. He was awarded the plum post of commander of the Kiev Military District. Sokolov, meanwhile, moved from commanding the Leningrad Military District, where he had been since 1965, to become a First Deputy Minister of Defense.

It was not long before Ivan and Margarita received their dividend for being part of the successful faction; in 1969 Ivan was appointed chief of staff of the Kiev Military District.

The Yershovs were now very much part of the Soviet military upper crust and could start to enjoy the rewards. During their later years in Moscow, their standard of living had already been far above that of most Soviet citizens. They had had a large apartment all to themselves and their three children, as well as access to some of the more exclusive special stores. Yershov's salary was augmented by the occasional cash bribe for services his influential position enabled him to deliver, while Margarita had earned something of a reputation as a *spekulyant*, or "speculator," owing to her sideline of selling goods bought at the special stores to less privileged friends at a handsome profit.

But with the promotion to Kiev, Yershov and his family became entitled to privileges that were positively feudal. In terms of actual cash money, they were not that rich; Ivan's salary amounted to a little less than 700 rubles a month, or about the same as his son-in-law Edward Lozansky was making from teaching and writing. The rewards of high rank in the Soviet Union are not calculated in straightforward financial terms but in perquisites.

As chief of staff for the military district, Yershov was allotted a free apartment in Kiev overlooking the river. Attendant cooks, maids, and chauffeurs were supplied by the army. Actually, this apartment was not used very often, except when Ivan had to stay in town overnight. Most of the time the family lived at another official residence, a comfortable country house a few miles out of the city.

Their favorite retreat, however, was yet another country

house, or dacha, beside a lake about 30 miles outside the city. The entire area around the lake, which was not shown on ordinary maps, was fenced off and guarded. The only other houses by the water were those reserved for the three other members of the Kiev Military Soviet—the commander, the deputy commander, and the chief political officer. All the houses were substantial eight-bedroom affairs, built since the war for the exclusive use of the military brass.

Lozansky recalls the atmosphere of semioriental feudalism that pervaded life by the secret lake. "In the course of the afternoon the wives of the other district generals, who were junior to Yershov, would be dropping by with little presents, maybe a basket of fruit or a freshly shot duck. They would be very, very deferential to Margarita or anyone else from the family, including me." These gifts were more than simple neighborliness. They were tokens of tribute, in return for which some favor might be granted, such as a desired posting to Moscow, a promotion, or the removal of some blot on a husband's official record. Everybody knew that influence of this sort was the way, indeed the only way, to get ahead in the Soviet military.

Favors go in both directions. Officers who cover up mishaps for fear of the vertical stroke cannot do so in complete isolation, so colleagues and juniors who are privy to guilty secrets must be looked out for and protected. Lozansky remembers one evening at his in-laws during which Yershov was frantically engaged in pulling strings and calling favors to keep the news of a particularly embarrassing misadventure from reaching the ears of higher and possibly unfriendly quarters in Moscow. Two junior army officers had gotten drunk while on an internal military flight and had conceived the scheme of hijacking the plane so as to visit their hometown in a different part of the Soviet Union. The pilot had managed to land the plane safely, but the incident would not have reflected well on Yershov if word had gotten out. Groups of officials who collude with and protect each other for the mutual benefit of their careers are known as "family circles" in the Soviet Union, and they flourish in the military no more or less than in other parts of the bureaucracy.

Officially, of course, the officer corps should have no independent politics of its own. According to the demonology of hawks like the American General Odom, it is no more than an "administrative arm of the [Communist] Party." Military policy is determined by the Party bosses and then faithfully executed by the armed forces hierarchy.

This picture accords with the necessary perception of an efficient Soviet military machine dedicated to implementing whatever plans are handed down from above. But it hardly gibes with what we can observe of the true situation within the armed forces, where miserable troops are reduced to drinking antifreeze and barrack bullies can ignore their sergeants with impunity. Whatever plans the Party might have for its military arm, knowledge is power, and the endemic habit of collusion and cover-up prevents any accurate picture of the situation from percolating upward. If Genady's general had punished him properly for striking an officer, the offense would have gone on record and the general would have suffered; if the regimental commanders in Alex Rantinor's division had not covered up the rapes and murders, "their man" would not have got his promotion and therefore would not have been so well placed to help their careers.

Kyril Podrabinek's account of why an officer will ignore the vicious abuse of the weaklings by the bosses is a succinct description of the whole system: "Who wants to admit that such things go on in his battalion or company or platoon? You'd be the first to be taken to task by your superiors, who also don't want to incur the displeasure of their bosses. Your whole career'll go to hell."

If these features of Soviet military life sound familiar, it is because the U.S. Army of recent years has been publicly and repeatedly criticized as a nesting place for self-seeking careerists trained to observe the ethic of "cover your ass." Despite the glare of worldwide publicity, the Army was quite successful in covering up the involvement of senior officers in the My Lai massacre during the Vietnam War, although this and other symptoms of moral sickness did prompt an official U.S. military interest in "ethics." At one such officers' ethics class in 1973, a participant has recorded: "One general was saying that he was right on top of things in his units, that no one would dare submit a falsified report there. A young major stood up and said, 'General, I was in your division, and I routinely submitted falsified reports.' The general's response was, 'When you speak to a general officer, stand at attention.'"

Although it involved nothing so serious as covering up the wholesale slaughter of innocent women and children, one further example of cover-up U.S.-style is worth recording, if only because of the subsequent career of its instigator. In the fall of 1967 seven trainee officers from the Third Regiment of the West Point Academy were discovered to have been smoking marijuana. The incident was covered up because neither the regimental commander nor his superiors at the academy "wanted it known at the Pentagon that the Third Regiment harbored a bunch of junkies and perverts." The regimental commander in question was Colonel Alexander Haig, who was about to take off on his meteoric rise to great rank and greater influence. Superficially the embodiment of the military virtues, Haig was to become one of the most swiftly promoted generals in U.S. history not through any martial triumphs but because of his skills as a courtier and his deft ability for intrigue. Ivan Yershov would have little difficulty in recognizing his type.

Tales like this about the Soviet military can only appear surprising because of the common expectation that things are different over there. It is hard to accept the notion that a totalitarian system can nurture indiscipline and the arts of collusion.

On a broader level, the concept of Soviet politics, in the sense of different interest groups jockeying for position, is equally unfamiliar to us. The official U.S. view appears to be that the military plays no independent political role in the Soviet Union. *Soviet Military Power* is emphatic on this point: "The key point to understand about the Soviet military control structure is that the reins of the instruments of state power and policy—not just the purely military—are in the hands of a tested political leadership." As we shall observe in the further career of Ivan Yershov, this conclusion could not be more wrong.

Apart from the *pied-à-terre* in town and the two country houses, the Yershovs also had a beach cottage in the Crimea. In the summer months, any member of the family who felt like a weekend beside the Black Sea could commandeer a military plane and fly down. But the cottage had purposes other than simple relaxation. It was very close to Lastochkino Gnezdo, literally "bird's nest," a very exclusive beach club patronized by senior ground forces generals. Here, the military chiefs would congregate with their wives, and it was here that Yershov, abetted by Margarita, set to work to consolidate his position in a family circle which seemed to be going places.

One habitué of Bird's Nest was Viktor Kulikov, the Grechko protégé who had been appointed commander of the Kiev Military District in 1967. His stay in that post had been brief, and in 1969 he was moved on to the far more important post of commander of the Group of Soviet

Forces, Germany. This position had traditionally been a stepping stone to higher things, and there was every reason to suppose that Kulikov still had far to go. Indeed his next promotion came almost immediately.

Grechko's predecessor as Minister of Defense, Marshal Malinovsky, had appointed his favored wartime subordinate Marshal Matvei Zakharov to be chief of the General Staff, a post that at that time ranked third in the military hierarchy, after the Minister himself and the commander in chief of the Warsaw Pact Forces. In 1971, Zakharov retired because of illness, and Grechko insisted that his protégé Kulikov be given this august position. An American officer stationed at the Moscow embassy who had met Kulikov around this time remembers him as "much more dynamic than most of that bunch. He reminded me of a U.S. Four Star [general] who is going places in the Pentagon and knows it."

Left behind in the shuffle for the time being was a dour and abstemious general called Nikolai Ogarkov, a former combat engineering officer who had risen to be first deputy chief of the General Staff despite a potentially disastrous incident early on in his career, when a mine-clearing unit he was supervising had been wiped out almost to a man while clearing a minefield left over from the war. As Zakharov's deputy, he had in fact been carrying on the ailing marshal's duties for some time. Now he had lost his sponsor and went into partial eclipse.

To Yershov and many others, it was Kulikov who was the coming man in military politics, someone it was well worth doing favors for. Ivan had never served in the same command as Kulikov, and their personal contact came about through a mutual friendship with General Sokolov. Yershov needed to find some way to make his mark.

When such an opportunity arose, it came not through some military crisis but for domestic reasons. Kulikov had a daughter, and in 1972 this lady decided to move back to Kiev, where her father had reigned as district commander a few years earlier. This was Yershov's chance.

Even for the elite, moving house in the Soviet Union is a cumbersome business. Yershov determined to devote himself to smoothing the return of Miss Kulikova to Kiev. For several months, the chief of staff of the military district used the resources of the units at his disposal, 11 army divisions and one air army of 100 aircraft, to render any necessary assistance. Army troops installed and removed furniture to suit Miss Kulikova's changing tastes, air force planes flew her back and forth from Moscow, army mechanics serviced her cars, army gasoline fueled them.

The effort paid off. The relationship between Kulikov and his eager protégé blossomed as the daughter communicated her satisfaction back to Moscow. Kulikov let it be known that if he succeeded Grechko as Minister of Defense, there would be a high-level billet for Yershov, possibly even that of a deputy chief of the General Staff.

From the time that Kulikov became chief of staff in 1971, it seemed very likely that he would indeed be the next Minister of Defense. The job traditionally went to a senior serving officer. In the early 1970s there appeared to be only two possible candidates to succeed Grechko—Kulikov or Marshal Ivan Yakubovsky, the commander in chief of all Warsaw Pact forces. Yakubovsky was senior by rank, but he was also a much older man and in poor health.

So the generals who gathered at Bird's Nest in the summers of the early and mid-1970s were confident that their circle would control the entire Soviet military apparatus in the not too distant future. For the time being, they disparaged the way things were going, particularly the SALT negotiations with the Americans. Edward Kozansky remembers them sitting by the beach—Kulikov,

Sokolov, Kulikov's putative rival Yakubovsky, and Yershov. They disparaged First Secretary Brezhnev's policy of détente, they disparaged their Eastern European Allies—"good for just one day of fighting," as Kulikov used to say; they spoke in terms of antagonistic respect of the Soviet navy and air force, whose officers they felt gave themselves airs, they derided the political officers as "priests."

They did not represent the entire high command of the Soviet armed forces, since they were exclusively ground forces men. Even within the ground forces they were simply a faction, albeit an extremely powerful one. General Ogarkov, for instance, who had served as deputy to Marshal Zakharov, was not among those present. Ogarkov was very much associated with the Brezhnev policy and had actually served as the senior military representative at the SALT talks.

The accident of Edward Lozansky's marriage, subsequent involvement in dissident activities and ultimate exile to the West allow us a unique glimpse into the private lives and conversations of these high military officials. But his evidence is not uncorroborated. The confirmation comes, strangely enough, from the Soviet press.

To accept that it is possible to track political disputes in the Soviet Union through their own public press, it is first necessary to understand that the Soviets have such disputes, that these disputes are ongoing despite the preeminence of a single leader such as Brezhnev or Andropov, and that nothing appears in the press by accident. Rivalries between factions or Politburo members are not announced in headlines or discussed in open terms, the way our media broadcast disputes between a Secretary of State and a Secretary of Defense, but they exist all the same, and the press does report them. Such reporting comes in nuances—a dropped signature here, a pruned speech there—but it is clear enough for those whose antennae are correctly attuned.

The published evidence of disaffection among the sections of the military over the SALT policy is not profuse, but like the visible portion of an iceberg, such evidence betokens larger events going on beneath the surface.

In the fall of 1969, just as the talks were beginning in Helsinki, *Pravda*, the official organ of the Communist Party, reported a speech by the Foreign Minister, Andrei Gromyko, in which he had mentioned that "some people" were not convinced of the correctness of undertaking such negotiations. In the spring of 1973, Defense Minister Grechko had been promoted to the ruling Politburo at the same time as Gromyko, who had been prominently associated with the SALT I treaty signed in 1972, and Brezhnev's ally, Yuri Andropov. In January 1974, *Pravda* began publishing extracts of Grechko's speeches rather than the full version, something that does not happen to members of the Politburo who are in good standing with the inner leadership.

In 1974 the dispute erupted into what, by Soviet standards, was a public slanging match. A frequently expressed precept of Soviet military doctrine had been that the best way to preserve peace was to prepare for war. In June 1974 *Pravda* reported a remark by Brezhnev that conveyed a different notion: the best way to keep the peace was by "waging peace"—meaning détente, SALT negotiations, and so forth. Shortly after, *Krasnaya zvezda* featured articles by both Grechko and Kulikov rejecting this concept and reaffirming the concept of military preparedness as the best way of preventing war.

This was followed by another argument on the question of why the balance of forces was swinging in favor of Socialism and the influence of military strength on that process. *Pravda* quoted Brezhnev's definition: this was happening, Brezhnev said, for a variety of reasons, including the decay of capitalism, the successes of the forces of national liberation in the Third World, and the increased military might of the Soviet Union. In riposte, Kulikov and Grechko stated that the balance of forces was swinging in favor of Socialism for one reason: the increased military might of the Soviet Union.

Despite these expressions of opposition (although neither side ever directly criticized the other), the arms control negotiations had continued. In November 1974, Brezhnev and President Ford met in the Siberian port of Vladivostok to sign another accord. Just prior to the meeting, Kulikov published an article on a historical subject with topical relevance. In discussing the role of the General Staff in World War II, he stressed the fact that it had invariably done all the staff work for important wartime conferences with the Allied powers and that it would have been a great mistake for other agencies to have become involved in the process. The implications were clear: the business of dealing with strategic arms should be left to the General Staff.

It is unlikely that Stalin would have tolerated such implicit criticisms from one of his marshals, but politics is more flexible in the Soviet Union nowadays. No senior military figure has been shot there since the head of the air force went to an untimely end in 1950; Brezhnev had to rely on less drastic measures to deal with the opposition.

Grechko died suddenly in April 1976. Expectations rose in Kiev, but they were soon dashed. Moving with unusual speed, the Politburo announced that the new Minister of Defense was to be Dmitri F. Ustinov, a bespectacled civilian Party bureaucrat and a long-time ally of Brezhnev. He was and is a very militarized civilian who had been in the defense production business since being appointed people's commissar for armaments in 1941 at the age of thirty-three. Along with Brezhnev, he had been in charge of setting up the Soviet strategic missile program in the late 1950s, and before being appointed Minister he had been the Communist Party central secretariat bureaucrat with responsibility for the defense sector. Nevertheless, he had come up a different channel from the men on the Crimean beach. He and they shared no memories of the Staff Academy or postings in the military districts, no common secrets of hushed up scandals or doctored reports. No one knew his wife.

In January 1977, Brezhnev carried out the second part of his coup against the Kulikov faction. Yakubovsky died, and Kulikov was appointed to his post as commander in chief of the Warsaw Pact forces, vacating the job of chief of the General Staff. That position now went to Ogarkov, the man Kulikov had shouldered aside in 1971. Along with this reshuffle, there went a crucial shift in the relative ranking of these high-level posts. Until 1977 the Warsaw Pact commander had ranked above the chief of staff, but under the new protocol, this order was reversed. In other words, Kulikov, although he had been promoted to marshal along with Ogarkov, had been demoted.

These reverses could not have come at a worse time for the Yershovs, because they had run into deep personal trouble and needed a high-level protector. The root of their problems was their daughter Tatyana's marriage to Lozansky.

In the beginning, Lozansky had seemed like a good prospect as a son-in-law, despite the fact that he was a Jew. He had already built up a good reputation as a physicist, and with the kind of influence Yershov could supply, he might easily have gone far. Even the obstacle of his Jewishness could be removed with a simple phone call to the relevant official, who could reclassify his nationality to Russian or Ukrainian. Although Lozansky made it clear that he was content to remain a Jew, the Yershovs assumed that he would eventually see the light, and in the meantime he was presentable enough to be introduced to their powerful friends.

Unfortunately, Lozansky went beyond noncooperation on the question of his nationality, and he began to get into serious political trouble. As a physicist, he was sympathetic to the plight of Andrei Sakharov, the "father of the Soviet hydrogen bomb," who had come out in open opposition to the regime. That might not have mattered if he had kept such thoughts to himself, but Lozansky began discussing Sakharov's political statements with his officer students at the Malinovsky Tank Academy.

It was only a matter of time before the security police found out, and when they did, trouble followed quickly for Yershov. To have a senior officer so closely touched by antistate activities was beyond the pale. If things had turned out differently for Kulikov, all might have been well and the matter covered up. But matters came to a head after Grechko's death, when the Kulikov faction was in eclipse, and those now in power at the Ministry of Defense had no compunction about taking severe measures against one of Kulikov's protégés.

From being chief of staff in Kiev, with expectations of even better things to come, Yershov was abruptly placed on the retired list. The apartment, the private planes, the country houses, and the beach resort all disappeared along with the job. Yershov's fall encompassed other members of the family; his son, who had been slated for a job in the diplomatic service and had been preparing for it at the Kiev diplomatic academy, was also dismissed and forced to take up more humble employment as an engineer.

Lozansky himself faced sanctions that were even more dire, such as a stretch in a labor camp. But the authorities chose to forgo the inevitable publicity that a trial would have engendered in the West. Instead, Lozansky was induced to go quietly into exile, with the promise that Tatyana would be allowed to join him later. This promise was not to be fulfilled for some years, and then only because Tatyana went on a hunger strike.

Just when things appeared to be at their bleakest for the Yershovs, an unlikely rescuer appeared—President Jimmy Carter. In March 1977 the newly installed Carter Administration sent a delegation headed by Secretary of State Cyrus Vance to Moscow to present proposals for a new round of SALT talks. Despite the dovish rhetoric of his campaign, Carter was sensitive to pressure from U.S. defense interests to adopt a stiffer line toward the Soviet Union. There were strong demands from influential representatives of these interests, like Senator Henry Jackson and Defense Secretary Harold Brown, that the SALT talks be a forum for forcing significant arms reductions on the Soviets. Vance accordingly proposed that the Kremlin agree to a sharp and unilateral cut in the most important component of their strategic arsenal: land-based missiles.

All factions in Moscow agreed that this proposal was unacceptable, and it was immediately and forthrightly rejected. But the episode had additional and far-reaching consequences for internal Soviet politics; it legitimized anti-SALT sentiment, thus boosting the fortunes of those who had opposed the Brezhnev line all along.

Public indications of this shift were subtle but telling. One of them was the promotion of Kulikov's associate Sergei Sokolov to marshal. Other indications were the signs that Brezhnev's old crony Ustinov considered it expedient to distance himself from his mentor and show some common cause with the hard-liners.

This change in the political winds served to rehabilitate Yershov, at least partially. Sokolov arranged a deal with Ustinov: if Yershov could see to it that Tatyana severed all ties with her exiled husband, he would be reemployed.

Tatyana was accordingly pressured into writing a letter to Lozansky renouncing him forever (a declaration she later withdrew).

By the end of 1977, Yershov was back in service with a job similar in title but not in substance to his former position in Kiev. He was appointed chief of staff of the civil defense troops. These are a force of some 100,000 men specializing in measures for the mitigation of the effects of nuclear war, such as clearing roads, evacuating city dwellers, and restoring essential services. The Soviet civil defense program has many ardent admirers in the United States, but in truth it is a lowly branch of the service, as indicated by the appointment of the recently disgraced Yershov to be the chief of staff. Telling indications of the overall status of civil defense are the modest perquisites that accrued to Yershov when he took over one of its most senior posts: one apartment in Moscow and one dacha of reportedly modest proportions on which he had to pay rent.

Yershov rose, and fell, and then succeeded in making a modest comeback not because of his abilities as a soldier but because of military politics. His association first with Sokolov and then with Kulikov was the determining factor in his career through the upper reaches of the Soviet high command. His story is important not only because it allows a glimpse of the flesh-and-blood dramas that lie behind the subtle nuances of *Pravda* and *Krasnaya zvezda*, but also because it helps us understand the real motivations and preoccupations of the Soviet military elite, which are not so very different from those of their counterparts on the U.S. side. As the military career of Alexander Haig indicates, a taste and ability for political intrigue can be more important for success in the military bureaucracy than martial prowess. There is a saying in the Pentagon that the smartest officers are the colonels who never make general; enlightened Soviet defense observers may well have fashioned a similar adage.

The process feeds on itself. As the marshals and generals become involved in factional struggles both within the military and with the civilian leadership, so officers are promoted primarily on the basis of their personal loyalty.

There could be no clearer example of this process than the astonishing story of Brezhnev's coup against the high command of the ground forces in the winter of 1980–81. The point at issue was Poland. To put it simply: key elements both in the military and in the Politburo wanted to intervene forcibly to put down the Solidarity trade union in all its manifestations (this was a year before the declaration of martial law in Poland). Leonid Brezhnev opposed the idea, and he got his way.

By the early winter of 1980, matters in Poland appeared to be coming to a head. The Communist government under Stanislaw Kania was steadily retreating before the independent Solidarity organization. That the Soviets might intervene with troops, as they had in Czechoslovakia, was commonly accepted both in Poland and in the West. U.S. intelligence reported actual signs of military preparations for intervention toward the end of November. Such visible indications that the tanks might roll as the calling up of reservists and troop maneuvers on the borders were obliquely confirmed in the Soviet press. But the press reports also indicated something else: the decision to prepare for action had met with opposition at the highest level.

On November 17 a *Pravda* article on the Russian Civil War, which had ended nearly sixty years before, contained this intriguing passage: "Differences of opinion between the Commander in Chief and the command of the fronts" (local military headquarters) had been resolved in favor of "mobilization [and]... urgent measures for strengthening the army." The Soviet commander in chief, as experienced *Pravda* readers could be expected to understand, was currently Leonid Brezhnev.

Krasnaya zvezda was in a more forthrightly warlike mood, although also taking care to cloak its comments on present-day events with allusions to distant history. In November 1980 it published an article about the Soviet-Polish war of 1920. This conflict is rarely mentioned in the Soviet press, since it is normally considered awkward to discuss past wars with present-day allies, especially wars that the Soviet Union had lost. Nevertheless, the story was addressed at length, concluding with a quote from Lenin himself: "War with Poland is forced upon us." The military newspaper also printed several pointed remarks about "fawning on foreign authorities" and the dangers of subordinating "military movements . . . to the wishes and plans of diplomats" at a time when Brezhnev was meeting with foreign statesmen and being warned of the consequences of a Polish invasion.

The trouble for the bellicose generals was that although they seemed to have won the political battle, they were less adept at getting ready for a military operation. The actual mobilization turned into a shambles. Reservists called up in key districts next to the Polish border promptly deserted in numbers too large to punish, and coordination between different units and headquarters broke down.

Military intervention had been successfully touted by the generals over the apparent objections of Brezhnev, but they then had been unable to get the troops ready. It did not take long for the wily President of the Soviet Union to make them suffer the consequences. Within two months, six senior Soviet army generals were removed from their key commands in the Warsaw Pact countries or western Russia and demoted to less important posts elsewhere. General Ivan Pavlovsky, an old Bird's Nest habitué and commander in chief of the ground forces since 1967, was dispatched into semiretirement, where he was shortly joined by General S. P. Vasyagin, chief of the political directorate of the ground forces. General Ye. F. Ivanovsky, commander in chief of the 900,000 Soviet troops in East Germany, was packed off to take charge of the Byelorussian Military District, which has precisely one resident full-strength division. General D. T. Yazov, the commander in Czechoslovakia, was sent even farther away, to the Central Asian Military District.

The fallen generals' successors all had close political ties to Brezhnev. V. I. Petrov, who got Pavlovsky's job as commander of the ground forces, moved up from the Chinese border command. Just before leaving for the east to take up that post in 1978 he had been personally received by Brezhnev, a unique honor for such an appointment and a sign of high favor. The new commander facing China, V. L. Govorov, had been a close associate of Brezhnev's closest friend among the military, the political General K. S. Grushevoy. M. M. Zaytsev, who got the key East German command, was one of a group of officers who had been moved up after Brezhnev's coup in 1976.

It might be assumed that this turnover, unprecedented in recent years, was simply a case of competent new men being called in to replace those responsible for making such a complete hash of the mobilization. But that does not explain the strange case of the general who was *not* fired.

General V. A. Belikov was the commander of the Carpathian Military District, where the preparations for the mobilization had been most chaotic. If anyone's head was to roll it should have been his. But while far mightier chieftains like Pavlovsky were summarily dismissed, Belikov retained his post, the only commander of a district bordering Poland who did. In fact, *Krasnaya zvezda* went out of its way in mid-January 1981 to inform readers that Belikov was still at his post. What distinguished Belikov from the other officers involved in the invasion buildup was that he was a protégé of Brezhnev. He had been one of the select group of officers who had moved up in 1976, at the time of the Ustinov appointment.

Commenting on this episode, Richard Anderson, the former CIA analyst whose minute scrutiny of the Soviet press first uncovered Brezhnev's purge, remarks drily: "One interpretation of Politburo decisions regarding top military appointments ascribes decisive weight to a general's performance. However, another explanation could be offered—namely, that politics makes the difference. Such an explanation seems to fit here."

Nations and leaders who entrust their military fortunes to generals selected on the basis of politics or personal favoritism have usually paid a heavy price. The British commander in France during most of World War I, General Douglas Haig, retained his post because of political influence in London, although he slaughtered hundreds of thousands of men to no useful purpose. Hitler kept his toady Field Marshal Wilhelm Keitel as chief of staff while Germany went down to defeat. Egypt might well have escaped its military defeat in the 1973 war if Sadat had not backed the fatal decisions of his incompetent but reliable crony General Ahmed Ismail. That the Soviets, supposedly so dedicated to military efficiency, should select their military commanders through the machinations described above tells us much about their real priorities.

It should come as no surprise that an institution as politicized as the military establishment should play a crucial role in the politics of the state. The Red Army, after all, was originally the armed instrument by which the Bolsheviks crushed their rivals in the Civil War that followed the Revolution. Since that time there have been a number of instances when the military has intervened decisively in power struggles within the military establishment.

The precise circumstances surrounding the arrest and elimination in 1953 of Beria, Stalin's much-feared secret police chief, are obscure and likely to remain so. However, it seems clear that units of the armed forces, under the command of Marshals Zhukov and Koniev, were brought to Moscow to counter the threat of Beria's praetorian guard of KGB troops. Khrushchev later recounted that the actual arrest of Beria during a Politburo meeting was carried out by the two marshals in person.

Zhukov again came to Khrushchev's aid in 1957, when a so-called "anti-Party group" of the latter's rivals mustered a majority on the Politburo to oust him. Zhukov used military planes to fly friendly members of the Communist Party Central Committee to Moscow, thus giving Khrushchev the necessary votes to repel his rivals.

Above and beyond such dramatic incidents, however, the military establishment influences Soviet politics in a more pervasive and permanent fashion. The manner in which this influence is exercised, as well as the reasons for it, has to do with the structure of the Soviet state and economy.

Political power in the Soviet Union stems from the support of the bureaucracy, the thousands of officials who run both the myriad facets of the state-controlled economy and of the ruling Party itself. A successful Soviet politician needs to have the support of a significant portion of this "electorate" to obtain and keep his position. Just as successful military politicians like Viktor Kulikov build up a "tail" of officers like Yershov who support them, cover up their mistakes, and so on, so the civilian officials also have "tails" that form their power base. Bureaucrats down the pecking order will join the "tail" of a politician if that man seems to be in a position, at least potentially, to advance the progress of their own careers and keep them out of trouble.

Now the Soviet Union is an economy of shortages. Various sectors must compete to obtain the necessary materials, such as steel, concrete, and machine tools, which they need in order to fulfill their part of the overall production plan. A manager or Party secretary who fulfills his or her quota within the plan can expect bonuses, promotions, and a higher standard of living, while for those who fail the reverse is true.

The military establishment is the exception to this rule; it does not have to compete for resources because it is assured of automatic priority for anything that is needed. Thus, an expanding military budget automatically ensures corresponding shortages in the civilian sector, such as consumer goods. This fact of life makes control of and support from the military establishment very attractive for a Soviet politician, because he is then in a position to dominate the direction of the economy. If he supports an expansion of the military budget, rivals who control and are responsible for civilian sectors will find greater trouble in fulfilling their plans. This, in turn, means that the rivals' "tails" have greater difficulty in carrying out their functions, with consequent impact on their own positions and careers.

The would-be successful politician is primarily interested in the industrial aspects of the military establishment—the weapons-making plants and factories. But, as I explain in the following chapter, it is the generals and marshals who call the tune as to what is produced in these plants and whether the product is accepted by them, the "customers." They are thus key players in any military-industrial political coalition.

Stalin, Khrushchev, Brezhnev, and Andropov all followed this pattern in their rise to the preeminent position in the Soviet hierarchy. Each has played for and secured the support of the military-industrial complex while consolidating his power and edging out formidable political rivals. The period of the first five-year plan in the early 1930s, as directed by Stalin, was marked by overriding emphasis on the priority development of defense-oriented industry. This was also the period in which Stalin finally triumphed over rivals who advocated a less frenetic pace of development, such as Bukharin. Between 1955 and 1957, Khrushchev followed the same course, supporting and encouraging military expansion, as opposed to the softer line of some political opponents, such as Malenkov. Brezhnev's rise followed the same pattern, while his erstwhile partner Kosygin, who bore responsibility for the consumer-oriented sectors of the economy, eventually went into relative political eclipse.

As we have seen, Brezhnev's relations with the military had their turbulent moments. This too can be seen as part of an underlying pattern in Soviet politics. As each leader eventually triumphs over his rivals, he apparently perceives the necessity to cut his powerful backer—the defense complex—down to size. Stalin did this in characteristic fashion by physically eliminating great numbers of the relevant officials. Such terrorizing tactics had gone out of fashion by Khrushchev's time, so Khrushchev had to be content with sacking them—in the first instance by cutting the size of the armed forces. Brezhnev lacked the power to do even that, and in any case it might have been a bad idea to try, since disaffection among the military appears to have played a part in Khrushchev's fall. Thus, when it came time for Brezhnev to try and curb his military monster, he had to be content with the modest arms control initiatives of the SALT negotiations, which, as we have seen, were repugnant to powerful factions within the military.

Toward the end of his life, Brezhnev was once again

in political trouble. The economy was stagnant, while agriculture, the perennial problem area, had suffered from a series of disastrous harvests. In his last important speech, Brezhnev turned once again to his original and most important power base. Addressing 500 generals assembled for the purpose in the Kremlin, he delivered a bellicose peroration, reaffirming his commitment to match the concurrent U.S. buildup (and thus expand the defense budget). Within a month, he was dead.

Yuri V. Andropov acceded to the key position of First Secretary of the Communist Party of the Soviet Union within a day of Brezhnev's death. In a speech delivered to the Party's Central Committee, which elected him to the First Secretaryship immediately afterward, he gave a clear indication that his consolidation of power was to follow the same pattern as that of his predecessors. "We know well that the imperialists will never meet one's pleas for peace," he told the officials. "It can only be defended by relying on the invincible might of the Soviet Armed Forces." Writing shortly afterward about the circumstances of the Andropov takeover, Dusko Doder, the well-informed Moscow correspondent of the Washington *Post*, reported that "the backing of the armed forces was decisive."

While Western observers might therefore hopefully speculate whether a new Soviet leader would follow a dovish policy, the traditional patterns of Soviet politics suggests that he would have to pursue a hawkish line, thus justifying heavy expenditures on the military-industrial complex. Only when he feels his position is unassailable will he be able to pursue an alternative course.

This kind of subordination of the issues of peace or war to the grubby considerations of internal politics should come as no great surprise to Americans. Agitation over the Soviet threat and the consequent necessity for increased largesse for the U.S. military-industrial complex is a standard feature of the American electoral cycle. When I asked former Secretary of State Cyrus Vance why the Carter Administration had opted for a far more hard-line foreign policy in 1979, he replied matter-of-factly that this development was inevitable because "we were getting into election politics at that point."

Richard Anderson has pointed out that "foreign nations can scarcely regard with equanimity the Soviet leaders' willingness to upset the world military balance for the convenience of their own internal struggles," a sentiment that applies equally well to the activities of U.S. politicians. Still, it helps us cope with the specter of the Soviet threat if we understand that Soviet postures are determined by politics rather than deep-laid schemes for aggression founded on ideological hostility toward the West. Such understanding also helps us understand the poor performance of the industrial portion of the Soviet military-industrial complex in producing weapons for an actual shooting war.

Five

The Weapons Makers

Tom Wolfe, in his book about the first American astronauts, *The Right Stuff*, makes reference to the mysterious nature of the Soviet space program, which in the late 1950s was scoring spectacular successes: "It gave off an air of sorcery. . . . It was revealed only that the Soviet program was guided by a mysterious individual known as the 'Chief Designer.' But his powers were indisputable."

The Sputnik era, when the Russians scored continuous triumphs—first satellite, first man in space, first rocket to the moon—reinforced for Westerners a change in the image of Soviet science and technology, which began when the Russians exploded their first nuclear bomb in August 1949.

Although the Russians had already been feared as a military threat, it had been assumed that the danger they posed lay crudely in vast numbers, which could to some extent be counterbalanced by the scientific sophistication of America and her allies. Sputnik did far more to shake this view than did the atom bomb, since that achievement could be written off as cheating—the Russians had stolen the secrets of the atom bomb from the United States by use of spies. What made both the bomb and the space rockets so much more intimidating was the "air of sorcery," the relentless anonymity that surrounded these endeavors.

That was a long time ago. We now know that the mysterious chief designer was Sergei Korolev, an early pioneer of rocket flight who had spent years in prison during Stalin's rule. We know that the chief scientist on the Soviet bomb project was Igor Kurchatov and that the most useful intelligence the Soviets received from America was an official and nonsecret U.S. government document called the Smyth Report. This told them the best way to go about enriching uranium for the bomb's core, without their having to try various costly alternative approaches as the Americans had done.

These are historical insights, information released by the Soviets because it is now old and of interest only to historians. Information about current Soviet weapons development and production, however, is a different matter.

In the winter of 1981, a Swedish televison team arrived in a small Moscow working-class apartment to film a profile of a typical Muscovite family. The project had official blessing, and the Swedes had been provided with a government guide to supervise the proceedings. Filming was about to commence, when a neighborhood policeman arrived. He vehemently accused the Swedes of attempting espionage and ejected them forthwith. There was nothing of interest to any foreign power in the apartment itself, but the view from the living-room window was of a high brick wall. Behind that wall was a factory engaged in work for the Ministry of Defense, which, in the eyes of the policeman, made the wall itself a state secret.

There are many such walls in the Soviet Union. No one in the West is quite sure of the full dimensions of the military-industrial complex that lies behind them. Between 4 and 7 million people are directly engaged in defense work. The U.S. Defense Intelligence Agency says there are 135 major plants to assemble the missiles, tanks, submarines, fighter planes, and other weapons. There are a further 3,500 related factories and installations that provide support for the big plants. If the Defense Intelligence Agency is right, it may know more than the deputy chairman of the State Planning Commission, which is responsible for drawing up the overall state plan for the Soviet economy. Asked by a foreign visitor how many plants were directly engaged in defense production in the Soviet Union, this official replied, "I don't know, and if I did I wouldn't tell you."

Again, no one knows precisely how many scientists and technicians are employed in developing new weapons for the Soviet military. The best estimates put the number at around 400,000 men and women.

Part of the difficulty in calculating the size of the Soviet military-industrial complex is due to the lack of a clear distinction between the military and civilian sectors of the overall economy. "Civilian" scientists may be asked to help on a problem relating to weapons research, sometimes without even being told for whom they are working. This was the experience of Elena, a graduate student in meteorology who was hired by a research institute to carry out what she assumed was some work of a benign nature on weather patterns. Only when a bureaucratic slipup resulted in the name of her real employer being written on her trade-union card did she discover that she was working for the Ministry of Medium Machinery, which is responsible for the production of nuclear explosives. From this she inferred that she was, in fact, helping determine radioactive-fallout patterns.

On a more mundane level, civilian factories may spend a great deal of time working on military contracts. When the Ministry of Defense decrees a styling change in military uniforms, the entire clothing industry has to be involved, causing a consequent shortage of civilian clothes in the stores. At the same time, defense enterprises have entered the civilian market. The Ministry of General Machinery supervises factories that make streetcars, refrigerators, and combine harvesters, as well as nuclear missiles and space rockets.

Surprising as it may seem, it is in the defense sector that the Soviet economy is closest to the U.S. economy. In contrast to America, the consumer does not enjoy much priority in Soviet business. Since most consumer goods are in short supply, the buyer must take what he is given and be thankful for it. But in the defense sector, it is the customer who is in charge. The military issue their requirements to the suppliers, in much the same way as in the United States. The military can then reject products that do not measure up to their specifications.

Every plant producing goods for the armed forces in the Soviet Union has a military representative permanently stationed on the premises. In the big plants, these officers, called the *voyenpredy*, are high-ranking generals. They have the power to reject anything that does not meet the officially prescribed standards of quality.

Subservience to the whims of the customer is not the only parallel between the Soviet and American defense industries. Just as names like General Dynamics, Lockheed, and McDonnell Douglas are synonymous with American warplanes and missiles, so too the Russians have big-name defense contractors. They are called design bureaus and are named after the designers who originally set them up. The famous MiG fighters are developed by the Mikoyan-Gurevich Bureau, named for Artem Mikoyan and Mikhail Gurevich. There are the Cholomei, Yangel, and Nadiradze missile "corporations." The Sukhoi Bureau designs and oversees production of Sukhoi fighters; likewise, the Tupolev Bureau designs bombers, and the Morozov Bureau develops tanks. As we shall see, the relationship of these "contractors" to their military customers and the manner in which the bureaus execute their contracts have many similarities with how American defense contractors conduct their business.

The dimensions of the Soviet defense-industrial effort are normally expressed in terms of cost, which is then frequently compared to the U.S. defense budget. Statements such as "the Soviets are outspending us by 50 percent" do not really tell us much, since they equate the number of dollars spent with military capability. Even when the estimated Soviet budget is broken down into categories of weapons—so much for missiles, so much for submarines, so much for tanks—we are not really much wiser, since plain figures do not inform us as to how efficiently the money has been spent. To cite an American example, we know that the cost of the U.S. M-1 tank increased from $500,000 to $2.8 million over ten years, but we cannot assume that the tank became five and a half times more threatening to the Soviets in that time.

The value of this kind of comparison between the United States and the Soviet Union is further diminished, since no one really knows what the cost of the Soviet defense effort actually is. The United States publishes its defense expenditures. The Soviet government also publishes a defense budget, giving a figure of just over 17 billion rubles, a figure which has hardly changed in ten years and which cannot be accurate. It would mean that Soviet defense costs amount to one-eighth of the U.S. defense budget.

Furthermore, the official Soviet figures show their defense budget declining slightly over the course of the 1970s.

It may be that Soviet authorities themselves do not know the precise economic burden of their defense industry on the overall economy. In a Western free-market economy, the cost of something is reflected in its price. But in Russia, the price of something is what the government says it is, although that may not necessarily bear any relation to the true cost. Defense plants, for example, may get their electricity at 10 percent of the price paid by civilian consumers. Thus, the energy bill for that plant will be low, while the economy bears the excess cost of producing the power.

The CIA, charged with the task of estimating the true size of the Soviet defense budget, strives to come up with a realistic figure by indirect means. Its method has been to rely on what is called the direct-costing method. The analysts count up all the physical components and activities of the Soviet defense effort, such as weapons, labor forces, and construction, and then estimate what these would cost in the United States. Using this method, the CIA argues that the Soviet Union heavily outspends the United States.

This "spending gap" has had a big effect on U.S. policymakers, which is disturbing because the calculation is based mainly on guesswork. The approach involves taking intelligence data on individual Russian weapons, such as the Backfire bomber, and asking a U.S. industrial concern how much it would charge to produce it. In the case of the Backfire, the authority to ask is the Rockwell International Corporation, which makes the closest thing to the Backfire in the United States, the B-1 bomber. Thus, the price that corporation charges the U.S. government for the B-1 becomes the basis for calculating the cost of the Backfire. If there is a cost overrun on the B-1, the CIA estimate of the Backfire goes up accordingly. This, in turn, means that our estimate of the overall Soviet defense budget goes up.

The pitfalls of this method become even more apparent when it comes to calculating manpower costs. Since the object is to find the "dollar equivalent" of Soviet expenditures, the CIA counts all the men in the Soviet forces and awards them the same pay scales as the American volunteer soldier. But an American enlisted man gets $573 a month basic pay, while a Soviet draftee gets the equivalent of $6.50 a month, so the CIA calculations manifestly exaggerate what the Soviets are spending on manpower.

In estimating "investment," the military term for weapons buying, the CIA used to make one crucial assumption—that the defense economy of the USSR operated on a more efficient level than the civilian sector. It is easy for Western visitors to see that ordinary civilian industry in the USSR is plagued by bottlenecks, shortages, and shoddy production. Given their habit of thinking postively about anything to do with Soviet defense, it may have been natural for U.S. intelligence agencies to infer that the part of the Soviet economy hidden behind high walls functioned in a different and better way from the observable chaos of the civilian sector.

The CIA revised its thinking in 1975, and the Soviet defense budget went up as a result. The intelligence authorities announced that, after careful reevaluation of their data, they found that the Soviets were not much more efficient at producing weapons than they were at producing cars or tape recorders. It therefore followed that it was costing the Russians much more than had been previously assumed to produce the same amount of tanks, submarines, and other weapons.

The intelligence officials' explanation for their change of mind was not quite the whole story. They had indeed been reexamining their assumptions about the efficiency of the Soviet defense industry—and had concluded that all their calculations were correct. Their complacency was spoiled by a report from a defector, which proved that the actual secret Soviet defense budget, available only to high-level officials, showed the price the Soviets paid for defense to be much higher than the CIA had estimated. According to former CIA employees, the intelligence analysts were extremely reluctant to accept this piece of hard intelligence, which pointed up the faults in their methods, and they did everything they could to disprove its authenticity.

In the end, they accepted it, with the result that the spending gap increased. This was widely misunderstood to mean that the Soviets were investing in more weapons. The truth was, they were investing more to produce the same amount of weapons because of inefficiency. Occasional press reports did point out why the Soviet defense budget had suddenly increased and the questionable basis of the dollar-equivalent methodology. But these caveats made little impression on the American consensus that the United States was falling behind in the race to spend money on defense. After all, as the hawkish Pentagon officials appointed by President Reagan like to point out, the Russians have built up their defense effort to the point where they are outproducing the United States in all important categories of weapons.

Soviet weapons building does appear to be large, large enough to justify the assertion, frequently repeated, of a "buildup." The "buildup," however, is not a recent phenomenon but one that started half a century ago. In the 1930s, the regime launched a major spending program in the defense industry. Throughout most of that decade, the Soviets were producing 3,000 tanks a year, more than today. They were also churning out 3,000 aircraft a year. In 1938 the Soviets started a major buildup in warship construction.

Apart from straightforward weapons manufacture, the Russians also pursued an energetic program of research and development in military technology. They were continually designing new types of fighter planes, very-long-range bombers, versatile tanks that could swim, even a mortar that could dig trenches.

This massive investment was carried out at the cost of immense sacrifices for the civilian population. But on the outbreak of war with Nazi Germany in June 1941, the Russians outnumbered their enemies by 6 to 1 in tanks, 5 to 1 in aircraft, and 2 to 1 in submarines.

By the end of 1941, nearly all this enormous arsenal had been destroyed. Superior German tactics, training, and equipment had more than made up for unequal numbers. Nevertheless, the buildup of the 1930s paid off. After the initial shock of the German invasion, the Russians managed in six months to shift over 1,300 major factories and more than 10 million people to new industrial centers behind the Ural Mountains, out of reach of the German panzers. By the beginning of 1942, with factories that sometimes lacked roofs and with workers living in tents, they were already producing four times as many tanks as a year before and 70 percent more aircraft. By the end of 1942, the Russians were producing almost twice as many aircraft as Germany and more than four times as many tanks, a feat made possible by the breakneck industrialization of the 1930s. For the Russian leadership of today, all of whom retain vivid memories of the wartime crisis, there could be no better confirmation of the virtues of putting enormous resources into defense production.

Since 1945, there have been two periods of temporary decline in Soviet defense production. The first was immediately after the war, when the Soviets had to divert resources to rebuild an economy in ruins. The defense production burgeoned again, however, when they began to invest in a new generation of advanced weapons, including the atom bomb. The second decline occurred in the late 1950s, when Krushchev decided that nuclear missiles had made large conventional forces obsolete. He subsequently cut the defense budget and reduced the physical size of the army. In a speech delivered in January 1960, Khrushchev claimed that the Soviet armed forces had dropped from 5,763,000 men in 1955 to 3,623,000 in 1958.

At the same time as Khrushchev was reducing the size of the conventional forces, which involved cashiering thousands of officers, he was building up what he regarded as the new and decisive instrument of military power—nuclear missiles. In December 1959 a totally new service was set up, the strategic rocket forces; the industry to supply the expensive equipment required by the new forces was constructed simultaneously.

After the Berlin crisis of 1961, the modest trend in arms reductions was reversed. By the mid-1960s, with nuclear-missile technology assimilated and Khrushchev retired, the defense industry settled down to a steady and lavishly funded rate of production, claimed to be between 12 and 14 percent of the gross national product. However, investment of large amounts of economic resources in defense production does not necessarily translate into increased weapons production and consequent military capability.

It is commonly accepted by both hawks and doves that the Soviets have been engaged in a massive rearmament program since sometime in the early 1960s. Doves may point to the array of threats facing the Soviet Union as justifying to a certain extent a rearmament program. Hawks consider it to be clear evidence of the malevolent and aggressive schemes being hatched in the Kremlin.

Such rhetoric tends to obscure the actual details of Soviet weapons production, which do not by any means describe an across-the-board buildup. It is true that during the 1960s the Soviets did sharply accelerate their production of land-based intercontinental missiles. But in other areas the picture is not so clear. If anything, the figures suggest that the Soviets have been building down rather than up. Estimates of Soviet aircraft production for 1960 range upward from an annual total of 5,000. Tank production during the early 1950s was estimated at 6,000 by U.S. intelligence and confirmed by official Soviet figures. By 1966, according to the Pentagon's own figures, tank production had fallen to 3,500 a year, and by 1981 it was down to 2,000. (In the intervening years the numbers did fluctuate, from a high of 4,500 in 1970 to a low of 2,000 in the mid-1970s, up to 3,000 in 1980, before falling again.) Fighter production is estimated at 1,350 for 1981, well down from the 1960 figure and about almost exactly the same as it was in 1937.

The familiar image of a steady buildup is further clouded by the fact that an increasingly large proportion of Soviet arms production is intended not for the supply of the country's armed forces but for export. The indications are that the Soviet Union's pressing need for hard cash has given rise to a policy of selling as much arms overseas as possible. Between 1977 and 1981, for example, the Soviet Union turned out 15,100 tanks and self-propelled guns. In the same period, it delivered no fewer than 7,050 of these weapons to foreign customers, including nearly one in every three of the brand-new T-72 tanks that came off the assembly lines. (There have indeed been reports that this led to a shortfall of T-72 deliveries to Warsaw Pact allies.) Between 1976 and 1981, more than one-third of the Soviet production of the most modern fighters and fighter-bombers has been diverted overseas, while one class of submarines, the Foxtrot, is manufactured solely for export.

Once upon a time the Russians were content to use arms transfers simply as a means of winning friends and controlling people, accepting payment in the form of barter deals or soft currency. By the early 1980s, the most poverty-stricken clients were being required to pay up. Even the indigent Ethiopians were obliged to find hard currency to pay for their Soviet arsenal. So important has this trade become to the Soviet economy that the prospect of a major order for the MiG-27 fighter-bomber by the Indian air force was enough to send Defense Minister Ustinov himself hurrying to New Delhi in March 1982 to tout his wares. The trip was to no avail, as the Indians ultimately selected a French plane, the Mirage 2000, which they considered to be superior.

All available information about Soviet defense production indicates that the industry, while not expanding in any dynamic fashion, is operating in a very comfortable and well-funded rut. A full order book does not necessarily mean either dynamic innovation or superior quality, as the recent history of the American automobile industry can confirm. As Detroit continued producing more of the same, the quality of both workmanship and design declined. The complacent industry became a dinosaur, easily overtaken by the Japanese.

It is true that during World War II, the threat of imminent defeat by the Germans galvanized all sections of the country to superhuman efforts. If the German threat was not sufficient to extract the maximum performance from everyone concerned with producing weapons, there were more personal sanctions. The aircraft designer Aleksandr Yakovlev recounted in his memoirs how Stalin ordered him to carry out a particular task. When Yakovlev tried to refuse, Stalin told him, "We are not afraid of coercion. We will not stop short of coercion when it is necessary. Sometimes coercion is useful. Without coercion, there would have been no revolution." Yakovlev took on the job.

The program to build an atom bomb, which went into high gear in 1945, had the overriding priority of a wartime project and the same threat of coercion. Lavrenti Beria, Stalin's much-feared secret police chief, was in charge of the overall project. Beria made use of thousands of slave laborers from the Gulag Archipelago, which he controlled. One of the chief scientists on the program, Vasily Emelyanov, later remarked, "What would have happened if we hadn't made it then? They would have shot us. Just shot."

Although it is hard to find examples of scientists and engineers actually being executed for failing to perform, there was certainly intense competition in the early postwar years between the different weapons-producing enterprises. This is best illustrated by the history of Russian jet fighters.

The Germans had been the first to put jet-propelled aircraft into production, although such aircraft came too late to have much effect on the course of the war. After the German surrender, both the Russians and the Americans started intensive efforts to build their own jet fighters, based largely on captured German prototypes and drawings.

Five Soviet design bureaus competed for the contract to build the first production jet fighter—the Sukhoi, Lavochkin, Alekseev, Mikoyan-Gurevich, and Yakovlev Bureaus. All built prototypes. Three were discarded in favor of the Mikoyan-Gurevich entrant, which became known as the MiG-15. After losing to the MiG, one of the contenders, the Alekseev Bureau, went out of business.

In 1951 and 1953 the Mikoyan-Gurevich Bureau once again beat what was left of the competition with the MiG-17 and the supersonic MiG-19. None of the losing prototype fighters were seen again. After 1953, the Lavochkin enterprise disappeared from the manned aircraft business. The Sukhoi Bureau would have suffered the same fate, since none of Pavel Sukhoi's planes scored in these competitions. But Sukhoi was an old acquaintance of Khrushchev, who rescued him from oblivion.

Of all the aviation chiefs, Yakovlev was personally closest to Stalin. In his autobiography, he gives a telling account of how he managed to avert the consequences of failure in the MiG-15 competition.

"We have the fine MiG-15," Stalin declared, "and I have no intention of creating any new fighters in the immediate future. It would be better to continue improving the MiG. . . ."

"I was highly upset by the situation that was arising in our Design Bureau," recounts Yakovlev. "Behind me there were several hundred people who might lose faith in me as a design team leader. . . . And so day and night, I was tormented by the question of what stand to take."

Finally, Yakovlev promised Stalin that he could develop a new plane totally different from the MiG-15; it would have a long range and be able to fly and fight in bad weather. Stalin accepted the idea, and Yakovlev set to work. His design team came up with what became the Yak-25. The new plane flew only after Stalin's death, which may have been just as well for Yakovlev, since the Yak-25 had neither a long range nor the ability to fight in bad weather.

Whether by coincidence or not, things changed after Stalin died. There were no more competitions to produce the best aircraft. Instead, everybody's plane got built, or at least no one went out of business just because of a bad plane. In 1955, the Sukhoi and Mikoyan-Gurevich Bureaus both produced prototype interceptors. The MiG-21 was judged to be the better plane; it had better acceleration, speed, and "handling qualities" and was the winning entry. It has since been produced in great quantities all over the world. But the Sukhoi plane did not disappear; it too was put into production. However, instead of being used to intercept bombers, for which it was originally designed, it was employed as a ground-attack plane and consequently did not perform very well in its new role.

This pattern has continued. No one goes out of business anymore; there are no penalties for failure. A direct result of this featherbedding is that the Soviets must operate a large number of different types of combat planes. The air defense forces, which are solely concerned with defending Soviet territory against enemy bombers, have no less than eight different kinds of interceptors. The implications are that each plane requires different training, supply lines, repair shops, and spare parts, all of which is costly and inefficient.

As there are no penalties for failure, there are no commensurate rewards for success. In the early postwar years, all the design bureaus had a system of strong material incentives for their employees to work hard and outperform the competition. But these bonuses are now a standard part of everyone's pay packet. "They have," says Richard D. Ward, a U.S. aircraft designer who has made a special study of the Soviet system, "a license to exist. They take care not to run any risks by trying an innovative idea. If they produce an unworkable design, as was the case with the original MiG-23 (now the standard operational fighter), they are allowed to keep on working until it is at least acceptable even if it isn't brilliant."

The original pioneers who built up Soviet aviation and who gave their names to the design bureaus are nearly all dead now—Artem Mikoyan, who profited by the fact that his brother Anastas was a long-surviving member of the Politburo; Andrei Tupolev, the bomber specialist who survived five years in Stalin's prisons; Pavel Sukhoi, who did well out of his friendship with Khrushchev. Yakovlev, who was reportedly adept at flattering Stalin, is still alive at the time of this writing and is still, at least in theory, in charge of his bureau.

The prospects for imaginative innovation in the future are not increased by the fact that, in some cases at least, the great bureaus have become family enterprises. Yakovlev's son Sergei has taken over day-to-day responsibility for his father's bureau. Tupolev's son "inherited" the Tupolev Bureau, and the Mikoyan-Gurevich Bureau is now headed by the firm's longtime chief engineer, R. A. Belyakov.

Innovation is further restricted by a comprehensive bureaucracy that superintends the work of the designers. Concepts and design ideas must be cleared through the Ministry of Aviation, the Central Aerodynamics Institute, the Ministry of Defense, and the General Staff. Designers must work from officially approved "designers' handbooks," which specify what kind of aircraft designs may be used—for example, sharply swept-back wings, high tails, or twin tails—and which dictate what kind of materials can be used in building the plane.

Such bureaucratic stagnation does not seem to be unique to the aircraft industry. Soviet tanks have not changed their appearance, or indeed many of their working parts, since Stalin laid down the basic criteria of what a tank should look like in 1938. This may have to do with the fact that the designer to whom Stalin delivered his instructions, Aleksandr Morozov, was still the most important Soviet tank designer until the early 1970s. All Soviet tanks currently in service bear his imprint.

The most important design bureaus are the missile-building concerns, and the most important among these are Yangel and Cholomei. The former is named for Mikhail Yangel, a Siberian-born engineer descended from German immigrants. He had more experience with missiles than any other Soviet designer. During World War II, Yangel had infiltrated the German V-2 rocket program as a spy for the Red Army. In the 1950s, he worked as a deputy to Sergei Korolev, the designer of the Sputnik rockets, before being given his own bureau.

V. N. Cholomei, the founder of the rival enterprise, had originally prospered as a designer of naval missiles. When Korolev, who had designed excellent space rockets, failed to produce anything but indifferent nuclear missiles, Khrushchev turned to Cholomei. As chief designer, Cholomei had access to Khrushchev on a personal basis. A revealing anecdote indicates the power these chief designers enjoyed. Cholomei wanted to build a dacha in an area just outside Moscow where no building was permitted. He appealed to the chairman of the Moscow Soviet, the man in charge of the Moscow government, to have the regulations waived but was turned down. He then took his request to Khrushchev personally. The Soviet leader listened carefully to his story and then phoned the chairman of the Moscow Soviet and told him, "I understand you have turned down comrade Cholomei's request. Aren't you forgetting you are an elected official?" Cholomei got his house.

By the 1970s, both Yangel and Cholomei were dead, but the great design bureaus they had founded were flourishing. Both bureaus were building prototypes of a long-range missile that had been ordered by the government. The Cholomei missile was adjudged to be superior to the Yangel version, since it was more reliable and could carry more warheads. It went into full-scale production in 1974.

So far, the Soviets have deployed more than 300 of the Cholomei missiles, which the Americans call the SS-19. But the inferior Yangel missile, known as the SS-17, was also put into production, although on a more limited basis. So far, the Russians have installed 150 of them in silos in the central USSR.

"I cannot think of any reason for putting a missile like the SS-17 into series production," says one former high-level adviser to the U.S. Defense Department, who has perused the intelligence information on the SS-17 and SS-19 competition. "Except," he adds, "to keep the Yangel people happy and prosperous." Yet the business success of Yangel in this instance is eclipsed by the record of the Nadiradze Bureau, founded by V. N. Nadiradze, which has been trying and failing to build a solid-fueled ICBM for twenty years.

In the 1950s, the early ICBMs produced by the Russians and the Americans used liquid fuel. The fuel itself is not complicated to make. However, it requires a rocket motor of complex construction, and furthermore, it is liable to explode. In the 1960s, the Americans changed over to missiles powered by solid fuel, which is far safer to use. Such fuel can be left in the missile for long periods and requires a less complicated motor. However, it is extremely difficult to manufacture. The Nadiradze Bureau was given the task of duplicating the American achievement. Its first attempt became known as the SS-13, which was not a success. While the Americans were building 1,000 of their equivalent missile, the Minuteman, the Russians deployed only 60 SS-13s.

The bureau tried again with the SS-15, which was apparently so unsatisfactory that it was dropped even before it was properly flight-tested. The succeeding SS-16 was, in the words of one U.S. military observer, "A dog of a missile—it was just no good."

Toward the end of 1982, however, the pressure on Nadiradze intensified. Under the terms of the SALT II agreement, the Soviets are permitted to develop one new ICBM, but once they had certified that the development of that missile had started, they were not permitted the option of dropping it and trying an alternative model.

On October 26, 1982, a solid-fueled medium-sized prototype ICBM lifted off from the Plesetsk test site in northern European Russia and headed for Kamchatka. It never got there, because a few seconds after launch the missile blew up. Once again, Nadiradze had blown it. An otherwise anonymous "Reagan Administration arms control expert" admitted shortly afterward to the trade newsletter *Aerospace Daily* that the failed test was "a certain sign of the failure of Soviet technology that . . . they still don't have a good operational solid-propellant missile."

Intercontinental nuclear missiles, by the very nature of their mission, are usually discussed in apocalyptic and impersonal terms. Reports of conventional weapons frequently include the name of the manufacturer—for example, the Lockheed Starfighter, the General Dynamics F-16, and the MiG-21. The provenance of the ICBMs is less familiar. We do not customarily hear of the Boeing Minuteman, the Martin Marietta MX, or the Yangel SS-17.

It is slightly surprising, therefore, to realize that behind these immensely destructive weapons there lie organizations, both in Russia and in America, which foul up on schedules, make fraudulent claims to their governments, and incur cost overruns.

In January 1967 Art Cruikshank, a U.S. Air Force general, then in charge of the development of the Minuteman II intercontinental nuclear missile, told a high-level Pentagon meeting of a discussion he had recently had with the contractor responsible for making the weapon's guidance system. "'Don't worry about it, Art,' he said to me. 'This system is like old wine—the older it gets, the better it is.' I said to him, 'Bullshit. It's like old cheese. The older it gets, the worse it smells.'"

Such droll insights into the real world of the missile business are rare even in the United States. They are rarer still on the Soviet side. Mikhail Agursky, a dapper engineer who now lives in Jerusalem, worked in Moscow for the Institute of Production Technology before he emigrated. The institute was responsible to the missile-building Ministry of General Machinery. It was run by Mikhail Kovalev, whose prevoius career had been in the manufacture of bullets. His main qualification for running the missile institute was not his insight into ammunition manufacture, which is totally irrelevant to rocket technology, but the fact that he was an old crony of future Defense Minister Dimitri Ustinov, who was in charge of the military rocket program. When setting up the Soviet missile-construction industry, Ustinov had been reluctant to draw on the powerful aircraft industry for support and facilities. Instead, he had turned to less qualified but more assuredly loyal bureaucrats like Kovalev.

In the spring of 1970, Agursky was summoned to a meeting in the director's office. Among those present was the chief engineer of the Yangel missile plant in Dnepropetrovsk. The engineer explained that they had a problem down at the plant. The Council of Ministers, which must authorize all important Soviet weapons projects, had just awarded Yangel a contract to produce the largest missile ever built in the USSR, or indeed anywhere. The problem was that the design bureau had agreed to have the missile in production in three years. The contract, however, contained no provision for the complex machine tools that would be necessary for the missile to be produced in quantity. Without these machine tools, the missile could not meet its schedule, since no Soviet firm could produce them in time.

There was, however, a West German machine tool firm which was fully abreast of the problems of large missile construction, since it had supplied equipment built to American specifications for the U.S. Saturn moon rockets. The Germans were eager to do business with the Russians and had promised to make delivery within a year.

Since this seemed a golden opportunity to keep the project on schedule, Agursky was surprised to note that the man from Yangel was reluctant to accept the German offer. He was even more puzzled that the missile bureau seemed so anxious to foist the responsibility for supplying the vital tools onto Kovalev, since his institute was totally ill-equipped for the task. "I told Kovalev, 'You're in a trap.' He said nothing but agreed to make the tools."

Only afterward did Agursky realize how naïve he had been. The omission of any mention of a machine-tool supplier in the contract had not been an oversight but a deliberate ploy by the Yangel people. They were well aware that in any event they had no hope of getting the missile ready in three years, but this way the schedule slippage could be blamed on the late arrival of the tools. The Germans with their irritating efficiency were threatening to spoil the whole plan.

The West German offer was rejected. The machine tools, produced under the auspices of Kovalev's institute, arrived late, and the missile went into production years behind schedule. When it finally did appear, the Americans called it the SS-18, and were so impressed with its potency, they made limitations on its production a focal point of the SALT II negotiations.

Kovalev did not suffer for his part in delaying this mighty addition to the Russian arsenal. At the time Agursky left Moscow in 1975, Kovalev still enjoyed the trappings of Soviet success. "He got 1,000 rubles a month, which is very high for Russia. He had a good apartment in Moscow. He went for vacations to one of the special resorts reserved for the elite. His children went to the best schools. He had a car, and could get food even when it was in short supply."

Willful obstruction of the kind described by Agursky would probably have been discovered and mercilessly punished in the days of Stalin and Beria. But even without the threat of coercion, it is possible that this kind of problem would not have arisen.

During and immediately after the war, defense work offered both intellectual challenges and a standard of living that were not to be found elsewhere. The civilian economy was being rebuilt on the basis of prewar 1930s technology. The exciting place for a scientist to be was in the weapons business, particularly in the novel fields of nuclear fission, radar, and jet engines. At the same time, the perquisites of defense work—high salaries, incentive bonuses, good housing, holiday resorts, personal cars—were not so accessible elsewhere.

In the 1950s, however, this began to change. As civilian opportunities expanded, the advantages of working in the defense sector became less pronounced and the disadvantages more apparent. The major disadvantage is the elaborate and comprehensive apparatus of secrecy which surrounds all aspects of Soviet defense work. In the high-level meeting to discuss how the Yangel Bureau might evade the contract deadline for the SS-18, the words "rocket" and "missile" were never used. Instead, the participants used nicknames or referred to "the product."

All information is classified in one of five categories: "open," "confidential," "secret," "top secret," or "top top secret." Every defense installation in the country has a resident KGB office to enforce the rules, and when a new employee is taken on, this office assigns the degree of secret information he or she is entitled to receive. There is no overall system to determine who should know what. The result is that a person working in one place may have a "secret" clearance, while a colleague doing the exact same work elsewhere might be classified "top secret."

A defense worker's security pass entitles that worker to enter only his or her particular place of work. Communications with other defense installations have to be cleared through the KGB. There is a "universal" pass which should allow the bearer to go anywhere, but it is so rare that there have been cases where people presenting such a pass have been arrested by security guards who thought the unfamiliar pass must be a forgery.

The records of any work that carries a classification of "secret" or higher must be kept in the KGB office attached to all defense-related enterprises. Thus, the scientists and engineers must record their labors in "secret" notebooks, the pages of which are numbered and must not be removed or defaced. Every office must have two typing pools, one for "open" work and one for "secret" work.

This security bureaucracy can and does lead to absurd situations. Agursky recalls how Kovalev and Kovalev's deputy once went to Paris to attend an international exhibition on machine tools. More interested in seeing the sights than in attending to the business at hand, the two men visited the exhibition simply to pick up all the brochures on offer, which were so numerous that they had to be transported back to Moscow in a separate suitcase.

Upon returning home, Kovalev and his deputy instructed Agursky to write up the required report on their trip. Agursky discovered that the brochures did not help much, so he wrote his 400-page reprot on developments in international machine-tool manufacture entirely from data supplied by ordinary Western technical magazines. After he had turned it in and it had been typed up in the "open" typing pool, the middle-aged lady who ran the KGB office announced that according to a recent decree, all reports on trips abroad must be classified as "secret." She demanded therefore that the typescript of Agursky's report be copied out in longhand into a "secret" notebook and then retyped in the "secret" pool.

After several days of delicate negotiations, Kovalev and the KGB lady agreed on a compromise to evade the regulations. The report was not retyped, but every page was stamped "secret" to make it appear as though the proper procedures had been followed. It was then filed in the KGB's library, available only to those with "secret" or higher clearances.

This stultifying system has very deleterious effects on the quality of Soviet defense research and development because any bureaucracy that is shielded from critical observation is prone to sterility and incompetence.

Dr. Thomas S. Amlie, a former technical director of the U.S. Naval weapons center at China Lake, California, describes how he was once charged with developing a new tactical air-to-air missile. One crucial component was the proximity fuze, which would cause the missile to explode when it neared the target. Amlie was anxious to scrutinize the work of the fuze-development team, which was in another location. "They told me their work was so sensitive, my top secret clearance wasn't enough. So I went and got a 'need to know' clearance. When I finally got to look at their work, I found that what they had developed would not and could not work."

In February 1982 the deputy director of the CIA, Admiral Bobby R. Inman, put the case for security restrictions on scientific inquiry. "Science and National Security," he wrote, "have a symbiotic relationship."

Writing in reply, the executive officer of the American Association for the Advancement of Science, William Carey, declared, "Censorship, secrecy, and the heavy presence of the police state all contribute to limit Soviet science to something less than world class productivity." He went on to suggest that the best way to abolish U.S. leadership in technological development was to follow the Soviet example.

The second effect of the compulsory obscurity in which Soviet defense scientists must work is that the more intelligent, ambitious, and professionally accomplished Soviet scientists and engineers are deterred from working in weapons-related fields. Some of these have no option in the matter. In 1969 the Soviet government decided that Jews were a potential security risk and should no longer be hired for defense work, although those already employed were not fired. This move entailed the abandonment of a considerable intellectual resource, since Jews, who constitute only 1 percent of the Soviet population, hold 14 percent of all the doctorates.

For those with a choice, defense work is unappealing for several reasons. The vast majority of Soviet citizens relish a chance to travel abroad. Scientists in classified work are almost never allowed to visit the West, whereas there are considerable opportunities for those involved in less sensitive areas. Dr. Zhores Medvedev, the famous radiobiologist exiled for his dissident activities, recalls how while he was still in the Soviet Union, he was offered a "secret" job. He turned it down, although it would have meant a salary increase, because he had just visited the West for the first time and he knew that if he accepted the offer, he would never travel again.

Scientists like to publish in technical journals. It is the way their work in their particular field becomes recognized and applauded. It is extremely difficult for those working within the Soviet military-industrial complex to publish in an "open" journal. Any manuscript would have to pass through several layers of security checks and most probably would never surface. The defense scientist does have an alternative: to publish in the secret journals issued by each of the military-industrial ministries, which are accessible to only a limited number of people.

It is often assumed that these irritants are compensated for by the higher salaries paid to people in defense work. It does appear to be the case that the pay is higher, but again, because of secrecy restrictions, defense workers are debarred from earning money on the side by teaching or writing.

While the brighter and more promising scientist might thus be discouraged from going to work for a weapons enterprise, there are attractions for more mediocre and less ambitious technical graduates who cherish the total job security offered by the defense industry. It is, for example, far easier to get a thesis accepted in a military institution, because it is subject to the same security restrictions as any other publication and therefore will be reviewed by a limited number of people.

Not least among the disincentives to working in defense is the unappealing location of most of the weapons centers. Although a good deal of defense work is carried out in Moscow, where most ambitious Soviets want to live, the greater share is located far away. Young scientists and engineers recruited into the defense industry have no choice about where they will be sent. Many of them end up in places like Petropavlovsk-Kamchatskiy, a major warship-building and missile-testing center on the Pacific coast of the Kamchatka peninsula. They may be sent to the submarine center at Severodvinsk on the White Sea or the missile-building plants in Krasnoyarsk in Central Siberia. In these isolated and inhospitable places, the climate is terrible, consumer goods are in short supply, and diversion is hard to find.

In order to remedy the effects of its own bureaucratic inertia, the defense-industrial apparatus draws on two outside sources for inspiration and technological assistance. The first of these is the civilian sector within Russia itself. Scientists working in civilian institutes and academies are frequently asked to help out on a problem, often without being told what the actual problem relates to.

One such case involved the computation of the trajectories for a space shot. The Soviet space program is, of course, under the control of the military, and the computations were therefore to be carried out at Computer Center No. 1 in Moscow, which controls the main computers used by the military.

The center, however, felt it would be preferable to give work of this importance to civilian experts from TSEMI, a big civilian mathematics institute. The mathematics experts were paid a handsome free-lance rate but were unaware that the problem they were working on had anything to do with space or rockets. They only found out later because their work and the consequent space test were so successful that the grateful authorities offered them a cash prize.

The second source of inspiration is the West. All Western technical journals are scrutinized by the Soviets, and those dealing with defense technology most closely of all. Importing Western technical ideas is an old Soviet practice. The Klimov engines that powered most fighters during World War II were an adaptation of the French Hispano-Suiza design. The first Soviet jet fighters were based on German-designed airframes and British engines. The first postwar Russian bomber, the TU-4, was an exact copy of an American B-29 bomber that landed in Siberia during the war. The story goes that the Soviet engineers found a small hole under the left wing with no ascertainable purpose. But since Stalin had ordered the plane to be copied perfectly, every single TU-4 had an identical hole drilled under the left wing.

Unfortunately for the Russians, not all Western weapons concepts are good ones. As we shall see, the Soviets have been peculiarly undiscriminating in the Western weapons fashions they have copied.

The diversion of a huge amount of resources into defense does not necessarily mean that the Russians receive a proportionate return on their investment. Edward Procter, a former deputy director for intelligence at the CIA, expressed it this way in 1976: "In research and development, the relationship between inputs and outputs is very tenuous. And you can work very hard on the problem and never solve it, and spend a lot of resources. It isn't that the Soviets don't desire to have advanced technologies, it is our feeling that they have not been able to acquire these technologies as rapidly as we have."

The secrecy should not serve as a blank canvas on which U.S. defense interests can paint notions of a perfect structure, employing the best and the brightest and operating with maximum efficiency to produce an ever-increasing number of deadly weapons. Rather, it seems that on the evidence, it is not sorcery that lies behind the Soviet effort, as Tom Wolfe suggested, but a stagnating bureaucratic organism hiding its frailties from the world.

This policy of concealment is, of course, greatly to the benefit of U.S. and allied defense interests. As Dr. Kosta M. Tsipis of the Massachusetts Institute of Technology points out, "The Russians are a wonderful threat to have because, you know, they're foolishly paranoid about it. They are inferior and that's why they try to keep themselves from being found out and that's a wonderful way to have a bogeyman for the American public to be frightened by."

The consequence for the American defense industry, whether inevitably or not, has been that it has come to resemble its Soviet counterpart more and more. Just as the Soviet design bureaus now exist in a comfortable environment well insulated from the chill winds of competition, so too are the giant U.S. defense contractors assured of a continuing prosperity. All too often, important weapons contracts are awarded not on the merits of proposed designs but because it is the turn of a particular corporation to receive a large order. Thus, for example, the Chrysler Corporation was awarded a contract to build the M-1 tank for the U.S. Army in 1976, even though the Army's technical experts had concluded that the design submitted by General Motors was preferable, while the Northrop Corporation got the order to build the YF-17 prototype (predecessor of the F-18) rather than Boeing. Important contractors go out of business as rarely as Soviet aircraft design bureaus.

Just as the production of particular weapons, such as the MiG-25, can continue in the Soviet Union regardless of their military utility, so do political and economic factors ensure the manufacture of American weapons that might otherwise be terminated. A Pentagon official who tried to cancel the contract for the F-18 naval fighter-bomber on the grounds of its spiraling cost and technical shortcomings confessed later that trying to kill the order was "like trying to pull Excalibur out of the stone."

Despite the openness with which the American defense establishment conducts its business, by comparison at least with the Soviets, there are signs that here too the systems may be becoming more alike. The number of "black," or secret, programs in the U.S. defense budget is increasing, and contracts are thus effectively protected from unfriendly scrutiny by the Congress or press, with all the attendant evils consequent on a richly endowed but unsupervised bureaucracy.

In short, as defense analyst Pierre M. Sprey has pointed out, "If you stop and think about it, you'll realise that our Defense Department buys weapons by almost the same system the Soviets do. That is, we have a very large state bureaucracy that buys weapons from another state bureaucracy; for in most respects, Lockheed, Raytheon, Westinghouse, Boeing and Northrop are extensions of the state."

As we examine the potential effectiveness of the products of the Soviet weapons makers in the hands of the officers and conscripts described in the preceding chapters, we shall find that the two sides have more in common than the way they produce weapons.

and confusion are thus effectively reduced to a minimum . . .

In sum, as defense analyst Steven M. Spiegel has pointed out, "If we step back and think about it, you'll realize that the Defense Department buys weapons . . . weapons they don't always want, more weapons . . .

As we examine the potential effectiveness . . . of the Soviet Union, we must . . .

Part III

Hordes, Tanks, and Other Weapons

Six

The Hordes

Only in recent years has the U.S. national security establishment begun to express publicly a presumption that the Soviet Union either has or very soon will have the means to fight and win a nuclear war. Even so, despite the alarms sounded by the likes of Professor Richard Pipes and Defense Secretary Caspar Weinberger, the conviction that a strategic nuclear exchange would result in the mutual immolation of both victim and aggressor remains widespread. Even President Reagan felt obliged to defer to this sentiment when he declared that "It's difficult for me to think that there's a 'winnable nuclear war.'"

There are no such doubts when it comes to more traditional modes of warfare. For more than thirty years, Soviet conventional superiority has been accepted as a self-evident truth. Ever since the late 1950s, it has been assumed that the only possible defense against an enormous Soviet superiority in men and equipment is nuclear weapons. "I must not conceal from you tonight the truth as I see it," Winston Churchill told an audience at the Massachusetts Institute of Technology in March 1949. "It is certain that Europe would have been Communized like Czechoslovakia, and London under bombardment some time ago, but for the deterrent of the atomic bomb in the hands of the United States."

Thirty-three years later, American Secretary of State Alexander Haig, himself a former NATO supreme commander, rose to denounce a proposal by four distinguished former national security officials that the United States renounce the first use of nuclear weapons. "Those in the West who advocate the adoption of a 'no first use' policy," he declared, "seldom go on to propose that the United States reintroduce the draft, triple the size of its armed forces, and put its economy on a wartime footing. Yet, in the absence of such steps, a pledge of no first use effectively leaves the West nothing with which to counterbalance the Soviet conventional advantages and geopolitical position in Europe."

This kind of casual dismissal of the armies, air forces, and navies of the NATO alliance is common across the political spectrum, from hawks to moderates. Opponents of present NATO plans for reliance on tactical nuclear weapons like to suggest that Soviet conventional superiority can be offset by a sharply increased Western investment in nonnuclear forces. Western scholars inclined to view Soviet actions in a sympathetic light make the same automatic assumptions about the East-West balance. Writing about the early Cold War period, for example, the historian Edgar Bottome has interpreted Soviet military policy thus: "In the case of the Soviet Union, this nation responded in the only manner possible in the face of the American atomic monopoly; it increased the size of the Red Army . . . *to a point where it could march across Eu-*

rope in the event of an American attack on Soviet territory."

Even if the locale of a possible Soviet invasion shifts away from Europe, the automatic presumptions do not change. When President Carter declared it to be a "doctrine" in 1980 that the United States would use force to repel any assault on the Persian Gulf, the Pentagon quickly leaked its conclusion that the only way to repel a conventional Soviet thrust southward through Iran would be to employ nuclear weapons.

Many factors are responsible for this ingrained attitude of mind, which has remained unaltered for more than a third of a century despite the numerous economic and political changes that have occurred in America, Russia, and Europe as a whole. One of them has undoubtedly been the determination of policymakers on both sides of the Atlantic to preserve an unbreakable link between Europe and the United States by means of the American nuclear deterrent. Such a link could only remain the linchpin of the Atlantic alliance so long as nuclear weapons were portrayed as the sole means of keeping the Red Army at bay, the point emphasized by Churchill in his MIT speech. But the idea that the Red Army was unstoppable by anything short of a nuclear blast was born in the war against the Germans. Most of the land fighting had after all taken place on the Eastern Front, and it was there that the Germans had deployed the bulk of their forces. Nevertheless, the Russians had succeeded in destroying the Wehrmacht in four years of bitter fighting. From the beginning of 1943 onward, they had advanced steadily and remorselessly, accepting terrible casualties and deploying enormous concentrations of men and equipment—a "steamroller" that crushed everything in its path. During the war, the Allied military leaders had been delighted to rely on the great mass and power of the Red Army; but despite the preeminent position it had occupied in their war plans, the American and British commanders had little opportunity to observe the Soviet army in battle. Allied liaison officers were almost always rigorously excluded from the battle zone by the Soviet authorities. Thus, when the Red Army changed from being an indispensable ally to a potential foe, the Western generals had to rely on the reports of the Germans about its fighting abilities and mode of operation. Such reports stressed the part that sheer numbers had played in the Soviet victory, an advantage against which German superiority in tactical abilities and technical equipment had been to no avail.

In 1945 the American General George Patton was removed from his position as military governor of Bavaria for stating that "we are going to have to fight [the Russians] sooner or later; within the next generation. Why not do it now while our Army is intact and the damn Russians can have their hind end kicked back into Russia in three months?" But within a short space of time, the United States demobilized its armies and dismantled most of its war machine to the point where not even the most bellicose and anti-Soviet elements in the U.S. military could have repeated Patton's boast of kicking the Russians back to Russia in three months. In 1947 a professional U.S. military journal published an example of what was to become the orthodox inferiority complex. "It has been estimated recently by reliable authorities," wrote the editor of the U.S. military publication *Armored Cavalry Journal*, "that Russia could probably invade and occupy the whole of Western Europe against resistance from present American, British and French troops in a matter of 48 hours."

If the battle had been between the forces of the United States and its allies of 1947, on the one hand, and the Soviet army that took Berlin in 1945, on the other, then this kind of wild statement might have had some, but not much, merit. The U.S. forces had shrunk from a total of 12 million men under arms in 1945 to just over 2 million in 1948. The U.S. Army alone, which had numbered more than 5 million at war's end, was reduced to a comparative rump of 690,000 men. The defense budget had gone down from $43 billion to $12 billion.

This rapid dissolution of wartime military might was well known to all in the West. What attracted less notice, although military leaders were aware of it, was that the Soviet Union had also demobilized. At the end of the war, the Soviet armed forces combined had almost the same number of men as the American forces. Although the official Soviet figure was 11.365 million, this cannot have been more than an estimate, since the Red Army kept no accurate record of precise numbers of lower-ranking personnel. During the war, Communist Party membership had shot up in the ranks, partly because that was the only way for a soldier to ensure that his family would be informed if he became a casualty.

By 1948 the Soviet forces had been reduced to a total of 2.8 million, including the large but militarily irrelevant forces devoted to maintaining order among the civilian population. This might have been quite sufficient for the subjugation of Western Europe, except that only a portion of the total force was available for the task, and the Western forces, although depleted, were by no means insignificant.

For a blitzkrieg-style attack westward, the Soviets would, then and now, have to rely on the forces already in place in Eastern Europe, backed up by reserves in the western Soviet Union. At the time that "reliable authorities" were postulating a Soviet occupation of Western Europe in 48 hours, the Russians had, at most, just over half a million troops in their occupation zones in Germany and Austria. They had none in Czechoslovakia (nor did they station any in that country until 1968) and a relatively small force in Poland. In the western districts of the Soviet Union, there were an additional half a million troops.

The force the Soviet generals faced on the other side of the line that was congealing down the length of Europe was actually almost exactly the same in numbers. In their occupation zones, the Americans, British, and French had half a million troops, a further 375,000 in France, Holland, and Belgium, and many more in Britain and the United States itself. The Russians, therefore, possessed no overwhelming superiority in simple numbers. Simple numbers, however, do not necessarily mean very much on their own in war.

In *Threats Misperceived*, an examination of the real military balance in Europe between 1945 and 1955, the defense scholar Matthew A. Evangelista has pointed out that the Western and Soviet forces in Central Europe during this period were very differently employed. The Western powers had speedily turned over most of the civil administration of the territories they occupied to local civilians, leaving their own resident armies to fulfill in the main purely military functions.

The Russians ran things very differently, retaining control of almost all civil administration in the hands of the Red Army. Above and beyond these duties, the troops were heavily engaged in extracting reparations, to which they felt legally entitled, for German war damage, reparations in the form of factories, railway lines, and even plumbing fixtures and baths. The forces in western Russia were also heavily engaged in nonmilitary activities. That part of the USSR had been almost completely devastated by four years of war, and the troops were needed to restore the transport system and other key services. To a certain extent, the domestic forces were also engaged in occupation duties, since the local population in many cases comprised newly assimilated and reluctant Soviet citizens. Large numbers of Poles had been incorporated into the USSR, the previously independent Baltic republics had been swallowed up, and nationalist partisans in the Ukraine carried on a guerrilla war until the early 1950s.

Had the Soviet forces not been thus distracted by these duties, they were still hardly fit for the kind of military gamble that the Western military were predicting. According to one contemporary observation, the troops were "of poor quality, indifferently clothed, and, as regards transport at any rate, ill found in equipment." During the war, the Soviets had relied on American lend-lease supplies for most of their trunks, and deliveries had abruptly ceased after the German surrender. Domestic Soviet defense production, including the manufacture of tanks, had been sharply cut back at the end of the war. Morale among the troops stationed in the occupation zones was bad, so bad, in fact, that huge numbers of them—possibly as many as 75,000—including many officers, deserted to the areas under Western control.

This is not to say that the Western forces were exemplars of military proficiency. One former officer who served at U.S. headquarters recalls the American occupation troops as being "useless or worse than useless. Right after the war the good combat troops left, and what we got instead were the sweepings of the jailhouses, and officers who had managed to evade combat service. We sort of automatically assumed the Soviets had kept some of their World War Two combat capabilities." With the wisdom of hindsight, it is clear that the armies on both sides were exhausted, very different from the forces that had advanced across Germany in 1945 and totally incapable of launching any kind of blitzkrieg on each other. Even at the time, information was available that indicated something of the true state of the Russian forces. Hanson Baldwin, the military correspondent of the New York *Times*, was able to give a reasonably accurate list of how many troops were stationed in different parts of Europe in 1947. General Omar Bradley, chairman of the U.S. Joint Chiefs of Staff, publicly numbered the Soviet Army at 2.8 million men in 1948, as did Emmanuel Shinwell, the British Minister of Defense, in 1950.

Such accurate assessments were ignored in favor of more lurid comparisons. Churchill, in his MIT speech, invoked the specter of the "Mongol hordes" that had briefly menaced Europe 700 years before, only to withdraw when their Great Khan died; "they never returned," he observed dramatically, "until now."

In the face of these imagined hordes, the Western European countries joined together in the North Atlantic alliance in 1949. It may be that the important reasons for the formation of the alliance were the undeclared ones— the establishment of West Germany as an independent state, the necessity of an institutional bond between the United States and Europe, or even the hope of rolling back Soviet hegemony in Eastern Europe. But these were not the stated reasons for the rearmament program that continues to this day. NATO was and is presented as a defensive alliance, a perennial military underdog. As the former senior Pentagon official Alain C. Enthoven has written: "NATO was born with a psychological 'complex' about conventional forces. The allies could never hope to match the Soviet hordes. Any attempt to do so would be enormously expensive."

Once it had taken root, this complex became totally resistant to any dose of reality. Enthoven and K. Wayne Smith, in their book *How Much Is Enough?*, recount both the conclusions and the fate of a high-level study of the NATO-Warsaw Pact balance commissioned from the Pentagon Office of Systems Analysis by Defense Secretary Robert McNamara in 1961.

Official military estimates then, as in the late 1940s and today, held that the Soviets had a force of 175 divisions of troops to face a far smaller (25 divisions in the early 1960s) number of ill-equipped, ill-trained and unready NATO divisions in the "center region"—Europe between Switzerland and the North Sea. The systems analysts, who were civilians rather than career military officers and derisively referred to by the latter as "whiz kids," set to work to examine the basic premises of this gloomy and unvarying conclusion. They drew attention to the fact that the total population of the NATO countries was far larger than those of the Warsaw Pact. They realized that the United States alone could potentially field far greater hordes of soldiers than the Soviet Union, since half the Soviet population was engaged in agriculture, presumably producing the food to feed the entire population, whereas no more than 10 percent of the U.S. population was fulfilling the same task. Further reexamining the obvious, they wondered how it was that the Soviets could have an army of 175 divisions and the United States a mere 16 when the Soviet army was only twice as large in terms of manpower (2 million to 1 million). Closer examination of those Soviet divisions revealed that at least half of them were essentially paper units, with little equipment and even fewer men. If these were to be counted in the force balances, then so should the U.S. reserve units, which numbered about 50.

By 1965, the "whiz kids" had reached a startling conclusion, one that was most unwelcome to the military: "NATO and the Warsaw Pact had approximate equality on the ground." The reaction of the Pentagon generals to this news was to call for reinforcements.

"Threat assessments" up to this point had tended to

discount the potential contribution to enemy strength of Russia's satellite armies. When these forces were considered at all, they were thought of as a marginal asset at best and possibly a liability in view of their uncertain loyalty.

"As the perceived size of the Soviet force began to shrink under closer analysis," Enthoven and Smith recount, "it became apparent that the Soviet forces alone were substantially outnumbered by the NATO forces, even after mobilization. Suddenly, despite the increasing independence of the East Europen countries from the Soviet Union, intelligence reports and service staff estimates began to count the satellite divisions as nearly equivalent to Soviet divisions. Indeed, it appeared that whatever headway the Systems Analysis Office made in reducing the number of Soviet divisions was offset by an equivalent number of newly found satellite divisions. One way or another, the number of well-equipped, well-trained combat-ready Pact divisions stayed at 175 in military threat estimates."

By the middle of 1968 Enthoven and his staff had finished their work. Their conclusions had been convincing enough for McNamara and his successor, Clark Clifford. They had, however, no impact at all on policy. NATO, it is true, did adopt the strategy of "flexible response," which meant tarrying awhile before introducing nuclear weapons into a European conflict, but at a meeting of the alliance's Defense Ministers in 1969, it was agreed by all that because NATO forces were outnumbered 2 to 1 on the crucial central front and would quickly be overrun in the event of an all-out ground attack, it was necessary to adopt new guidelines that provided for quicker use of tactical nuclear weapons.

Having survived that high-level assault, the presumption of Soviet invincibility on land and in the air remains as strong as ever today. In the spring of 1982, NATO headquarters in Brussels published a booklet called *NATO and the Warsaw Pact: Force Comparisons*.. It lacked the attractive artwork and photographs of the Pentagon publication *Soviet Military Power*, but it strove for an air of objectivity by listing both Warsaw Pact and NATO strengths. Once again, the Soviet Union, aided by its allies, appears to possess forces of overwhelming strength, trained and equipped to smash through the comparatively puny forces of the North Atlantic allies in Europe. NATO is now accorded a total of 84 divisions, while the Warsaw Pact has remained close to the traditional number, with 173. The Pact is depicted as having three times as many tanks, six times as many antitank guided weapons launchers, three times as many artillery guns, and more than twice as many combat aircraft.

The study is introduced by the NATO secretary-general, Dr. Joseph Luns, who notes with practiced gloom that "the numerical balance of forces has moved slowly but steadily in favour of the Warsaw Pact over the past two decades. During this period the members of the North Atlantic Alliance have lost much of the technological advantage which permitted NATO to rely on the view that quality could compensate for quantity." In case anyone should miss the dangerous implications of this trend, the introduction also points out that "Warsaw Pact military doctrine as shown by its literature and military exercises calls for large-scale penetration into enemy territory in order to secure strategic objectives. . . . Warsaw Pact forces are therefore organized and equipped in accordance with the fundamental principle that they must be able to take the offensive in any conflict."

Despite Dr. Luns's declaration in his introduction that his publication is "factual, objective, and unbiased" in presentation, such assessments can never be objective, since they are built up of facts, bolstered by prejudices, assembled toward a particular end. The minimizing of one's own forces and the maximizing of those of the enemy are standard gambits in "bean counting," practiced with varying disregard for veracity by all participants. Thus, in a particularly egregious example, *Force Comparisons* blandly omits all mention of the very considerable French armed forces in West Germany and France itself on the grounds that "although France is a member of the North Atlantic Alliance it does not participate in its integrated military structure." While this explanation may be technically correct, it also provides a handy way to eliminate nine fully manned and equipped divisions from the Western side of the East-West balance.

Numbers may look simple and straightforward, but they never tell quite the whole story. The United States has 2.2 million men in its armed forces, while the Russians have 5.8 million. How ominous that equation can be made to sound!

But who are these 5.8 million Soviet servicemen?

Nine hundred and twenty thousand of them are construction and railroad troops, the conscripts considered politically too unreliable or otherwise unusable as combat troops who serve their time swinging a pick and shovel on construction sites or working on the BAM railroad, an extension of the Trans-Siberian; 650,000 are occupied with the important but specialized tasks of internal security and guarding the borders and are irrelevant to any East-West confrontation; and 100,000 are civil defense troops, readying themselves to deal with the aftermath of a nuclear war. The last are also assigned to fight American paratroop landings inside the USSR, and as long as the United States continues to reject the possibility of doing that, these troops will not enter into combat.

Unless one includes the personnel of the U.S. Army Corps of Engineers, who carry out public works, and the few active-duty Pentagon officers assigned to civil defense, it must be concluded that the United States had no equivalent of these 1.7 million Soviet troops, since their tasks are considered militarily irrelevant.

That leaves 4.1 million Soviet troops assigned to combat functions confronting 2.14 million U.S. servicemen, still an unequal balance. But again, the simple numbers conceal much.

The Soviet troops of national air defense number 560,000 soldiers, who man the enormous antibomber network of radars, missiles, and interceptors. The U.S. Air Force has only 8,000 men assigned to this function.

A Soviet force of 495,000 men guards the long border with China. The United States has no comparable second front, although it does keep 125,000 men on the coasts of Asia and the Eastern Pacific. The Soviets also use 30,000 to occupy Poland and 70,000 to occupy Czechoslovakia. It is assumed that these will augment an offensive against Western Europe. In practice, they would probably be needed to guard Soviet supply lines across these countries.

The Soviets often use many more troops to provide the same or smaller capabilities than the United States. Soviet strategic offensive forces are roughly equal in capability to their U.S. counterparts. But the Soviets use 472,000 men to operate their ICBMs, missile submarines, and bombers. In contrast, the United States requires only 71,000 for its Strategic Air Command and Fleet Ballistic Missile Force.

All professionals employed by the Soviet Ministry of Defense at headquarters level are military officers. These number approximately 250,000. The equivalent figure for the Americans is 60,000, which is the number of military personnel at headquarters level in the Washington area. While this still betokens an inflated and inefficient U.S. military bureaucracy, it is still far lower than the number of Soviets required to do the same job.

Soviet military air transport cannot transport as much or as far as the U.S. Military Airlift Command, and yet while the United States does the job with 37,000 active-duty personnel, the Soviets need 100,000.

Long ago the United States abandoned the idea of defending its coasts with short-range rockets and artillery. The Soviet navy, however, keeps 10,000 coastal rocket artillery troops in service.

The list of men taken up with duties that the United States and its allies do not consider necessary for a fighting force goes on and on. Thus, the Soviets have 70,000 political officers, unmatched by anything on the U.S. side, unless one counts the 3,290 chaplains. The Soviet military commissariats (draft boards) employ 40,000 military personnel. Soviet military academies are at any one time educating 160,000 cadets, while the U.S. equivalents hold 13,000.

Discarding the kinds of troops that the United States does not have because it does not think it needs them, as well as the excess numbers required to perform functions that the U.S. services can manage to do with fewer men, the net is about 2 million on either side.

This kind of exercise is important because the arguments over the military potential of the superpowers and their allies have become so sterile. Because the notion of the Soviet hordes has been so successfully implanted in Western consciousness, it is necessary to use common sense and simple arithmetic to dispel it, although it should be remembered that numbers alone are of little help in assessing a nation's real military effectiveness. If they were, Israel would not be the dominant superpower in the Middle East, Germany would not have thrashed the combined armies of France and Great Britain in 1940, and Britain could not have hoped to have retaken the Falkland

Islands from the Argentines in 1982. Manpower numbers on their own tell us little.

Comparing the numbers of divisions is even less profitable. A division is not a fixed number of men; rather, it is a unit of military administration, used in different armies in different ways at different times. The U.S. Army currently has about 17,000 men in an armored division, that is, a division which is predominantly equipped with tanks; the West Germans have 15,000; and the Soviets have perhaps 11,000. During World War II, both German and Russian divisions fought on, although they had sometimes been reduced to 5,000 men or less. The size of the U.S. Marine Corps is fixed by a law at three divisions of ground troops (the result of a fierce fight over the very existence of the corps after the war), so each division has expanded to 35,000 men.

The strength of individual Soviet divisions can also vary. Most officers and men of the Soviet army (ground forces) serve either in tank divisions or motor-rifle divisions. As the name suggests, the 38 tank divisions in the ground forces consist primarily of tanks. At full strength, each division should contain 325 tanks and about 11,000 officers and men, some of whom make up a supporting infantry detachment. The 117 motor-rifle divisions also contain a contingent of tanks, numbering 288, but the bulk of the divisions' 13,000 men are foot soldiers, although they are called motor-rifle troops because they are supposed to be carried into and even during battle in armored vehicles. In addition, there are artillery divisions, independent units of big guns and short-range rockets (the limit is 600 miles), as well as an elite force of eight airborne divisions, lightly equipped and reserved under the direct control of the Ministry of Defense for rapid offensive operations. Until 1980, there was also a subdivision of the troops of the air defense of the ground forces, but in that year they were absorbed by the separate air defense service, the PVO.

None of this neat tabulation of functions and strengths should be taken to mean that Marshal Petrov, commander in chief of the ground forces since his predecessor, Marshal Pavlovsky, was fired in 1980 for political insubordination, is in control of 177 or more divisions (although the eight airborne divisions are outside his direct command), all equally and fully "organized and equipped in accordance with the fundamental principle that hey must be able to take the offensive in a conflict."

The force that Petrov commands from his headquarters in Moscow, nicknamed the Pentagon by Muscovites, is paradoxically the largest and politically most powerful of the five Soviet services, while at the same time it is inferior to some of the others in prestige and the quality of the people in it. Each of the individual U.S. services could and did claim an indispensable contribution to victory after the last world war: the Navy had played the major part in the war against Japan, the Army fought across France and into Germany, and the Air Force gained its independence from the Army by successfully spreading the notion that strategic bombing had helped bring the Axis powers to their knees.

As far as the Russians were concerned, it was the ground forces, aided by the tactical support of the air force on the battlefield, which had defeated Germany. The navy had played little part in the fighting, there was next to no strategic bombing force, and the strategic rocket forces and the troops of national air defense were not even created until some years after the war.

Despite the prestige of the wartime triumphs, the ground forces were to suffer many political reversals in the ensuing years. The troops of national air defense were created as a separate force in 1948, which meant that there was now a separate bureaucracy competing for resources. The navy also underwent a resurgence, receiving enormous funds for a major shipbuilding program between 1948 and 1955, after which it suffered a political eclipse for some years, until the admirals once again successfully garnered the political support for further expansion.

Most seriously, the ground forces lost control of the strategic rocket program, as did the U.S. Army, in the late 1950s. While the air force emerged as the victor in the United States, Khrushchev decided that the new weapons called for a new service, the strategic rocket forces, which he proposed to pay for by trimming the ground forces budget. Khrushchev further made it clear that he considered much of the ground forces equipment and thinking to be obsolete in the face of the new weapons. One one occasion, he went so far as to publicly deride the army's favored weapon: "When I went out into the training field," he told *Pravda*, "and saw the tanks attacking and how the anti-tank artillery hit those tanks, I became ill. After all, we are spending a lot of money to build tanks. And if—God forbid, as they say—a war breaks out, these tanks will burn before they reach the line indicated by the command."

Despite such barbs, the ground forces generals and marshals were able to preserve their position. They strove to make the case for adapting traditional instruments of land warfare, such as the tank, for use on a nuclear battlefield. At the same time, they sought to prove that future wars would not necessarily be dominated by the nuclear missiles of the strategic rocket forces. These efforts gradually bore fruit. The important theoretical textbook *Marxism-Leninism on War and the Army* contained this passage in its 1965 edition: "Our military doctrine gives the main role in defeating an aggressor to the nuclear rocket weapon. At the same time it does not deny the important signifi-

cance of other kinds of weapons and means of fighting."
Three years later, in a new edition of the same book, the
concluding sentiment about "other kinds of weapons and
means of fighting" had been stiffened up with an added
statement: ". . . and the possibility in certain circumstances
of conducting combat actions without the use of nuclear
weapons."

In 1967, for the first time since the 1950s, the Warsaw
Pact carried out exercises that did not involve the simulated
use of nuclear weapons. At the same time, according to
Pentagon figures, tank production was rising sharply, from
about 2,500 a year in 1967 to 4,500 in 1970. The ground
forces had made a big comeback.

Politically, of course, they had never been eclipsed but
had merely suffered setbacks. Despite the indignity of the
strategic rocket forces being named the primary service,
the chiefs of the General Staff continued to be selected
from the ranks of ground forces generals. The army has
the major role in maintaining Soviet hegemony in Eastern
Europe, both through its control of the Warsaw Pact apparatus—again, always commanded by an army man—
and the recurring necessity of reinforcing satellite discipline with tanks and live bullets. It appears that it was the
ground forces high command that pressed for action in
Hungary in 1956 and in Czechoslovakia in 1968. It was
the senior officers of the ground forces who pressed for
intervention in Poland in the winter of 1980–81 and who
were fired or transferred by Brezhnev in his political coun-
tercoup. Almost all the Soviet forces in action in Afghanistan are from the army, aided by helicopters and light
bombers of the air force's frontal aviation branch.

The other side of the paradox is that the ground forces
are the "backward service." A retired Soviet naval captain,
sipping Guinness in a Manhattan Irish bar, dismisses the
army as "intellectually inferior—an army colonel is the

equal of a naval lieutenant." A lot of this kind of sentiment could be written off as arrogance common and traditional in all navies, except that the Soviet army generals seem to acknowledge it too. Lozansky remembers how defensive the immensely powerful military chiefs on the Crimean beach were about their colleagues from the other services. "They disliked them, but they were envious at the same time, they seemed to feel they were smarter."

The army gets the last pick of the conscripts. The navy, air force, and strategic rocket forces are, for example, far more exclusively manned by reliable, Russian-speaking, and well-educated Slavs than the ground forces, which must make up its numbers with less desirable racial minorities.

This kind of division is not unique to the Soviet system. Studies during World War II discovered that the most effective type of combat soldier was a man of average or higher intelligence, with good mechanical skills. But these are just the attributes that are absolutely vital for the operation and maintenance of a jet fighter, a ship's radar system, or the fuel system of an ICBM. Before the United States abolished the draft, the conscription system applied only to the Army, while the other services were able to fill their ranks with volunteers.

The threat of the hordes as postulated by Churchill and other cold warriors of the late 1940s has endured despite a constant stream of information to the contrary. When facts about the Soviet army as it really is are substituted for legend, it turns out that it is not a giant confronting a Western pygmy but a force of roughly equal size to its adversaries. Such facts, as we have seen, have been readily available to policymakers throughout the Cold War but have been customarily ignored. "Comforting old myths" as Enthoven and Smith point out, "do, indeed, die hard."

Seven

Mobilizing the Hordes

Compared with most other armies, the Soviet ground forces are old-fashioned. In the nineteenth century the Germans pioneered the system of mass conscription in peacetime. Young men were called up for a period, taught the rudiments of drill and how to handle their relatively simple weapons, and then sent home at the end of their service. They then formed part of the reserve, ready if needed to rejoin the colors and do their duty. By the eve of World War I, all the continental armies operated on this system, and the intricacies of the mobilization procedure were the main concerns of the general staffs of the day. So complex were these procedures indeed that once the mobilization system was put in motion it was very difficult to stop and became one of the reasons for the outbreak of the war.

Most armies today have substantially altered this system. Although many countries retain conscription and reserves, the reservists are regularly called up for retraining. Israeli reservists can count on spending a portion of each year in uniform. The West Germans, French, and Dutch also recognize the fact that worthwhile military skills grow stale with disuse. Even in the United States, National Guard divisions train regularly. Without constant refresher courses, the skills that are retained by veterans amount to little more than a familiarity with military routine, which raw recruits can pick up quickly enough anyway.

Only the Russians among the world's major military organizations have retained the nineteenth-century system. Officially, Marshal Petrov has a force of 169 divisions at his disposal (the eighth airborne units are outside his direct control). Of this number, only 54 divisions are fully equipped and manned, and these are called Category 1 units by NATO intelligence. The rest are divided into Category 2 and 3 units, which vary from units having most of their equipment and perhaps half or two-thirds of their men to units having virtually no equipment and little more than a small nucleus of officers. The official Russian military term for these low-readiness units is *kadrirovannye*, or "cadre," but officers prefer to pun on the word and call them *kastrirovannye*, or "castrated." In time of war, these 115 reserve divisions would be brought up to strength with veteran conscripts recalled for duty.

In theory this is a formidable system. Since the regular forces release 1.8 million draftees back into civilian life every year, the Soviet Union should have millions and millions of veterans trained and ready for service. But, as noted, almost none of these men will have had any retraining since they were discharged; none of the veterans I have talked to had ever been recalled for routine retraining. Some had seen extra service during emergency mobilizations, but these exercises, as we shall see, do not inspire much confidence in the efficiency of the system.

There have been three large-scale mobilizations of Soviet reservists in the past twenty-five years: in 1968, for the occupation of Czechoslovakia; in 1979, for the invasion of Afghanistan; and in 1980, for the aborted intervention in Poland.

By July 1968, there were at least 500,000 officers and men of the ground forces poised to occupy Czechoslovakia. The reservists of western Russia, from the Baltic to the Ukraine, had been summoned from their civilian jobs, tugging on the uniforms they had been presented with on the day they left the service. The call-up included machines as well as men; as already mentioned, every truck in the Soviet Union has a military as well as a civilian function. In 1968 both trucks and drivers were frequently called up together. Since the call-up happened at the beginning of the harvest season, the results for the economy, especially the food supply, were unfortunate. The effects were so severe that General Sergei S.Maryakhin, who was in charge of all support services for the invasion, had to admit to the problems in *Krasnaya zvezda*: "It is no secret," he wrote, "that the exercises urgently required the requisition of thousands of units of powerful technical equipment and motor transportation from the national economy and the removal of thousands of reservists from [working in] the fields, at a time when the heavy work of the harvest was at its peak throughout the country."

While the economy staggered from the disruptive effects of the mobilization, the army did not find it easy to assimilate the influx of the reservists. In *The Liberators*, his satirical but invaluable memoir of life as a Soviet officer, the pseudonymous defector Viktor Suvorov describes the condition of his unit in the Ukraine at this time:

After receiving its 'battle technology' [the military euphemism for the unit's collection of clapped out trucks commandeered from the civilian sector] the infantry was forbidden to leave the cover of the forests. On the roads and fields, only tank crews, the artillery and one parade battalion of armored personnel carriers were training. All the remainder were standing along forest cuttings and forest clearings. Viewed from outer space, it must have looked menacing, but not from the ground. The military hierarchy was afraid of frightening the locals by the look of our army: fat, untrained, and undisciplined soldiers, who had forgotten all they ever knew, in worn-out vehicles of all possible types and painted all the colors of the rainbow. . . . From outer space the Americans saw new divisions increasing like fungi. Their reconnaissance noted mighty tank columns on the roads and calculated that innumerable infantrymen lay hidden in the forests. And so it was, in fact, but this infantry was neither organized nor controlled and, what is most important of all, was incapable of fighting.

Any doubts about the effectiveness of this force were speedily dispelled once the Soviet army had entered Czechoslovakia. For political reasons, the Czech army chose not to resist, although the Soviets had cleverly weakened their capability anyway by inducing it to use up most of its ammunition in extensive joint maneuvers during the early summer. This lack of opposition was fortunate for the Russians.

The armored columns drove into Czechoslovakia in four main thrusts, from the Ukraine, Hungary, Poland, and East Germany. Simultaneously airborne units captured Prague Airport. The airborne element was the only part of the operation which could have been claimed to be a success. The first plane was able to land in the early hours of August 20 by the simple stratagem of pretending to be a civilian airliner in distress. Once the troops who burst out of the plane had overcome the unsuspecting Czechs in the control tower and other key points, the way was clear for other troop planes to land. Otherwise, the invasion quickly degenerated into chaos. Units got lost, armored units ran out of fuel, and troops ran out of food, while almost from the moment they crossed the border, the columns got stuck in enormous traffic jams, which would have provided tempting targets in a shooting war. Even after all the units had eventually found their positions, other problems appeared, as the troops began to wonder why they had been sent to occupy the country in the first place. Despite stringent precautions on the part of the authorities, several hundred men took the opportunity to desert across the frontier into Austria.

After two months, the units that had poured into the country in August were withdrawn and the reservists sent home. They were replaced by fresh divisions of conscripts; these moved straight into secluded camps, which were sealed off as much as possible from the local population and where their successors in the five Soviet divisions of the Czech garrison remain to this day. Suvorov, whose unit was one of those withdrawn in October 1968, pithily recalls: "As they left Czechoslovakia, our divisions reminded one of the remnants of a defeated army, fleeing from the hot pursuit after a shattering defeat."

The next opportunity for the Soviets to mobilize for an invasion did not come for another eleven years, and when it did, the enemy was shooting back.

For the move into Afghanistan in December 1979, the authorities mobilized reserve units close to the border, in accordance with accepted practice. This meant that at least two of the divisions dispatched to Kabul were made up not of Russians but of Central Asians, Category 3 "castrated" units, which had been hurriedly filled out with local former draftees. Unfortunately, most of these men had spent their draft years in noncombatant units, wielding a pick and shovel or working on the railroads. But when they were demobilized, they automatically went on the books of the local division, which was where they had to report when they got the call for the Afghan operation. Thus, the motor-rifle divisions used in the initial phases of the invasion looked warlike enough, but the bulk of the men in them had had little experience in the care and maintenance of tank transporters, field artillery batteries, tanks, and all the other modern weapons.

To add to the problems of General Ivan Yershov's old mentor, Marshal Sergei Sokolov, who was in charge of the operation, these Asian troops were not only untrained, they were also politically unreliable. Perhaps the Russians had thought that using troops linked by race, culture, religion, and even language to the Afghans would help things along, but the collaboration went in quite the wrong direction. The Central Asian troops were observed passing ammunition to the locals, buying Korans in the bazaars, and possibly even handing over their personal weapons. There have even been reports that some Soviet Central Asians are prepared to oppose their government in more direct ways. Louis Dupree, an adventurous scholar in Afghan studies, spent some time in the main Kabul jail in 1978, when there were already some Soviet troops helping the Marxist Afghan government battle the insurgents. While incarcerated, he reports having met some Uzbeks, an ethnic group on the Soviet side of the border, who had come down to fight against their own government.

By the end of March 1980, the Soviet authorities evidently had concluded that the use of Asian troops in Afghanistan had been a mistake. They withdrew them and sent the reservists home, along with thousands of others who had been mobilized but kept in camps inside the Soviet Union. Since that time, the Soviet forces in Afghanistan have been almost exclusively made up of units of militarily more proficient and politically reliable Slavic conscripts.

This problem of unreliable border populations is not necessarily unique to Afghanistan. As a residue of the expansion of Russian power during the nineteenth century and after the Second World War, the Soviet border tends to slice through peoples with ethnic, cultural, religious, and political ties to each other. More than 1 million Poles live just inside the Soviet Union, as do 3 million Rumanians (known as Moldavians), 10 million Iranians (called Azeris), and huge numbers of Kazakhs and Uighurs, separated by the border from their fellow tribesmen in China.

When the young Moldavians, Azeris, Western Ukrainians, and the like are drafted, they tend to be dispatched to the noncombatant branches of the service; but once on the reserve lists, they are eligible for duty with the nearest combat unit. This leaves the authorities with the invidious choice of either accepting large numbers of ill-trained and potentially disaffected troops into the forces during a mobilization or simply exempting them from reserve duty altogether, thus denying the state large numbers of potential soldiers.

The third operation by the Soviet army to gear itself up for military action ended, probably happily for all concerned, without any troops actually being sent across the border. By mid-November 1980, as I described in Chapter 4, the Politburo had authorized a mobilization of the Carpathian, Baltic, and Byelorussian Military Districts prior to intervening in Poland. In at least one of these districts, the Carpathian, the mobilization was a disaster. Reports reached Moscow that large numbers of reservists had failed to answer the call. Many could not even be located by the military authorities (15 percent of the Soviet population changes address every year). Those who did turn up were housed in tents, and since winter had set in, this may have been the reason that so many of them promptly deserted and went home. There were, in fact, so many deserters, that the authorities gave up trying to catch and punish them. Other aspects of the operation displayed a severe lack of coordination. Units were shifted back and forth around the countryside for no apparent reason, and trucks were pointlessly requisitioned off the roads in the middle of the night.

As previously discussed, the foul-up gave Brezhnev the lever he needed to turn the tables on the interventionists in the Politburo and the army high command. The shake-up in the senior ranks of the ground forces which ensued was accompanied by fierce criticisms by military spokesmen of the readiness of the forces. General Borisov, who took over command of the Soviet forces in Czechoslovakia in January 1980, went on record with unprecedented accusations to his subordinates of "drunkenness, abuse of rank, corruption, mismanagement, waste, bureaucratism." Marshal Nikolai Ogarkov himself spoke out several times in the next few months about the need to shape up the army's reserve system. But, as ever, politics took precedence over military efficiency, since General Belikov, the commander of the Carpathian Military District, where the worst scenes of disorganization took place, was not sacked owing to his close association with Brezhnev.

Predictably, the U.S. Defense Intelligence Agency refused to countenance that anything could have gone wrong with the Soviet reserve system. The agency was asked by a Congressional committee to comment on reports from Kevin Klose, the Moscow correspondent of the Washington *Post*, about the disorganization and desertions. Klose insists that he and other Western journalists got the story "from what had always been very reliable sources, who were detailed and specific enough about what had happened to be totally convincing." Despite this, the Defense Intelligence Agency took refuge in conjecture. "While it is possible that the situation occurred as described, it is not considered likely," the military intelligence service stiffly informed the Joint Economic Committee. Sticking closely to the conditional tense, it pointed out that "administrative and internal security organs would act to preclude an incident of such magnitude, and to ensure punishment of the individuals involved." Like the military journalists who assumed a Soviet conquest of Western Europe in 48 hours in 1947, the military establishment continues to prefer theories to facts, one such theory being, to quote Thomas C. Reed, an influential adviser to President Reagan's National Security Council, "the Soviets can mobilize 200 divisions within 30 days."

The bleak record of Soviet mobilization efforts has to be balanced off against the fact that it is not an entirely useless system. Creaky though it is, the organization does exist, some of the men do turn up, and a proportion of them are trained. In 1941, when the Germans invaded the Soviet Union, the country did mobilize 5.5 million men in eight days. Conditions were different then of course; it was much harder for Soviet citizens to move house without the express permission of the authorities, and the army was organized along more primitive lines, with simpler weapons than today. The condition of the U.S. reserve system does not present an overly bright picture, although some of the NATO allies, such as the West Germans and the Dutch, have what are by all accounts well-organized and practiced systems.

Nevertheless, the fact remains that an awful lot of those 177 or so Soviet divisions so frequently advertised by the Pentagon would have a meaningful part to play in any conflict with the United States and its allies only after a very long shakedown period, much longer than the "30 days" so carelessly tossed off by Reed. Despite their enormous losses in World War II, the Soviets were able to find the reserves necessary to throw back the Germans. It is unlikely that a contest between East and West would last four years, or even six months, the length of time that some intelligence officials report it took for the Russians to get ready for Czechoslovakia and Afghanistan. A nuclear war would probably be quite short; a conventional one would in all likelihood not last long either. Apart from anything else, the Soviet economy of today would be far more disrupted by the effects of mass mobilization than the far more primitive Soviet economy of World War II. The Israelis, who are practiced at mobilizing quickly, find that their wars cause really serious trouble to the economy if they last much longer than a month. It therefore looks as if the Soviets, if they have to go to war, will fight with what they have.

Eight

Tanks and
Other Armor

Civilians who drive on the public roads which crisscross
Fort Hood, the enormous U.S. Army base in the rolling
countryside of central Texas, get used to passing tanks.
Enormous steel vehicles, measuring about 25 feet long,
12 feet wide, and 10 feet high—all tanks project an
impression of raw power. The tracks on which they move,
like a bulldozer, seem able to crush anything that gets in
their way, such as an ordinary automobile, without the
slightest effort. The tanks at Fort Hood all share one common characteristic—a protruding turret on top carrying a
long cannon and one or more machine guns. Most of them
are American, either M-60s, the main American tank for
twenty years, or newer and larger M-1s, which emit a
high-pitched whine from their gas-turbine engines, quite
unlike the throaty rumble of the diesel-powered M-60s.

Sometimes the passersby notice tanks that look different, un-American. These tanks are smaller and lower, with
rounded egg-shaped turrets and a very long cannon that

impart a streamlined appearance missing from the more boxlike M-60s. It is not surprising that they should look different. They were designed and built in the Soviet Union.

These Soviet tanks have reached Fort Hood by a long and roundabout route. Produced at the great plants in Kharkov or Nizhny Tagil, they were supplied by the Soviets to their Syrian and Egyptian allies in the Middle East. Thrown into battle against the Israeli army, they were captured undamaged and passed on to the U.S. Army as a small recompense for the vast shipments of American weaponry dispatched in the opposite direction.

Along with other examples of captured Soviet equipment—lighter armored personnel carriers for the infantry, antiaircraft guns, machine guns, rifles, and trucks—these tanks can give the U.S. forces hard data on the actual performance and characteristics of their enemy's equipment. However, they are used for more than mere education of the intelligence specialists. The Army maintains Opfors (Opposing Forces) units at bases around the country, consisting of American soldiers who wear quasi-Soviet uniforms, operate and maintain the Soviet equipment, and "fight" in exercises against ordinary U.S. units according to the precepts of Soviet tactical manuals.

Standing in the rather scruffy parking lot of the Fort Hood Opfors unit, which, like military vehicle parks everywhere, is littered with bits of machinery at various stages of disassembly, one can easily imagine how frightening the Soviet tanks must have been to the peaceful citizenry of Prague when they first appeared there in August 1968. Seen up close, Soviet tanks project an air of sinister elegance. Like most Russian weapons, they look dangerous, unstoppable.

But once one climbs inside, the perspective changes. All tanks induce, in this writer at any rate, a feeling of acute claustrophobia. Even when engaged in an exercise no more warlike than a spin about the Fort Hood firing range, members of a tank crew go about their duties in conditions more cramped than those of even the smallest sports car. Their comfort must come as an afterthought, after the requisite gadgetry for operating the tank and its weapons has been crammed inside. Tanks are usually manned by four men: commander, driver, gunner, and loader. The latest Soviet models are manned by three men, in which case the loader is replaced by a system which loads the shells into the main cannon automatically. When enemy fire is not too intense, the commander and driver stand and sit, respectively, with their heads and torsos sticking out of the relevant hatches. Otherwise, when the hatches are closed against enemy fire, they view the world through narrow window slits, which means that they must direct the movements of a vehicle that may weigh more than 50 tons with about the same amount of vision that a driver of an automobile gets from the rearview mirror. When the world is a madhouse of exploding shells and bullets clattering against the armored hull, with infantry armed with antitank weapons or other tanks possibly lurking about ready to send a shell or missile exploding among the tightly packed crew, it is no wonder that tanks should appear less omnipotent from the inside. Even if the crewmen are not killed by an enemy shot, the tank may be put out of action by a damaged track or engine. If that happens, the crew must climb outside, possibly under fire, and try and repair the damage or else go off and find somewhere to hide. The people of Prague may have been frightened by the tanks of 1968, but some of them soon learned that the machines could be put out of action by a bottle of kerosene with a flaming rag stuffed in the top.

These facts of life hold true for all tankers everywhere. A U.S. Army public affairs officer who once showed me around an M-1 commented briskly on the "unequalled space and comfort afforded the crew" by this, the army's most up-to-date tank. Even so, I could only think of how hellish it would be to be bolted up inside, hardly able to move, while unseen enemies outside were trying to kill me.

Yet that M-1 has interior space of ballroom proportions compared to the Soviet T-62 tank I explored at Fort Hood. I was unable to find out what it is like to sit inside with the hatch closed because I am over 6 feet tall, and Soviet tanks are so small that there is no headroom for anyone taller than 5 feet 6 inches. The amiable GIs of the local Opfors unit pointed out that the Soviet designers appeared to have gone out of their way to make even this cramped space as dangerously uncomfortable as possible. The inside was festooned with small fittings and brackets. Unless the crewmen held on very tight, they were bound to suffer gashes and bruises, or worse. Soviet crewmen often get severe spinal and kidney injuries in this way.

The driver sits up front. He steers the tank by braking one or the other of the tracks with the two levers on either side of his seat, an operation which requires considerable effort. American tanks have automatic transmission, while Soviet tanks do not. The whole process of operating the driving controls is so exhausting that the tough-looking men of the Opfors unit said they felt worn down after an hour or so. To avoid decapitation by the cannon as it swings about, T-62 drivers commonly drive with the hatch closed. Conditions for the former Arab drivers of the Fort Hood tanks must have been indescribable in the boiling heat of the Middle East, and there are reports that some Syrian and Egyptian tankmen in the 1973 war became asphyxiated or went into shock.

The rest of the crewmen sit in the turret: the gunner and commander to the left of the gun, one behind the other, and the gun loader to the right. A Soviet tank gun loader's job is not an enviable one. He must manhandle heavy, 50-pound, shells either from a rack near his feet or from the main storage area behind him into the breech of the main gun. To ram the shell home in the breech, he must get behind it and use both hands and then get out of the way very quickly before the gunner fires, since the gun recoils with lethal force. On a T-62, an automatic mechanism ejects the heavy casing of the spent shell through a small porthole in the rear of the turret each time the gun fires. But the casing often misses the porthole, in which case it ricochets back inside the tank. The commander has a metal guard to protect his head if this happens. The loader does not. The perils of his position are further increased if a device called a gyrostabilizer is switched on. This device is supposed to keep the gun trained on a target while the tank is moving, which means that the gun breech and turret can swing about unexpectedly, crushing the loader if he is not quick on his feet.

I asked a distinguished Israeli general what he admired about Soviet tanks. Moshe Peled, who had directed a crucial and successful counterattack against the onslaught of Syrian T-62s in the early days of the 1973 war and had gone on to become commander of the army's armored corps, replied that the tanks' small size was the most advantageous feature. Tanks, it seems, spend most of their time trying to remain out of sight of the enemy except when firing a shot from the cannon. Since Soviet tanks are smaller and lower than their American and other Western counterparts, they are harder to spot, and this attribute has been hailed as an example of Soviet deliberate "design philosophy."

If the Soviet tank designers have really been striving to make their tanks as small as possible, they have certainly accepted sacrifices in the cause, or at least required the hapless tank crews to accept them. Tanks use a lot of fuel, but there is so little room inside a T-62 that the extra fuel is stored directly next to the crew and underneath the plates next to the turret. This means, as the Israelis discovered, that a severe blow from a shell can make the tank explode even if the shell does not penetrate the armor. The tank has room for only so much ammunition—40 rounds, as opposed to 63 in the more commodious M-60. Because there is so little room inside the turret, the gun can only be reloaded if it is pointed up so that the breech is down and clear of the back wall of the turret. This procedure has to be repeated after every shot, which means that the rate of fire is slowed down, while the gun loses accuracy as it is taken off the target.

The lack of space inside the turret even detracts from the Soviet tank's major asset—its small size. A favored way for tankers to conceal themselves is to drive up the far side of a ridge to just below the crest and depress the main gun as far as it will go. The enemy will thus see little more than the gun itself and the part of the turret above the gun. But because there is so little room inside the Soviet turrets for the rear end of the gun to move up and down, the gun can be depressed only to a limited degree, which means that the tank has to drive onto the ridge crest and expose more of itself to the enemy.

Listening to the GIs at Fort Hood explain these unwelcome attributes, it seemed more and more curious that the Soviet designers should deliberately opt for all these drawbacks simply to keep down the overall size of their product. Could there be another reason?

The orthodox view of Soviet weapons is that although they are less sophisticated than their U.S. counterparts their very simplicity makes them more reliable and easier to maintain. This notion is as ingrained as the overall assumptions about Soviet conventional superiority. In the one brief passage of their book *The Armed Forces of the USSR* devoted to weapons design, the hawkish scholars William F. Scott and Harriet F. Scott characterize Soviet weapons as being "rugged, well constructed, and capable of doing the task assigned."

The men of the Fort Hood Opfors unit were unimpressed with this view. "It's very cramped inside," the captain in charge pointed out. "They use a manual transmission which is very hard to drive, very tedious for the driver. In fact, the drivers are issued with sledgehammers to get the gears into gear." One sergeant asked me, "If Soviet tanks are so well designed, how is it that to take out the engine you have to take the turret off first, and that takes half a day?"

It was, in fact, the engine and transmission that seemed to cause most of the problems. The day I arrived, the commanding captain was despondent because the enlisted man who knew how to repair the transmissions of their tanks had announced he was quitting the Army. Since that particular piece of equipment apparently broke down at least once a week, the entire unit was in danger of grinding to a halt. The engines themselves were just as fallible, considered by the Fort Hood soldiers to be simple, even crude, in design but very unreliable.

The Soviets themselves do not expect these engines to be long lasting. The official operating manual issued when the T-62s now sitting in Texas were factory-fresh stipulated that the engine must be given a total overhaul after 250 hours of operation. The tanks are discarded entirely after 500 hours. The American M-60s, by comparison, require no major maintenance to their engines, or even to the more delicate transmission, until they have been driven for at least 500 hours. To put military technology overall into perspective, it should be pointed out that a long-distance Western commercial truck engine, which approaches the power output of a tank engine, is expected to last for 10,000 hours without an overhaul.

Even the Soviet engine's offical life-span of 250 hours may be overoptimistic. The Czech army adopted the practice of totally rebuilding the engines of the tanks they received from Russia after it was discovered that they wore out, because of sloppy construction, after 100 hours. All tanks are unreliable but, despite public testimonials to the ruggedness and reliability of Soviet tanks, unpublicized Pentagon estimates indicate the Soviet tanks are expected to break down about once every 100 miles, as compared with once every 150 miles for the NATO vehicles.

This raises a crucial point. If the Soviets cannot equal the standards of Western tank reliability, perhaps they also cannot make their engines more powerful. In other words, Soviet tanks remain small, with consequent reductions in the effectiveness of the crew and weapons, because the Soviets cannot build an engine powerful enough to move anything bigger.

Both the reputation and the design of nearly all modern Soviet tanks are derived from a model called the T-34. It was commissioned in 1938 by Stalin himself over the objections of his senior military experts, who had hankered after something far more complex. Designed by two young engineers, Mikhail Koshkin and Aleksandr Morozov, the T-34 went into production at the end of 1940. Alone among the thousands of tanks the Soviets had on hand when the invasion came six months later, the small force of T-34s that had been built by that time proved able to take on and defeat the German panzers. The T-34 had thicker armor and a more powerful gun than the German tanks, and its engine, derived, curiously enough, from a diesel engine developed by the French in 1928 for use in dirigibles, provided important advantages. Up until then, no one had used a diesel engine in a tank, but this one, which gave a power output of 500 horsepower, was able to provide more miles to the gallon than anything the Germans had, and the diesel fuel was less flammable than the gasoline in other tanks at the time.

The T-34 was simple to build and required no great technical skills to operate. The Russians could and did produce enormous numbers of them—40,000 during the course of the war—at very low cost. Later on in the war, the Germans developed the Tiger and Panther tanks, which, although technically superior to the T-34, proved to be complex, unreliable, and extremely difficult to maintain.

The T-34 was lauded by experts as the most effective tank of the war, and its success is often ascribed to its being "crudely built, but rugged and reliable." Such descriptions are a little misleading. The tanks were certainly crudely built, which is not surprising, since the wartime labor force consisted mostly of women working back-breaking hours on a minimal diet. The design paid little heed to the comfort or even safety of the crew. The commander and loader—the commander also served as gunner—had their seats fixed to the turret ring, which meant that they did not revolve with the turret. This, in turn, required them to shift in their seats, since the gun recoiled 14 inches with lethal force when fired. The driver could see very little out of his window slit, so that unless the tank was on a straight course, the commander constantly had to shout driving instructions. At the same time, the hard-pressed commander had to determine the range of the targets and aim and fire the gun, while making very sure that he was not in the path of the recoil. Only troop commanders' tanks—one in every four—had radios, so the others, in addition to their other exacting duties, had to keep an eye peeled for signal flags from the troop commander for any special instructions.

The Germans were certainly highly impressed with their

enemy's tank, but apart from its diesel engine, powerful gun, and thick armor, they considered its most formidable attribute to be its ability to keep moving in peculiarly unpleasant and difficult Russian conditions—heavy snow and thick mud. The Soviet tank could do this because it had a wider track, which could better bear the weight of the tank on soft surfaces, and while the finely crafted running gear of the panzers was frozen stuck, the sloppy tolerances of the crudely built T-34s enabled these tanks to keep moving. It was this kind of ruggedness that gave rise to the legend of the T-34's reliability. The individual components may have been few—the Russians worked constantly at reducing the number of moving parts—but they frequently broke down. The transmissions were so delicate that tanks would be sent into battle with spare sets roped to the decks. When American analysts had the opportunity to make a close examination of T-34s captured in the Korean War, they found that some components had a working life of about 14 hours.

The T-34 bequeathed its reputation for rugged reliability to the models that the Soviets have produced since the war. It also passed on many of its salient design features (possibly because one of its creators, Morozov, remained the principal Soviet tank designer)—relatively small size, low profile, extreme discomfort for the crew, and the engine. The succeeding tanks—the T-54, T-55, T-62, T-64, and T-72—are indeed larger and heavier because the caliber of the gun and the thickness of the armor have grown. The power of the engine, however, has not increased to anything like the same degree.

While the T-34 had a 500-horsepower engine to propel its 26 metric tons, the succeeding T-54 and T-55 were more than a third heavier, while the power of the engine had increased only 16 percent, to 580 horsepower. The next in line, the T-62, weighed 36 metric tons, although the engine output remained unchanged. Thus, each succeeding model was progressively more underpowered and sluggish.

Then, in the mid-1960s, the Russians decided to break with tradition. They introduced a new tank, the T-64, which was radically different in many ways from its predecessors, including a new engine. The designers, were unable, however, to go so far as to produce a totally original design. For inspiration they turned to an engine developed at about the same time for a new British tank called the Chieftain. This was not a particularly happy choice, since the Chieftain engine turned out to be not powerful enough for the load it had to carry and prone to incessant breakdowns. The Iranian army found it so poor, in fact, that it canceled its order. The CIA even singled it out for special opprobrium. Testifying before Congress, former CIA director Admiral Stansfield Turner remarked that, by comparison with Soviet tanks, "the heavier weights [of NATO tanks] have not hampered mobility because they have adequate power. The British Chieftain is an exception."

Adapted and fitted in the T-64, the British design lived down to its reputation. Viktor Suvorov, whose unit was issued with T-64s early in 1967, recalls that "the engine itself was not only bad, it was disgusting. Several teams of workers and engineers, and a gang of designers, were sent along simply to maintain our one tank regiment. But they could not hope to solve problems arising from the engine's design, try as they might."

Although the Soviets still have many tank units in Eastern Europe equipped with the T-64, there are indications that the authorities concur with Suvorov's unflattering verdict. It is either being produced in very limited numbers (it is very hard to kill a defense program in Russia; remember the MiG-25) and may even have been taken out of production altogether. More conclusively, the next model they developed, the T-72 (unlike aircraft, Soviet tanks are not given nicknames by NATO), was similar to the T-64 in most important respects save for the engine. For that, the Soviet designers reverted to the venerable design first used in the wartime T-34.

Soviet technical publications and the Pentagon concur in estimating the power of the T-72 at 780 horsepower, but there are grounds for skepticism. It is very hard to take a forty-year-old engine and suddenly discover a way of getting it to produce an additional 200 horsepower. One possible method would be to use a turbocharger—literally forcing the fuel-air mixture into the cylinder. But since the forty-year-old engine was not designed for such pressures, use of this device would have the effect of wearing out the engine at an accelerated pace. In this case, the T-72's rate of engine breakdown would exceed even the impressive figures for the rest of the Soviet tank arsenal.

The surest indication that the Soviet tank designers have not succeeded in developing a more powerful tank is the unchanged situation of the unfortunate crewmen. The most radical innovation in the T-64, apart from the "disgusting" engine, was the elimination of the loader and his replacement by an automatic mechanism. In theory, this represented an advance of the kind Dr. Luns has in mind when he refers to NATO having "lost much of the technological advantage" it formerly enjoyed. Unfortunately, the automatic loader has proved to have its drawbacks, because like many of the "technological breakthroughs" in modern weaponry on both sides of the Iron Curtain, it is more elegant in conception than in reality.

The loader works in this way. Ammunition is divided into two parts—the propellant charges and the projectiles themselves—which are arranged vertically in a circular tray beside the gunner. To load the gun, a mechanical arm comes down, picks up both charge and shell, and inserts first the projectile and then the charge into the breech, which then slams shut automatically. Unhappily for the gunner, the mechanical arm sometimes selects either his leg or arm and loads that into the breech instead. One U.S. Army officer has been quoted as suggesting "this is how the Red Army Chorus gets its soprano section." As late as 1979, long after the system had been introduced into service, Soviet tank gunners in East Germany were under orders to dispense with the automatic loader and do the whole business by hand, loading both shell and charge separately, as well as aiming and firing the gun. This effectively reduces the tank's rate of fire to one or two shots a minute, as opposed to seven or eight for a U.S. tank.

It is, in fact, the guns that make the main difference between one Soviet tank and the next. Tanks carry two kinds of weapons: machine guns, which are very important for use against enemy infantry and aircraft, and the more prominent main cannon, used for combat with other tanks. One of the basic imperatives in tank development is to build a gun powerful enough to penetrate the armor of your enemy's tank, while making your own armor strong enough to repel his projectiles. The larger the caliber of a gun (the diameter of its barrel), the larger the projectile it can fire. Soviet tank guns have traditionally been bigger than their Western contemporaries. Nowadays, the guns on the T-72 and T-64 tanks are 125 millimeters in caliber, as opposed to the standard 105-millimeter guns found on all American tanks. Since the Soviet vehicles are otherwise smaller than their Western equivalents, the long protruding gun barrel gives them an impressively threatening aspect.

Size is important in tank guns, but so are a lot of other things. Much depends on the velocity of the gun—meaning how fast its projectiles travel. Even more hangs on the quality of the ammunition—whether it is stable in flight, so that it hits the target at the proper angle, and whether it is good at penetrating the enemy armor, which can be as much as 50 centimeters thick. None of these attributes can be of any use if the gun is inaccurate in the first place. Big guns can throw a projectile farther than smaller ones, but this does not count for much in tank warfare, since tanks tend to fight at close quarters. Even in the open sandy expanse of the Middle East, Arab and Israeli tanks have usually fought at distances of considerably less than half a mile, although their guns had ranges of more than three times that distance.

Russian tanks have bigger projectiles to hurl at their opponents—which means of course that they can carry fewer of them and have a lower rate of fire. Further, the better penetrating power of the bigger cannon is wiped out by poorer accuracy and ammunition that is less efficient in penetrating armor. The standard 105-millimeter gun, originally designed by the British, which is used in most NATO tanks, is "rifled" with grooves inside the barrel to make the projectile spin in flight, thus helping its accuracy and stability in flight. Soviet tank guns also used to be rifled until the development of the T-62 in the early 1960s. At that time the Soviets decided to make the gun bigger than any other in the world but also to make it "smooth-bored." By eliminating the rifling, they achieved a longer, thinner projectile and a higher velocity but paid a penalty in accuracy and stability. The T-64 and T-72, with their enormous 125-mm gun, continue to embody the Soviet preference for size over precision, although, as Suvorov recounts, the troops were not impressed by its capabilities:

From the very first look we all liked the 125 mm. gun. It was the most powerful gun in the world and no tank had ever had anything like it before. Because of its amazing initial velocity, its shells could tear away the turrets of tank targets and hurl them a distance of about ten meters (tank turrets weigh eight or even twelve tons).

But now, upon closer acquaintance, our delight with the T-64s had begun gradually to fade. The gun was certainly all powerful but, in their endeavor to increase the initial velocity of the shell, the designers had made it not rifled, but smooth bored, as in the T-62, and this immediately adversely affected its accuracy. In fact, it was an all-powerful gun, which always missed its target.

On the occasions when the T-64 or T-72 does hit the target, the results may be less than satisfying. Antitank rounds come in two basic varieties: those that penetrate the target armor by means of a shaped-charge explosive, which literally melts a hole through the steel, and those that rely on kinetic energy to pierce the armor. U.S. Army tests of both the big Russian 115-mm T-62 ammunition and its smaller Western counterparts indicate that all that impressive bulk does not really make much difference. Assuming the projectile hits the target perfectly nose-on, which is vital for full effectiveness and which is by no means a foregone conclusion in the case of an unrifled gun, the T-62 gun should be able to send a kinetic-energy projectile — which is basically solid metal — through 228 millimeters of armor at 1,000 meters' range. The 105-millimeter gun used in all American tanks can send the same type of projectile through 275 millimeters of armor at the same range.

The same kind of detailed information is not available about the performance of the bigger and more modern Soviet tank guns, although there is a persistent rumor among interested circles that U.S. Army intelligence has had an undamaged T-72 in its possession since sometime in 1981. The unverified story is that the tank was obtained with the assistance of British intelligence as a by-product of the fighting in Afghanistan, driven across that country's border with Pakistan by Afghan army defectors.

Precedent suggests that the T-72 gun should compare unfavorably with the 105-mm gun on American tanks, as does the evidence of former Captain Suvorov and the results of its use in combat by the Syrian army.

The Israeli army encountered the T-72 for the first time during its invasion of Lebanon in June 1982, and this model appears to have performed with no more success than the earlier models of Soviet tanks in Syrian hands—the Israelis succeeded in knocking out at least ten T-72s in the very first engagement. When I asked the Israeli tank general Peled how they had managed to defeat the most modern Soviet tank so easily, he replied that it was not a matter of any Israeli secret weapon (despite reports to the contrary emanating from the Pentagon) but simply a matter of the effectiveness of the trusty 105-millimeter gun on Israeli tanks old and new. He might also have mentioned that these effects were achieved without the latest American-designed ammunition, particularly one variety of kinetic round which is made of a particularly dense and highly incendiary material called DU, for depleted uranium, a nonradioactive by-product of the nuclear industry. Although the Russians have abundant supplies of DU, they appear not to have mastered the technique of milling it for this purpose and instead rely on a substitute of inferior density and grossly inferior incendiary qualities called tungsten carbide, or on steel, which is even less satisfactory.

Despite its inauspicious combat debut, the reputation of the T-72 will quite probably continue to shine brightly as far as the Pentagon is concerned. Even while Syrian T-72s were still smoldering in the Bekaa Valley in Lebanon, the U.S. Army was reported as assessing the T-72 to be superior to its latest tank, the M-1, in many respects, including its gun and rate of fire.

It may be that this conclusion was based on an objective examination of the purloined T-72, but history indicates that even such hard evidence can be treated in a very subjective manner. Back in the 1960s, when the T-55 was the main Soviet battle tank, the U.S. Army insisted, on the basis of engineering calculations derived from measuring covertly obtained sample tanks, that the T-55's 100-millimeter gun was quite powerful enough to knock holes in U.S. M-48s; similarly, the Army claimed the American tanks could destroy the T-55 with the U.S. 90-millimeter weapon. When the two tanks finally confronted each other in the 1967 Middle East war, it transpired that neither of them had the wherewithal to punch holes in the other's frontal armor. The Army, it seemed, had not wished to test its theories about the effectiveness of either Soviet or American tanks by actually carrying out any practical firing tests.

These two modern Soviet tanks, the T-72 and T-64, have received more than a passing mention here because their treatment at the hands of the threat estimators is such a perfect example of the way in which Soviet military power as a whole is customarily portrayed by Western military officialdom. No matter that the enormous gun is no more effective than the far older Western weapon and that the automatic loader "eats" crewmen, the Pentagon will pay tribute to these "unique and innovative features." The T-72 engine may still have a block made of highly flammable aluminum because a French designer sometime in the late 1920s decided that would be suitable for the dirigible engine (the progenitor, remember, of the T-34 motor). The T-64, which, along with the T-62, is the tank used in all the Eastern European Soviet units, may have a "disgusting" engine, and a gun which "always misses the target," yet such imperfections are not allowed to diminish the threat of a Soviet armored onslaught on Europe. Nor, presumably, when the Pentagon planners concluded that a Soviet invasion of the Middle East oil states could only be halted with nuclear weapons did they pay heed to the considered judgment of the Indian army, which refused to buy more than a token number of T-72s on the grounds that the vehicle could not stand up to desert conditions (sand).

As so often in the matter of the East-West military balance, the explanation for this attitude must be found in the exigencies of internal U.S. military politics. After producing the M-60, the U.S. Army tank developers fell on hard times. In the mid-1960s, they began developing, at great expense, a tank of baroque complexity called the MBT-70. They justified this on the basis of an entirely spurious set of assumptions about the threat of the T-62. After repeated test failures, including a disastrous automatic loader, and mushrooming overruns, the Congress canceled the program and directed the Army to design a cheaper, less complex tank. Thus balked in their endeavors, they turned their efforts at the beginning of the 1970s to an allegedly simpler design called the XM-803; this too was canceled when the Congress found that the cost matched that of the MBT-70. Returning to the drawing board the Army came up with the M-1. This they opted to power with a gas-turbine engine, a variation on the jet engines normally used in aircraft, which at least had the merit of novelty. Although the main cannon chosen for the early models of this new tank was the tried and true 105-millimeter gun, the army announced plans to change at a later date to a 120-millimeter smoothbored gun of German design.

The mounting expense of the M-1 program generated heavy Congressional criticism, to which the Army responded by invoking the specter of the T-64 and T-72. Only the M-1, it was claimed, could hope to stem a steel tide of these sophisticated behemoths.

The result has been what might be construed as a friendly gesture by the U.S. Army generals to their counterparts in the Soviet ground forces, because the M-1 has deficiencies which go a long way toward offsetting those of its Soviet counterparts. Even as it went into full-scale production in 1980, Army tests showed that on average it broke down once every 43 miles. The extra fuel required by the gas-turbine engine means that its cruising range is two-thirds that of the venerable M-60. When the new and bigger gun is introduced, with a consequent increase in the size of the individual shells, the tank will be able to hold no more ammunition than the 40 rounds carried by the T-72, a drop of 23 from the M-60's ammunition capability.

American tank soldiers may yet come to remember the M-60 with increasing nostalgia, just as Soviet tankers are inclined to favorably compare the twenty-five-year-old T-55 with its more complex successors.

As more evidence becomes public about the performance of the T-72 in battle, American pronouncements about its capabilities will probably become more objective. There appears to be a pattern to official assessments of Soviet weapons. Newly developed or developing U.S. systems are usually described as superior to their Soviet contemporaries but threatened by imminent Soviet developments. For example, the May 6, 1982, issue of the in-house Pentagon journal *Pentagram News* describes the M-1 as "a better tank" than the T-72, but "the Soviets are working on a new tank, the T-80, which is expected to be its equal." The M-60 fits neatly into this scheme of things, being considered "better than the T-54, 55, and 62, but slightly inferior to the T-64 and T-72." One should note the absence of any suggestion that weapons may develop retrogressively or that newer does not necessarily equal better.

Tanks are agreed by both friends and enemies to be the cutting edge of Soviet conventional military might, but they do not operate in isolation. They are an integral although preeminent part of what the U.S. military anticipate will be "a combined arms team that can move in a quick armored thrust across Europe" made up, according to former Defense Intelligence Agency director Harold Aaron, of "self-propelled personnel carriers which can fire on the move, tanks, and self-propelled artillery."

If the Soviets were to embark on such a "quick armored thrust," they would have to transport most of their infantry in a vehicle called a BTR-60 (from *BroneTranspoRter*, "armored personnel carrier"). Although first introduced in 1961, it is still the most widely used troop carrier in the Soviet army. Consisting of a long boat-shaped steel body riding on eight massive wheels, it presents a formidable appearance, but appearance is not the best way to judge weapons, particularly Soviet ones. This 12-ton vehicle, which can carry 14 soldiers as well as its two-man crew, is powered by a gasoline rather than diesel engine, reportedly because at the time it was developed the Soviets were short of diesel fuel. They were also, however, short of a sufficiently powerful gasoline engine, so they used two small engines that had been originally developed for a farm truck in the 1930s. This complicated matters, since with two engines they also had to include two clutches, two transmissions, two distributors, and two starters. For this Rube Goldberg arrangement to perform properly, all the parts in each system must work reliably and in synchronization. If the synchronization breaks down, which, according to Viktor Suvorov, happens every day, one of the engines has to be urgently disconnected, leaving just one 90-horsepower engine to propel the 12-ton "coffin on wheels," as it is invariably called by the soldiers. The U.S. Army Soviet-equipment specialists, headquartered in Aberdeen, Maryland, have found the engine system so complex and unreliable that they have long since adopted the expedient of substituting American engines in their fleet of BTRs.

Troops only ride into battle in a BTR and its Western contemporaries; they cannot fight from it. In the early 1960s, however, American and then Soviet generals began dreaming of an armored vehicle from which troops could shoot, like a rolling fort. Accordingly, for their succeeding vehicle, which was introduced in 1967, the Soviets produced a troop carrier which would not only carry troops in armored safety through the thick of battle but would also allow them to shoot from portholes and from a small turret. The BMP, as this carrier is known (from *Boyevaya Mashina Pekhoty*, "armored vehicle infantry"), has aroused considerable enthusiasm among U.S. Army generals. "This is probably the best infantry carrier in the world," Defense Intelligence Agency director General Harold Aaron told a Congressional committee in 1978. "Built around 1967, it can carry a Soviet squad [eight soldiers]. Sure they are rather constrained, but the average soldier is only about five feet six inches tall. The BMP has a 73-millimeter gun, which can knock out a tank at about 800 meters. It has a Sagger missile on top that can reach out 3,000 meters. It can travel across water. It is a good system."

Viewing a BMP from the outside, one can easily understand the general's enthusiasm. Moving on tracks rather than wheels, it resembles a tank, except that the gun and turret are small in proportion to the rest of the vehicle. The men inside sit back to back, ready to blaze away with their automatic rifles through small rifle slits in the sides, while the gunner uses the cannon and missile to do in enemy tanks. Thus protected, they should be impervious to shot or shell, or even, because of a complex air-filtration system, to poison gas and radioactive fallout. When the occasion demands it, the men can dismount through the two rear doors.

It would require a Saul Steinberg to illustrate the difference in perspective between looking at this battlewagon from the outside and sitting crouched inside it in the middle of a battle. The men peer out through their rifle slits or small periscopes, but individually they can see very little. Should they choose to fire, they will choke on their own gun gases. They probably know that the 6 millimeters of armor over their heads is too thin to keep out artillery shrapnel and machine-gun bullets and that because they are totally enclosed, any kind of shell or rocket that penetrates the armor, or an exploding mine underneath, will probably kill them all. BMP crews in Afghanistan have paid dearly for the designers' folly in incorporating extra fuel tanks in the rear doors. The guerrillas have discovered that a heavy machine-gun burst will light the fuel and trap the crew, unless they can get out of the roof hatches in time. The gunner, like his ill-fated colleagues in the T-64 and T-72, must cope with an automatic loader, which has a tendency to "eat" arms. In any case, the turret "gun" is not a proper gun. Rather, it is a short-range rocket launcher that fires a much punier projectile than the ordinary shoulder-fired RPG-7 rocket carried in every Soviet infantry squad. The projectile fired from the BMP is so unstable in flight that it gets blown about by any strong crosswind, making it extremely difficult for the gunner to aim. It may be for this reason that on the BMP-2, which was exhibited for the first time in the Red Square parade in 1982, the Soviets have substituted a 30-millimeter high-velocity cannon. Since the engine is half of the standard tank engine, there is no reason to believe that it will be any more reliable.

The avidity of both the Soviet and American high commands to send their men into battle encased in such vehicles is curious. Since a troop carrier must be large enough to carry a squad or so of men, it cannot have armor thick enough to keep out much more than arms fire, yet if it has a roof it will always be enough to trap the inmates and the results of any interior explosion together. The rank and file have a better appreciation of this than generals and weapons designers; it is very hard to find any combat pictures from the Vietnam War of the American version of the BTR—the M-113—in which the men are not riding on top of the vehicle. The troops decided that sitting exposed to the elements and snipers was preferable to crouching inside the coffin, and judging by news footage of the 1982 invasion of Lebanon, Israeli troops using American-supplied M-113s have made the same choice. Passengers in the U.S. vehicle do indeed face a hazard that the Soviet designers have spared their men—the M-113 armor is made of aluminum. When hit by infantry antitank weapons, part of the aluminum vaporizes and explodes; the rest melts and spatters the troops inside with lethal fragments, which burns and melts in flaming droplets when hit. Despite this, the U.S. Army is pressing ahead with its own version of the BMP. Known as the Bradley Infantry Fighting Vehicle, it can only carry six troops in addition to the commander, gunner, and driver. Although supposedly able to emulate the BMP's ability to swim rivers, it has tended to sink in tests. The breakdown rate is high, and the dangerous aluminum armor has been retained, and indeed thickened, which makes it even more lethal. Nevertheless, according to *Pentagram News*, "it is believed to be superior to the Soviet BMP."

Even a relatively cursory examination of some of the weapons crucial for any kind of Soviet armored invasion shows their equipment in a very different light from the way in which it is normally presented. Their weapons are often commended for being "simple" and "reliable," and simultaneously are commended for incorporating advanced systems which diminish the West's technological advantage. The cursing GIs at Fort Hood attempting to repair their Soviet tanks regarded them as simply designed but not reliable. Using two weak engines to power a vehicle for lack of one powerful engine to do the job may be a simple conception, but is hardly simple or reliable in execution. A device which loads shells automatically into a gun may seem technologically sophisticated until soldiers start losing legs and arms.

Each of these vehicles has its individual foibles, but there is a common theme: the lack of efficient and reliable power trains—the combination of engine and transmission and driveshafts. The importance of this cannot be overestimated, particularly for an army that is, by common agreement among friend and foe, organized for a rapid offensive thrust into enemy territory. Stalin said at the outset of World War II that "modern war depends on engines." His words, relevant in 1941, are even more to the point today. The "combined arms team" that so impresses Pentagon officials like General Aaron includes many different kinds of mobile weapons besides the tanks and troop carriers. However, these weapons also share many of the same disabilities and even in a large number of cases the very same engines as the weapons discussed above.

For example, graphic illustrations of a Soviet combined arms army on the march depict an impressive array of accompanying antiaircraft weapons, which protect the ground forces against attacks at high and low altitudes. Discussion of these weapons in Western technical literature tends to focus on the operation of the guns and missiles themselves, with only passing mention of their means of transport. Yet it appears that two of the most important mobile systems for defense against low-flying aircraft—the SAM-6 surface-to-air missile and the ZSU-23-4 multiple-rapid-firing cannon—travel on an overloaded version of a light tank chassis powered by a half-version of the ubiquitous and unreliable tank engine. A larger antiaircraft cannon called the ZSU-57, which drives on the full-sized engine, was purchased by the Iranians in the late 1960s. After some unhappy experiences, the Iranian high command ordered that these supposedly mobile guns never be required to travel more than 18 miles under their own power, as they invariably broke down.

Even if the delicate 1930s technology of the power train can be kept working without mishap, the delicate machinery of the missiles and their radars may not. The SAM-8, which plays a major role in the Soviet scheme of mobile air defense systems, is considered by Western analysts to be very similar in design and operation to the Franco-German Roland missile, a system considered too delicate by the U.S. Army to accompany a division on the march.

The formidable reputation of Soviet SAMs really dates from two wars, the Vietnam War and the 1973 Yom Kippur War. The systems deployed by the Vietnamese will be discussed in Chapter 13, devoted to the Soviet troops of national air defense, rather than here, since the SAM-2 and SAM-3 missiles are too bulky to be moved from place to place with advancing or retreating troops and therefore are not considered to be mobile defense systems.

The impact of the SAMs during the Yom Kippur War came mainly from the fact that this was the first time that the previously omnipotent Israeli air force had suffered any kind of setback. Yet on close examination, it turns out that out of the 100 or so aircraft lost by the Israelis, only one-third were downed by missiles; the rest were killed by guns or fighters. Of the missile kills, very few came from SAM-6s—the Egyptians were only able to move two batteries of four launchers each across the Suez Canal during the entire war. Even without being moved, these particular missiles did not prove very effective in downing the Israeli planes. Even according to official Pentagon estimates, it took 55 missiles for every kill, although internal Israeli military sources insist that the true number was over 100 firings per kill. More recently, the Israelis are said to have incapacitated, in one strike, 19 batteries of Syrian SAM-6s during their 1982 invasion of Lebanon without the loss of a single aircraft.

Another, much smaller, SAM that emerged with a towering reputation from the 1973 Yom Kippur War was the hand-held SAM-7, designed to give the ordinary infantryman the ability to shoot down a jet plane. In fact, this weapon proved even less successful than the larger SAM-6—out of about 5,000 fired, only two scored definite kills, with four possibles. The reason for these unimpressive results becomes clear to anyone who looks beyond the mystique at the way the system actually works. It is heat seeking, which means that it homes in on the heat from the target's engine exhaust; but there are other sources of heat on the battlefield, such as the sun or decoy flares dropped by the intended victim. Even if the SAM-7 nevertheless hits the target, it may not destroy it. Like all handheld weapons, the missile is limited in its size and range by the amount a man can carry and fire from his shoulder: about 30 pounds. This limit means that the SAM-7, like similar U.S. weapons, such as the Redeye and Stinger, cannot pack enough rocket propellant to catch a jet fighter maneuvering at 500 miles an hour, nor can it carry more than 1 pound of explosive warhead. As a result, only about 28 Israeli planes were struck by SAM-7s—or Strellas, to use the Soviet nickname—and, of these, most suffered no more than a damaged exhaust pipe.

Because of its small size, the Strella has acquired an especial mystique as a guerrilla weapon. Afghan guerrillas, in particular, have made repeated pleas in interviews with Western journalists for supplies of these, as a counter to the Mi-24 Hind helicopters used by the Soviet forces in Afghanistan. It is less clear how effective these weapons actually prove to be when they do reach guerrilla hands. Certainly, when first used by the Vietcong against U.S. helicopters in 1972, they scored a hit on American aircraft and helicopters for every three missiles fired. The effect soon wore off, however, as the Americans learned that the missile could be neutralized by dropping a hot flare to attract its heat-seeking guidance system, a solution that was followed by bolt-on shields which cloaked the heat from the aircraft's exhausts. Nevertheless, these weapons have remained popular with guerrillas—the Afghans claim to have used one to shoot down a helicopter carrying the Soviet General Pyotr Shkidchenko in January 1982. The Afghans admit that the Strellas do have limitations. If a guerrilla fires at a helicopter and misses, he is in trouble, because the flash and smoke of the launch will have betrayed his position. There are reports that some sharpshooting Afghans actually prefer .455-caliber (which is a very large bullet) elephant guns as antihelicopter weapons to the sophisticated guided missiles; these guns can inflict lethal damage on the helicopter's rotor, and they do not give away the attacker's position.

Although nineteenth-century elephant rifles may be an extreme expedient, guns remain the most deadly enemy of attacking aircraft, even in the age of missiles. During the Vietnam War, no less than 85 percent of the 3,000 planes lost by the Americans were downed by guns. Missiles accounted for 8 percent, and the North Vietnamese air force MiG interceptors for another 7 percent. Guns are effective because they and their ammunition are cheap compared to missiles, so it is possible to have a great many of them. They can provide continuous and overlapping fields of fire, and they can be aimed by human beings rather than highly fallible mechanical guidance systems.

It is important to note that individual guns are not particularly effective—historically, antiaircraft guns have used about 8,000 rounds for every plane hit. It is when they are used *en masse* that they can be deadly to an attacking force; the Hanoi air defense system that wreaked such execution on the fighter-bombers of the U.S. Air Force and Navy included more than 5,000 guns at the height of the war.

Given the proven effectiveness of guns, it is not surprising that one of the components of the Soviet ground force's mobile air defense system most heavily publicized by the Air Force generals concerned with attacking invading tank columns is the ZSU-23-4 system, more mellifluously known by its Soviet nickname, Shilka. It is a rapid-firing cannon with four 23-millimeter barrels, which are aimed by radar. The whole system is mounted on a tracked vehicle powered, as noted, by half of the familiar tank engine. The American generals speak somberly of the Shilkas, which are designed to move with a division near the front line, being able to put up a wall of lead so potent that one out of every three planes coming within range will supposedly be hit, a capability which is expressed in the original jargon as a "PK (probability of kill) of .3," thus making it very hard for the U.S. planes to hit Soviet tanks. As a result, the U.S. Air Force has concentrated on developing complex and expensive antitank weapons that can be launched from beyond Shilka range.

The Shilka is, in fact, a more sophisticated and expensive version of an earlier Soviet antiaircraft gun, which consisted merely of two 23-millimeter barrels mounted on a two-wheel trailer. This older system cannot propel itself, and it is aimed by human eye. By comparison, the ZSU-23-4 appears far more "advanced." It has its own engine to move it about, which appears less impressive to anyone who has a practical knowledge of the engine's performance, such as the men of the Fort Hood Opfors detachment.

The Shilka's guns are trained on the target by the system's computer, which receives information on the target's speed, height, and direction from the radar. Since even rapid-fire cannon shells take a certain amount of time to reach the target—up to 6 seconds at maximum Shilka range—the computer must calculate where the target will have got to a few seconds after the gun has fired, in much the same way as a duck hunter "leads" his target duck with his shotgun.

Unfortunately, pilots being fired on do not behave like ducks. They jink and weave as violently as possible. A jet aircraft flying at 400 miles an hour can move a long way in even 3 seconds, and there is no way that even the very best computer and radar can anticipate the direction in which the pilot is going to decide to turn before he does so, by which time it is too late.

Such doubts about the dubious benefits of radar guidance, which apply to all antiaircraft weapons aimed in this way, are reinforced by the results of the Pentagon's own tests with the weapon. The United States possess a large number of working models of the ZSU-23-4, which have been used for an intensive series of tests, in which U.S. Army gunners fired thousands of rounds at remotely controlled drone targets and tracked hundreds of passes by real fighters. The tests took place under what are called "benign" conditions. The gunners were always forewarned of the approach of the targets, which flew past without exhibiting the realistically violent maneuvers that might be expected from planes flown by pilots in fear of their lives. The conclusion officially drawn from these tests was that the Shilka was just as deadly as had been feared and that it would claim, on the average, one victim from every three passes by enemy aircraft within range. However, unofficial reports from reliable sources attest that the actual results of the tests indicated something rather different: the effectiveness of this weapon, even in the most favorable conditions, was about 100 times worse than the Pentagon had chosen to believe. Furthermore, the weapon is almost entirely useless against a maneuvering target.

Such a conclusion was and is entirely unwelcome to the U.S. Air Force, since it questions the logic of a very expensive program to develop and buy "standoff" weapons that are to be launched from aircraft well out of range of the deadly Shilkas. Prominent among these is the Maverick, a "smart" missile which homes in on enemy tanks. Although the Air Force has announced plans to buy 61,000 of the latest version of the Maverick, at $70,000 each, its detractors claim that the missile has been subjected only to the most benign tests, bearing no resemblance to real battlefield conditions. U.S. Air Force General John Vogt, who tried to subject an earlier version to operational tests while he was commander of U.S. air forces in Europe, found that the missile "craps out entirely in bad weather." To fire a Maverick, a pilot must fly straight and level for 10 or 20 seconds, which puts him in grave danger from guns or SAMs.

As a result of this manifestation of the American military appetite for complex and impractical high-technology systems, the Soviets may be spared some of the consequences of their own initiative in developing a complex high-technology cannon. All radar-guided guns and missiles share a common inability to track maneuvering targets, but the Shilka has some uniquely Soviet rough edges: apart from the ancient engine laboring under the hood, the gun barrels have a tendency to wear out after a short space of time, while the gun itself has an unfortunate habit of loosing off bursts of its own accord, which must be most unpleasant for any friendly forces that happen to be in the way.

All in all, there could be no neater example of the way in which the military machines of the superpowers advance along parallel lines. The Soviets have invested in the Shilka, which is so expensive that no more than 16 are allotted to a division. Thus, they have discarded the traditional advantages of guns—overlapping fields of fire, numbers to spare, and simple equipment. Some independent-minded analysts with practical experience in air-to-ground fighting in Southeast Asia consider, as one put it, "this gun makes the life of the fighter pilot that much safer."

Meanwhile, to evade the Shilka, the U.S. Air Force has withdrawn most of its ground-attack antitank planes to a safe distance and equipped them with the expensive and ineffective Maverick, while even more complex and costly standoff weapons are under development—all to absolutely no purpose and at great increase in risk to the pilot.

Weapons like the T-72 or the ZSU-23-4 represent some basic facets of Soviet weapons design: simple but unreliable mechanisms grafted onto ambitiously complex features which ruin combat effectiveness. It is fair to say that this is not the orthodox view of Soviet weaponry, which is best summed up in the words of former CIA director Stansfield Turner: "Soviet equipment tends to be more simplistic in design than ours, but it is generally reliable for the purpose for which it is intended." It is hard to see how such a conclusion could survive any disinterested acquaintanceship with, for example, the armored personnel carrier turret, the T-72's automatic loader, or the clutch and transmission of the Shilka.

The general reputation of Soviet weapons for ruggedness and reliability is more likely derived from a small number of untypical examples. The most familiar of these must be the Kalashnikov AK-47 assault rifle, the basic weapon of the Soviet infantryman. It is the most famous of all Soviet weapons, the only one, with the possible exception of the MiG-21 fighter, that is widely known by name among nonspecialist Westerners. Its fame and reputation are principally derived from its popularity among guerrilla movements around the world. The AK-47 is indeed rugged and reliable. It can stand up to any amount of wear and tear, can be handled and maintained by poorly trained fighters, and does not jam in the thick of combat.

The Kalashnikov rifle is named for its designer, Mikhail T. Kalashnikov. Kalashnikov served at the front during the war, which enabled him to study the virtues of an automatic rifle introduced by the Germans in 1943 called the Sturmgewehr. That weapon marked a fundamental breakthrough in automatic rifle design, not because of the actual mechanism but because it used a light cartridge. Military rifle designers have traditionally equipped their troops with guns that are ideal for accurate shooting in the restful single-shot conditions of the firing range over ranges of 500 yards. These guns are less useful in combat, where very few men have the time or the inclination to carefully aim their weapons, where the rate of timing is crucial, and where most combat takes place at a range of 50 yards or less. This being so, the ordinary infantryman is better suited to an automatic weapon firing in bursts, like a submachine gun, so he can react instantly without having to take careful aim. But the traditional rifle cannot be made automatic, because the bullets are heavy and the cartridges in the bullets have a powerful powder charge for long-range accuracy. As a result, the heavy recoil in automatic fire with such cartridges makes a shoulder-fired weapon unmanageable. What the Germans did was to reduce the amount of powder in the cartridge so that the recoil was correspondingly diminished, which meant that the weapon could fire in bursts. Kalashnikov had the insight to appreciate the significance of this and incorporate it into the design of his own rifle, which first appeared in 1947. With few modifications, it has remained the basic infantry weapon of the Soviet and allied forces until the early 1980s.

The U.S. Army meanwhile had failed to produce a Sergeant Kalashnikov, or at least no one with his ideas was able to overcome the deep-rooted prejudice of the Army Ordnance Command in favor of big marksman-type rifle cartridges, which, in turn, necessitated big, heavy rifles, which cannot be fired in bursts. Large weapons of this kind have an added and deleterious effect on the soldiers' effectiveness because they decrease the amount of ammunition that infantrymen can carry. By the time a combat soldier is loaded up with the basic necessities of existence—rations, first-aid kit, water, and so forth—he has an upper limit of about 18 pounds for his rifle and its ammunition. Within that limit, the bulk of the weight can be accounted for by the ammunition or by the rifle itself; but if one is increased, the other must go down. The M-14 rifle, which was standard issue for American troops until the mid-1960s, allowed its owner to carry only an additional 100 rounds of ammunition, while the AK-47, with its lighter ammunition, meant that the Soviet soldier or a guerrilla could carry 180 rounds.

During the Vietnam War, the Americans changed rifles, despite bitter resistance from the Army's in-house bureaucracy, which had traditionally controlled the development of small arms. The new M-16 was smaller and lighter than the gun it replaced, mainly because it used a much smaller (though more lethal) bullet, which made it possible to reduce the overall size and weight of the weapon. U.S. soldiers could now patrol the jungles carrying no fewer than 300 rounds of ammunition. The success of this development was marred by the unremitting struggle of the small-arms bureaucrats against the M-16 (which had been privately developed by a brilliant American named Gene Stoner). Their resentment at this infringement of their prerogatives was carried to the lengths of actual sabotage of the gun, for which American troops in the field paid a heavy price.

The Russians appreciated the significance of the M-16's breakthrough, but only up to a point. In the mid-1970s, Mikhail Kalashnikov's institutional descendants (Kalashnikov died in 1972) introduced a modified rifle, the AKS-74, to replace the original gun. It used a smaller-caliber bullet, so the weight and size of the barrel and ammunition went down and the amount of ammunition that a Soviet soldier could carry went up somewhat. But to take the full weight advantage of the small caliber, the Soviets would have to have redesigned the original Kalashnikov firing mechanism, which they did not do. This may well be because the Soviets now lack a gun designer with the brilliance of a Kalashnikov or a Stoner, a salutary reminder of the fact that weapons technology does not necessarily proceed on an upward curve. Furthermore, U.S. Army tests have revealed that the manufacturing quality of the AKS-74 ammunition is of such a low standard that the rifle's accuracy is much poorer than that of the M-16.

This new rifle is a good example of an important aspect of the way weapons are designed in the Soviet Union nowadays: loyalty to a basic design, whether it be good, like the original AK-47, or bad, like the tank engine, coupled with a profound respect for American innovations regardless of their utility. While the Soviet soldier will doubtless find the new AKS-74 adequate, this imitative trait is leading the Soviet forces into more serious trouble elsewhere.

In 1962 the Soviets introduced the RPG-7 antitank rocket launcher. In essence the conceptual descendant of a very successful World War II German development, the Panzerfaust, this hand-held rocket launcher is simple to use and maintain and is extremely effective against tanks. In the 1973 war, the Israelis lost more tanks on the Syrian front to RPG-7s than to any other weapon.

The Americans meanwhile have failed to produce a light antitank weapon as successful as the RPG-7. For many years after the war, they relied on the bazooka, despite the fact that GIs had found it next to useless against German tanks and abandoned it in favor of the German Panzerfaust whenever they could. The reason it was useless was because the designers had made the explosive warhead too small to deal with anything but the softest target. The bazooka's lineal descendant, introduced in the early sixties, was the LAW (Light Antitank Weapon), which was designed to be fired from a disposable cardboard launcher; but it was still too light to inflict any damage on enemy armor. U.S. Marines who tried to use it against the vintage T-34 tanks operated by the North Vietnamese, which had very thin armor by today's standards, found that the charge, as one veteran bitterly recalls, "would just scorch the paint."

Undeterred, the U.S. Army decided to replace the LAW with yet another light antitank rocket of the same basic design called the Viper. The main differences are that the Viper has a longer range and a more expensive plastic launcher-container, which is thrown away after use. Unfortunately, as one observer put it, "the Viper suffers from a peculiar disability . . . the weapon stands virtually no chance of knocking out a Soviet tank under most battlefield conditions." Once again, in insisting on a throwaway launcher light enough to be carried easily, the designers have made the warhead too puny.

Critics of the Pentagon's appetite for expensive—the Viper is supposed to cost $1 billion—and fundamentally useless weapons might at this point compare the unhappy lot of the U.S. infantry squad with their more fortunate Soviet counterparts equipped with the proven and successful RPG-7. Only one awkward fact disturbs this scenario—the Soviets have copied the LAW. They too are introducing a light antitank weapon, which has a much smaller and therefore less effective warhead than the RPG-7. It too is carried in a cardboard disposable launch tube although, true to form, the Soviets have incorporated a uniquely deleterious feature: once the end of the tube is opened for firing, it cannot, unlike the U.S. original, be closed again, even if the target goes away.

The Soviet infantryman will pay a heavy price in combat for his superiors' admiration for the products of the U.S. antitank industry. But it is in the Soviet air force that we find the clearest examples of how U.S. fashions influence the other side.

Nine

The Air Force— Keeping Up with the Joneses

In its issue of June 7, 1982, *Aviation Week* and *Space Technology*, a journal with long-standing and deep ties to official U.S. Air Force thinking, ran an article delineating what it called "The systematic improvement in Soviet-built aircraft faced by U.S. and allied air forces in Central Europe."

"The Soviet Union is producing and fielding inventory aircraft with major performance improvements at twice the U.S. aircraft production rate," the article declared. "The range and payload improvements in these aircraft are being complemented by an all-weather capability." It appeared that the Soviet Union was not only producing "present-generation aircraft with qualitative improvements," but was about to go into production with newer and better designs. These were reported to include a fighter equal in performance to the McDonnell Douglas F-15, another fighter "considered to be the Soviet counterpart of the McDonnell Douglas/Northrop F-18" and a "Soviet version of the Fairchild Industries A-10 close support aircraft."

The aircraft already in service that most worried *Aviation Week* were the MiG-23 Flogger, which has become the main Soviet fighter, a modified Flogger called the MiG-27, the longer-range Su-24 Fencer bomber, and the MiG-25 Foxbat, which has reportedly so improved in performance that NATO has confusingly renamed it the Foxhound.

"Because of this Soviet modernization program," the military journalists conclude, "the NATO technological lead is decreasing." This conclusion embodies the most basic and long-held assumptions of orthodox Pentagon thinking: the Soviets are building an air force that increasingly resembles the U.S. Air Force in equipment and tactics. Since the U.S. Air Force represents the distillation of wisdom on the proper use of air power, Soviet emulation represents a greatly increased threat. Since Soviet defense policy is governed also by rational if malevolent motives, the appearance of aircraft akin to current U.S. planes represent a vindication of the decisions that produced these planes in the first place.

Forecasts of the imminent appearance of Soviet lookalikes of the American F-15, F-18, and A-10 fighters should be treated with some skepticism. Soviet prototypes as yet unseen by Westerners are often presented by the U.S. military as representing a perfect reflection of current Pentagon procurement programs. The Pentagon pamphlet *Soviet Military Power* includes an artist's impression of the long-awaited though as yet unseen Soviet T-80 tank. The illustration looks quite unlike any other tank the Soviets have ever produced, but it does bear a close resemblance to the U.S. Army's M-1, which has been the object of fierce criticism in the press and Congress. Soviet threat watchers with long memories may recall that in the mid-

1960s U.S. Air Force intelligence repeatedly leaked news of a new MiG fighter that promised to be a carbon copy of the F-4 Phantom, then the newest frontline American fighter. When the new MiG-25 fighter was finally unveiled at the 1967 Domodedovo air show outside Moscow, it bore not the slightest resemblance in appearance or function to the F-4. The occasion in 1958 when *Aviation Week* published what purported to be a drawing of a nuclear-powered bomber "being flight tested in the Soviet Union" at a time when the American nuclear-powered bomber program was under terminal attack was an even more extreme example of the same syndrome.

The Soviet planes that are now in operational service, such as the MiG-23 and the Su-24, do, however, indicate that some of the U.S. Air Force's assumptions are correct. The Soviet air force of the 1970s and 1980s has come to resemble its U.S. counterpart in many respects. It is the wisdom of this emulation that is open to doubt.

The modern U.S. Air Force is founded on the presumption that high technology can conquer all. The service is not unique in this respect, but it has pursued what James Fallows calls "the magic weapon" with even greater fervor than the army or navy. The demand has been for systems, particularly electronic systems, that can remove all physical constraints on the business of destroying the enemy and that can reduce combat to an automated process that can proceed with industrial predictability. If it is difficult under normal circumstances to shoot down an enemy plane that the pilot has difficulty seeing, then a missile that can guide itself by means of radar "beyond visual range" is required. If the enemy army can move about unmolested under cover of night or bad weather, then a way must be found for a bomber to proceed to the target automatically, without human intervention. Since bombs that are simply dropped are prone to miss their targets, it is necessary to have them guide themselves precisely to the final impact.

The magicians had a chance to test their ideas in combat during the Vietnam War. The results were disappointing. The A-6 radar-guided bomber, for example, was supposed to be able to find its way to the Ho Chi Minh trail at night, drop its bombs on the enemy truck traffic moving in the darkness far below, and return, with the pilot doing little more than take off and land. As it turned out this expensive and complicated technology accounted for a small number of North Vietnamese trucks "killed" per mission (0.6 to be exact), while the ancient propeller-driven A-26 plane, which carried out the same function under the guidance of a crewman peering out the door with a simple night telescope, accounted for four times as many. The loss of several planes to beyond-visual-range radar-guided missiles fired by other U.S. planes made it clear that these weapons could only be used if the pilot could first see and identify his target as a foe. Even then, the Sparrow missile scored no better than about one kill for every ten missiles fired. The destruction of the Thanh Hoa bridge with precision-guided bombs in 1972 was publicized as a great victory for the new technology, but it took several missions with several varieties of these weapons before the bridge was hit, and as it happened, the North Vietnamese were not using it anyway.

Despite all this, the U.S. Air Force emerged from its defeat with undiminished faith in the benefits of complex technology. Development proceeded through the 1970s and beyond on even more "advanced" air-to-air missiles, "all-weather" navigation and bombing aids, and precisely guided bombs.

Heretics who point out that the dominant trends had not been vindicated by results in real-life combat situations are not popular. It was only with deep reluctance that the U.S. Air Force succumbed to Congressional pressure and released the study *Defense Facts of Life* in 1980 by a Pentagon official named Franklin Spinney. The study was an incisive critique of what the search for the magic weapon has done to U.S. military effectiveness. Spinney demonstrated in withering detail that "advanced" aircraft systems are not necessarily more effective and that, in fact, as the technology incorporated in them becomes progressively more ambitious, the effectiveness of the total force actually declines. This is because the newer planes, such as the U.S. F-15, are so replete with complex mechanisms that they break down with increasing frequency and are also more difficult to repair than their predecessors. Because the planes are so expensive to buy and the technology embodied in their components is so little understood, the number that can actually be bought and added to the force is steadily declining. As a result of the amount of time these planes are out of action and awaiting repair, the pilots have less and less opportunity to practice.

Spinney is not alone in his criticism. There are others in the Pentagon and in Congress who decry the counterproductive effect of the search for the magic weapon. Although they have failed to shake the basic foundations of the prevailing orthodoxy, they have scored occasional victories, such as the development of the F-16 fighter. Conceived by two middle-ranking Air Force officers, John Boyd and Everest Riccioni, and a civilian Pentagon analyst, Pierre Sprey, who collectively became known as the Fighter Mafia, the F-16 was meant to be a lightweight fighter that would embody the combat-proven virtues of small size, so as to remain inconspicuous to the enemy, great agility, so as to outmaneuver the enemy in dogfights, and simplicity, so as to increase the amount of time it could be employed usefully in the air. The Air Force did not like the F-16, and even though forced to buy it as a result of a combination of skillful bureaucratic maneuvers on the part of the Fighter Mafia and fortuitous political circumstances (the United States needed an inexpensive fighter to sell to NATO), the air generals have done their best to incorporate as many items of high technology as the plane's limited volume allows.

It is against the background of this kind of criticism that Pentagon officials point to the appearance of new Soviet planes, which, far from being lightweight fighters, appear to have all the signs of what the Air Force likes to believe are "advanced systems"—radars that enable the planes to operate "all-weather," and so forth. More fundamentally, it seems as if the Soviet "frontal aviation," as their tactical units (as opposed to strategic units) are called, are at last beginning to adopt American ideas for the proper use of air power.

Traditionally, the Americans and Russians have viewed and employed air power in very different ways. The U.S. Air Force has always regarded its most important mission to be deep strike interdiction, that is, bombing, behind the lines and in the enemy's homeland. For reasons rooted in their long struggle to gain institutional independence from the U.S. Army, the American air generals have held that wars can be won in this way independently of the other services. Although the generals acknowledge the necessity of supporting ground troops at the battlefront, this "close-support" role has always had a lower priority.

For a period in the 1930s, the Soviet air force was also suffused with the doctrine of Douhetism, as the philosophy of strategic bombing is known, after one of its original proponents. This doctrine died out, literally, after Stalin executed most of its senior advocates in his military purge of 1937–38. Consequently, during World War II, the Soviet air force was mostly engaged in supporting the ground forces by bombing and strafing close to the front. To this end, it developed a slow but toughly built and armored dive bomber called the Sturmovik, which was produced in greater numbers than any other plane of the war. The ultimate Soviet success in the air was over the Eastern Front with this machine, as well as with the Yakovlev and Lavochkin fighters, was due to the Soviets' ability to turn out cheap and simple machines in great volume. On a plane for plane basis, the Germans always had the upper hand; some Luftwaffe pilots individually accounted for hundreds of Soviet kills, but the Soviets won with numbers and, of course, indomitable courage.

After the war, the Russians continued turning out great numbers of fighters, but the priority changed. The interception of American nuclear bombers, for which purpose the troops of national air defense were set up as a separate service in 1948, became the most urgent mission, and so all fighter planes were designed with this in mind. It is interesting that when Stalin declared that the MiG-15, designed as an interceptor, was adequate for Soviet requirements and that therefore there was no need to build any other combat planes, the designer Yakovlev kept his bureau in business by suggesting another interceptor rather than a plane for some other purpose.

A fighter that is optimized for interception must be able to accelerate and climb quickly in order to catch the enemy bomber. Since bombers are too large to take much evasive action, there is no particular incentive for the fighters that must catch them to be maneuverable. As the pilot pursues the target under the strict supervision of a controller monitoring him and his target through ground radar, there is no reason for him to be able to see much out of the cockpit. But a fighter plane that cannot maneuver is at a severe disadvantage in air combat with other fighters, especially if the pilot lacks either the training or the means to search all points of the sky for the enemy. A ground-attack plane must be rugged and able to maneuver close to the ground, like the old Sturmovik, and the ability to climb high and fast is of little help.

Thus, although frontal aviation during the 1950s and 1960s was meant to carry out the traditional functions of "air superiority"—the downing of enemy fighters and the provision of close air support—the equipment it received had been designed with another mission and indeed another service in mind. The Su-7, for example, which had lost out to the MiG-21 in the 1955 interceptor competition, was put into production anyway and designated a ground-support plane. Later on, the MiG-21 was supplanted as an interceptor of nuclear bombers by the Su-9, so it was handed down to become the main frontline air-superiority plane.

Paradoxically, the early MiGs did have some of the attributes of a good air-superiority fighter, although almost certainly for reasons of luck rather than good judgment. The design team of Mikoyan and Gurevich had to make them able to climb high and fast. The easiest way to do this is by increasing the power of the engine, but because the MiG engines were not quite powerful enough, Mikoyan and Gurevich gave their planes a large wing area in relation to the total weight for added lift. This had the added effect of helping the plane turn quickly. Again, because of the engine limitations, the MiGs were extremely small, a very important advantage in air combat, when victory is usually determined by who sees whom first. Because the planes lacked technological sophistication, they could be easily, if frequently, repaired.

The MiG-15 was the first Soviet operational jet fighter. It went into service late in 1948 and in that innocent era was christened Fagot by Western intelligence. Thrown into combat in Korea with North Korean, Chinese and occasionally Russian pilots, the Fagots displayed some advantages over the American F-86 Sabres. They could turn faster, and their engines were more powerful in relation to the planes' weight. Nevertheless, the eventual score was a lopsided 14 to 1 in favor of the American planes. The major reason for the resounding defeat of the MiGs may have been the superior skill and training of the American pilots, but deficiencies in the MiGs themselves certainly contributed. Although the MiGs could carry out individual maneuvers better than the Sabres, they could not shift from one maneuver to another as quickly. Even to exploit the MiG's ability to turn faster than the Sabre required a greater level of pilot skill, because like other Soviet fighters, the MiGs were "bad handling," that is, difficult and dangerous to fly.

The MiG-15 was succeeded by the MiG-17, a plane very much like the MiG-15 but with a more powerful engine and consequently better acceleration and speed. The MiG-19, which first flew in 1953, was the Soviets' first attempt to produce a truly supersonic plane. It was not a success, as evidenced by the fact that it was produced in far smaller numbers than the MiG-15 and MiG-17, and the Russians passed on most of those they did build to its allies as "aid." Richard Ward, a fighter-plane designer for the General Dynamics Corporation and a noted authority on the Soviet aircraft industry, remarks caustically that "they tried to use a single Soviet-designed engine, but that turned out to be so unsatisfactory they had to use two engines based on an old German design instead. But when they switched on the two afterburners to go supersonic the back of the plane would catch fire, so they could only use one at a time." (An afterburner is a tube on the back of a jet engine. Fuel is injected into it, which combines with and is ignited by the hot exhausts, generating extra thrust.) American pilots who flew MiG-19s obtained years later from North Vietnamese defectors reported that it was so "bad handling" that it was acutely dangerous to fly.

The MiG-21 Fishbed, which first appeared in 1955, was a much more successful product. It could go to supersonic speeds on its single engine without encountering the mishaps of the MiG-19. The handling, though still bad, was better, although U.S. Air Force and Navy pilots who flew the 12 MiG-21s presented by Egypt to the United States in 1978 reported that below altitudes of about 15,000 feet, where the air is denser, the control stick becomes very difficult to move: "Like pulling on a telegraph pole" was one comment. Displaying its heritage as an interceptor, the MiG-21 has extremely bad cockpit visibility.

Like the Kalashnikov rifle and the T-34 tank, the MiG-21 is often cited as an exemplar of what are supposed to be the peculiarly Soviet virtues of simplicity and reliability, although as we have seen with the T-34 tank, simplicity and reliability are not necessarily the same thing. The Fishbed is indeed simple, having a small number of uncomplicated working parts compared to contemporary U.S. fighters, like the F-4 Phantom. This makes the plane easy to maintain, since there is little difficulty in removing and replacing the defective components. On the other hand, these individual parts are not in themselves reliable; such key items as the brakes on the undercarriage wear out and must be changed after very few landings. More importantly, for reasons and with consequences we shall examine later in this chapter, the engines wear out extremely quickly.

Notwithstanding these defects, the Fishbed has become the most widely produced and used jet fighter in history. Apart from the thousands produced for service with the Soviet military, thousands more have been bought by or given to Soviet customers and allies around the world. This popularity, for the most part, has not been matched by the plane's combat record. The Israeli air force has consistently outclassed the Fishbed in the Middle East wars in 1967 up to the engagement with the Syrians over the Bekaa Valley in 1982, destroying an average of 20 for every Israeli plane lost. In the 1971 Indo-Pakistani war, the Pakistanis, flying F-86s of Korean War vintage, scored an "exchange ratio" of 6 to 1 against MiG-21s of the Indian air force. Only in the air war over Vietnam did the MiG-21 manage to give a good account of itself. At one point, the North Vietnamese were downing more enemy planes than they had lost themselves, U.S. planes that were the most modern and sophisticated fighters in the world embodying all the latest ideas in high technology.

If the Soviets had shown little sign of understanding why they had done so badly in the Korean air war, the Americans paid equally little attention to the reasons for their winning it. The Sabres that fought in the earlier conflict were small, highly maneuverable, and simple. The F-4s, F-105s, and A-7s that flew most of the raids over North Vietnam were large, less maneuverable, and vastly more complex. The F-4s carried the most up-to-date radars to spot the enemy from farther than the eye could see, but meanwhile their "advanced" J-79 engines trailed clouds of black smoke, which made the Americans themselves visible to the naked eye from 20 miles away. The Navy's F-4s had to fight without guns, the traditional fighter weapons, because high officials had determined that the new long-range radar missiles would wipe the enemy out of the sky before he could come within gun range. Part of the F-105's size and complexity was due to the fact that in the 1950s and 1960s the Tactical Air (fighter) Command had built all its planes to carry nuclear bombs, in order to better compete for funds with the Strategic Air Command. Even without the nuclear mission, the F-4's performance suffered because the planes were produced as "multimission" aircraft, carrying the necessary apparatus for air combat, bombing, and reconnaissance.

Some observers, such as the Fighter Mafia, deduced from the combat results that the emphasis on high technology had not worked very well and suggested alternatives like the F-16. The majority of U.S. Air Force officials thought differently. This high-technology-oriented policy was endorsed and emulated by the Soviet air force establishment.

The notion, widespread among military professionals and the public alike, that "more modern" and "advanced" aircraft are necessarily superior to old weapons survived the Vietnam War intact. Writing on the implications of recent conflicts in June 1982, Colonel Jonathan Alford of the International Institute for Strategic Studies in London noted that in the recent fighting over Lebanon "American equipment and Israeli pilots have once more seemed more than a match for Syrian pilots and Soviet aircraft." However, he pointed out, "the evidence appears to show that the Syrian aircraft used were mostly rather elderly MiG 21s rather than modern MiG 23s or MiG 25s." Newer, Alford automatically assumed, must be better.

The Israelis, who have had more direct experience of combating Soviet aircraft of all types than any other air force in the world, do not agree. Yalo Shavit, who retired as an air force general in 1980 and remains heavily involved in defense issues, summed up the difference between the "rather elderly" MiG-21 and the "modern" MiG-23 and MiG-25 this way:

The MiG-21s we flew against in the 1967 war and the MiG-21s we see today are supposed to have been given many improvements, but in reality there has not been much difference. It's still basically the same plane, with the same faults.

But the 21 is at least a fighter plane, even if we have found it easy to beat. The MiG-23 looks great on parades; when it flies past the reviewing stand in formation it looks great, like an arrow.

But in combat it is so clumsy, so hard to maneuver—as a fighter plane it is no improvement at all, even a step backwards.

Charles B. Myers, formerly an Air Force fighter pilot and one-time director of the Pentagon's Office of Air Warfare, gave me a similarly caustic assessment of the MiG-23, which is rapidly replacing the MiG-21 as the main frontal aviation fighter: "I would put [the MiG-23] in the category of 'meat on the table' in fighter-pilot language. It's a fairly large airplane. It's rather complicated in that it incorporates a swing wing and all of the quote unquote 'advanced technology.' Also, the increased complexity will probably evolve a brand of airplanes that are more difficult to maintain, more costly to maintain. You might say that they are busily shooting themselves in the foot with their technology." He could have added that it is the first Soviet fighter to emit black smoke from its engine, an attribute that proved so disadvantageous to the F-4.

Most of the "advanced technology" referred to by Myers is not immediately visible from a casual glance at the MiG-23. But the swing wing is. It is a prominent feature not only of this plane but of every single combat aircraft introduced into Soviet service in the 1970s—an idea, the Soviets had decided, whose time had come.

Swing-wing aircraft were originally conceived in Germany toward the end of World War II, but the concept did not find practical expression until fifteen years later, when it was taken up with enthusiasm in the United States. The attraction lay in the prospect it offered for incorporating the benefits of two different kinds of aircraft in the same plane.

Aircraft with large wingspans have "high lift." This gives them the ability to take off and land at slow speeds on short runways, as well as to coast aloft without using much fuel. Aircraft with sharply swept-back wings, on the other hand, present little "drag" to the air through which they are flying and can therefore go much faster. Swing-wing aircraft can utilize the advantages of high lift by extending their wings straight out or folding them back into an arrowhead shape for low-drag high-speed flight.

The Americans designed three planes using the swing-wing concept in the 1960s: the F-111, which was originally intended to serve as a fighter-bomber for both the Air Force and Navy and ended up as a purely Air Force plane; the F-14 fighter, which the Navy adopted after dropping out of the F-111 program; and the B-1 strategic nuclear bomber, laid down by the Air Force after its effort to buy the ultrahigh-speed and high-altitude B-70 had been canceled by the Administration.

Unfortunately, swing wing, or variable sweep as it is technically called, did not live up to expectations. A. Ernest Fitzgerald, who as a Pentagon official was heavily involved in the F-111 contract, later wrote, "key people in the Pentagon apparently were misled by the 'optimistic' (read 'wholly false') assessment of the potential of the variable sweep concept which was central to the whole idea of the F-111."

It emerged that the mechanism which swung the wings and bore their weight had to be much stronger and therefore heavier than the designers had allowed for. Thus, the weight of the plane increased, cancelling the expected benefits of high speeds and low fuel consumption. In addition, the wings presented far more drag in the swept-back, or folded-back, position than had been forecast. Finally, the whole arrangement significantly boosted the cost of the plane.

Fitzgerald declares that "the inherent problems were widely known, but except for one engineer at Grumman Aircraft, where the Navy's F-111B version was being assembled, no one was willing to criticize the concept openly.

The Grumman engineer was dead right in his criticism, but he was declared crazy and eventually driven from the industry." In the United States, as in the Soviet Union, it is difficult to stop a weapons program.

That swing wing had been a bad idea was not officially admitted until the United States moved on to the design of newer aircraft in the late 1960s and early 1970s, at which time the whole concept was abandoned. The F-15, F-16, and F-18 all have wings fixed in the traditional manner and perform much better as a result.

The U.S. Air Force still has to live with the legacy of the F-111. Although intended as a multimission plane, which could take part in air combat, act as a close-air support attack plane, and carry a large bomb load great distances, it can do none of these things well and some of them not at all. Because of its greater than expected weight and the unsatisfactory power (thrust) of its TF-30 engines, it has little ability to maneuver not only in the demanding circumstances of a dogfight but even for the less exacting function of dive bombing or strafing. In fact, it turns at a slower rate than the Boeing 707 airliner traveling at comparable speeds. Originally intended to carry 48 500-pound bombs, it has a maximum load of 12. It had been expected that the F-111 would be able to make a low-level 400-mile dash to the target at a speed faster than sound, but at best, it can travel 30 miles at that speed and height. At normal height and cruising speed, it has a combat radius of 600 miles, allowing for some use of its afterburners during the mission.

In 1973 the F-111 program finally petered out. The Air Force stopped buying F-111s, even though no more than a quarter of the hoped-for number had been built. That same year, the first multimission swing-wing MiG-23s appeared on Soviet air bases. One year later, the Su-24 Fencer went into production, a plane extraordinarily similar to the F-111 in all major respects. Large and with swing wings, it duplicated in amplified form the less welcome characteristics of the F-111. For example, the F-111 is sluggish in accelerating, partly because its thrust-weight ratio—an index obtained by dividing the weight of the plane by the thrust of the engines—is low, at 0.74, about the same as a straightforward bomber's. The Su-24's ratio is still lower, at 0.52, while its wing area, which must be high in relation to a plane's weight for maneuverability, is about 20 percent less than that of the F-111.

It is the electronic equipment (technically, avionics) carried on the Su-24 and other modernized Soviet fighters that evokes the most fervent admiration in the Western defense community. In a June 1981 article about the Fencer, *International Defense Review* commented that "the fact that the avionic systems of currently produced Soviet aircraft are virtually on a par with those of Western aircraft is exemplified by the Su-24 Fencer's navigation and weapon aiming system, which is certainly comparable with F-111A/E technology and was designed only a few years afterwards."

The key ingredient of these avionic systems is the radar that allows the plane to be "all-weather," which simply means the ability to find and accurately bomb targets that the pilot cannot see because of darkness or bad weather. Although the military journalist quoted above intended to be complimentary, his remarks seem ironic in view of the F-111's all-weather bombing record. As evidenced by combat results from Southeast Asia, the F-111 can deposit half its bombs no closer than three-quarters of a mile from the intended target. This may be less than satisfactory, since the lethal radius of its bombs against any kind of structure is about 30 feet or less.

International Defense Review sums up the Fencer as "perhaps the greatest threat to Western Europe." A U.S.

Air Force official intimately involved in the F-111's development takes a more sanguine view. "The best thing that ever came out of the F-111 program," he told me in all seriousness, "is that the damnfool Russians went out and copied it."

"All-weather" systems are not the only feature on the newer Soviet planes to find commendation in the West. By 1978, the Pentagon's Military Posture Statement was describing the MiG-23 Flogger as the "first Soviet aircraft with a demonstrated ability to track and engage targets flying below its own altitude." This function, colloquially referred to as "look-down, shoot-down," is extremely difficult to achieve. The problem lies in the nature of radar. Radar works by beaming out electronic pulses akin to radio waves, which bounce off objects and return. Unfortunately, they bounce not only off the object that may be of interest to the radar's operators but also off all solid matter lying in the path of the pulses. For a radar that is looking up in the sky, this represents no problem, since the only objects painted by the pulses will be aircraft moving against an empty background. But when the radar is beamed from the sky toward the ground, the pulses will reflect not only off the target but also off the land or sea. Unless these are absolutely uniformly flat, which is unlikely, the resultant background clutter will effectively muddle up the screen.

There is a theoretical solution to the problem, which the United States has spent billions of dollars trying to implement but with results that have been less successful than claimed. In a complex procedure known as Doppler processing, the radar listens not just for the strength of the echo reflecting back from the target but also to its frequency. A moving object will reflect at different frequencies as it moves in relation to the listener, just as the pitch of an ambulance siren increases and then diminishes as it moves toward and away from you. The largest operational

U.S. look-down system is the AWACS (Airborne Warning And Control System), which is housed in a heavily modified Boeing 707 airliner with a large radar antenna on top. The equipment was officially reported to have passed its tests with flying colors, but it appears that the range at which it could spot low-flying planes was extremely small and the regularity with which it picked them up was very unreliable. The Saudi Arabians were reportedly much displeased when they became aware of these limitations after they had agreed to buy five AWACS planes at tremendous cost. U.S. Air Force AWACS planes dispatched to patrol the skies over the desert kingdom until the home-owned models arrived repeatedly failed to spot low-flying interlopers. In March 1982, for example, an Iranian pilot who defected from Iran flew deep into Saudi Arabia and landed at the Dahran air base completely unnoticed by the AWACS planes.

The United States has been flying fighters with miniaturized look-down radars since the late 1960s, and all the current frontline fighters have them. As might be expected, such radars suffer from the same limitations as the larger AWACS. On one occasion during the Southeast Asia war, a U.S. F-4 pilot fired a Sparrow missile at an Australian destroyer because his look-down radar had informed him it was a low-flying helicopter. Luckily for the seaman in whose bunk the Sparrow ended up, the fuze was not working and the missile failed to explode.

According to Dr. Thomas S. Amlie, who developed radar weapons systems for many years as technical director of the Naval Weapons Center at China Lake, California, "our planes can track and shoot at a target flying below them only under very particular circumstances, which include the fact that the target plane must be flying toward its attacker."

In view of the U.S. experience, it appears that the

advent of Soviet aircraft equipped with look-down radars might not be such a menace as *Aviation Week* and other official spokesmen would have us believe. It is, however, doubtful if there are more than a few Soviet combat planes so equipped. Although the 1978 Pentagon Military Posture Statement publicized the fact that the MiG-23 was endowed with a look-down system, it did not mention that only a very limited number of these planes were actually fitted with it. Most of the Floggers have done without. The MiG-27, which is variously described as an improved Flogger or a ground-attack version of the air-superiority MiG-23, carries no interceptor radar—with or without look-down—nor does it carry an all-weather attack radar. *Aviation Week*, seeking to highlight the burgeoning threat, describes the MiG-27 as equipped "with Doppler, laser, and electro-optical systems for all-weather attack." There is some confusion of terms here, because the Doppler system referred to is an altimeter used as a simple navigation device, and laser beams cannot pierce the moisture that invariably accompanies bad weather in Europe, nor can an electro-optical system, which is merely the military term for a television camera. So if the MiG-27 is indeed all-weather, as claimed, it must carry out its mission by some unknown technical means.

The other plane reportedly endowed with look-down capability is the MiG-25. In honor of the addition of this capability to the original MiG-25, NATO has changed the codename for Foxbat to Foxhound. The look-down, shoot-down radar in the Foxhound is supposed to have successfully enabled this plane to shoot down low-flying targets simulating U.S. cruise missiles while flying at 20,000 feet armed with the "AA-9 air-to-air missile." Such a test may indeed have taken place, with the happy results reported. This does not, however, really tell us much about the effectiveness of the Foxhound's missile.

Readers will already be familiar with the concept of "benign" testing of new weapons systems. A particularly relevant example in this case is the 1982 test of a new U.S. air-to-air missile called AMRAAM. Like the AA-9, the AMRAAM intercepted a target drone flying at low level after being fired from a high altitude. The U.S. Air Force, however, "not wishing to bore anyone with technical details," as one observer put it, neglected to report that the target drone was emitting a signal that attracted the intercepting missile. Stratagems of this kind have traditionally given air-to-air missiles glowing reputations, which on the basis of later results in combat, turn out to have been entirely undeserved. The U.S. Air Force Falcon infrared air-to-air missile, for example, was deemed on the basis of its development tests to have a probability of kill, or PK, of 99 percent. In combat during the Vietnam War it turned out to be effective about 7 percent of the time and pilots eventually refused to carry the Falcon on their planes. There is no reason to believe that Soviet missile developers are any less proficient than their American counterparts at augmenting the test performance of their wares—former Defense Secretary Harold Brown once remarked that "if their developers lie like our developers, we've got nothing to worry about."

Air-to-air missiles do not, in any case, appear to be the Soviets' strong suit. Their basic heat-seeking short-range air-to-air missile, the Atoll, is still no more than an exact copy of a 1950s model of the U.S. Sidewinder.

A more fundamental problem for the Soviets is their inability to increase the comparatively short range of their planes. The newer models, festooned though they may be with large radars, are still obliged to operate far closer to their bases than the U.S. equivalent, as we can see by comparing the F-111 and Su-24 look-alikes. The F-111 can attack targets 600 miles from base while carrying 12

500-pound bombs but with no auxiliary fuel tank. The Su-24, carrying ten bombs and bearing two large auxiliary tanks attached to the wings, can manage 400 miles. Neither of these planes can manage such distances if they are flying close to the ground, where the dense air causes higher drag and lower fuel efficiency. Under these conditions, the Su-24 may just be able to manage 200 miles, which is half the combat radius on a "lo-lo-high" mission (flying out near the ground and flying home at altitude) ascribed to it in official U.S. Air Force briefings. The combat radius of the MiG-23/27 is even more constrained, to a limit of about 250 miles under any circumstances. The MiG-25 is still listed in official Pentagon publications as having a combat radius of more than 500 miles, even though Viktor Belenko almost crashed on landing in Japan because, after a 400-mile one-way flight from Siberia, he had used up all but the last drops of fuel in his MiG-25's tanks. No U.S. fighter pilot ever sighted a MiG-21 more than 100 miles from its base during the entire Vietnam War.

The root cause of what are colloquially known as the "short legs" of Soviet aircraft is not a problem of the design of the engines but of the technology and fabrication processes involved in the construction. As noted earlier, Soviet engines wear out quickly. According to General George Ezzat, the chief of repair and engineering for the Egyptian air force, the most up-to-date engines in their Soviet-supplied MiG-21s must be removed and sent away for major overhaul after every 300 hours of operation. This is a far higher replacement rate than even that of the very complex F-100 engine that powers the U.S. F-15 and F-16 fighters, which has been criticized for requiring substantial overhaul every 800 hours. This extreme fragility of the Soviet engines is directly linked to the limited range of the planes.

The crucial factor affecting the life of a jet engine is its resistance to high temperatures. Jet engines provide power by taking in air through the front and then compressing it with a series of fans and mixing it with the fuel. The resultant mixture then burns and heats itself and in doing so greatly increases its pressure. It then pushes itself toward the rear end of the jet, turning a turbine in the process and finally being exhausted at high speed through a nozzle, giving the aircraft a push in the opposite direction. The turbine extracts some of the energy from the heated air and uses it to drive the compressor fan. The hotter the zone where the fuel and air mix and burn, the higher the thrust. Most jet engines will run at temperatures somewhat below the maximum possible, as otherwise the engine will burn out eventually at the core and will have to be replaced.

The reason the F-100 engine must be overhauled every 800 hours is that it burns at the exceedingly high temperature of 2550° F. Another older and much more primitive American military jet engine, the J-85, which is used to power the F-5 fighter (a plane sufficiently similar to the MiG-21 that the United States uses it to simulate the Soviet plane in exercises), burns at 1800° F and must be replaced every 850 to 1,000 hours. But the latest MiG-21 engine, the R-13-300, which is reportedly more reliable than its predecessor and which burns at the same temperature as the J-85, must be replaced every 300 hours, about three times as often.

Soviet fighters can go as fast as the U.S. planes, but they use up more fuel in the process. By doing so, they run up against another constraint on range: Soviet planes can carry less fuel than American aircraft of equivalent weight and size and for the same reason—the engines are less temperature-resistant.

Soviet designers are well aware of how the more efficient Western engines are built. They have had plenty of opportunity to study them in detail from samples captured in Vietnam and earlier. Indeed, the MiG-15 and MiG-17 were powered by engines copied in every detail from the Rolls Royce Derwent and Nene engines exported in 1947 with the permission of the British government (to Stalin's astonishment). The problem then and now derives not from the design but from the refining and machining of the metals that have to withstand the extreme conditions inside a jet engine. In the same way, the metal spars and panels that make up the airframes of Soviet aircraft must be thicker and therefore heavier than comparable Western components to provide the same amount of strength and support. A comparison between two heavy-duty cranes, one Soviet and one Western, provides a simple example of the problem. Although both are designed to take the same weight, the Soviet version will be considerably larger than an American, European, or Japanese version because it relies on brute size rather than quality steel for its strength.

The amount of fuel a given aircraft can carry is called its "fuel fraction." This is the amount of weight-carrying capacity that is left over after irreducible elements have been taken into account, like the weight of the pilot and his seat, as well as the weight of the instruments, the armaments, and the basic structure of the aircraft itself. Since the heavier materials mean that the structure takes up a larger fraction of the total weight, the fuel fraction is correspondingly reduced.

This problem is so basic to Soviet engineering across the board that to suggest that a new generation of Soviet combat planes can suddenly appear with vastly more efficient engines or improved fuel fractions is like suggesting that Italians can suddenly turn into careful drivers or the French become polite to strangers.

Large and unmaneuverable aircraft like the swing-wing Floggers and Fencers are not best suited to the exacting business of attacking enemy troop concentrations on or near the battlefield. The Soviet air force's preference for these types has so far left it without a plane of the necessary small size and agility for avoiding ground fire, such as it had with the wartime Sturmovik. The Soviets did modify the venerable and unsatisfactory Su-7 into the variable-sweep Su-17 at the height of the swing-wing mania, but the Egyptians, who were offered a squadron of them before the 1973 war, concluded that the Su-17 represented little, if any, advance over the Su-7.

For inspiration as to the soundest approach to the problem, the Soviet air force has turned to the U.S. Army. The U.S. Army places a great amount of hope and resources in the attack helicopter as a potent battlefield weapon, a policy the Soviets now appear to be adopting with equal enthusiasm.

The basis of the U.S. Army's deep interest in helicopters is an agreement on the division of responsibilities between the services called the Key West Agreement. Drawn up in 1947, the agreement allotted control of essentially all fixed-wing aircraft to the Air Force, a preserve that has been jealously guarded by that service ever since. Thus constrained, the Army has found its way into the air only with helicopters. Accordingly, it has developed them not only for tasks like medical evacuation and covert commando raids but also for missions traditionally carried out by aircraft, such as attacking enemy troops and tanks with guns and rockets.

Helicopter gunships met their baptism of fire and their Waterloo in Vietnam. They did wreak some damage among irregular and lightly armed opponents, but any time they ran into concentrated gunfire from the ground, they proved to be highly vulnerable. In the course of a war in which the Americans only occasionally encountered opposition of the concentration and scale of a conventional battle and in which they were unchallenged in the air over South Vietnam, they lost nearly 5,000 helicopters, or about one-third of their total force every year. The heavy losses came about because helicopters are by their very nature slow, unmaneuverable, and highly vulnerable to any kind of damage, particularly damage to the whirring rotor blades that keep them aloft.

The Vietnam experience did not cause the U.S. Army to abandon the attack helicopter. The Key West Agreement still stands. But in an effort to mitigate the machine's vulnerabilities, the Army commissioned the AH-64 Apache, a model so complex and sophisticated, that as of 1982 it was projected to cost $17 million per copy. Although this makes it three times more expensive than any helicopter ever built, the alternative for the Army of resigning all aerial battlefield support to the Air Force is still more unpalatable.

The interservice rivalry that has fostered the gunship in the United States does not apply in the Soviet forces, since the Soviet air force already has control of all flying machines, including helicopters. But despite the absence of the peculiar circumstances that forced the Americans down this particular route, the Russians adopted the idea with enthusiasm around the beginning of the 1970s, as American helicopter losses were steadily mounting in Vietnam.

So far, the Soviets have produced and deployed two basic models for combat operations: the Mi-8 Hip, which is used more often as a transport than a gunship, and the Mi-24 Hind.

Although helicopters were pioneered by the Russian-born aeronautical engineer Igor Sikorsky (who left for the United States after the 1917 Revolution), the Soviet Union has always lagged far behind the United States in helicopter development; Soviet models of the 1950s were so unreliable and dangerous that Khrushchev was advised not to fly in them. The problems were only partly solved by President Eisenhower's gift of two Sikorsky helicopters to the Chairman. Today, Soviet helicopters remain unreliable and underpowered: by comparison with Western machines, their engines supply 40 percent less power in relation to the weight of the airframe.

In appearance, the Hind is impressively menacing, like most Soviet weapons. Not only is it very large, with rotor blades spanning almost 60 feet, but the snoutlike projecting gun pod in the front, together with the stubby wings for carrying bombs and rockets, makes it look something like a huge and vicious insect. Hinds have been well publicized in the West for their role in the Afghan war. Guerrillas interviewed by Western correspondents are routinely quoted as describing it with frightened respect. "We are not afraid of the Russians," one guerrilla told the New York *Times* in January 1982, "but we are afraid of their helicopters."

Nevertheless, it is hard to view the Hind as the "nemesis of the *mujahedin* [holy warriors]" as *Time* magazine has called it. Losses have been high; the Defense Intelligence Agency has privately conceded that up to 250 Hinds had been lost, mostly to enemy fire, within the first 18 months after the Soviet invasion. Although the Hind does have some armor plating on the sides and bottom, this only really protects the machine and crew against small-arms fire; even then, the rotor blades and portions of the engine remain exposed to a well-placed rifle bullet. The machine's unwieldy bulk and inadequate engine are drawbacks in any situation but especially so in the thin air of the Afghan mountains, where the engine and rotor blades provide less lift. *Aviation Week*, which rarely fails to give favorable reviews to Soviet weapons systems, has reported that the Hind cannot maneuver sharply, because if it does, the main rotor blades collide with the tail; it has also reported that losses in Afghanistan as a result of pilot error and bad weather have been "significantly high." A firsthand observer of the Afghan fighting reported in December 1982 that "the vaunted Soviet Mi-24 helicopter gunship has proven vulnerable to the severe stress of sustained aerial combat and increasingly accurate ground fire. The Mi-24 helicopter has three vulnerable points, difficult to armor or protect: turbine air intakes, tail rotor assembly and an oil intake inexplicably, but conveniently, located beneath the red star on the fuselage."

Soviet gunship units stationed in Eastern Europe will not have the problems of high altitude, but they will face bad weather and the greater danger of concentrated fire from an enemy far better armed than the ragged *mujahedin*. When a pair of Hinds attacked a Pakistani army border post, in a rare encounter with regular troops, the Pakistanis promptly downed one of them with heavy machine-gun fire. The Arab armies attempted to use the slightly older Hips in the 1973 Middle East war, but apart from some commando raids in the early hours of the war, the results were disastrous. An Egyptian helicopter force that moved into the Sinai during the first few days was wiped out by Israeli fighters and ground fire, as was a later foray with five Hips against an Israeli bridge over the Suez Canal.

The combat record of helicopters in the wars in Vietnam, the Middle East, and Afghanistan does not suggest that the modernization of Soviet forces facing Europe with attack helicopters represents any significant increase in the threat. Rather, it should make clear to the Soviets the pitfalls of blindly emulating the military Joneses across the Atlantic, who do things for their own reasons, not all of them connected with military effectiveness.

It would be untrue and unfair to suggest that it is only the Soviets who follow the American lead in pursuit of the magic weapon. The European allies of the United States have also spent themselves into severe trouble by following in the footsteps of the U.S. military technologists. The British, for example, agreed to buy the F-111 for the Royal Air Force in 1966. In 1968 the British were undergoing one of their perennial financial crises and the Treasury was anxious to save some precious hard currency by cancelling the F-111 purchase order. By that time, the plane's technical misfortunes were widely known in the United States, and the U.S. Navy was in the process of abandoning the plane. Yet according to the posthumously published diaries of the Labour Party politician Richard Crossman, who was a member of the Cabinet at the time, the British Minister of Defence, Denis Healey, and his officials fought doggedly to retain the order, claiming that the F-111 was essential to the defense of Britain and the West. Despite their entreaties, the government decided to pull out of the deal, but for financial rather than technical reasons. In fact, the British defense establishment's faith in swing-wing technology was so little disturbed that the following year the British agreed with the West Germans to develop and build a very expensive and complex swing-wing fighter-bomber called the M.R.C.A. Tornado, a smaller and even more expensive version of the F-111.

Crossman records that in the Cabinet arguments over the F-111, Healey used to justify his arguments by allusion to secret information withheld from the uninitiated and therefore difficult for his colleagues to refute. It is this mystique surrounding modern high-technology defense hardware that makes it difficult for the lay person to question whether the emperor has, in reality, any clothes. Lookdown radar, all-weather bombing systems, or beyond-visual-range missiles appear to embody such arcane concepts (not to mention terminology) that the claims advanced for them by their military and commerical proponents all too often go unchallenged.

When it comes to the maintenance of such systems, however, and the training of servicemen for their use, the most technically obtuse observer can understand that a weapon system will be of little use if it has broken down or if its operators are not trained either to operate or repair it.

Ten

Organizing the Troops for War

The American military scholar and writer S. L. A. Marshall once wrote a short book, *The Soldier's Load and the Mobility of a Nation*, in which he pointed out the practical consequences of burdening down the individual infantryman with too much equipment and supplies. GIs landing in France on D-day had drowned in 2 feet of surf because they were too enervated by fear and fatigue to stand up under the weight of their 80-pound packs (which in some cases included four cartons of cigarettes per man) once they had fallen. In the same way, Marshall argued, the American armies in Europe had been hamstrung by their reliance on an overelaborate system of supply, a problem that the Russians did not share. "Whereas the supply discipline of the United States Army is regulated by the pressure to give the troops the maximum possible of the comforts which the middle-class American has learned to expect, the Russian army," Marshall points out admiringly, "can operate in war on a minimum subsistence level." He cites examples of how Soviet truck drivers, bereft of equipment for repairing tires, would do the job anyway "with the help of an empty oil can, a piece of crude rubber and the help of a heavy stone from the roadside." Broken-down tanks would be repaired with improvised methods, including the use of chopped down trees for hoisting out motors or other heavy items; wooden bridges were thrown across major rivers with no other tools than axes, hammers, and clamps. The Russians had no need of an elaborate mail system because the soldiers were discouraged from writing or expecting letters.

Marshall exaggerated the self-sufficiency of the war-time Red Army in his disgust at the decadent luxury of the U.S. system. Although the Russian soldier may have gone without mail and harvested the wheat for his bread himself, he was still dependent on the supply system for ammunition, spare engines, and other parts for his tank and for fuel for everything from the combat planes to the transport trucks, which themselves had had to be laboriously shipped all the way from the United States. For this reason, Soviet advances during World War II tended to run out of steam. Months of preparation for an onslaught against the Germans would result in initial and crushing success. All forces would then have to halt, while supplies were once again laboriously built up.

The Soviet serviceman of today still leads a spartan existence, as we have seen. Genady, the radar operator who was posted at an early-warning station on the arctic island of Novaya Zemlya, received mail and newspapers from Leningrad only once every six months, and sometimes not even then. Today's weapons demand far more care and attention, and as the Soviets strive to emulate the military high technology of the Americans, they must encounter one of the most salient aspects of these "modernized" weapons systems: it is very hard to keep them working.

The effect of the trend toward weapons of greater complexity on the U.S. Air Force has been exhaustively documented and publicized. In 1979, for example, the F-111D, the most sophisticated and complex plane in the Air Force, was out of action, or nonmission capable, 65.6 percent of the time, while the far simpler A-10 attack plane was grounded for only 32.6 percent of the time. The U.S. Army's new M-1 tank, which the Soviet Ministry of Defense admiringly describes as having "twice the combat capabilities" of the older M-60 tank, breaks down at least twice as often. In *Defense Facts of Life*, the Pentagon analyst Franklin Spinney bluntly states that "increasing weapons complexity reduces combat readiness." The F-15 fighter plane, which he uses as an example in *Defense Facts of Life*, is nonmission capable far more of the time than the F-4 it is partly replacing, so that it breaks down more often, requires more skilled ground crews to repair it, uses up spare parts at a faster rate, and, because it is ready to fly so much less frequently, allows the pilot less time for flying practice.

"Modernized" Soviet equipment, such as their swing-wing planes, may be crude by comparison with the American originals, but they still represent an enormous leap in complexity over the previous generation of weapons. The old MiG-21 carried a minimum of electronic systems in comparison with the array of radar, navigation, and laser systems to be found on the MiG-23. The ZSU-23-4 is aimed, however falteringly, by means of a radar and computer, whereas its predecessor relied on the human hand and eye. The latest Soviet tanks sport not only the infamous automatic gunloader to replace the harried human who formerly carried out that function but also a laser range finder for more accurate gun aiming. Soviet weapons, never reliable, are now becoming increasingly complex.

The care and maintenance of even the simple old-fashioned systems were never the Soviets' strong point. "If we can be said to treat our weapons like handkerchiefs," Steven Zaloga of the Defense Market Survey Corporation points out in an apt simile, "they use theirs like Kleenex— use them up and throw them away, or at least send them back to the factory for total overhaul."

In a way this is a reasonable solution for the Soviets, considering their limited resources in skilled manpower. A U.S. tank battalion or fighter squadron is meant to do as much repair work as possible on its own machines. Only if a broken-down machine cannot be repaired *in situ* will it be sent back up the line to a central depot. The Russians have never been able to do on-the-spot repairs; their available manpower is drawn from conscripts who are serving for a maximum of two years and who for the most part have never driven a car, let alone repaired one, before they joined the army. Their solution has been to rely on what is called depot maintenance: keeping what skilled mechanics they do have at a central repair facility well behind the lines. Anything more than the very simplest of mechanical problems is simply referred back there.

This system may have worked when the weapons were simple. Airfield mechanics did not have to be highly trained to remove a MiG-21 engine, crate it up, and send it to the depot while simultaneously unpacking its replacement. But things are more difficult today. As David Isby remarks in *Weapons and Tactics of the Soviet Army*: "While the education of the Soviet soldier has increased arithmetically, the complexity of many of his weapons has increased geometrically." Now there seems no reason to believe that the Soviet experience with high-technology weaponry has been any happier than the American experience. Defense

Secretary Harold Brown's lament in February 1980 about the latest U.S. fighter planes that "the highest effectiveness we had hoped for has in part, however, been compromised by lower reliability that higher complexity had brought with it" cannot be too far different from the private thoughts of Marshals Ustinov, Ogarkov, and Kutakhov (the air force commander in chief).

Many consequences emanate from the Soviets' problems with maintaining their weapons. One of them is the number of weapons the Soviets must produce. Just as the Detroit automobile industry used to produce a lot more cars because the cars wore out so quickly, so the Soviet Union produces a large amount of weapons to keep the "market" in the armed forces fully supplied. Depictions of the military threat facing the West customarily focus on the far larger stocks of weapons of all kinds produced by the Soviet Union. But it is not at all clear that all those planes, tanks, and armored troop carriers that loom so ominously in the official NATO and Pentagon pamphlets could ever actually be used at the same time against NATO. For example, the Defense Intelligence Agency reports the Soviets as having produced 9,300 of their vaunted modern tactical aircraft—the MiG-23/27, MiG-25, and Su-24— between 1973 and 1980. During this same period, they exported 3,000 of these planes. That left 6,300, which presumably went into service with the air force and air defense forces. But the most authoritative official U.S. estimate of the number of these planes actually serving with operational units puts the figure, as of January 1981, at 3,575, leaving 2,725 unaccounted for. It is just possible that the difference can be explained by exaggeration of Soviet aircraft production by U.S. intelligence. The alternative explanation is that the Soviets are so pessimistic about the reliability of their most up-to-date combat aircraft that for every one they have in operational service they keep one spare; when a breakdown occurs, the first is withdrawn and the other substituted. There is, however, reason to believe that this in itself is insufficient to maintain the regiments of tactical fighter planes at their authorized strength. Semyon, a dour ex-mechanic who served on an air base in East Germany tending Su-7s, not the most up-to-date plane in the Soviet air force even in his time, which was 1971 and 1972, told me that "for every one plane we had that was able to carry out its combat missions, there would be another one or even two that had something wrong with it and couldn't fly. That was from the authorized strength of the regiment, which was 38 planes. There were another dozen or so aircraft which were kept on the field as spares." If that was the situation with a 1950s vintage plane like the Su-7, an Su-24 base can hardly be in a better situation.

The policy of withdrawing and replacing a system that has broken down has wider implications, because the Soviets do exactly the same thing with whole divisions. When an American or West German division loses men and equipment in combat, the normal procedure is to "repair" it with fresh troops and tanks or other weapons to make up the losses. But when a Russian division is ground down to the extent that it is no longer effective as a fighting force, it is simply withdrawn altogether and replaced. Quite obviously, this system requires a lot more men and weapons than the Western approach. If a division of, say, 300 tanks goes into combat and loses 150, then the U.S. Army would simply feed in another 150. The Soviets, on the other hand, would withdraw the division with the remaining 150 and send in a fresh division with 300. This being the case, the numerical superiority that the Russians have in such indicative items as divisions and tanks begins to appear in a new light. In the Central European region, the area of most interest to threat assessors, NATO has 53 divisions, counting regular troops and those reservists available for immediate recall. By the same criterion, the Warsaw Pact has 55 Soviet and Eastern European divisions in the same area, although, as Harold Brown once said of the Soviets' allies and the native Russian reservists, "the political reliability of the former and the combat readiness of the latter are open to doubt." Disregarding these doubts, it looks very much that if the Soviets really do have to keep far more of their divisions in reserve than any of the Western armies, then they are not only not superior in the number of units they can deploy, but they are actually behind.

The imbalance between the tank forces of NATO and the Warsaw Pact countries is another traditional yardstick of the gross numerical inferiority of the Western side. The numbers here are more contentious, since they vary according to which authority one consults. The NATO publication *Force Comparisons* gives a figure of 13,000 NATO tanks pitted against 42,500 Warsaw Pact tanks along the whole frontier, from Norway to Turkey. John M. Collins, the senior specialist in national security affairs at the Library of Congress and faithful recorder of official Defense Intelligence Agency information, lists the balance as slightly more even, but only just. He gives NATO 15,730 tanks, against 42,035 on the Warsaw Pact side. The widely quoted *Military Balance*, published by the International Institute for Strategic Studies in London, allots 17,000 tanks to NATO and 26,300 to the Soviet Union and its allies. A "specialist" at NATO headquarters told the New York *Times* in September 1982 that the Warsaw Pact has 26,000 tanks "now deployed in Europe . . . compared with the 17,000 tanks of the Atlantic alliance."

All these authorities agree that the Soviet side leads in tanks by a greater or lesser margin. But, given their system of replacement rather than repair, the Soviets must maintain huge reserves just to get themselves on equal terms on the battlefield.

Obscure but crucial organizational considerations like these are hard to depict on a graphic display, which may be why they are not featured in the official Pentagon and NATO assessments of the extent of the Soviet tank threat. The Soviets, on the other hand, have every reason to bear in mind the uselessness of a broken tank that cannot be repaired. In June 1941 the Red Army had six times more tanks than the Germans. But out of this enormous Soviet force of 23,000 tanks, 6,500 were so worn down they needed to be totally rebuilt and 10,000 required a major overhaul. The Russians managed to hang on until new factories started producing, but only just.

To make sure that tanks and other weapons remain in as good condition as possible, the Soviet military follows a rigid policy of using them as little as possible, keeping them packed away like a family's best china, to be used only on special occasions. The weapons are removed from storage only when needed for major exercises once or twice a year, and even then they must conform to a mileage limit.

This sounds sensible enough in theory, but in practice the procedure imposes some crippling drawbacks. First of all, the stored tanks do not necessarily stay in good condition. Former tankers recall that when the time came to start them up at exercise time, significant numbers had major defects. A likely reason for this is the Soviet addiction to preventive maintenance. Under this system, components are not serviced according to their condition but according to a rigid schedule which pays no attention to whether they are in need of repair of not. Thus, on a given day, all the engine oil systems on all the tanks will be opened up and checked, an unnecessary process which will inevitably harm a certain percentage of those systems which were otherwise in good condition.

There is a second and more serious effect of this moth-balling policy: it means that the men's training is restricted, and this is perhaps the most vital Soviet military weakness of all.

Training is far more important for success in combat than technical or even numerical superiority in weapons. The German panzer army that invaded France in 1940 had fewer tanks than its British and French adversaries, and the machines it did have were inferior in armor and fire-power. Nevertheless, it totally crushed the enemy within six weeks. Israel's early victories against its Arab neigh-bors demonstrated the same point, as do, in a narrower arena, the routine victories scored by the U.S. Air National Guard in mock battles against flyers from the regular Air Force. The Guard is manned by part-time volunteers flying aircraft discarded by the Air Force because of obsoles-cence, and yet in a mock dogfight Guard pilots flying the relatively venerable F-4, widely regarded as an unsatis-factory plane for air combat, will frequently overcome full-time pilots flying the F-15, which is specifically designed for this purpose. The difference lies in training and ex-perience, because the Guard pilots are themselves Air Force veterans and have accrued as much as four times the flying hours of their younger opponents.

Though the Soviet soldier may lead a harsh and mis-erable life and though his equipment may be for the most part technically inferior to that of any Western army, he should at least be well trained. The official daily timetable for the troops allots the hours between eight in the morning to two in the afternoon to training, as well as other periods for weapons maintenance. This routine goes on six days a week for two years, unbroken by little, if any, furlough time. In addition, the newly arrived conscript is supposed to have absorbed some basic skills, such as operating and maintaining a rifle or a radio, before he even arrives in the army through the military training programs for school-children and the DOSAAF organization. It is doubtful whether this actually makes a difference. S. Enders Wim-bush, who interviewed large numbers of former Soviet conscripts for the Rand Corporation think tank, reports that "considerably more than half" of his sample never took part in any DOSAAF activities. The Soviets them-selves have indirectly confirmed the basic uselessness of the preinduction program. Up until 1967, all conscripts served three years, the first month of which was spent in basic training, whereupon the draftee was assigned to an operational unit. When the system was changed to a two-year draft, the authorities announced that the month for basic training would be eliminated, since an expanded DOSAAF and military training program in the schools would teach the recruits all they needed to know before they joined up. Fifteen years later, all conscripts must still undergo three weeks to a month of basic training.

Once he is in uniform, the conscript does indeed spend a lot of time training, but very little of it has much to do with realistic combat situations. The main purpose of the program is to teach the young men to follow orders, and one of the means for inculcating this is drill—marching in formation. Drill was invented as a military technique by the armies of classical times, when contemporary tactics required sword and spear carriers to preserve unbroken formations. It has little relevance on the modern battle-field.

The men also spend a great deal of time learning about their weapons but far less time actually practicing with their tanks, armored personnel carriers, or artillery pieces. It would be hard for them to get such practice because most of the weapons spend almost the entire year, as noted, in storage. Each unit does have designated training tanks for the men to train on, but there are not many of these. A platoon, which would normally have three tanks, must make do with one. The problems of training are further compounded because the tanks used for training are sometimes of a different model from the ones that the unit would actually use in war. As recently as 1980, the Soviet units in East Germany, supposedly the elite of the army, kept most of their T-64s in storage except for major maneuvers and trained on T-62s, which had different gunsights, guns, engines, and gun-loading mechanisms.

The authorities are no more anxious to use up expensive ammunition than they are to wear out the precious and delicate tanks. That at any rate is the reason given to the tank crews for their infrequent opportunities for live firing with their weapons. American tank officers lament the insufficient practice their men get from firing only 90 or so shells from their main guns every year. Soviet tankers unanimously recall that they were given no more than six such opportunities a year. The rest of the time they practiced with what are called subcaliber munitions: far smaller and cheaper machine-gun cartridges fired from the tank cannon, adapted for that purpose by the insertion of a tube down the inside of the barrel. Since a 12.7-millimeter shell will have totally different characteristics as far as range and accuracy are concerned from a full-sized 115- or 125-millimeter projectile, it is hard to see what purpose is served by this kind of penny pinching.

Soldiers awaiting their turn on the training machines receive plenty of classroom instruction on such subjects as the recognition of friendly and enemy tanks, but there are some curious omissions. Maps are treated as state secrets in the Soviet Union, and thus ordinary soldiers are not taught how to read them; in fact, maps are kept locked away and are released for exercises only upon an officer's signature. Officers are instructed in the mysteries of map reading—a skill routinely imparted to American boy scouts—but not always with total success. In the early 1970s an American army officer traveling in East Germany (American military personnel are allowed to do so under the postwar occupation agreements) found himself helping lost Soviet units. According to General Aaron, former director of the Defense Intelligence Agency, it happened this way:

> Our attache was out in a green jeep which we provided him for better cross-country mobility and he came on this Soviet formation in the field. Our people were dressed in green clothing that looked in some respects like their military clothing. Suddenly a Soviet lieutenant came up. Our attache thought he was going to throw him out of the maneuver area. The Soviet officer was waving a map and said, "I'm trying to get to this town. Can you help me?"
>
> And our attache, who speaks . . . Russian, said, "Well, let me see your map."
>
> Our attache was showing him how to get to this road and that road. Next comes up a Soviet colonel who had made the same mistake and also was lost.
>
> So a lot of people don't understand that they lock these maps up, they can't read the road signs [because in Eastern Europe the signs are in roman rather than Cyrillic script], and sometimes they may be going across that border and may end up on another route going back to Moscow.

The Soviet solution to the problem of unskilled conscripts is to devolve all tasks requiring the slightest technical aptitude upon officers. In 1975, General Daniel O. Graham, who later achieved fame as a founder of the hawkish pressure group Committee on the Present Danger, drew the attention of a Congressional subcommittee to this: "The Soviets rely on junior officers to do things we would never have a junior officer do in the United States. I mean you see a junior officer running a switchboard, out in the field. We would have a corporal."

When the men are given live-firing exercise on the firing range, the conditions appear to bear little relation to the unpredictable realities of combat. "We knew that firing range in our sleep," reminisces Sasha Dorman, the tank officer. "Three tanks would advance down three parallel roads. At a certain moment, always the same moment, three targets would pop up from the same places. The drivers knew exactly when the moment would come, the gunners knew the range and angle by heart, so it was not too difficult to hit it."

In the spring of 1981, in an effort to get a firsthand comparison between the American and Soviet ways of doing things, I took Sasha down to visit the Opfors unit at Fort Hood. We arrived in the middle of an exercise, in which the Americans dressed as Russians were busily engaged in a mock battle with a visiting Canadian unit. It had been intended that the Opfors' Soviet tanks would be taking part in the action, but they had all broken down before our arrival, and U.S. tanks had had to be substituted.

Nevertheless, there was some of the smell of combat about. Tanks rumbled back and forth, attack planes whistled overhead, helicopters roared this way and that, and the air was continually rent by explosions.

The U.S. captain in charge of the exercise greeted my companion affably but remarked with some diffidence that he supposed these maneuvers were a far cry from the massive Soviet exercises occasionally displayed on television. Sasha insisted that this was by no means the case and expressed his admiration at the way that a relatively junior officer should be directing affairs, changing the plan, and communicating even with the aircraft that were circling overhead, ready to provide close air support when asked.

On a Soviet maneuver, explained this Russian ex-tank officer to his audience of American officers, some of whom were dressed to look like Russian tank officers, things were organized very differently. In accordance with the abiding Soviet military principle that appearance is more important than substance, every last detail is planned in advance, with as little as possible left to chance. Sasha recalled a maneuver that he had experienced which the Minister of Defense himself, Marshal Grechko, was supposed to attend.

Things had been difficult from the beginning, Sasha explained, because so many of the mothballed tanks had refused to start. The tanks had certainly appeared to be in fine condition, lined up neatly under cover in the old stables of what had once been the headquarters of a tsarist cavalry division. They had been painted and polished, with the wheels picked out in gleaming white until they looked the equal of the tanks of the Fourth Guards Kantimir Division, which spends its entire year getting ready for the November 7 Red Square parade. But the trouble was that no senior officer had wanted to tempt fate by checking to see if all those immobile tanks were in as fine a condition on the inside as they appeared to be on the outside.

Working day and night, the men had got most of their complement of 325 tanks to the railhead on time, and the whole division chugged across southern Russia to the maneuver grounds in the Ukraine. It arrived four days before the maneuvers were due to start, which gave everyone time to prepare.

The first evening, Sasha's battalion commander, a major, summoned him and all the other platoon commanders. The approaching mock battle, he told them, was of paramount importance not just for the maintenance of vigilance and preparedness on the part of the armed forces of the Soviet Union in the face of imperialist aggression but also for the reputation of the unit and the careers of its officers. This had little meaning for Sasha and his friend Fyodor, who were officer draftees committed to serving two years in the army before returning to their civilian careers. Fyodor cared so little about his military career that he was drunk most of the time and absent without leave in the nearby town of Polotsk the rest. But for the career officers it was different. A bad showing, especially in front of the Minister of Defense, might mean a posting to the Chinese border; certainly there would be less prospect of a transfer to East Germany or Poland.

This was why the senior officers were determined to leave nothing to chance and why, in the gathering darkness, the assembled platoon commanders now had to traverse the area in which they would be fighting the mock battle a few days later, an encounter which would supposedly reveal the strengths and weaknesses of the units taking part under the stress of the ebb and flow of unpreprogrammed combat. But in reality, the "battle" was as carefully choreographed as a classical ballet: "Your tank will be here, you will surprise and destroy an enemy tank on that hill there, but ten minutes later you will be taken on the flank by another enemy tank firing from those trees there."

The next day Sasha took the individual tank commanders and gunners from his platoon over the same ground and went through the same intricate rehearsal. But the preparations were not over yet. That evening, all the officers assembled again. This time they joined the officers of the other two battalions in the regiment, while the colonel who commanded the regiment took them through all the moves and countermoves they were to make yet again. On the following day, Sasha and his men resimulated the part they were to play in the mock battle, after which he joined his exhausted fellow officers for a final walk-through under the anxious gaze of the divisional commander. Nothing, it seemed, had been left to chance.

No one had bargained for snow. Although the weather was cold, the first snowfall was not expected for another week or so. But on the morning that the two sides were due to join battle in an inferno of thunder flashes and smoke clouds, a near-blizzard was raging.

Squinting desperately through the white haze from the open turret of his T-55, Sasha tried to recognize the landmarks he had memorized so carefully over the previous few days. It was very difficult—everything had changed in appearance—and Sasha and his crew kept getting lost. Occasionally Sasha glimpsed another tank, but he could not be sure if it was an enemy tank he was meant to kill or one that was going to kill him. Inside his own tank, the crew were even more fuddled than he was, possibly because they had followed the standard and expressly forbidden practice of T-55 crews of reversing the turret fume extractor, designed to suck exhaust gases from the gun out of the turret, so that it sucked in warm exhaust from the engine. There was no way to stop this; the crews always insisted that they preferred the possibility of being poisoned to the certainty of freezing to death.

By late afternoon, Sasha's adherence to the plan had become academic, since the whole exercise was called off. Some of the tanks were unable to return to base because the fuel trucks had gotten lost. The officer in charge later explained that this happened because his radio was expropriated by an artillery colonel whose own radio had malfunctioned. What with this and other disasters of the day, the high command was not pleased and the commanding officers' careers suffered accordingly.

Other accounts of training exercises convey the same

message: the Soviet military trains so as to leave nothing to chance because it cannot cope with chance events. When the unexpected occurs, the system breaks down.

In 1967, for example, the Soviet military decided to mark the 50th anniversary of the October Revolution with an enormous series of maneuvers centered on the crossing under fire of the Dnieper River, a feat which the Red Army had actually carried out under real battle conditions during the war. Operation Dnieper, as the exercise was called, was to be the largest such exercise in the history of the world, with well over half a million men taking part.

The centerpiece of the operation was to be the crossing of the Dnieper, a sizable river, by tanks traveling completely underwater on the riverbed. Such Soviet submarine tank tactics are the object of envious attention on the part of Western military observers. They are made theoretically possible by fixing a snorkel to the tank, so that while submerged it can draw in air for the engine and crew. The problem is that even a 40-ton tank is extremely buoyant underwater because of the large volume of air within, as a result of which the slightest excess pressure on the steering lever will instantly cause the submerged tank to make a sharp turn. Consequently, the chances of a tank being able to navigate its way across a riverbed so as to emerge immediately opposite on the other bank are remote.

Accidents could not be considered for Operation Dnieper, since the entire Politburo and numerous high-ranking foreign guests would be watching. Therefore, for four months before the exercises were due to start, thousands of men labored to pave the Dnieper's riverbed with concrete furrows, so that the tanks would be automatically guided across. The scheme worked perfectly, as can be seen from the film of the exercise, which to this day provides the staple stock footage used on Western television programs of the Soviet Army in action. In wartime, needless to say, it would be difficult to spend four months paving the bed of a river while the opposite bank was in enemy hands. If it were not in enemy hands, then the whole exercise would be pointless anyhow, since a bridge would be constructed.

It is clear that the Soviet military are themselves aware of the disadvantages of such totally unrealistic, if theatrical, training exercises. Writing about pilot training in *Krasnaya zvezda* in 1976, the air force general Pavlov complained that "in training, the pilots imitating the target fly only in a straight line, without changing altitude or speed... without mincing words, these comrades would have a hard time under combat conditions." Another air force general, Anatoly Konstantinov, wrote in the same newspaper a year later that "the officers in training were placed in a situation where they did not have to concern themselves with which targets to fire at first, which rate of fire to use, etc. They knew all this beforehand, including the 'enemy's' action, the target's flight profile, their routes and other data." General Nosov drew the attention of *Krasnaya zvezda* readers to what happens when the plan is changed. In a 1976 article he complained that when the target was suddenly changed during a particular bombing exercise, the pilots "could not make an accurate bombing approach on the designated targets" because, complained the general, they had been "systematically trained to carry out attacks on targets which were predetermined at the airfield."

Part of the reason for this rigidity, which even the generals decry, is due to the ways in which performances are evaluated. Officers are graded according to their proficiency in carrying out the plan, whatever the realities of the situation. Thus, the incentive is to avoid the unexpected at all costs and rehearse the men before a mock battle: make sure the pilots know exactly where they have to fly ahead of time; run the tanks as little as possible so that the unit does not have to report breakdowns. While air force units do not follow the tankers' practice of keeping most of their machines in mothballs, they do their best to avoid accidents, a policy which precludes all but the simplest flying maneuvers in training.

Demanding flight training is the only effective method of training pilots for combat and is the reason that the U.S. Air National Guard pilots, some of whom have an individual average of about 1,600 hours of flying time, can so regularly outperform full-time pilots whose total experience in the air typically averages no more than one-third that amount.

The lack of flight training for the regular U.S. Air Force is regarded with concern within the service. Spinney, in his *Defense Facts of Life* study, pointed out that in 1979 the average American Air Force fighter pilot made no more than 11 or 12 flights a month, for a total of 16 hours in the air, or about 10 hours a month less than they had received ten years before, when the Vietnam air war was at its height. In contrast the Israeli air force, generally deemed to be the world's best, gives its pilots over 30 hours a month of flying training.

Yet even the modest U.S. figure far exceeds the Soviet norm. Testifying before a Congressional committee in 1981, General Lew Allen, the chief of staff of the U.S. Air Force, conceded that Air Force flying hours were still decreasing, but pointed out the consolation that "Soviet pilots receive only half the approximately 14 hours of flight time accorded U.S. pilots of F-4, F-15, and F-16 aircraft. . . . It is one of the great advantages that we have. They are much less flexible . . . [and] operate under very rigid sets of rules and under very intensive ground control. They are just obviously not quite so proficient."

The preeminent proficiency of the Israeli defense forces

comes in the first instance from a lot of practice in combat. There can be very few of their officers who have not had experience of a shooting war, and even in the periods when the Middle East is officially at peace, there are ample opportunities for trainees, particularly combat pilots, to learn their business under realistic conditions. Even without the extra stress of combat, the Israelis strive to educate their men to take decisions quickly and without reference to higher authority. In his book *Sinai Victory*, S. L. A. Marshall recounts one such exercise, devised by the Israeli General Staff as a corrective for officers who "undeviatingly responded to orders" rather than adapting their plans as circumstances changed. The trainee commander, a middle-ranking officer, such as a colonel, would be taken out on an exercise and told that he had 22 hours to prepare a plan of attack against an enemy-held objective, like a town or a hill. After he had pondered and prepared a carefully thought-out scheme, he would be told that the situation had totally changed and that a new plan must be ready in 30 minutes. When he had presented his revised version, he would be told that the situation had drastically altered yet again and that he had to make an instant decision on what to do next.

This is a far cry from the type of training exercise described by Sasha or the Soviet Generals Pavlov and Konstantinov. The Israelis, following Clausewitz's maxim that "since all information and assumptions are open to doubt, and with chance at work everywhere, the commander continually finds that things are not as he expected," stress flexibility. The Soviets, who profess to be great admirers of Clausewitz, discourage it.

These kinds of problems are more than a product of the long years of peacetime inactivity for the Soviet forces between World War II and the occupation of Afghanistan. Centralization of command and a consequent inability of junior commanders and troops to think for themselves were an abiding feature of Soviet forces during the world war. In 1944, Marshal Zhukov issued a directive in which he complained that "we are not training our troops in the proper use of features of the locality in the attack [meaning taking cover under fire], we are simply training them to rise up and shout 'hurrah' and advance toward the enemy." General Von Mellenthin, a senior staff officer during World War II and a product of the German General Staff Academy, where the emphasis was on training officers to adapt to changing situations, renders this disobliging verdict on Soviet military professionalism: "The rigidity of Russian attacks was almost proverbial. . . . The foolish repetition of attacks on the same spot, the rigidity of artillery fire, and the selection of terrain for the attack, betrayed a total lack of imagination and mental mobility. Our wireless intercept service heard many a time the frantic question: 'What are we to do now?'"

Von Mellenthin's onetime commander, General Hermann Balck, is even sharper in his criticism, although he does draw attention to the Russians' ultimate advantages in defending their homeland. "The Russian is a unique type. You can risk things with the Russians that you couldn't risk with any other power in the world," the old general told an interviewer in 1979.

At Budapest [in January 1945] I attacked 45 Russian divisions with about 7 to 9 of my divisions. It worked pretty well. If I had had two more armored divisions I could have cleaned up the whole Budapest area. But Hitler could never make up his mind to weaken a sector in order to have overwhelming strength at a decisive point.

The Russian is passive and slow-moving, terribly slow-moving. You have to get inside the Russian psychology. Then you come to very different conclusions, including tactical ones. When facing the Russian you can't sit down and calculate that he has so and so many divisions or weapons or what not. That's all baloney. You have to attack him instantly and throw him out of his position. He is no match for that.

To discuss the Russian approach, we have to look at not only the last war but earlier wars. We can start with Charles XII of Sweden. He defeated the Russians at Narva, defeated them everywhere. What did the Russians do? They built up an army and trained their commanders and troops in serious warfare. Finally, they reached the point where they were a match for the Swedes. They could afford the time to do this because they had boundless men and because they could withdraw as far as they wanted to. No one ever reached Moscow without paying a price.

In the Second World War, it was much the same thing. The Russians were unbelievably sluggish and incompetent to employ their overwhelming masses. Here's how it was at the Chir River in front of Stalingrad where I had the 11th Panzer Division. The Russians had their Fifth Tank Army under Koniev. Koniev would launch a tank corps to attempt a breakthrough. He would give the orders on the spot and move on. So the attack would go on. Naturally it cut through our thin defenses like a knife through butter. Then the attack would stop; the Russians didn't know what to do next. You had to wait for this moment and then counterattack them immediately. In the blink of an eye they'd be destroyed. In the meantime Koniev would have moved on to the next corps. Same game all over. Attack, etc. . . . then they in turn would get wiped out. In this fashion, with one division I eventually broke up the whole Fifth Tank Army.

Despite this disobliging summation, Balck concedes the all-important caveat that given time and space, for which they paid dearly, the Russians did in the end learn to defend themselves in World War II as they had in the time of Charles XII: "It was possible to do this [wipe out the tank army] only because the Russians hadn't trained their commanders yet. Then in the next year their commanders improved. They were better selected and received more training and experience. That made things more difficult for us." (Although in January 1945, outside Budapest [see above] Balck still did well despite odds of 5 to 1.)

The all-important question for today is whether the Soviet army has retained the improvement in skills noted by Balck during the war. The threat, after all, is not that the Soviets might be able to resist an invasion of the USSR by the forces of the West, but that they might launch an invasion of territories under Western control, either in Europe or in the Middle East. In such an event there would be no time for the Soviets to carry out on-the-job training for their commanders and soldiers, just as there would be little time to mobilize and retrain the bulk of their reserves.

There is certainly no doubt that the Soviets have conducted the most searching postmortems on every conceivable aspect of their war against the Germans. In the specialized magazine *Voenno-istoricheskii zhurnal* (Military Historical Journal), as well as in a torrent of books and articles in other publications, they have gone through every engagement of the four-year struggle, examining not just the famous battles like Kursk and Stalingrad, but also minor encounters previously ignored or unnoticed by historians. In doing so, they hope to ascertain the determining factors for their victory or defeat: the balance of forces on either side, the disposition of the forces, the amount of ammunition, and so forth.

The information is then reduced to numerical symbols, so that every battle can be described by a mathematical formula. By this means they hope to discover the "correct" response to any given battle situation. Thus, the "norm" is established, a set, lifeless formula, which, if applied correctly, should enable a commander to determine what he has to do to win—align his forces in such and such a position, attack one or other of the enemy strongpoints, or, which is most often the case, call for reinforcements.

All military staff colleges, both East and West, apply such formulas to a certain extent, but the Soviet practice differs in the degree and intensity with which this method is applied. This is why Soviet training exercises follow such a stereotyped and repetitive pattern. The officers are drilled in the varying preset formulas for dealing with a number of different situations. Artillery officers, for example, are schooled to follow a set of guidelines which determine the amount of destruction that will be achieved by firing a given number of rounds at a given target. Therefore, the officer will know that if he is firing a 122-mm howitzer at a group of enemy troops under cover occupying a hectare of ground (just under 2½ acres), he will need precisely 47 shells if he opens fire without preliminary "ranging rounds" or 35 if he had been able to calibrate the range more correctly. If, on the other hand, the enemy are not so well dug in, then the corresponding number of shells required decreases to 35 and 26, respectively.

These calculations are known as Projectile Expenditure Rates (PER) and they are based on wartime experience confirmed to the artillery's satisfaction by years of subsequent tests. Yet, as David Isby drily remarks, "The nice neat charts of PER and weapons effectiveness appear similar to those prepared before the First World War and which proved to be completely invalid when put to the test of combat."

All the armies that took part in World War I had spent years in detailed study for such a conflict, preparing, as they thought, for every eventuality. As it turned out, nothing happened the way they had expected, and it took years of bloody impasse before they thought of new ideas to deal with the situation. After it was all over, Prince Rupprecht of Bavaria, one of the senior German commanders, declared: "There is no panacea. A formula is harmful. Everything must be applied according to the situation."

Soviet Army Operations, a handbook prepared by the U.S. Army Intelligence and Threat Analysis Center (not an institution normally given to underestimating the Soviet threat), makes the same point rather less succinctly. "There are obvious disadvantages in using such a comprehensively regimented and structured system," it notes in commenting on the Soviet addiction for preset formulas. "Primarily, there is no provision for the unexpected. When initiative is seen in terms of finding a correct solution within normative patterns, a sudden lack of norms may place a commander, at whatever level, in an unexpected and perilous situation. The Soviet leader who can assess his situation and select the 'proper' tactical guidelines based on appropriate norms is lauded. However, despite all the exhortations for a commander's use of initiative, he will be condemned if his initiative fails and he has not followed prescribed norms."

The objection to such criticism of the Soviet way of doing battle is that no one has seen the Soviets put their ideas into practice since the Germans and Japanese surrendered in 1945. Attacks on the modern U.S. military way of doing business, such as *Self-Destruction*, *Crisis in Command*, and *National Defense*, are bolstered by copious examples drawn from the Vietnam debacle of ill-led troops, mendacious commanders, and ineffective weapons.

Since 1980, the counterinsurgency war in Afghanistan has given us some inkling of the efficiency or otherwise of the modern Soviet army. Such reports as have arrived from that remote battlefield give no indication that the Soviets are showing themselves to be any different than as described in this book. There could be no clearer example of their inability to react quickly to novel situations, for instance, than their use of antiaircraft weapons in Afghanistan. The point is, of course, that the enemy the Russians went in to fight, and are still fighting, has no aircraft or helicopters. Nevertheless, the Soviet divisions that poured down the passes in December 1979 came equipped with their full complement of long- and short-range SAMs and guns. It took upwards of a year for the realization to dawn that there was no Afghan rebel air force, but that, on the other hand, the rebels were finding good use for antiaircraft weapons captured or stolen from the Soviet forces or those of the Afghan government. Only then were all such weapons withdrawn from the country.

There are a number of problems with using the Afghan war for assessing Soviet military capabilities. First, it is extremely difficult to get reliable reports of what is going on in Afghanistan, and second, the motley groups of poorly armed tribesmen against which the Soviets are fighting bear little resemblance to the kind of opposition they would face in a direct assault on the West, which is the threat that frightens the policymakers and strains the budgets of the NATO powers.

The fact that the Soviet forces are nevertheless getting some combat experience has led some observers to conclude that they are mending their ways. A report in the Washington *Post* of February, 13, 1983, for example, concluded that "More than 400,000 Russian troops have been rotated in and out of Afghanistan, among them many thousands of junior commanders whose hard-won combat experience is now being shared with those bound for fighting there." Chief among the lessons learned in the stress of combat, so the author maintained, was that of the importance of encouraging initiative at unit and subunit level. The article cites as evidence reports in the Soviet military press in which veterans of Afghanistan complained of fatal adherence to textbook tactics and the need for "small, fast-moving units led by warrant officers and sergeants trained 'for independence in making decisions.'"

Such worthy sentiments might be more convincing were it not for the fact that they have been a recurring theme in the military press long before Soviet forces arrived in Afghanistan. Though the truth of exhortations to initiative and independence may now have been borne out in blood, it does not follow that the Soviets have taken or will undertake the necessary and far-reaching reforms of their system to set matters to right. Indeed, the fragmentary reports coming out of Afghanistan suggest that nothing much has changed. A British photographer in the company of a group of Afghan guerrillas who ambushed a large Soviet column on the main Kabul–Jalalabad highway in April 1982 was relieved to report that although the column was escorted by a large number of troops riding in BMP armored personnel carriers, the troops made no attempt to dismount and outflank the Afghans—although this would have been very easy to do.

The American forces were taught many lessons in Vietnam—the uselessness of tactical bombing, the vulnerability of attack helicopters, the bad effects of rotating junior officers through brief spells of combat command, and much else besides—and yet the weight of institutional inertia ensured that most of these lessons were ignored or speedily forgotten.

Wars fought by countries that have been armed with Soviet equipment and trained according to Soviet precepts provide another indication of the real worth of threat dispositions. They have not provided the Kremlin with much grounds for complacency.

The Syrian army that attacked the Golan Heights in October 1973, taking an outnumbered and complacent Israeli force completely by surprise, was nevertheless halted and then thrown back after a few days. Part of the reason was that so many of the Syrian tanks broke down or ran out of fuel—80 percent of the tanks captured by the Israelis were completely undamaged. More importantly, once the Syrians had achieved their initial objectives as laid down in the overall plan, they halted of their own accord, even though their enemy was off balance and in a state of confusion. By the time the Syrians had formulated a new plan and were ready to proceed, the Israelis had gathered the necessary reinforcements and were counterattacking.

Another army organized and equipped according to the Soviet model is that of Iraq. When the Iraqis suddenly attacked Iran in September 1980, in an attempted emulation of the Israeli blitzkrieg of 1967, they repeated the 1973 Syrian experience. The American magazine *Armed Forces Journal International* subsequently reported that they "continuously halted after their first tactical successes ... they entered and abandoned Susangerd twice, and gave up critical positions near Dezful [two key centers on the Iranian border] because they lacked clear orders and responsive command. ... At the start of the war [the Iraqi command] controlled NCOs and junior officers so rigidly that they would not move without orders, waiting rather than take the initiative. They were particularly unwilling to advance without orders or to maneuver round a position once ordered to advance. This cost Iraq many casualties in the first few weeks of fighting in Khorramshahr and Abadan."

The Egyptian army that crossed the Suez Canal in 1973 was also a Soviet military client, and it did indeed carry out a difficult operation with great success. But much of this success was achieved by ignoring Soviet precepts. The Egyptians had reorganized their reserve system according to the Swedish rather than the Soviet model. They deployed their antitank weapons in a manner that contravened the tactical precepts of their Soviet suppliers. Even so, once the carefully planned initial phase of the crossing itself and the occupation of a limited portion of the Sinai had been completed, the Egyptians lost the initiative. Their inability to respond to a successful Israeli countercrossing led to the encirclement of a large part of the Egyptian army and a shattering military defeat.

The drawbacks to the Soviet tradition of rigid command and the discouragement of low-level initiative are so obvious that even the most hawkish threat inflators, such as the U.S. Army intelligence commentators quoted above, feel bound to refer to them. Thus, whenever there appears the slightest hint or sign that the Soviets might be mending their ways, the news is enthusiastically broadcast among Western military commentators, echoing the excitement among technical specialists that greeted the appearance of Soviet "all-weather interdiction/strike" combat aircraft.

Armed Forces Journal International, which never deviates too far from the prevailing winds of Pentagon ideology, took care to suggest that however poorly the cumbersome Iraqi forces might have performed, the Soviets themselves would do better. "Regardless of the recent Soviet emphasis on 'daring thrusts,'" states Anthony Cordesman, the author of a detailed report on the Gulf war in the June 1982 issue, "Iraqi armored units have followed the most rigid Soviet tactics of the World War 2 era."

"Daring thrusts" conjures up images of low-level units under the command of low-ranking colonels leading deep raids into the enemy's rear in the best traditions of the wartime German panzer leaders. If it were true that the Russians had abandoned the ponderous preplanned massive advance, what they call the echelon attack, in favor of these thrusts, then the threat would have become that much more formidable. Happily there seems to be no real sign, or chance, of this happening. In fact, the phrase "daring thrust" is a translation of the Russian *smelyi reid*, which is more correctly translated as "an audacious march by a motorized column." Some Soviet military writers have proposed the institution of such units, although General Meremsky, who is in charge of all ground forces training, took the trouble to denounce the notion in a signed article in 1976. Deep-penetration raids have always been present to a greater or lesser extent in Russian military theory, from the beginning of the nineteenth century through the 1930s (although Stalin shot its chief proponents during his 1937–38 purge) and today. The Afghan experience has renewed calls for giving greater responsibility to lower-ranking officers and to NCOs.

The problem for the Soviets is that however desirable such an innovation might be, it remains impossible to put into practice. To do so would involve changing the rules of Soviet society so far as the armed forces are concerned. It is a society that is run from the top down, in each and every respect. The brothers Zhores and Roy Medvedev, perceptive Russian observers of the Soviet system, affirm this point in arguing against the possibility of an adventurist military leadership going to war without the approval of the leadership:

If the government and party apparatus do not allow any freedom of action even for editors of small and obscure provincial publications; if they refuse to allow any film or play to be presented without a special session at the Ministry of Culture; if they ban the formation of any professional association without state and party authorization; and if not a single person can go abroad without approval of several different party "travel commissions" (not to speak of local and regional policy authorities), then how can one imagine that these military experts who manage the

Soviet Union's ICBMs could possibly launch them in an emergency without collective decisions at the highest levels of the party and state?

It might be suggested that in an area as important as the military, the state command apparatus might be prepared to relax its grip and allow the lower levels some leeway. It is worth looking at agriculture in this regard, which, despite its appalling record, is another item of high Soviet priority. The necessity of decentralizing the cumbersome agricultural system has been obvious to many ever since Stalin collectivized and centralized it in the early 1930s. In his book *The Russians*, Hedrick Smith, the former New York *Times* Moscow correspondent, recounts the story of a would-be reformer named Khudenko, who in 1972 worked some marginal farmland as an experiment to test his theory that a self-reliant group, unencumbered by command and control from above, could do better at growing crops. Unfortunately for him, the experiment was too successful; his farm proved to be 20 times more productive than the state-run units. As a result, Khudenko was arrested, tried on trumped-up charges and subsequently sentenced to prison, where he died. In the view of the bureaucracy, the discrediting of their methods and possible diminution of their power was too high a price to pay for the solution of Russia's food problems.

In essence, initiative seems to be something that the Soviet military bureaucracy realizes is a good idea and should be implemented—so long as it is not accompanied by any genuine freedom of action or thought. "On what does the effectiveness of creativity on the battlefield depend?" asked a *Krasnaya zvezda* writer rhetorically in 1971. "It depends on a firm knowledge of the regulations." Even more ironically, when Marshal Grechko, the then-Minister of Defense, listed initiative and independence as among the six principal requirements of a trainee officer, he emphasized the point by adding, "These qualities are *compulsory* for a military man."

In the face of these prevailing attitudes, there is little chance that officers who see the necessity for reform will ever make headway. Marshal Kutakhov, who as commander in chief of the air force is now a pillar of the system, published this poignant lament when still occupying the relatively lowly position of air commander of a minor military district:

> You see, our every good beginning at some time takes a turn, somehow the rational substance evaporates from it, and only the formal shell remains. This results from the fact that we make a living and creative task to fit a kind of procrustean bed and regulate everything without exception.

Eleven

What the Red Army Is Supposed to Do

The threat posed by Soviet land and supporting air forces, by common consensus among U.S. and allied military commanders, is that they could launch a surprise attack that would smash through NATO lines in West Germany and roll westward to the Rhine and beyond. One report "by a senior officer of NATO's armed forces" which received wide circulation and approbation in 1976 concluded that lead elements of a Warsaw Pact invasion force could crack the NATO defense "crust" three hours after leaving their bases. "A second wave would cross the frontier seven hours later and a third six hours after that ... without political warning on which so much NATO planning depends." Within 48 hours, in the view of this eminent but anonymous scenarist, lightly opposed Pact spearheads would be west of the Rhine and still rolling.

The Third World War, a somewhat lugubrious fiction co-authored by a group of retired British generals which appeared in 1978, postulated a similar Russian attack in 1985, which is stopped only because NATO had invested in a massive rearmament program. The book enjoyed an immense success and reportedly so impressed the then-Leader of the Free World, Jimmy Carter, that he kept it at his bedside.

In common with most expert descriptions of the NATO–Warsaw Pact balance, these gloomy scenarios pay very little attention to the actual state of the Soviet forces. *The Third World War* does have a denouement in which racial strains cause the breakup of the Soviet Union, but the more immediate problem of nationalist tensions within the units on the battlefield passes unnoticed. The T-72 tank acquits itself honorably, untroubled by breakdowns or carnivorous automatic loaders, and is only checked in its onward advance by the deadly accuracy of TOW and other precision-guided antitank missiles. Soviet tactical combat aircraft were now "of broadly comparable performance to their allied counterparts" because "the men in the Kremlin had woken up at last to what air power was really all about." While the Soviets did face problems in inculcating "boldness of initiative and independence of judgment" in their junior commanders, they had nevertheless adopted "the concept of the 'daring thrust'—bold action in depth by a force of combined arms . . . similar to that of German blitzkrieg in the Second World War."

Although the Soviet generals may have their own doubts about "daring thrusts," their overall assumptions about land warfare as expressed in the Soviet military literature bear out the gloomiest prophecies of their Western counterparts. As General V. G. Reznichenko, a senior pedagogue at the Frunze Military Academy, writes in a typical burst of aggressive rhetoric, "The offensive is the basic form of combat action, only by a resolute offensive conducted at a high tempo and to a great depth is total destruction of the enemy achieved."

This "high tempo" is to be achieved by the use of overwhelming masses of mechanized formations, capable of fighting and advancing continuously by day and night and moving forward at the rate of 70 miles a day, a pace that would indeed bring them to the Rhine in 48 hours and the English Channel in a week. If the Soviet forces did indeed move at this rate, they would be advancing faster than any other force in history. The record was set in August 1945 by the battle-hardened veterans of the Soviet Sixth Guards Tank Army, which stormed through Manchuria in ten days at the rate of 51 miles a day. But that offensive was against a totally outnumbered and demoralized Japanese army (the attack started 3 days after the nuclear destruction of Hiroshima), and for the first four days the Russians were totally unopposed. General Heinz Guderian's panzer columns moved no faster than 12 miles a day in their "dash to the sea" across northern France in 1940, the same speed as Patton's Third Army during its celebrated offensive in the opposite direction over the same flat country four years later.

A detailed examination of the forces with which the Soviets would have to set this breathtaking precedent makes the possibility still less likely. These forces would not have the overwhelming numerical superiority or the tactical experience of the army that took Manchuria; in fact, they would be facing an enemy that in most respects has approximate equality in numbers. Nor would they be organized to deploy forces with the flexibility and independence of action that made the truly daring thrusts of Guderian and Patton possible.

Despite the impression it has successfully projected of mass and brute force, the Soviet army is a delicate instrument, in both its equipment and organization. As we have seen, its weapons have in the past been simple but unreliable and are now becoming complicated and still more unreliable. While operating within these mechanical constraints, the commanders must rely on a force of short-term conscripts that, at best, can be trained to perform tasks in which they have been repeatedly rehearsed by officers who are themselves no more capable of deviating from the "norm." As a study prepared by the U.S. Defense Nuclear Agency concludes: "The impression gained is that the whole system depends on everything going just as prescribed, that the loss of a communication link or a command echelon would be more than disruptive, perhaps even catastrophic."

Some defense analysts have managed to discern a grave threat to the West in the very existence of this brittle Soviet vulnerability. Joshua M. Epstein, a defense scholar who has ably chronicled the myriad Soviet deficiencies in flexibility and training, suggests that these problems, in fact, are an incentive for the Soviets to launch a surprise attack in the hope of crushing NATO before the machine begins falling apart. The problem for the Kremlin leaders in considering this kind of gamble is that they have no real idea of the precise readiness of the forces they have built up and maintain at such expense. Thanks to the system of the vertical stroke, the officers are accustomed to concealing the true state of the efficiency, training, and discipline of the men in their units, as well as the state of the equipment, from their superiors, who, in turn, collude to conceal the true facts from their superiors, and so on up the line. Richard Anderson, who pioneered the examination of these aspects of the Soviet military while serving at the CIA, declares bluntly:

The high command know that things are in a bad state down below, but they don't know precisely how bad. Furthermore, they don't want to know, because then they would have to account for the situation to their superiors in the Kremlin. Even so, the Politburo must have a shrewd idea of what is really going on, especially after the fiasco of the Polish mobilization.

Soviet leaders are willing to take a calculated risk, but they are much less willing to take a risk that they do not believe they can calculate accurately. And when they do not have an accurate picture of the true condition of their forces a key variable in their calculation is missing.

There is an ironic twist to the firm conviction on the part of our military leaders in the West that the Soviets could launch a blitzkrieg invasion of Western Europe. The French military leaders of the 1930s were also worried about an invasion from the East, but they were confident that it could be halted by the massive and enormously expensive line of fortifications known as the Maginot Line, which in the event proved to be totally useless against German mobile tactics. As a response to the threat of a modern and more terrible blitzkrieg, the NATO planners have re-created the Maginot Line. They have not gone so far as to build a continuous line of concrete fortifications the length of Germany, although that has been suggested, but their defensive arrangements are based on static lines which allow little or no freedom of maneuver to the defenders.

NATO's defensive strategy is designed to work in the following manner. On receipt of warning that the Soviets are about to attack, the NATO units are to move out of their barracks, which are situated according to wherever the various Allied armies happened to be at the outbreak of peace in 1945, and proceed to their designated positions just behind the border, where they dig in and wait for the

Russians to arrive. This "forward defense" line, which extends the entire length of the border, is open to the criticism that Napoleon once made of a similar plan for defending the borders of France. "Who are you trying to guard against," asked the emperor, "smugglers?"

Once the Russians have attacked, it is expected that the NATO troops would be pushed back slowly from their forward positions, fighting along the way for every inch of ground and doing their best to maintain an unbroken line of defense. The main duty of the defense, according to the prevailing philosophy, is to "attrit" (a Pentagonese word derived from the English "attrition") the enemy by firepower, either conventional or nuclear. The outcome of the battle will be decided according to who "attrits" whom faster. If the defenders manage to kill enough Soviets and knock out enough tanks, then the attack will have failed and the Russians will have lost. If, on the other hand, the Soviets succeed in grinding down the Western forces by attrition as they slowly drive them back, then they will have broken through, and a helpless Europe will lie at their feet.

It is this outlook, which the Pentagon analyst Franklin Spinney calls the "attrition mindset," that has spawned the obsession with numbers—of tanks, men, aircraft—that dominates all assessments of the East-West military balance. It is a bureaucratic approach to warfare, one of the many indications of the increasingly strong similarity between the military bureaucracies of the superpowers. Like the Soviets, NATO strategists make their dispositions on the assumption that the outcome of a battle is determined by the initial size of the opposing forces and the comparative lethality of the enemy's weapons. This preoccupation tends to ignore the human factor, the decisive contribution to the outcome of any conflict. It also ignores the result of a previous strategy of forward defense in Europe. Once the Germans had bypassed the Maginot Line by advancing through the forest of the Ardennes, which had been thought to be impassable to tanks, the considerable French forces tied up in the frontier fortifications were effectively marooned, isolated from the crucial battles taking place far to their rear. If today the Russians were to break through NATO's "cordon defenses" at any particular point, then the other troops on either side of the breakthrough would be as isolated and useless as the French divisions were in 1940. It is extremely difficult to move forces sideways or backwards to deal off a breakthrough of this kind, a better solution being to hold large reserves in the rear, far enough behind the front line so that the troops can be moved to deal with an enemy attack once its main direction becomes apparent.

NATO generals do not ignore the desirability of large reserve forces, but they complain that they do not have the necessary manpower. This raises a curious paradox. NATO and the Warsaw Pact countries have roughly equivalent numbers of men in their total forces in Central Europe; in fact, with the inclusion of the French forces, NATO has 200,000 more men in its air and ground forces. Yet the Soviet alliance manages to deploy more combat forces, men who can actually fight, as opposed to support, the forces in the field. For example, with a total of about 120,000 men in Afghanistan, the Soviets field five combat divisions. The United States also has five divisions in Europe, which require no less than 276,000 men for their operation and support. A U.S. tank division includes about 17,000 men, while a Soviet tank division has no more than 11,000. Yet they both have the same number of tanks. Looking at these figures, it is easy to see what defense analyst Pierre Sprey means when he refers derisively to the "lightly armed hordes from the West." To be fair, the European contingents within NATO are a model of efficiency compared to the American contingent, since with 2½ times as many troops they provide 4 times as many divisions as the United States.

What are all the rest of the uniformed Americans stationed in Europe doing? They are helping run the bureaucracy that renders the combat forces as immobile and ponderous as if they were interned in the concrete bunkers of the old Maginot Line and as deprived of freedom of movement and initiative as their putative enemies across the border. One man who can provide an interesting perspective on the effectiveness of NATO combat organizations is a retired German soldier, Heinz Gaedcke. During the war, he was a young one-star general in the Wehrmacht, fighting on the Russian Front, and when the West German army was rebuilt as the Bundeswehr under American auspices in the 1950s, he joined again and rose to three-star rank.

"When I see the enormous staff apparatus that we have now constructed, partly under your influence," he told an American interviewer in 1979, "I often ask, 'My God, how is this going to work?'

"Here is how we controlled our divisions in the West and the East in World War 2: My division commander and I would sit together in a half track vehicle with the map on our laps, exchange opinions—'Should we go to the left or to the right, should we do it tonight or tomorrow at dawn?'—then we'd scribble our instructions, give them to the driver next to us, and he'd pass the orders along to a couple of radio operators in the back of our vehicle.

"Now we've built the division staff into a little city with operations centers, communications centers and whatnot—with everything in formal writing and transmitted by teletype machines. I must add that what we now understand the daily command briefing to be—this assembly of 10, 12, or 15 experts ranging from weather to religion—simply didn't exist in World War 2.

"There are lots of other disadvantages to these huge staffs. You get far too many vehicles which are hard to move and that attract the attention of enemy aircraft. The whole apparatus becomes sluggish and slow."

However easy it may be to deride Soviet rigidity and inflexibility, particularly in the way that they conduct their exercises, this veteran German General Staff officer does not find much to commend in the American model as transmitted to the modern Bundeswehr. "When I attend the maneuvers, it seems to me that these exercises are too rigidly conducted. . . . If you will permit me to be a little critical, I have generally found that American tactical and operational command tends to follow a rigid pattern, a school situation. And, unfortunately, since World War 2 we Germans have imitated a good deal of this."

Rather more violent examples of American rigidity, and the bloody consequences, occurred during the Vietnam War. In December 1972 the Nixon Administration decided to pressure the North Vietnamese to negotiate by unleashing the giant B-52 bombers of the Strategic Air Command against Hanoi for the first time. The Air Force command, in its wisdom, decreed that the bombers would go in at regular intervals, flying at identical heights and speeds. After dropping the bombs, each plane would turn for home at precisely the same spot, always turning in the same direction. The pilots protested to no avail that these orders made life very easy for the antiaircraft crews on the ground, who were able to predict the bombers' position with a minimum of effort. Only after the resultant devastating losses had provoked an actual mutiny among the fliers were the plans changed to allow a modicum of variation and flexibility.

Such efforts have not blunted the urge of U.S. military bureaucrats for ever-greater "command and control" of the lowest fighting units from on high. The AWACS, for example, is more than a radar plane for spotting enemy intruders. It is also a device for monitoring and directing the activities of individual fighter pilots engaged in an air battle over Central Europe from the flying command post or indeed, by means of a satellite radio link, from a comfortable control room in the Pentagon. The disastrous attempt in 1980 to rescue the American hostages in Iran involved an AWACS plane in just this manner; the small group of men launched into the heart of enemy territory were under the constant supervision of the chairman of the Joint Chiefs of Staff, the Secretary of Defense, and the President of the United States himself, all of whom were sitting half a world away in Washington.

Present-day U.S. military doctrine represents no more of a fundamental departure from the habits and practices of most (but not all) U.S. generals and armies during World War II than does the Soviet variety. In the war against the Germans, both the Americans and the Russians basically relied on overwhelming firepower and superior numbers to defeat their opponents, who by the concluding phases were almost invariably fighting with far fewer men and weapons. Today, while it is official U.S. policy to affirm that our forces are underequipped and outnumbered in the face of the Soviet hordes, it is also official policy to fight as if the same aims and practices that led to victory in 1944–45 after a long drawn-out campaign still applied today. General Gaedcke remarks that among the other bad habits the modern German army has picked up from the Americans is that of fighting for a territorial objective, such as a hill or a wood.

What happens when we take that? Why, then we go on to Objective Number Two. There is no sign here of the idea that was bludgeoned into all of us old General Staff officers: Possessing the terrain doesn't matter; what matters is to shatter the enemy and then the terrain will fall into your hands by itself.

Perhaps the reason for your more rigid approach is that you had such overwhelmingly superior numbers, particularly in artillery and aircraft. Using these, Objective Number Two was wiped off the face of the earth. Then came your infantry who took possession because nobody else was left. We were always in a state of insufficiency. We had to figure out how to grab the enemy with the fewest possible forces. Once we had achieved that, then we let the terrain objectives fall by themselves.

As we have seen, the United States has convinced itself that it must face the enemy with an "insufficiency" that does not exist so far as the total numbers of men in uniform are concerned, let alone the potential manpower untapped in the general population. The response has been and continues to be to reduce the number of men actually available to fight the enemy. Not only does the size of the headquarters staff continue to swell, but each new generation of weapons that is introduced is more expensive, not just in terms of money but also in terms of men. The M-1 tank, for example, will require almost twice as many maintenance troops to keep the overall force working as does the older and simpler M-60.

There is no lack of sensible suggestions for ameliorating the present position of the NATO alliance without any increases in cost. Steven Canby, a Washington-based defense consultant, argues that "United States and Western military inferiority is purely self inflicted. It is a case of dated doctrine causing too few combat units, misuse of technology and manpower, and poor strategy and integration with allies." He points out that NATO could achieve decisive military superiority by trebling the number of combat troops that would be available in an emergency. This could easily be brought about by training a large number of ready reserves, which would be lightly armed and used as screening forces in the forward positions now occupied by the very expensive and top-heavy mechanized formations of the regular forces. These mechanized troops, in turn, would be held farther back, ready to counterattack deep into the enemy's rear once the scope and the direction of the attack became apparent. Cutting out the excess "fat" of the NATO units, particularly the American units, would also free large numbers of men for the more relevant tasks of fighting the enemy.

The NATO planners are not prepared to adopt anything so innovative, at least not as far as the all-important U.S. contingent is concerned. In 1977 the governments of the alliance agreed under U.S. prodding to set in motion a Long-Term Defense Plan in order to redress their perceived inferiority *vis-à-vis* the Warsaw Pact countries. The essence of this plan involved no fundamental reassessments of strategy, simply a commitment to continue the traditional policies but to spend more money doing it. Since this had the effect of encouraging governments to increase the number of top-heavy units armed with complex high-technology weaponry at the expense of forming combat-ready reserve units (a much cheaper process), it might be said to have helped degrade rather than increase NATO's military strength.

The arguments of such military reformers as Canby carry all the more weight because they are based on the assumption that the Pentagon assessments of Soviet strength are correct. Canby's suggested reforms hold out the prospect of military superiority over the Soviet Union even though he assumes that the Soviets presently enjoy an advantage in terms of tanks and aircraft twice as great as what they actually have, that they are trained and ready to use blitzkrieg-style infiltration tactics, and that they have reserves of "structured units capable of being quickly mobilized for combat" rather than the "fat, untrained and undisciplined soldiers who have forgotten all that they ever knew" so vividly recalled by Viktor Suvorov, formerly of the Novograd-Volynskii Motor-Rifle Division.

Pentagonese for the process of comparing the relative ability of the Soviet and U.S. alliances to fight each other is "net assessment." A detailed look at the real state of the armies of the two military blocks leads inescapably to the conclusion that neither army is particularly prepared for what General Balck called "serious warfare," and that the military men who control their respective machines are not basically very interested in changing this state of affairs.

The Americans plan on the basis of a perceived threat that bears little resemblance to the Soviet army as it really is. But they have organized and equipped their forces in a way that magnifies whatever combat capability the Soviet Army does possess. The Russians, while struggling to cope with the problems of their backward technology and cumbersome society, are doing their best to make themselves like the Americans.

The welter of misconceptions and falsifications chronicled in the above section deals only with warfare as it has traditionally been practiced and understood. The tangled realities of the Soviet threat and the U.S. reaction to it become yet more surreal when we come to consider the role played by devices of unknown performance and effect—what the Soviets call weapons of mass destruction.

Part IV

Weapons of Mass Destruction

Part IV

Weapons of Mass Destruction

Twelve

Missiles and
Bombers

Nuclear weapons are different. So much is a truism. Their
potential for gross destruction is so much greater than any
other engine of war that the word "weapon," which conjures up images of warfare as it has been known in the
past, seems totally inappropriate and even misleading. It
is a paradox of our age that nuclear explosives are nevertheless regarded as weapons, for the use of which their
military controllers construct battle plans, tactics, and
training plans just as if they were another and more useful
form of artillery. Nuclear strategists earnestly calculate the
imponderables of "victory" and "defeat" in wars fought
with nuclear weapons, and scientists and engineers labor
to build "better" variations of them, while those who oppose even the contemplation of their use discuss the progress of such a conflict in similarly precise terms.

There is clearly something illogical about all this precision. These are experts in tank warfare as it has been

practiced around the world since 1939; air combat between fighter planes has emerged as an "art" of war with certain dominant characteristics since World War I; the behavior of men and groups of men under fire has been charted and analyzed since at least the time of the legendary Chinese military thinker Sun Tzu in 600 B.C. It is this lexicon of experience that enables us to pass judgment on modern military forces and, for the purposes of this book, on Soviet tank engines, fighter tactics, and troop training methods. Nothing is certain in warfare, but conventional conflict is a matter we know something about, even conflict with Russian armies and Russian weapons.

No one knows anything about nuclear war. There are precisely two firm pieces of evidence as to what happens when nuclear energy is used for offensive purposes—the Hiroshima and Nagasaki explosions; as it happens, they produced differing results. The Hiroshima bomb, although of lesser destructive yield than the one used against Nagasaki, killed many more people. Nevertheless, the military forces of at least six nations—the United States, the Soviet Union, Britain, France, China, and Israel—have managed to persuade their governments that these devices are weapons of war to be used with calculable effects.

While even a relatively small nuclear arsenal, such as that of the British, could theoretically create more destruction and human suffering than the two world wars, it is the Soviet and American nuclear forces that receive most of the world's attention and evoke the most fear. The American military has the longest experience in building and maintaining nuclear weapons, but in the eyes of U.S. policymakers, there is something especially novel, fearful, and repugnant about the way in which the Soviets construct and deploy them. It is proclaimed that the Soviet Union, indifferent to the horrific consequences of a nuclear exchange, has both the will and the means to fight and win a nuclear war. U.S. Defense Secretary Caspar Weinberger delivered a typical expression of this sentiment in a letter to American and European newspaper editors in August 1982, informing them that "whatever [the Soviets] claim their intention to be, the fact remains that they are designing their weapons in such a way and in sufficient numbers to indicate to us that they think they could begin, and win, a nuclear war." Earlier in the year, Harvard's Professor Richard Pipes, ensconced as the resident Soviet expert on the National Security Council staff, explained to the Washington *Post* why the Administration thinks the Soviets have such an ominously insouciant view of nuclear conflict: "We used to believe that if you threatened the Russians with the destruction of 100 to 200 cities that would be sufficient deterrent. This notion is now being abandoned. . . . The Russians have made it clear that they would not really accept such rules of the game by developing a civil defense program, air defenses, and so on."

More than with any other instrument of power, perceptions about nuclear weapons have come to be regarded as no less important than the reality. We can look to the following tortuous exchange in a 1979 Congressional hearing as illustration of this novel approach to military assessment. The subject under discussion between a senior Senate aide, Richard Kaufman, and the director of the Defense Intelligence Agency, Lieutenant General Eugene Tighe, was the ability of the Soviets to launch a surprise first strike with their nuclear missiles and thereby cripple the ability of the United States to retaliate.

Tighe: It is the perception that they have, more than anything else, that is important. I think you will find a great deal of people disagreeing over whether or not they actually have a first strike capability.

Mr. Kaufman: Your assessment that they have a first strike

capability depends on your perception of what the Soviet perception is of the United States' will to retaliate?

Tighe: If the Soviets think they have a first strike capability, it is my judgment that they have it. I believe they believe they have that first strike capability.

Mr. Kaufman: That depends on perception . . . and not only on objective capability?

Tighe: That is right.

In all this welter of perceptions, the true facts, such as they can be ascertained, about the forces that the Soviets have built up with a nuclear mission in mind gradually fade into the background. Whatever General Tighe may have us believe, perceptions should be based to some extent on reality.

The Soviets do not brandish their capacity to launch a nuclear war in quite the same way as the United States does. The military officer carrying the "football"—a briefcase thus nicknamed because the original U.S. nuclear strike plan was code-named Dropshot—with the necessary codes and plans for sending the missiles on their way, who follows the U.S. President wherever he goes, has no visible Soviet counterpart. What is known is that the Soviets have gone to extreme lengths to ensure that their forces will not be able to launch a nuclear weapon without the proper authority. Nuclear stockpiles are under the custody not of the regular armed forces but of the KGB. U.S. missile-launch silos are manned by two Air Force crewmen, who must act in concert if the missile is to be successfully fired. Soviet silos contain four men: two regular servicemen, who launch the rocket, and two KGB soldiers, who carry out the separate function of arming the missile's nuclear warhead. In former years, these safety precautions were extended to keeping the warheads physically separated and under KGB guard away from the actual rockets that would carry them.

Whereas the United States has nuclear stockpiles littered about the world at its various bases, the Soviets have been extremely loath to keep any nuclear weapons outside their own territory. Hence, the short-range missiles, artillery guns, and bombers based in Eastern Europe that would fire or carry nuclear warheads and bombs are without their ammunition. The warheads are stored beside the USSR and only mated up with the delivery systems in times of extreme crisis or for the occasional exercise. While there are many reasons why the Soviet navy does not send more than a very small part of its nuclear-missile-firing submarine fleet to sea at any one time, as we shall see, one of them must be the difficulty of maintaining tight control over these submarines when they are away from base. The Australian defense scholar Desmond Ball suggests that the reason that Soviet nuclear forces overall are far less ready to fire than their American equivalents is that "the Soviet Union lacks the very complex and expensive command systems required to combine a high state of launch readiness with adequate safeguards against unauthorized firing."

Ultimate authority for using the weapons rests with the Defense Council, an obscure and semisecret body that has ultimate responsibility for all aspects of Soviet defense. It is not clear if the chairman of the Defense Council can actually launch the missiles on his own, although, as we shall see in Chapter 14, Brezhnev may have used the threat of a surprise attack to arrogate such power to himself.

The most important and powerful arm of the operational nuclear forces of the Soviet Union is the strategic rocket forces. Although it is the newest of the five services, dating back only to 1959, it is officially referred to as the "primary" service, and its commander—currently General Vladimir F. Tolubko—takes precedence over the commanders of the other four services. The 413,000 strategic rocket troops are responsible for all nuclear missiles with a range of more than 1,000 kilometers (620 miles).

The cutting edge of this formidable force is made up of the 1,398 ICBMs secreted in concrete silos hardened to withstand the effects of nearby nuclear detonations and distributed around the USSR in 26 complexes. Most important among these are the 820 missiles that were deployed in the 1970s. These are divided into two types: medium and heavy. The SS-17 and SS-19 medium missiles can carry multiple warheads aimed at separate targets, up to four warheads in the case of the SS-17 and six in the case of the SS-19. The only other difference between them is that the SS-17 has what is called in missileer jargon a cold launch, which means that the missile is ejected from its silo by compressed gases before the main engines ignite, thus limiting damage to the silo. The SS-19, on the other hand, fires straight out of its silo, which must then be entirely rebuilt before it can be used again. The heavy missile is the SS-18, a cold-launched behemoth towering 100 feet inside its silo and carrying as many as ten independently targeted warheads.

In addition to these fourth-generation ICBMs, the strategic rocket forces also maintain 578 missiles in service, which were first deployed in the 1960s. These are the SS-11s and SS-13s. The SS-11 carries three warheads, but these cannot be aimed independently, they simply straddle a single target like buckshot. The SS-13 was an unsuccessful development with severe technical problems, and only 60 were ever deployed.

In addition to these long-range missiles, the strategic rocket forces also control some 700 medium-range weapons, which can reach Western Europe and China. The most modern and famous of these is the SS-20, which travels on and is fired from a mobile launcher. It can carry up to three independently targeted warheads, although it

does not invariably do so. This missile is gradually replacing the SS-4s and SS-5s, which were first installed in
western Russia and the Soviet Far East at the end of the
1950s. These venerable systems, each carrying a single
warhead, stand for the most part out in the open, unprotected by silos.

Together the long-range strategic missiles (so called
because they can reach the United States) can carry up to
5,540 warheads, which means that the strategic rocket
forces control about 75 percent of the total operational
Soviet strategic arsenal of nearly 8,000 warheads and
bombs. The rest is divided between long-range aviation—
a branch of the air force—and the navy. The naval component amounts to 950 missiles, which are deployed on
62 submarines and which are capable of delivering up to
1,900 warheads. Soviet submarine-launched missiles are
prefixed SS-N- in the terminology of the Western military,
and there are four basic types. Of these, only the
SS-N-18 carries more than one warhead, the older SS-N-5,
SS-N-6, and SS-N-8 being restricted to one each.

Long-range nuclear bombers have never been as important to the Soviets as they are to the Americans, mainly
because the Soviets lack the tradition of strategic bombing
on which the U.S. Air Force is based. An additional reason
is that the Soviets were never very successful in building
bombers with the necessary range, for reasons explored
in Chapter 9. Before he died, Stalin had commissioned
the aircraft designer Vladmir Myasishchev to build him a
bomber that could fly to the United States and back. The
plane was not completed until after the old dictator had
died, which was perhaps lucky for Myasishchev since his
plane did not perform as required. Khrushchev recounts
what happened when the hapless designer came to report:
"This plane failed to satisfy our requirements. It could
reach the United States, but it couldn't come back. Mya-

sishchev said it could bomb the United States and then
land in Mexico.

"We replied to that idea with a joke: 'What do you
think Mexico is—our mother-in-law? You think we can
go calling any time we want? The Mexicans would never
let us have the plane back.'"

The Bison, as the Mya-4 was dubbed by NATO, was
accordingly relegated to medium-range missions over Europe and the Far East but has nonetheless been counted
as a strategic bomber, as is the propeller-driven TU-95
Bear, which was the other main Soviet long-range bomber
project of the 1950s. More recently, the TU-22M Backfire
bomber has been graced with the title of strategic bomber,
although like the Bison, it can only bomb the United States
under circumstances that would certainly have aroused
Khrushchev's derision. With the Backfires included, this
motley force of strategic bombers amounts to 215 planes,
carrying as many as 430 bombs. Long-range aviation also
disposes of several hundred medium-range bombers, such
as the 1950s-era TU-16 Badger, which have no pretensions
to a more demanding role.

Before we examine the strengths and weaknesses of the
Soviet nuclear forces in detail, it must be said that there
is no doubt they pose a credible threat of overwhelming
nuclear retaliation to the United States, as the somewhat
larger American strategic arsenal of almost 10,000 warheads does to the Soviet Union. This has not always been
the case. Although Americans who went to school in the
late 1950s and early 1960s may recall sheltering under
their school desks in simulation of a Soviet nuclear attack,
there was very little chance that the Soviets could have
carried out anything so devastating. Even when they had
begun to supplement their inadequate bomber force with
truly intercontinental missiles in the mid-1960s, the force
still remained highly vulnerable to a surprise American

attack, which might have knocked out Russia's ability to retaliate. The SS-6, which was the first operational Soviet ICBM, had been originally designed by Sergei Korolev to begin the exploration of space by launching Sputniks. To Korolev, although he probably did not tell the Kremlin so, the business of designing the means for delivering nuclear warheads onto cities on the other side of the earth was a tiresome necessity for generating funds and backing for the space program. Thus, the SS-6 had severe drawbacks as a weapon. It was so large that it could not be based away from a railroad line, the only means of transporting it; it needed 20 hours before each launch to fill up its highly volatile fuel of nitric acid and alcohol. Moreover, the missile had to be guided by radio signals beamed from ground stations, which could easily be jammed or destroyed by enemy action, and it could only just reach the northeastern corner of the United States.

It is an indication of the irrelevance of the enormous arsenals currently maintained by both the Soviet Union and the United States to deterrence that even the minimal threat of Soviet retaliation was enough to deter the United States from launching an attack on Russia at a time when it possessed the maximum nuclear advantage over the Soviets. This is not mere conjecture. There is at least one recorded instance when the United States seriously comtemplated a nuclear strike on the Soviet Union, only to be deterred by the possibility of a very limited degree of Soviet retaliation. The occasion was that of the 1961 Berlin crisis. According to Fred Kaplan's chronicle of the nuclear-war planners, "Wizards of Armageddon," the Kennedy Administration actually instituted a top-secret high-level study of a possible "counterforce" strike against Soviet military targets. The group revealed that conditions were ideal for such an attack. The United States would, at a stroke, be able to knock out almost all of Russia's nuclear-war-making potential. Soviet retaliation would be extremely limited, killing probably no more than 3 million Americans—at worst no more than 15 million. As Kaplan observes: "At the Rand Corporation (where this kind of nuclear warfighting analysis had been pioneered) the attack plan would have been heralded a monumental success. . . . Virtually the entire strategic community would have considered two, three, or even fifteen million fatalities, in the abstract, 'acceptable,' or anyway not 'unacceptable,' losses under the circumstances. But now, in the real world, in the context of a real crisis with real decision-makers, the reaction was much different. Nearly everyone was aghast."

In other words, nuclear superiority, which the United States undoubtedly possessed at the time, turned out to be utterly meaningless.

After the mid-1960s, it was too late for any such sanguinary American options. The Soviets had managed to deploy a few primitive missile submarines at sea, and more importantly, they had followed the American lead in protecting their land-based missiles in hardened concrete silos. It was now impossible to target the rockets of the strategic rocket forces with any degree of certainty that they would all be destroyed, an uncertainty that persists to this day and will do so into the foreseeable future.

It is this situation that renders the phrase "nuclear weapons" such a contradiction in terms. If neither side can use its "weapons" and the mere fact of possession of a limited number can ward off the threat of attack by the other side, then there is no point in employing the same methods of military assessment that are used in planning conventional forces, like tanks or fighter planes. Intricate war plans are of little use when dealing with weapons of such indiscriminately destructive power; numbers and performance make little difference beyond a certain minimal level. A Washington *Post*/ABC poll taken in April 1982 indicated that the American public has managed to grasp this elementary point. A majority of those questioned thought that the Soviets had an advantage in nuclear weaponry; an even larger majority thought that such an advantage made absolutely no difference because "both sides have more than enough to destroy each other no matter who attacks first."

Unfortunately, the military, either in Washington or in Moscow, does not care to see things that way. The bellicose World War II general George Patton regretted the advent of the atomic bomb because it would give "pacifists, politicians and fools a chance to say: 'All we need is a bomb, no Army.'" Patton underestimated the skill of the military bureaucracy, which has managed to secure itself both.

Nevertheless, the military must still grapple with the problem of unprejudiced observers who persist in the notion that nuclear weapons are for deterring rather than fighting wars and who might be disposed to withhold funds accordingly. Addressing the presumably sympathetic readers of *Air Force Magazine* in May 1979, the chairman of the U.S. Joint Chiefs of Staff, General David Jones, expressed his frustration at this attitude: Public opinion, he complained, is a prisoner of the "assured destruction" doctrine, which holds that "as long as the U.S. can wreak substantial damage on Soviet society—that is, destroy a given number of cities with some certainty—that's all we need in terms of strategic equilibrium. Under this view, anything beyond that point is regarded as overkill and unimportant. "This is the sort of thinking," according to General Jones, that leads to the belief that the Soviets "can continue to enlarge their strategic forces and 'waste their resources' without ill effect on our national security."

Despite the general's complaints, his profession has been remarkably successful in persuading its civilian masters that there is no such thing as overkill. Since the dawn of the nuclear age, the military mind has been at work trying to devise plausible scenarios for nuclear-war fighting in which traditional operational considerations, such as numerical superiority, the importance of offensive momentum, the relevance of defense, and even the possibility of victory, all play a part.

The Pentagon's word for refinement in the pattern of a nuclear exchange, as opposed to the cruder concept of mutual and assured destruction, has become known as "counterforce." As the name suggests, this embodies the notion of attacking the other side's war-making potential—weapons, command centers, communications, military industry—with any attendant civilian casualties merely an unfortunate and unlooked-for by-product.

Once in a while it is revealed that the American nuclear forces are targeted according to a counterforce war plan. These intermittent revelations, such as the Nixon Administration's National Security Decision Memorandum 242, the Carter Administration's Presidential Directive 59, or the torrent of leaks in 1982 over the Weinberger Pentagon's schemes for "protracted nuclear war," usually cause a media furor before being quietly forgotten by everyone but specialists (although the approach of the Reagan Administration to the whole business has been so unabashed that public repugnance may be longer-lasting this time).

What the military and their allies in the executive branch and the press have been far more ready to discuss are the counterforce plans reposing in the safes of the Kremlin and General Tolubko, plans which the entire national security apparatus, uniformed or otherwise, of the last two U.S. Administrations has accepted as being perfectly feasible. Briefly put, the presumption has been that the Soviet Union either possesses or shortly will possess warheads of sufficient quality and quantity to wipe out almost all of the 1,000 U.S. Minuteman land-based missiles in one lightning preemptive first strike. This, it is suggested, could actually give the Russians a nuclear victory, since the United States would then be reduced to its bombers and submarines. Since the bombers are slow and vulnerable and the submarine missiles supposedly too inaccurate for striking at enemy silos, the President would lack the option of a counterforce retaliatory strike against the enemy's remaining land-based missiles. His unpalatable alternatives would be either to dispatch his submarine missiles against Soviet cities, thereby inviting a return salvo against the U.S. civilian population, or to surrender.

Common sense dictates that this bizarre scenario is nonsense. One need have no knowledge of the number or types of weapons arrayed on either side to wonder how the Soviets could be so precisely sure of the mentality of the American President and his advisers that they could launch the initial attack in the absolute certainty that he would choose surrender rather than a city-swapping duel. Dr. Richard L. Garwin, a distinguished defense consultant and a former member of the scientific advisory board of the U.S. Joint Strategic Target Planning Staff, has pointed out an even more serious flaw in the argument: "The prelude is completely unnecessary. The Soviet Union could say, without destroying Minuteman, 'Look here, Mr. President, surrender or we will destroy American cities.' It wasn't necessary to destroy Minuteman in order to say that. The compelling nature of the argument would be just the same."

Nevertheless, it remains the case that the most senior officers of the U.S. military profess to view the vulnerability of the U.S. Minuteman missiles to an attack by accurate Soviet missiles as a deadly threat. Addressing the subject at his Senate confirmation hearings in May 1982, the newly appointed chairman of the Joints Chiefs of Staff,

Army General John Vessey, Jr., stated flatly that the Soviets had more nuclear explosive power than the United States and the ability to threaten American missiles. "In that sense," he told the Armed Services Committee, "they are superior to us." His predecessor, General Jones, had recently fielded a trick question much favored by doves—"Would you care to swap your forces for those of the Soviets?"—by asserting that he would be quite happy to exhange U.S. land-based missiles for their Soviet equivalents.

As these high-ranking generals made clear, it is the quantity and quality of the Soviet missiles that have provided the rationale for the alarms over a Soviet first strike. Before taking a closer look at these missiles, it is worth considering the precise mechanics of such an intricate maneuver.

The task facing General Tolubko would be to find some way to deposit nuclear explosives close enough to the 1,000 Minuteman silos dotted about the northern and central plains of the United States to destroy almost all of them. If he leaves a significant portion undestroyed, he will have failed, because the United States will still have a sufficient number of land-based missiles left to carry on nuclear-war fighting and strike back at the Soviet reserve of ICBMs. In the surreal context of this particular argument, the U.S. missile-firing submarines must be ignored, even though just two of the comparatively old-fashioned Poseidon submarines would demolish 200 Soviet cities. The reason is that sea-launched missiles are thought not to count in counterforce scenarios because they are acknowledged to lack the necessary "hard-target" (silo-bursting) accuracy for such a delicate business.

Not only must Tolubko's warheads find their target silos, they must do it simultaneously. Warheads that arrive on the battlefield a little late may fall victim to the phenomenon known as "fratricide," meaning that they are destroyed or blown off course by earlier explosions. If some of the missiles are held back so as to arrive after the turbulence of the initial detonations has subsided, the delay will give the Americans time to launch their undamaged missiles through the resultant "window."

Since each of the targets will require the attention of at least one Soviet warhead, the Soviets must dispatch a minimum of 1,000 warheads. This, in turn, requires the deployment of a minimum of 100 missiles, since the heavy SS-18 presently carries ten warheads, while its SS-17 and SS-19 siblings carry four and six, respectively. For the operation to stand any chance of success, the missile systems must be both reliable and accurate, and this is where things get difficult.

Launching a rocket missile requires that every one of a great many individual working parts and systems must work in the way it is designed to work and at precisely the right moment. Launch silos consist of a lot more than a hole in the ground lined with concrete. The electronic apparatus that switches on the missile and that ensures that it cannot be fired accidentally or illegally is extremely complex. A malfunctioning computer or an electrical connection that does not work can mean that the whole missile, with its three or more rocket stages, will fail to ignite. When the crewmen turn their launch keys, the primary rocket engine must ignite, or in the case of the SS-17 and SS-18, the compressed gas mechanism that "pops" the missile out of its silo must do its job before ignition takes place. Once ignited, the engine must not blow up, and the control mechanism guiding the movable nozzles that steer the engine must function properly. Once the first rocket stage has used up all its fuel, it must drop off cleanly, the second-stage engine must start up without a hitch, and so on, until all the stages have burnt out—and the thrust shut-off valves on the engines must function at precisely the right time, or the missile will miss by miles.

When the time comes to dispatch the warheads to their separate targets, they must not jam or knock into each other. The computers and gyroscopes of the guidance system on the so-called post-boost vehicle must all be working perfectly so as to eject the multiple independently targeted reentry vehicles (MIRVs) at exactly the right moment.

Even if all the various subsystems have functioned to perfection, the whole effort will be for nothing if the fuze that sets off the actual bomb in the warhead does not work.

We have all watched something like this process, with the exception of the bomb fuze, occurring on television during a space shot. The difference is that space shots are planned weeks or months in advance, and the preparations are in the hands of an experienced crew, which has carried out the same operation many times before. Furthermore, the space technicians have only one rocket to care about, while a first strike requires that all these processes, from first-stage ignition to the final explosion, be repeated hundreds of thousands of times in an operation for which there can be no full-scale rehearsal and no second chance.

Experience with more familiar military weapons systems does not suggest that the prospects for such flawless performance are good. The fatal breakdown of three out of the eight U.S. helicopters dispatched on the Iran rescue raid in 1980 brought the problems of military unreliability home to a worldwide audience. We have already noted the unreliability of more mundane Soviet weapons, such as tanks and aircraft. Such weapons, at least, can be tested under the same conditions as they would encounter in wartime, so that the commanders may proceed with a rough knowledge of how often their machines are likely to break down. Nuclear weapons systems are not and cannot be subjected to the same kind of realistic testing.

In this respect, the Soviets do display a slightly more realistic attitude than their counterparts in the U.S. military. While the U.S. Air Force never test-fires even a single missile out of an operational silo, the Soviets do. This practice is indeed construed by U.S. policymakers as yet another indication that the Soviets are both ready and able to fight a nuclear war with the aim of winning. On June 19, 1982, for example, the then-Secretary of State Alexander Haig chose the occasion of a meeting with Soviet Foreign Minister Gromyko to publicize the fact that the Soviets had carried out multiple tests of various nuclear missiles the day before. *Aviation Week*, an unofficial mouthpiece of the Pentagon, later reported that "demonstration by the Soviet Union of a strategic nuclear weapons offensive and defensive capability integrated with command control and communications over a 7-hr. period June 18 had led the U.S. to conclude that a nuclear war-fighting capability has been tested successfully."

What the Soviets had actually done was to launch two aging SS-11 ICBMs from their operational silos in the western and central Soviet Union across Siberia to the desolate Kamchatka peninsula, which juts out into the Pacific from the coast of Siberia. At the same time, they also fired a medium-range SS-20 missile, also at Kamchatka, an SS-N-8 missile from a submarine in the White Sea, two antiballistic missiles, and an antisatellite missile.

This was indeed very impressive, particularly since the United States has not fired more than one ICBM at a time since 1971. Beyond the fact that the Soviets had managed to get a number of missiles into the air more or less simultaneously, it is difficult to see this as a demonstration of a nuclear-war-fighting capability.

The test was not unique, since the Soviet Union has carried out similar exercises at least once before in the last five years. The two SS-11s were not the kind of missiles that would be used in a first strike. That role is reserved, according to the Pentagon scenarists, for the larger and MIRVed SS-18. SS-11s were used because these missiles are being phased out, and it is somewhat hazardous to manhandle a Soviet missile, especially an old one, from its silo. The Soviets, therefore, display an admirable sense of economy in using the junking process to exercise a crew in firing a missile off into the wastes of Kamchatka. Since the Delta class submarine is in the process of changing over from the older SS-N-8 missile to the MIRVed SS-N-18, the navy was probably also using the occasion to get rid of an obsolete weapon. Buried deep in Pentagon leaks about this demonstration of the Soviets' "alarming capability" was the revelation that the antisatellite missile had missed, as apparently had the antiballistic missiles.

If other Soviet exercises are anything to go by, such as Sasha Dorman's tank maneuvers in the snow, this limited series of test shots was undertaken only after lengthy rehearsal and preparation. We do not know if it took place on schedule.

According to U.S. intelligence analysts who have had access to the secret reports on Soviet ICBM test shots from operational silos, the failure rate is extremely high. According to one senior weapons engineer who has seen highly classified intelligence data on the tests, it would be "inconceivable" for the Soviets to risk a first strike in view of their reliability problem. "Their accuracy stinks, and reliability is so bad you can't believe it," he told a reporter in 1983. Although the Defense Department typically assumes that Soviet missiles are 80–85 percent reliable, "it would be closer to the mark to call that their unreliability."

Far from being ominous, the fact that the Soviets do carry out semirealistic tests of their nuclear-war-fighting equipment is very comforting. It means that General Tolubko and his staff have some idea of just how unreliable their missiles actually are. The Americans, in contrast, prefer to remain in happy ignorance. The U.S. Air Force has not fired an ICBM out of a silo that would be used in wartime since the 1960s, when there were four such attempts. The results were not auspicious—three missiles failed to show any sign of life whatsoever and the fourth exploded in the first seconds of its flight. Since then, the Air Force has been content to undertake operational testing by removing a designated missile from its silo, transporting it to a special test launch facility at Vandenberg Air Force Base in southern California, giving it a very careful going over by experts, and then firing it into the South Pacific.

On the basis of this experience and of tests of individual missile subsystems taken in isolation from all the other working parts, the U.S. Air Force has assured itself that 98 percent of its Minuteman ICBM force—that is, the total force apart from a dwindling number of aged Titan II missiles—is fully operational and ready to go. The Soviets are more modest about the proportion of their force that is kept on peak-readiness alert. Some reports suggest that it may be as low as 25 percent. The exact figure is hard to pin down, but it is almost certainly no higher than 70 percent. The remaining 30 percent are "stood down" for overhaul at any one time, unavailable for action. The ICBMs that fail in the practice launches are selected from the ones that are on peak-readiness alert. If we assume that the alert figure is 70 percent, that cuts Tolubko's operational force from 1,398 ICBMs to about 980. Taking the reliability rate as 50 percent, which is a very conservative figure, the number of Soviet ICBMs that could be expected to perform to specifications comes out at about 490. This would be quite enough to obliterate the fabric of American society, but it leaves very little margin for error in any kind of counterforce operation.

Doom-laden pronouncements about growing Soviet strategic capabilities seldom take much account of matters like reliability. Nor do they take account of the fact that the Soviets are still at least twenty years behind the United States in the development of rocket engines, despite their tremendous efforts to catch up.

The original German V-2 rockets were powered by an engine using liquid fuel. In such engines, two liquids, a fuel and an oxidizer, are pumped into a combustion chamber. There they mix and burn, producing high temperatures and high-pressure gases, which exhaust through a nozzle in the tail of the rocket with great speed, causing the rocket to recoil in the opposite direction, thus driving it forward. The oxidizer is necessary to make the fuel burn. (A jet engine needs no oxidizer because its fuel is oxidized by the air.)

All early rockets, both Soviet and American, were propelled in this way. The problem with liquid propulsion is that the liquids tend to be highly volatile and are liable to explode. They are also dangerous to handle in other ways; they give off, for example, a highly corrosive and toxic gas. Furthermore, liquid-fueled engines require an extremely intricate arrangement of pumps and other circuitry in order to ensure that the two liquids flow into the combustion chamber in the correct proportions. Their major advantage is that they deliver a great deal of thrust per pound of fuel.

At the end of the 1950s, the Americans adopted a new method of propelling their military rockets. Instead of liquid fuel, they developed a way of powering the missiles with a solid propellant. Solid fuel, which can be very crudely compared with gunpowder, does not need a series of delicate pumps to operate. It is simply molded in the rocket, where it can safely remain for lengthy periods until it is fired, when it burns in the same simple and straight-

forward fashion as a Fourth of July firecracker. The snag
with solid-fueled rockets is that the fuel itself is very difficult to design and manufacture. It must be of absolutely
uniform consistency throughout, as otherwise it may mo-
mentarily fail to burn or else explode.

The first operational U.S. solid-fueled missile was the
submarine-launched Polaris. The U.S. Navy had rejected
the idea of liquid fuel for their missiles on the grounds
that it was simply too dangerous. To this day, there is a
ban on any weapon propelled in this fashion being carried
on a U.S. ship. Soon afterward, in 1963, the first Minuteman solid-fueled land-based missile went into service
with the U.S. Air Force. With the exception of a diminishing force of Titan II missiles, which were put into service in the presolid era, all U.S. strategic missiles are now
solid-fueled.

With one very limited exception, all Soviet rockets, on
the other hand, are still liquid-fueled. The experience of
the U.S. Air Force with its remaining liquid-fueled missiles—the Titans—serves as a vivid reminder of what
opearting such vehicles actually entails. "It is dangerous,
it is dangerous," Sergeant Jeff Kennedy of the U.S. Air
Force told the CBS-TV program *60 Minutes* in 1981. "It's
dangerous to the people that work on it. It's dangerous to
the people that are in the surrounding area around the
missile, for the simple reason that once the tank's punctured, that's it. There's nothing we can do to prevent it,
to stop it. . . . There's so many places for a Titan missile
to leak, it's just unbelievable. It's not uncommon to have
three or four Titan missiles leaking at once." The danger
stems from the fact that the vapor given off by leaking
fuels is highly poisonous and has a tendency to explode.
Sergeant Kennedy was speaking from the wisdom of personal experience. In September 1980 an airman working
on a Titan at a base in Damascus, Arkansas, dropped a

9-pound wrench, which fell 66 feet down the silo and punctured the skin of the missile. The fuel began to leak. Nine hours later the missile exploded, blowing the 750-ton concrete lid a distance of 1,000 feet, and Sergeant Kennedy, who had just emerged from the silo, 150 feet. Sergeant Kennedy subsequently explained to me that although some of the Titan's problems can be ascribed to its age—the seals on the fuel tanks might be better designed nowadays—the basic system is inherently fallible because it is liquid-fueled. "There is always something going wrong with it; a leak or some other malfunction. In theory the missile could stay fueled up and ready to go for eighteen months at a stretch. In fact, I never saw one that we didn't have to offload [its fuel] within two months, and that is a very cumbersome process."

The U.S. Air Force gave a vivid confirmation that the drawbacks of the Titan are mirrored in the Soviet liquid missile force in 1979. In that year a terrible accident took place at McConnell Air Force Base in Kansas when the oxidizer component of a rocket's fuel leaked and exploded. The Strategic Air Command subsequently showed Sergeant Kennedy and other key technicians a satellite photograph of a Soviet silo where exactly the same thing had happened two years before.

Since all liquid rocket fuels, both U.S. and Soviet, are poisonous and volatile, it is easy to see why the Soviet rocket scientists and their military customers should be anxious to develop solid-fueled missiles. In about 1957 the Nadiradize Design Bureau began working on a missile very similar to the Minuteman. Dubbed SS-13 by the Americans, the missile was not a success, although, as is often the way with failed Soviet weapons developments, it was nonetheless produced and deployed in limited quantities. Years later, a ballistic-missile expert with the Defense Intelligence Agency, James Miller, gave his views on the SS-13 to a Congressional committee: "This was the first Soviet attempt at an ICBM in the solid propellant field, that is, the 13. It did not prove out very well. They had problems with their (security deletion) and they had problems with their (security deletion). Therefore there were only a limited number of them deployed, 60 of them, which we think may still be deployed."

Undaunted and apparently unpenalized for its failure, the Nadiradize Bureau kept on trying. By the mid-1970s, it was testing another solid-fueled missile, which the Soviets called the RS-20 and the Americans listed as the SS-16. But the passage of time since the ill-fated SS-13 development had apparently not been sufficient for the Soviets to discover the techniques of solid fuel. The tests were a humiliating series of bangs and fizzles, with the third and topmost stage of the missile providing the most problems. By 1975, testing had ceased altogether. Fortunately for the developers, the SALT negotiations now intervened to save the Soviets from further embarrassment. The American side had been much exercised by the specter of the SS-16, not only because it might put the Soviets on a technological par with the United States, but also because there was some indication that the Soviets might make it mobile and therefore harder to target. The Soviet delegation was more than happy to assuage the American feats by agreeing to forgo any further testing, construction, or deployment of the missile. Defense Secretary Harold Brown revealed in 1980 that the SS-16 "has been flight-tested only once since 1975, and then unsuccessfully."

Nadiradize and the strategic rocket forces did manage to salvage something of their reputation from the SS-16 debacle. By removing the third stage of the SS-16, they had a missile that could manage a flight of 3,000 miles— not enough for the serious business of intercontinental warfare but sufficient for use against targets in Western

Europe and China. There was a market for such a missile because the medium-range SS-4s and SS-5s, which had first been installed in their silos in the late 1950s, were, in the words of one report, "crumbling in their silos." Furthermore, the SS-11 force, which despite its intercontinental range had been given some medium-range targets, was also due to be phased out in the late 1970s.

The SS-20, as the SS-16 sibling was called, incorporated some novel features for a medium-range missile. It was MIRVed, carrying up to three independently targeted warheads. It was also mobile, being fired not from a silo but from a self-contained transporter. Although initially attracting little attention in the West, the SS-20 achieved fame and notoriety around the time (1977 onward) that the campaign to find a European home for the new U.S. Pershing and cruise missiles began in earnest. In blithe disregard of the earlier NATO decision to base medium-range nuclear missiles at sea on submarines rather than on land, the Pentagon was able to argue successfully that the appearance of the SS-20 signified a "gap" in the Russians' favor in land-based medium-range missiles. These worries were increased by the Carter Administration's bungling of the issue of the neutron bomb. This device, yet another answer to the universally accepted "fact" of overwhelming Soviet conventional superiority, had been requested for deployment in West Germany by the then chancellor, Helmut Schmidt, in response to suggestions from Washington that he do so. President Carter then changed his mind and declared that the neutron bomb would not be sent to Europe, leaving Schmidt with the feeling that he had been made a fool of.

While this was happening, the Soviets had developed and were in the process of deploying their new SS-20 as a replacement for the antiquated SS-4s and -5s. At the same time, the United States was developing new medium-range missiles of its own—the Pershing II and the cruise missiles. The SS-20 provided a welcome justification for the production of these new systems. As with the neutron bomb, Schmidt was encouraged to play his part by requesting their deployment in Europe. Before long this deployment had become a "test" of the cohesion and strength of will of the Atlantic alliance. As a result, some observers came to believe that the SS-20 represented the "real issue" as far as the Soviet military threat was concerned, either being ignorant of or ignoring the fact that Western nuclear policy regarding Europe is and has always been predicated on the assumptions that NATO is incapable of defending itself against Soviet conventional forces without resort to nuclear weapons, and that in the event of a Soviet conventional attack the NATO response must be nuclear, whether the Pershing IIs and cruises are deployed or not.

As is so often the case with nuclear weapons, the military aspects of SS-20 deployment and the proper NATO response have been obscured by political considerations. It was certainly true that the SS-20 represents an improvement over the SS-4s and SS-5s. Most of these older missiles were vulnerable to enemy attack. Only a few were protected by concrete silos. They were liquid-fueled with all the consequent problems of reliability, and they carried only one warhead apiece. The SS-20 is powered by solid fuel, is possibly less vulnerable to enemy attack because it is fired from mobile transporters, and carries up to three individually targetable warheads. However, as one former very high-ranking CIA official put it to me, "If you are an inhabitant of Paris or any other European your chances of dying in a nuclear attack have not been increased or diminished by the replacement of the SS-4 or SS-5 by the SS-20."

The political furor that arose in the late 1970s and early 1980s over the issue of medium-range nuclear systems in

Europe owed its origins less to a quantum leap in the effectiveness of Soviet mid-range missiles than to European, particularly West German, concern about U.S. commitment to the defense of its NATO partners in the event of a Soviet attack on Western Europe. The SALT negotiations had been limited to the two superpowers without reference (at American insistence) to medium-range systems based in Europe. The worry was that in the cozy atmosphere of U.S.–Soviet détente the Western European allies were being left in the cold—maybe the Americans and the Russians could agree to limit intercontinental weapons, but where would this leave Europe itself?

The issue of the "Euromissiles" had, by 1983, come to dominate relations between the U.S. and its European allies, particularly West Germany. As is so often the case in debates about defense, any accurate assessment of military realities was given very short shrift, for the simple reason that the military significance and utility of either the U.S. or the Soviet medium-range missiles was not the main issue. One interesting depiction of the real stakes involved was expressed by Richard Perle, the Assistant Secretary of Defense for International Security Affairs. In May 1983 he told a group of Washington journalists, in an "off the record" discussion, that the cruise and Pershing II missiles had no military utility for the defense of Europe, and that in fact the decision to deploy them had been a great mistake in view of the political problems it was causing the Western alliance. However, explained Perle (one of the most obdurate hawks in the Washington national security establishment), deployment must now be pushed through because the credibility of the Western alliance was at stake.

The rules of the game required, however, that everyone pretend that the presence or absence of SS-20s, Pershings, or cruises made some difference to the military balance in

Europe. The Soviets raised far more objections to the Pershing IIs because, they asserted, its accuracy and speed meant that it could be used to eliminate command and control centers around Moscow as part of a general strategic first strike. This seems a curious alarm to raise. However ineptly the Soviet high command may comport itself, it should not be beyond its capabilities to arrange an alternative command center elsewhere in the USSR, out of range of the Pershings, to direct Soviet nuclear retaliation in the event of such a preemptive first strike.

Having raised such a hue and cry over the Pershings, the Soviets felt it necessary to threaten dire reprisals in the event of their deployment.

One of these threats was to deploy nuclear weapons, complete with warheads, in Eastern Europe for the first time. This put the U.S. in a spot, since it was anxious to reassure the West Germans that there would be no invidious consequences from the planned Pershing deployment. Secretary Weinberger therefore suggested that this was an empty threat, since the Soviets "already had" nuclear weapons in Eastern Europe. The missiles in question were recently developed short-range missiles: the SS-21, with a range of about 60 miles; the SS-23, which had a range of 200 miles; and the SS-22, with a range of about 550 miles. It is easy to see why, for political reasons, the Americans should wish to denigrate a Soviet threat that, theoretically at least, was just as ominous as the SS-20 (the SS-21, 22, and 23 were supposedly endowed with superb accuracy and would have a very short flight time from Eastern Europe to West Germany). Nevertheless, the dispassionate observer should reflect on the fact that while the SS-20 had served to justify the introduction of the Pershing and cruise missiles—the development of which long predated the appearance of the SS-20—the prospect of the other new Soviet missiles was dismissed by U.S.

policymakers as being of little account because they threatened the deployment of the U.S. missiles.

Nor, of course, was there much inclination on the part of the press and public at large to question official U.S. assessments of the SS-20's technical capabilities. Spectacular claims were advanced for the accuracy of the new missile. The CIA concluded that it could land within 400 yards of its target after a flight of 3,000 miles. The estimate was misprinted in one 1980 Agency report so as to suggest a possible SS-20 accuracy of 40 yards. This absurd figure was duly reprinted in a widely syndicated newspaper column, a fine example of the credulity traditionally attached by the press to any intelligence leak that promotes the specter of Soviet military prowess. Another press report described the SS-20's transporters as "huge, wheeled vehicles capable of rapid movement" without the authors apparently pausing to reflect how fast such a vehicle, carrying a load of as much as 40 tons, might actually be able to go.

What was not apparent from all the publicity surrounding the SS-20 was that U.S. intelligence actually knew very little about it. No one had ever seen one because the Russians had never taken the SS-20 out of its protective canister while it was in view of a photosatellite. The missile had been launched on its test flights from a site in the north of Russia, which made it very difficult for the U.S. monitoring stations along the southern borders of the Soviet Union to observe. In addition, the radio signals emitted by the missile during test flights had been encoded to an unprecedented degree, which made precise intelligence estimations of its accuracy even more difficult than usual.

The significance of the SS-20's accuracy lay in the assumption that the Soviets could thereby employ it in a first strike against NATO military emplacements without causing significant damage to adjacent civilian centers. However, as the doleful aphorism goes, "towns in West

Germany are two kilotons apart." The smallest yield for the SS-20 warhead, according to such publications as the International Institute of Strategic Studies's *Military Balance*, is 150 kilotons. Therefore, even if the SS-20 were as accurate as has been claimed, a precisely accurate strike on a West German base would have unpleasant consequences for the civilian population.

Such caveats found no place in official assessments of the SS-20 "threat," nor did anyone ask why it was that if the Soviets could develop such a superb solid-fueled missile for use on land, they were still sending their ballistic-missile submarines to sea with a cargo of liquid-fueled rockets.

For a brief period in the late 1970s, it seemed that there might have been a breakthrough in sea-borne missiles. The Soviets equipped one missile submarine with a new, solid-powered missile called the SS-NX-17 (the X denotes an experimental program). Once again the hope was unfulfilled, as the SS-NX-17 was withdrawn and not seen again. In 1980 Cholomei, which has always had a lock on Soviet naval missile development, began testing the SS-N-20, a large and solid-fueled naval missile code-named Typhoon, after the extremely large submarine that is being built to carry it. In January 1982 the Washington *Post* reported: "After observing seven tests, U.S. intelligence sources believe the Soviet Union has run into difficulty in developing its new long range submarine launched Typhoon missile." Two of the tests had been observable failures: in one test the missile had failed to get off the launch pad, and in the other, it appeared to have been destroyed in flight. On October 26, 1982, the Soviets finally carried out the long-awaited test of a new solid-fueled land-based ICBM. It blew up shortly after launch.

Grubby realities, such as incompetent defense contractors or weapons which fail to work, find little place in the considerations of members of the defense intelligentsia pursuing their well-funded existence in institutes and think tanks. Nor does military officialdom care to dwell on such verities, especially when they suggest that the threat may have been inflated. In these circles, questions relating to the primitive design of Soviet missiles tend to be answered with abstract generalizations about "differing and equally respectable philosophical approaches to problems of technology." Dr. John Kincaid is not a defense intellectual or a high defense official. He does, however, know a great deal about rocket engines because he designed most of the basic systems now used by the U.S. Navy. "Whoever thinks that the Soviets have stuck with liquids because they chose to do things that way doesn't know what they are talking about," he declares. "No one would mess around with liquids if they didn't have to. The reason the Russians do it is because they are so goddamn backward."

Threat scenarios take little note of possibilities that the Soviet or American nuclear forces might not perform as advertised. It is true that these matters are hard to quantify, since the Americans prefer not to test at all, and the comprehensive Soviet test reports, even if honestly prepared, are kept a close secret by all concerned. What features far more prominently in assessments of the threat to U.S. missile silos is the purported accuracy of the Soviet ICBMs. According to the most solemn pronouncements of U.S. defense officials, this has been steadily and ominously improving.

As with all missiles, the accuracy of Soviet ICBMs is denoted by what is called the circular error probable (CEP). CEP, strictly speaking, is not the measure of how far the missile lands from its intended target but the radius of a circle in which half the projectiles fired at a particular target will land. The hope is that the target will be somewhere near the middle of the circle. A low CEP means that missiles or warheads of a particular type will land close together; it does not mean that they will necessarily land close to the target, since the center of their impact pattern—the center of the CEP circle—may be a long distance from the target. This simple fact has the gravest implications for the whole elaborate structure on which theories about nuclear war, and the multibillion-dollar budgets that these theories are used to justify, are based.

The chances of a Soviet reentry vehicle, which is the small cone-shaped capsule containing the nuclear warhead, destroying a U.S. missile silo are computed by calculating the missile's CEP together with the yield of its explosive charge and the hardness of its target. If a particular type of missile system promises to provide a low CEP, then the size of the bomb can be correspondingly reduced, assuming that the potential victims do not strengthen the protection of their silos. Accuracy is therefore deemed to be more important than the size of the bomb, since a doubling in accuracy will have the same theoretical effect on the probability of the silo surviving as increasing the yield of the bomb by a factor of 8.

The estimation of Soviet accuracy is thus a task of high priority for U.S. intelligence, since an improvement of as little as 200 feet in the CEP can be taken to mean that 90, rather than 80, percent of the U.S. ICBM force is at risk, with momentous consequences for U.S. policy. Despite this, these crucial assessments are made on the basis of fragmentary information and highly subjective analysis.

Most Soviet missiles are tested from Tyuratam in the deserts of Kazakhstan east of the Aral Sea. They are invariably fired eastward, landing either on the Kamchatka peninsula or, on longer range flights, in the northern Pacific. During the missile's flight, instruments on board record the performance of the various subsystems, particularly the guidance mechanisms, and radio the information back to the scientists and engineers on the ground. This "telemetry," as such signals are called, has an attentive audience at the American monitoring stations along the southern borders of the USSR in Turkey, China, at sea off the Pacific coast and via the satellites kept in orbit for this purpose.

Soviet accuracy cannot be determined by simply watching to see where the missiles land. There is no giant bull's-eye painted on Kamchatka. All the Americans can do is listen in on the telemetry to find out how true the missile's trajectory is to the instructions in its computer memory. The fewer the number of correctional commands and the smaller the size of the correction issued by the guidance system, the more efficient and hence accurate the system is judged to be. The CIA is the principal agency for this mode of esoteric intelligence analysis. As it has refined its techniques, it has detected a similar refinement in Soviet missile-guidance expertise. However, its analysis does not take place in isolation. Just as the CIA must turn to defense contractors for help in estimating the cost of Soviet weapons systems, so does it rely to a certain extent on contracted assistance from U.S. missile-guidance manufacturers in determing Soviet missile accuracy. Some defense analysts consider this practice to be akin to "letting the fox into the chicken coop," as one analyst puts it. "These firms have been selling improved missile accuracy for American systems; it's only natural that they should discover the same thing happening over on the Soviet side." Thus, some analysts who have had access to the full telemetry data from the Soviet tests insist that the information shows their accuracy to be "at least twice as bad" as the official conclusions suggest.

The debate over the accuracy of the SS-9, a very large missile which first appeared in the late 1960s, illustrates how even this kind of highly technical intelligence can be warped by considerations of military politics. The SS-9, which was twice the size of a Minuteman, eventually carried three warheads, each up to 5 megatons in explosive yield. The CIA nonetheless concluded that it did not pose a threat to the Minuteman silos because its CEP was no better than 0.5 of a nautical mile. (CEPs are commonly expressed in terms of a nautical mile, which is 2,025 yards. So 0.5 is 1,012½ yards.) The CIA's conclusions were overridden by the Department of Defense, where there were powerful interests in search of a rationale for installing an antiballistic missile (ABM) system for protecting the Minuteman silos. Pentagon officials therefore chose to interpret the data on the SS-9 test shots as indicating a potential CEP of 0.25 of a nautical mile. Calculated together with the mighty wallop of the 5-megaton warhead, this provided satisfactory evidence that the Minuteman silos of the day were potentially vulnerable. Later analyses suggested that the CEP was more like 0.7 of a nautical mile, but by that time, the ABM program was under way.

The SS-17, SS-18, and SS-19, which constituted the next generation of Soviet missiles, were initially presumed to have a potential accuracy of little better than the SS-9, although they carried more warheads. Since more warheads meant smaller warheads of lower individual yield, there were grounds for complacency. This unalarmist conclusion was hotly contested by elements within both the U.S. and the Soviet military establishments. During the 1974 Moscow summit, a Soviet official approached members of the U.S. delegation and told them that the new missiles had already scored CEPs of 0.27 of a nautical mile — far better than the 0.5 figure advertised by the CIA. The Soviets may have spoken up out of simple chagrin at seeing their efforts held in such little regard, or else, as one former CIA analyst jokingly suggests, "the Politburo may have been challenging the military's internal reports of progress in missile accuracy on the basis of what they read in the American press. Experience has probably taught them that one is no more believable than the other."

In any event, American assessments of the Soviet CEPs shrank steadily from the mid-1970s on. A turning point in this process came when CIA director George Bush, conscious of the CIA's unwholesome reputation in some quarters for dovishness, appointed a team of nonprofessional analysts specially selected for their hawkishness to second-guess the professionals' conclusions. Team B, as this eccentric grouping was called, criticized the CIA's estimates of Soviet accuracy as overoptimistic and suggested that the Russians were at least as proficient as the United States in this technology.

Experts who paid closer attention to the details of Soviet missile development were less impressed. The most threatening component of the new Soviet ICBM force appeared to be the SS-18 Mod (for modification) 2. It was this version that could carry at least ten warheads, each capable of zeroing in on a Minuteman silo with uncanny accuracy. But in secret testimony before the House Armed Services Committee in 1979, the chief of the Ballistic Missile Systems Branch of the DIA, James Miller, indicated that there might be less to this fearsome weapon than met the eye. "The Mod 2 had serious problems," he told the Congressmen. "The guy who designed the postboost vehicle [the section that carries and ejects the individual warheads] is probably in Siberia because everything you could do wrong in the design of a postboost vehicle he did. . . . He really goofed it."

In the unclassified version of Miller's testimony later released to the public, the description of the designer's malfeasances are deleted for security reasons, but it appears that his mistake had been to rely on an unwieldy mechanical arm to eject the reentry vehicles instead of a microrocket, as employed by the Americans. The Soviets are now reported to have remedied this deficiency.

By 1980, Defense Secretary Harold Brown was lending the full support of his high office to the notion that the Soviets either already were or soon would be in a position to destroy the Minuteman silos. The age of total Minuteman vulnerability was supposed to dawn when the favored candidates for the mission—the SS-18 Mod 2 and the SS-19 Mod 1—had achieved a CEP of 0.1 of a nautical mile, or about 600 feet. The precise date of this turning point has been a matter of some dispute. Brown's even more hawkish successor, Caspar Weinberger, stated on at least one occasion in 1982 that Soviet missiles are "now more accurate than ours." Since the official CEP of the latest Minuteman warhead is itself supposed to be 0.1 of a nautical mile, this would imply that the era of Minuteman vulnerability had at last arrived. Unnamed Pentagon officials were, however, quick to assure the press that no Soviet missile could presently match the Minuteman for accuracy.

Weinberger had some justification for his confusion. The arcane methods and language (few people apart from professional navigators think in terms of nautical miles) of missile accuracy estimation lend an air of authority and precision to what at best is a highly subjective process. "You look at the data in one way and you think yes, that is a firm indication that the Soviets are getting much better CEPs," one former high-level strategic analyst explains, "but if you look at it in another way, with a different set of assumptions, you can come out with a quite different conclusion. It all rests on the assumptions you bring with you, and you better believe there is encouragement to assume that the Soviets are getting better."

It was Team B, curiously enough, which underlined the speculative nature of the whole business. The panel argued that since it was impossible to make a precise estimation of the enemy test missile's performance, there was no evidence to support the official CIA position that Soviet ICBMs were less accurate than the American ones. This being so, it chose to believe that the Soviets were actually more proficient than the Americans in this respect and that the hour of Minuteman vulnerability was at hand.

However much one might disparage Team B's own paranoid fantasies about the malign efficiency of the Soviet military machine, it must be admitted that the team had a point in questioning the quality of the CIA's estimation of Soviet strategic military developments, an area in which U.S. intelligence as a whole has not distinguished itself.

In the beginning, there was a tendency to underestimate Soviet capabilities. The important question of the immediate postwar era was the length of time it would take the Soviets to develop an atom bomb. Authoritative testimony came from General Leslie R. Groves, director of the Manhattan Project, who concluded on the basis of intuition bolstered by prejudice that "those Asiatic Russians" could not do it in less than twenty-five years and so informed the President. The American nuclear scientists, who knew little about intelligence but a lot about making bombs, concluded that the Soviet Union could go nuclear in four or five years. They were right.

From then on, official caution was discarded. By virtue of luck rather than good judgment (there were no actual intelligence sources on the subject), the predicted date for the first Soviet hydrogen bomb was off by only one year. In 1955 the intelligence community concurred that the Soviets would have 500 long-range nuclear bombers by 1960. The actual number turned out to be 190. In 1957 the CIA concluded on the basis of reports from its U-2 spy planes that there would be 500 Soviet ICBMs in place by 1960. Air Force intelligence read the data differently and insisted that the number should be twice as high. The actual number was four. Throughout the early 1960s there was general agreement that the Soviets would have developed and deployed no less than 10,000 antiballistic missiles (ABMs) by 1975. The number never exceeded 64. So fixated was the CIA on the prospect of all those ABMs that it failed to anticipate the very large buildup in Soviet ICBMs that did occur in the 1960s.

Inaccurate predictions about Soviet atom-bomb developments or missile deployments could be and were disproved on the evidence of spy planes and satellites. Missile silos can be counted, and so can nuclear explosions. The accuracy of missiles is a different matter. Unless and until the SS-18s start raining down on the Minuteman silos of North Dakota and elsewhere, there will be no firm conclusion because, as we shall see, even the fullest access to the files of the Tyuratam test center would tell us little about the accuracy of a Soviet missile fired not at Kamchatka but over a completely untried route.

Intercontinental missiles are not steered to their targets by any exterior guiding agency. From the moment they leave their silo, there is no way anyone can interfere with or correct their course. This is because the missile depends for guidance on what is known as inertial sensing. The simplest way to understand this is to think of a glass of water sitting on a table in an airplane with no windows. If the plane tilts up or down or rocks from side to side, the motion will be apparent in the movement of the water in the glass without any necessity to look outside. All that the inertial system does is to compare the movements of a very much more sophisticated version of the glass of water with information programmed into its computer before the flight. The computer will indicate what these movements should be if the rocket is going in the right direction. Undesirable variations can be corrected accordingly up until the moment that the last rocket engine is switched off. Once that point is passed, after about 3 minutes of flight, there is nothing more that can be done. Everything depends on the guidance system having positioned the missile correctly, since it will continue on that course like a bullet after leaving the barrel of a gun or a spear after leaving the thrower's hand. If the flight of the missile were to take place under conditions that were entirely predictable, the guidance computers could have all the necessary information fed into them before the launch, and no silo would be safe. But under the real conditions of a flight over the North Pole—the projected route for all ICBMs—and down onto the other side of the world, the missiles will encounter forces that either are imperfectly understood or are by their nature unpredictable.

The earth is not a perfect sphere. It varies significantly in composition and density, which means that the force of its gravitational pull is not constant from place to place. For example, the gravitational pull over an island in the Aleutians is different from what it is over Vandenberg Air Force Base on the California coast. And these gravity "anomalies" are far from accurately mapped. The inertial guidance system cannot tell the difference between the effect of its own motion and the effect of gravity. If an unprogrammed variation in the earth's gravitational field pulls the missile fractionally down while the engine is still burning, the guidance system will have no way of distinguishing that motion from the "sensation" it would perceive if the missile moved suddenly upward. Detecting what it records as an unprogrammed upward motion, the system will adjust the missile's trajectory accordingly, sending it off course.

There is no reason to believe that the Soviets are any less aware of this factor than the U.S. Air Force, which has spent a lot of time and effort in trying to construct a gravity map of the relevant regions. The missile generals claim that this effort has been successful, but Dr. J. Edward Anderson, who speaks with the authority of a pioneer in the guidance technology under discussion, suggests otherwise. Debating the subject with the commander of Air Force Systems Command, General Robert T. Marsh, in the specialized journal *Strategic Review*, Anderson pointed out that "an error or six seconds of arc [one six-hundredth of a degree] in computing the direction of gravity over the boost phase will cause an impact error of 300 feet." An average error of 4.2 parts per million in computing the gravitational forces over the entire course of the missile's flight would also, he calculated, cause an erosion in accuracy of 300 feet. "It is believed that [even] this accuracy is not possible to achieve reliably either by gravity field measurement or the use of a model constructed from any prelaunch information presently available."

It is theoretically possible that one day it will be possible to measure all the pertinent variations in gravity and program them into the guidance computers. It is inconceivable, even in theory, that it will ever be possible to program the computer with all the necessary information about the state of the weather over the target area on the day that the missiles are launched. This is of vital importance, since the weather, meaning all possible variations in atmospheric conditions, can make a great deal of difference to the course of an incoming warhead. For example, it has been calculated that a 30-mile-an-hour wind speed averaged throughout the height of the atmosphere (which is a low estimate considering that winds aloft can reach three or four times the speed of surface winds) could cause a warhead to drift 1,320 feet outside its lethal radius from the target.

Loath though the missile industry may be to admit that unpredictable factors can upset precise calculations, it has, in fact, tried to compensate for wind. Older warheads, such as the ones on the 1960s-vintage SS-11, had squat conical shapes, which presented a lot of drag to the atmosphere. This caused them to slow down as they descended to earth and thus rendered them particularly susceptible to the effects of wind. Both Soviet and U.S. designers, therefore, began streamlining the shape of later-model warheads, so that they passed through the atmosphere much faster and were less buffeted by the wind. But now the warheads travel fast enough to be affected by a collision with an object no more solid than a hailstone or even a drop of rain, in just the same way as an unprotected motorcyclist will have his face stung by a gentle drizzle. In a 1972 test of the new-model U.S. Mark 12 streamlined warhead, the vehicle ran into a tropical storm and almost disintegrated.

Such are the conditions which would affect the Soviet missiles launched in a first strike into the unknown. The uncertainties are even present in the test shots that produce such confident estimates of both Soviet and American CEPs, despite the fact that the missiles have been firing over the same test ranges for more than 20 years. Dr. Richard Garwin, a scientist well versed in the classified esoterica of strategic weapons technology, is quite blunt about the limited relevance of these test programs to the requirements for an operational launch over the North Pole.

In every ICBM you have an inertial package, accelerometers and gyros and things like that. You've got to fire your missiles from operational silos to points in your enemy's country. Now, obviously you've never done this before and so you have to base your calculations on test shots—in our case from Vandenberg to Kwajalein Lagoon [in the southwest Pacific], that is, east to west; and in the Russians' case west to east. Judging from how far each test shot falls from the target you adjust your accelerometer or your gyro to compensate for the inaccuracy, until in the end your test shots are landing in the prescribed area. But every time you fire a new model missile over the same range or the same missile over a slightly different range, the bias changes. Sometimes it is greater, sometimes it is smaller, but it never has been calculated beforehand. So you have to go back to adjusting the gyros and so on to try and eliminate the novel bias. But if we were firing operationally, both we and the Russians would be firing over a new range in an untried direction—north. And a whole new set of random factors would come into play— anomalies in the earth's gravitational field, varying densities of the upper atmosphere or unknown wind velocities. [The Russians] may adjust and readjust in testing and eventually they may feel sure that they have eliminated the bias. But they can never be absolutely certain. We certainly cannot be; and although we are less well informed about the Soviet ICBM test program than our own there is no reason to suspect that they are any more successful than we are at dealing with the problem. If you cannot be sure that you will be able to hit the enemy's silos then there is no point in even trying.

It is important to understand that the uncertainties summarized by Garwin are not surmountable by some quantum leap in weapons technology. It would be possible, for example, to steer the warheads precisely onto their targets by means of radio signals from the ground or from orbiting satellites, except that it would be a relatively simple matter for the enemy to jam these signals without even going to the trouble of destroying the transmitting stations. A warhead could steer itself onto the target if it was equipped with a radar to scan the target area, which it could then compare with a radar image of the target stored in its computer memory. This indeed is the guidance method employed in the U.S. Army's Pershing II missile. But again, such ingenuity is easily frustrated. The enemy need only periodically change the shape of the target silo as it is perceived on radar by rearranging a series of aluminum sheet radar reflectors for the incoming missile warheads to be totally spoofed.

Nor can relief be found by increasing the yield of the warhead. There has been a great deal of perturbation among hawks about the enormous destructive power of the big Soviet missiles, a factor otherwise referred to as large throw weight. But the throw weight of a missile is, in fact, nothing more than the weight of all the various components, such as the guidance systems and heat shield that sit on top of the rocket engines. It does not necessarily have anything to do with the power of the actual bomb. For example, the latest U.S. warhead, the Mark 12A, is only 2 percent heavier than the slightly older Mark 12, yet it has twice the explosive yield. In addition, it should be said that no one outside certain select and secretive Soviet circles actually knows the yield of the nuclear devices carried by Soviet missiles. Like much else to do with nuclear weapons, the intelligence assessments are purely a matter of conjecture, based on the size of Soviet underground tests and extrapolations from practice and experience with U.S. warheads.

Paradoxically, the sum of all the *uncertainties*—unpredictable weather patterns, the inconsistency of guidance systems even when traveling over familiar routes, the dubious reliability of missile systems—leads us to one *certainty*: a precisely orchestrated Soviet counterforce strike against American missiles as they are now deployed is absolutely impossible.

No less a figure than Dr. James R. Schlesinger, a former CIA director, Secretary of Defense, and senior strategic analyst at the Rand Corporation, tried to make this very clear in testimony presented to the Senate Foreign Relations Committee in April 1982:

The precision that one encounters in paper studies of nuclear exchanges reflects the precision of the assumptions rather than any experience based on approximation-to-real-life test data. Specialists, in their enthusiasm, tend to forget how conjectural the whole process remains. To a greater or lesser degree we are employing speculation regarding delivery system reliability and accuracy, reliability of the nuclear weapons, and the impact of weapons effects. This introduces vastly greater than normal uncertainties into such paper analyses. We must be careful therefore not to ignore these dominating uncertainties and thereby to ascribe high probability to the outcomes projected in these paper studies. To do so would be to fall into the error that Alfred North Whitehead once described as "the fallacy of misplaced concreteness."

Happily no one has ever fought a nuclear war. Not only have ICBMs never been tested in flying operational trajectories against operational targets, they have not been tested flying north and this may or may not introduce certain areas of bias in the estimates of accuracy. Nuclear weapons have never flown 6,500 miles through space with the accompanying acceleration and deceleration and therefore we have no real test data regarding failure rates. Consequently, neither the Soviet Union nor ourselves have appropriate test data to buttress the estimates regularly made about either nation's strategic forces. For leaders on either side, that may be enticed into considering the utility of a major nuclear strike, I would hope there would always be somebody there under such hypothetical circumstances to remind them of these realities.

For these reasons, perhaps the dominant element in measuring nuclear forces against each other is the unknown and immeasurable element of the possibility of major technical failure. It would tend to dominate any outcome. Given the spotty Soviet history in dealing with modern technologies, one would hypothesize that this must be a constant worry of the Soviet leaders— regardless of what others abroad may say about the supposed superiority of their forces. We ourselves know a great deal more about helicopter operations and maintenance than we do about actual missile operations. Yet if we recall the abortive rescue operation in Iran in 1980 even we—with a far more impressive history of technical success—should bear in mind the salient element.

Schlesinger's warnings about the "dominating uncertainties" strike at the very heart of the military's basic policy for dealing with the existence of nuclear weapons. For without precision, the entire rationale for nuclear-war fighting and thus the assumptions that nuclear devices can be used as weapons like any other fall totally apart. This is a concept the military on either side cannot entertain.

The ongoing confrontation between East and West has made it possible for the armed bureaucracies to justify each and every initiative in the field of weapons development as a defensive maneuver. Thus, the costly programs under the Reagan and Carter Administrations could be presented as a response not only to Soviet actions— the development of more accurate missiles—but also to Soviet plans for nuclear war. Influential and hawkish intellectuals, such as Richard Pipes and Amoretta M. Hoeber (who was appointed Assistant Secretary of the Army in 1981), have argued passionately that the Soviets do not view nuclear war as a simple matter of mutual obliteration and therefore something to be avoided at all costs. To support their contention that the Soviets conceive of nuclear war as something that can be fought and won, they and others quote liberally from the pages and statements of Soviet military spokesmen.

What these hawks choose to ignore, of course, is that the clearly stated policy of the *U.S.* military is also to treat nuclear war as just another kind of conflict. Robert McNamara spelled this out in a secret speech to the NATO Defense Ministers as long ago as 1962: "The United States has come to the conclusion that to the extent feasible, basic military strategy in general nuclear war should be approached in much the same way that more conventional military operations have been regarded in the past." In 1981 another Defense Secretary, Harold Brown, made it clear that little had changed: "U.S. nuclear forces have always been designed against military targets. . . . In particular, we have always considered it important, in the event of war, to be able to attack the forces that could do damage to the United States and its allies."

Statements by national security officials of the Reagan Administration on the subject of nuclear war make the opinion of their predecessors seem positively demure. Caspar Weinberger's Fiscal Year 1983 budget statement proclaimed bluntly that "U.S. defense policies ensure our preparedness to respond to and, if necessary, successfully fight either conventional or nuclear war." The influential White House aide Thomas Reed told a gathering of defense contractors in June 1982 that "prevailing with pride is the principal new ingredient of American security policy." His remarks, according to the New York *Times* report of the speech, had been personally approved by President Reagan.

That being said, a selective perusal of Soviet statements on the subject suggests that similarly chilling notions are current in Moscow. "Mass nuclear missile strikes at the armed forces of the opponent and at his key economic and political objectives can determine the victory of one side and the defeat of the other at the very beginning of the 'war,'" declare the authors of *Marxism-Leninism on War and Army*, published by the Ministry of Defense in 1972. "Therefore a correct estimate of the elements of supremacy over the opponent and the ability to use them before the opponent does are the key to victory in such a war."

The more one examines the slogans penned for internal

consumption by various members of the military establishment on either side, the more apparent it becomes that the military feels the need to reject notions that nuclear war is unthinkable. Field Manual FM 287, issued in February 1980, declares staunchly that "the U.S. Army must be prepared to fight and win when nuclear weapons are used," a statement not too far removed in spirit from these words written by the Soviet General A. S. Milovidov in 1974: "There is profound error and harm in the disorienting claims of bourgeois ideologues that there will be no victor in a nuclear war."

Statements by political leaders to the effect that the whole notion of fighting and winning nuclear wars is hard to take seriously parallel these bellicose military statements. Brezhnev declared in October 1981: "It is a dangerous madness to try and defeat each other in the arms race and to count on victory in nuclear war in the hope of emerging a victor from it. No matter what the attacker might possess, no matter what method of unleashing nuclear war he chooses, he will not attain his aims. Retribution will ensue ineluctably."

Only those who preserve an unshakable faith in the monolithic structure of the Soviet state, with every political element, both military and civilian, subordinated to a single long-term plan, can believe that statements like Brezhnev's are merely disinformation, designed to lull the West into a false sense of security. Since it is evident that the Soviet state is not a monolith and that the military is a bureaucracy far more intent on promoting its own internal self-interest than in addressing the realities of war, there is little need to pursue such elaborate conspiracy theories.

A telling example of what really concerns the military bureaucracy is to be found in the attacks on the retired General Nikolai Talensky in 1965. Talensky had been so bold as to write an article stating: "In our days there can

be no more dangerous illusion than the idea that thermonuclear war can still serve as an instrument of politics,
that it is possible to achieve political aims by using nuclear
weapons and still survive." This heresy brought an immediate and vehement response from serving officers, who
rushed into the military press to criticize him by name,
something that rarely happens to eminent Soviet generals.
They did not, however, take issue with Talensky's views
on nuclear weapons; the objections were to his having
stated them in public. Such loose talk, his attackers made
clear, was tactless in the extreme because it could dangerously undermine the case for a strong and prosperous
military establishment in the Soviet Union. For example,
General K. Bochkarev, deputy commandant of the General
Staff Academy, complained that if ideas like those expressed by Talensky took hold, "the armed forces of the
socialist states . . . will not be able to set for themselves
the goal of defeating imperialism and the global nuclear
war which it unleashes and the mission of attaining victory
in it, and our military science should not even work out
a strategy for the conduct of war since the latter has lost
its meaning and its significance. . . . *In this case, the very
call to raise the combat readiness of our armed forces and
improve their capability to defeat any aggressor is senseless* [my emphasis]."

It may seem hard to believe that a country's armed
forces could treat nuclear strategy as simply another counter
in the game of winning funds and influence. But the changing attitudes of the U.S. Navy toward nuclear weapons
show that this kind of game playing is not confined to the
USSR. When American nuclear weapons were the sole
prerogative of the U.S. Air Force, the U.S. Navy argued
forcefully against their acquisition. "We consider," Admiral Ralph Oftsie told the Congress in 1948, "that strategic air warfare is militarily unsound, morally wrong, and

decidedly harmful to the stability of a future world war."
When submarines armed with long-range Polaris nuclear
missiles became a practical possibility, Admiral Oftsie
returned to Congress to testify with enthusiasm in favor
of strategic attacks on enemy cities, using Polaris.

Some people in the West, particularly those who are
aware of the more lurid aspects of American nuclear-war
planning, tend to argue that the Soviets do indeed plan
their forces rationally but that their initiatives can be explained as simply a reaction to bellicose moves by the
Americans.

It is certainly true that the United States has set the
fashion in strategic weaponry. The United States was the
first to build an atom bomb, the first to develop intercontinental bombers, the first to put missiles in silos, and the
first to MIRV its ICBMs. In every case, the Soviets have
followed suit as best they could. This rationale does paint
Soviet behavior in a more reasonable light. But in many
instances, the original initiatives were prompted by reasons
that had little to do with increasing U.S. capabilities *vis-
à-vis* the Soviet Union. In such cases, there was no particular reason why the Soviets should have slavishly followed along.

For example, in 1964 Defense Secretary Robert
McNamara informed the U.S. Air Force that its force of
Minuteman ICBMs would be frozen at a limit of 1,000
missiles. The Air Force, irked at this constraint, immediately began exploring the possibility of putting more than
one warhead on top of the missiles, a process later called
MIRVing. MIRVed missiles are much less accurate than
those carrying only a single warhead, since the action of
jettisoning each MIRV has the effect of throwing the post-
boost vehicle carrying the remainder slightly off course.
Still, this stratagem allowed the Air Force to evade the
spirit of McNamara's order. In fact, McNamara endorsed

the MIRV development program, because it helped him enforce the 1,000-missile limit.

The strategic rocket forces of the Soviet Union were not bound by McNamara's edicts, and so there was no reason why they should also have adopted MIRVing, but they did so nonetheless. While this may have saved some money on rockets and concrete silos, these items form such a small portion of overall defense budgets that cost could not have been the determining factor. Even by CIA estimates, the annual cost to the Soviets of their *entire* ICBM construction program rarely exceeded $6 billion during the 1970s, or about one-thirtieth of their overall defense budget.

Dr. Herbert York, who helped lay down much of the basic framework for present-day U.S. strategic forces from various august Pentagon posts, has a sardonic explanation for the present size of the Soviet strategic forces:

The Russians today have a strategic force of roughly 2400 missiles and bombers. The reason they have that many is because that is the number we planned to build in the early 1960s, when our present force was laid down, and they have simply copied it. The reason we decided on that number at that time was because we were changing over from a strategic force [composed purely] of bombers, and we couldn't have proposed to replace it with anything smaller. The reason we had [that number of] nuclear bombers in the 1950s was because the force had been based on the number of bombers we had for attacking the enemy in World War II. That number had been determined by the number of planes we could build in the war years, the number of crews we could train in that time, the number of airfields we could maintain overseas, and so on. It does not seem such a rational basis for planning Soviet strategic forces.

Victories won by various factions in disputes within the Pentagon can be very useful to their counterparts in

Moscow, though the benefits for Soviet defense are harder to detect. In the early 1950s, the U.S. Army, regretful at being excluded from the "nuclear club" then exclusively inhabited by the U.S. Air Force, succeeded in developing a heavy artillery gun that fired nuclear shells a distance of 20 miles or so. The Soviet ground forces insisted on being allowed to follow suit, and so an even more enormous nuclear cannon was duly constructed. These guns were so heavy that they could only travel on well-built roadways; and were in fact kept in permanent storage except for the annual Red Square parades. Khrushchev thought that the construction of these useless weapons was "pointless imitation . . . showing the smallness of the military mind."

Notwithstanding the many examples of pointless imitation, there are some significant differences between the organization of the Soviet nuclear forces and their American counterparts. The circumstances of domestic U.S. military politics have ensured the continual existence of a nuclear "triad" of Navy missiles, Air Force missiles, and Air Force bombers. The U.S. Army, swatted out of the strategic nuclear business by the Air Force in 1956, managed to sidle back in by the early 1980s with its long-range Pershing II missile, purportedly capable of hitting Moscow if launched from West Germany.

In the Soviet Union, by contrast, the strategic rocket forces have scooped the pool. Their force of 1,398 land-based ICBMs carries three-quarters of the available Soviet strategic megatonnage, as opposed to the U.S. ICBM's 25 percent share in the triad. Soviet technical deficiencies undoubtedly contributed to this ascendancy; the Soviets were unable to build a satisfactory bomber, and the submarines were forced to rely on the dangerous liquid-fueled missiles. Nevertheless, technical problems need not in themselves cramp the style of an ambitious military clique.

The U.S. Air Force has turned the supposed vulnerability of its missiles to advantage, even though the obvious response might be to put all U.S. missiles on invulnerable submarines.

The Air Force has managed to persuade successive Administrations and Congresses to allow it to develop a new missile—the MX—which will be based in a mode that will somehow frustrate the Soviet targeteers. At the time of this writing, the preferred stratagem is a concept called dense pack, in which the missiles' silos will be bunched close together on the assumption that the fratricidal effects of the first Soviet warhead to explode would discommode other warheads following close behind before they could destroy the adjacent silos.

Even if the Soviet bomber and submarine industries were able to come up with technically more accomplished products, it would be hard to shake the political dominance of the strategic rocket forces. These forces were set up at a time when Khrushchev was trying to trim the size and appetites of the other services. They were given responsibility for all land-based missiles with ranges of more than 1,000 km (620 miles).

The ground forces were the major losers in this shake-up. Khrushchev announced a major cut in troop levels only a month after the official inauguration of the strategic rocket forces. Naturally disinclined to accept the premise that nuclear missiles had rendered them obsolete, the ground forces commanders set out to demonstrate that these devices should complement rather than replace more traditional weapons and modes of land warfare. For example, Chief Marshal of Armored Forces Pavel Rotmistrov argued forcefully from the late 1950s on that tanks could easily be adapted so as to play a useful part on battlefields irradiated by nuclear explosions.

Eventually it was agreed that despite the "revolution in

military affairs" caused by the new weapons, there was a place for everybody in Soviet military doctrine, and thus the army was instructed that "units and sub-units must be prepared to fight with or without the use of the nuclear rocket weapon." Exhortations of this kind have been greeted with enthusiasm by Western military analysts. In a typical compliment to the farsighted efficiency of the Soviet commanders, a Pentagon consultant wrote in 1977: "More than in any Western army the Soviets attempted to integrate nuclear weapons into their theatre warfare operational concepts."

It is certainly true that Soviet military academics discuss the use of nuclear weapons on the battlefield as do the authors of U.S. military manuals. Nevertheless, as one researcher has pointed out, "Statements in these Soviet volumes which deal with the nature of tactical nuclear warfare are phrased in a tone which is a mixture of the exhortative and the predictive—such and such shall happen," which is "nothing short of bizarre and unrealistic. They might best be described as being dreamlike."

That this should be so is not surprising. It is hard to see how realistic plans could be drawn up for integrating weapons that have never been used and rarely tested into the operations of a force that is otherwise based on the lessons of the Great Patriotic War. Observers who have attended U.S. Army exercises which simulate the introduction of nuclear weapons report a similar atmosphere of unreality, which is compounded by the fact that U.S. units train on the assumption that Soviet practices conform to their own. U.S. tactical nuclear weapons tend to be low in yield and, to a certain extent, accurate in their delivery. What little is known of the Soviet tactical weapons that GIs would actually face in a war suggests that these weapons are considerably more crude. One of the principal Soviet tactical missiles, with a range of about 50 miles, is the Frog (free rocket over ground). During the 1973 Mideast war, the Egyptians fired a number of these with nonnuclear warheads at Israeli bases on the Sinai. None of them did any damage, and one missed by 18 miles. Others, used by the Syrians against military targets in the north, were so far off course that the Israelis thought they were aimed at civilian settlements and reacted accordingly against Syrian population centers, a useful example of the unpredictable consequences that can attend the use of these types of weapons.

While the Soviets have followed the U.S. example in equipping themselves with nuclear battlefield weapons and devising speculative rationales for their employment, they do at least acknowledge that such weapons would be unlikely to be used in isolation. Americans find it easier to conceive of a "tactical" or "theater" nuclear war in Europe, from which the continental United States might be insulated by the broad expanses of the Atlantic Ocean and unspoken agreement between the superpowers. The Soviets have made it clear that they do not believe in this kind of finesse. To them, any kind of nuclear exchange will mean a general exchange, whether the first warhead to arrive is a U.S. Army Pershing II, deployed in support of beleaguered ground troops, or a Strategic Air Command Minuteman. Such a position makes it all the more pointless that the Soviet ground forces should be equipped and trained to fight nuclear battles in a war that is otherwise presumed to have conventional patterns of conflict—taking ground, knocking out enemy command centers, and so forth.

"Tactical nuclear warfare," wrote General Arthur Collins, a former deputy commander in chief of the U.S. Army in Europe, "is not a rational form of warfare. Proponents for nuclear warfare, both civilian and military, are prone to stress weapons effects on the enemy. They have not been nearly as objective and thorough about what might happen if the tactical nuclear weapons were used on our forces. That is why the doctrine is not persuasive when subjected to critical review."

It has, of course, been the argument of this book that there is very little military rationale to be found in any of the activities of the superpowers' armed forces. The prevailing attitude toward nuclear "weapons" is the most obvious example of this, but the care and attention devoted to chemical weapons must run as a close second.

Chemical weapons have been used in combat between regular armies only briefly, and that was a long time ago. Developed by the Germans early in World War I because they anticipated a shortage of high explosives for more conventional ordnance, they were very successful when first used in 1915 against unprepared and unprotected troops. But as soon as the opposing armies on the Western Front had adopted the use of protective clothing—primitive face masks—their effectiveness dropped sharply. One aspect of the relative usefulness of a weapon can be quantified by the number of enemy troops that a given amount can put out of action, compared with the casualties meted out by an equivalent amount of some other weapon. By this criterion, a ton of mustard gas, the most lethal agent employed in World War I, was inflicting no more damage by 1918 than a ton of high-explosive shells. Research into these lethal agents has made great strides since that time; modern nerve gases are odorless, colorless, and kill in minutes. However, the development of protective masks and suits has more than kept pace, with the result that the comparative lethality of these weapons has not improved.

The other drawback of chemical weapons is that they are extremely hard to use in any precise manner. This point was forcefully demonstrated during one 1980 U.S. Army exercise in West Germany. The war-game scenario called for the introduction of chemical weapons, so the army released some nonlethal tear gas. Unfortunately, the wind changed and the gas blew across the fields and into a nearby village, resulting in the hospitalization of three shocked and indignant hausfraus. Furthermore, while a bomb or shell is lethal only at the moment it explodes, the effects of chemical agents persist over time in ways that may inconvenience the user, especially if he is trying to advance.

The disadvantages of chemical weapons are less significant if the intended victims are unprotected civilians or guerrillas (or vegetation, as in the U.S. defoliation program in Vietnam). Poison gas has enjoyed great popularity with "advanced" nations engaged in campaigns against troublesome Third World populations. The British took large stocks with them during their expedition into Afghanistan in 1919; the Italians deposited large quantities on the Abyssinians in 1935–37; and the Egyptians employed it during their counterinsurgency campaign in Yemen in the mid-1960s. Whatever the official purpose of the U.S. defoliation program may have been, the effects of Agent Orange on any humans who came into contact with it were certainly horrible enough. Thus, reports that chemical weapons have been used by Vietnamese forces to put down the natives in Laos or by the Soviets in Afghanistan certainly gibe with the grand tradition of the chemical warriors. But the specter invoked by the Pentagon concerns the capability of the Soviet military to attack and defeat modern Western armies, not poorly equipped Third World tribesmen.

Despite their questionable effectiveness, chemical weapons enjoy vigorous support in both the Soviet and the U.S. forces. Both armies maintain units of specialized chemical troops. The Soviet chemical corps is larger, numbering 100,000 men, as opposed to the 8,000 in the U.S.

Army. This does not indicate a great disparity of commitment to this kind of armament. It simply means that all chemical weapons in the Soviet forces are the responsibility of specialized troops, while in the U.S. forces the ordinary soldiery is also trained to handle them.

Although the scale of the Soviet chemical effort is impressive, it is important to understand that this effort involves more than just poison gas. For example, the Soviets consider smoke, a commonplace technique for hiding troop movements, to be a chemical weapon. As Christopher Donnelly of the Royal Military Academy at Sandhurst points out, "this fact alone may be enough to account for the wide differences in Western estimates of Soviet stocks of chemical munitions." The Soviets also class napalm, as used by the United States in Vietnam, and tear gas, as employed by the British in Ulster, as chemical weapons. In view of this, the uproar over chemical weapons in Afghanistan must seem somewhat hypocritical to the Soviets.

The Pentagon brochure *Soviet Military Power* refers to the Soviet forces as being "better equipped...than any other military force in the world to conduct offensive and defensive chemical warfare operations." This conveys a rather distorted picture, since their specialized chemical warfare equipment has considerable shortcomings. The rubber suits and masks designed to protect soldiers against the effects of both poisonous chemicals and nuclear radiation are not normally worn for more than two hours at a stretch, and when exercises are held in which troops wear suits and respirators for up to 10 hours at a time, these are reported in triumphant terms in the Soviet press. One reason that rubber suits cannot be worn for very long is that they become exceedingly hot. The Soviet method of dealing with this is to pour a bucket of water over the perspiring soldier every half hour.

The bulk of a chemical unit's equipment is defensive,

designed to wash off chemical agents that may have contaminated its own side's tanks and other vehicles. The Soviets have a device for this purpose, the TMS-65, which consists of a modified jet engine mounted on the back of the truck. It does the job by blowing hot water or decontamination fluid onto the contaminated tank. The appearance of a TMS-65 at the Kabul Airport in the early days of the Afghan invasion caused great excitement in the Western press, since it was presumed to indicate that the Soviets intended to use chemical weapons on a large scale. As it turned out, the vehicle was there to perform a more innocent function—blowing snow off runways. But even when it is being used for chemical-warfare purposes, the results may be counterproductive. According to Dr. Julian Perry-Robinson of the University of Sussex, "This could be used to clear off some highly volatile agents, but for a lot of the most commonly used agents like Soman [a semi-persistent nerve gas] the only effect would be to burn it into the surface of the tank which would then be covered with a coat of highly poisonous glue for some time afterwards."

The rudimentary nature of the Soviets' defensive chemical measures is sometimes seen as a sure indication of their aggressive intentions. Since these measures would be of little help in the event of a NATO chemical attack, it is argued, the Russians must therefore be planning first use of chemical weapons, in which case their protective equipment would allow the Soviets to advance through the areas they had just attacked.

Unfortunately for this scenario, the same logic can be applied to show that the United States is purely concerned with offensive chemical weapons. Anyone who has seen the U.S. Army film of a training exercise at Vogulsang in West Germany, in which headquarters staff attired in full protective gear are shown attempting to carry out their normal functions, must rapidly conclude that the Americans are fully resolved to use chemical weapons for offensive purposes only. In actual fact, it would be a mistake to look for a coherence in the activities of the chemical bureaucracies in the United States and the Soviet Union which is not there. Close examination reveals yet again that the objectives of these warriors hardly extend beyond the provision of dubious justifications for the support and increased prosperity of their respective organizations.

The convenient assumption that Soviet shortcomings merely provide telling evidence of aggressive intent has a wider application. When I asked Senator John Tower, chairman of the Senate Armed Services Committee and a prominent conduit of taxpayers' largesse for the Pentagon, whether the notoriously low state of readiness of the Soviet strategic nuclear forces did not provide grounds for complacency, he replied that this indicated that the Soviets did not fear an attack from the West and could count on readying their own forces for an attack at a time of their own choosing.

It is this kind of thinking that detects coherence and deliberation in every aspect of Soviet military activity and which has elevated the Soviet military institutions designed for defense in a nuclear war to the status of major threats to the peace and security of the United States and its allies.

Nuclear deterrence rests on the assumption that one side, if attacked, can retaliate and obliterate its attacker. The 650,000 men in the Soviet air and civil defense forces are dedicated to the task of frustrating a nuclear strike on the USSR. In the view of hawks, such as Richard Pipes, such defensive preparations provide clear evidence that the Soviets do not accept "the rules of the game" in nuclear deterrence. If the Soviet Union could indeed frustrate an enemy nuclear attack, something the United States as yet makes no pretense of being able to do, then it would indeed have an advantage in a superpower confrontation. A closer look at the forces maintained ostensibly for this purpose suggests that the Soviet leaders have few grounds for complacency, if indeed they take the idea very seriously in the first place.

Thirteen

Air Defense

The troops of national air defense were set up as a separate force in 1948, a year before the first Soviet nuclear test explosion. This was also long before the missile age, so the only way the Americans could exercise their nuclear monopoly was by using bombers. It therefore seems reasonable that the Soviets should have set up as a viable response to the American threat this force of two striking arms—antiaircraft units and interceptor planes—which reached a size of 550,000 men in the early 1950s. Bombers, unlike missiles, can be intercepted and shot down. The antibomber mission was of such overriding importance that up until the early 1970s all Soviet fighters were designed primarily to intercept incoming bombers rather than to combat enemy fighters or support ground troops.

During the 1950s the Americans also constructed an air defense force of considerable dimensions, but when both sides began deploying ballistic nuclear missiles, the U.S. force was downgraded as expensive and irrelevant. Meanwhile, the Soviet air defense service, or PVO (*Protivo-vozdushnaya oborona*) as it is commonly called after the Russian initials, kept right on expanding, acquiring new fighters and missiles to deal with the diminishing threat of enemy bombers and steadily eating up 15 percent of the Soviet defense budget.

The Americans, noting the strong emphasis placed on strategic defense by the Soviets, assumed that they would take the logical step of constructing defenses against ballistic missiles. Such forebodings appeared confirmed when the Soviet Union began developing a new kind of defensive missile system. By 1964, U.S. intelligence was predicting that every major city in the USSR would have protection against U.S. missiles before too long and that there would be no less than 10,000 such missiles in place by 1975. Confirmation of these gloomy estimates came from the official statements of Soviet leaders. Khrushchev boasted that the Soviet Union had a missile that could hit "a fly in outer space," while Marshal Sergei S. Biryuzov, the commander of the strategic rocket forces, claimed in 1963 that Russia had successfully solved the problem of destroying rockets in flight.

A Soviet air defense missile code-named Griffon, which was under development in the mid-1960s, aroused particular concern within U.S. intelligence. It was obviously intended for use against targets at high altitude. By this time, U.S. bombers were practicing to fly into Russia at extremely low altitudes, so that if Griffon were an anti-bomber weapon, it would have nothing to shoot at. It was therefore concluded that the missile must be an ABM. Later analysis of the radar systems that helped guide the missile revealed that the Griffon was indeed intended as a defense against (nonexistent) high-flying bombers. Apparently unruffled by the utter pointlessness of this weapon, the air defense service proceeded to build and install no less than 1,800 Griffons.

In 1964 the Soviets did display a missile genuinely intended as an ABM in the annual Red Square parade, while at the same time the air defense service began to make grandiose references to a new command called the PRO, antirocket defense. Eventually 64 of these missiles, which the Americans code-named Galosh, were deployed around Moscow.

Although the Americans considered the Galosh primitive by the standards of their own (projected) ABMs— its radars, for example, had to physically rotate to follow targets rather than tracking them electronically—*all* ABMs suffer from an overriding and insuperable defect. The designers are not optimistic enough to imagine that they can actually hit the incoming warheads or even get close enough to destroy them with a conventional explosion. ABMs are therefore designed to carry nuclear warheads, so that their blast will be sufficient to destroy everything within a radius of several miles. Unfortunately, a nuclear explosion generates more than just a blast; it also creates a huge cloud of electrically charged particles, which, among other things, renders the sky totally opaque to radar. Thus, the first Galosh might just possibly be able to destroy one enemy warhead; but thereafter, the entire system around a particular target, such as Moscow, would be entirely "blind" and therefore useless.

The consequences of an ABM detonation are, however, more far-reaching than that. The science writer William Broad has pointed out what would have happened if the U.S. Spartan antiballistic missile had successfully intercepted a Soviet warhead: "Upon nearing the Soviet warhead, at a height of perhaps 160 miles, the Spartan would have silently turned into a ball of nuclear fire. Unfortunately, the fireball would have also bathed the United

States with a high voltage wave [electromagnetic pulse], which would in turn have knocked out unprotected communications equipment from coast to coast and shut down the U.S. power grid." The effect of an exploding Galosh on Soviet communications and power supplies could be no less severe.

While there are efforts in the United States at least to overcome the EMP problem by devising a nonnuclear ABM, such projects belong in the realm of science fiction rather than reality. Such a missile would have to intercept a target traveling at a speed of about 7,000 meters a second with an accuracy, in order to destroy it, of about 20 or 30 feet. Given the spotty record of conventionally armed antiaircraft missiles in hitting aircraft traveling very much more slowly and at lower altitudes, these projects seem far-fetched, to say the least.

Since there appeared to be little prospect of overcoming these problems, both the Soviet and American high commands were not too reluctant to agree to the 1972 treaty banning any further deployment of ABMs beyond the limited systems which were already in place. The PVO, however, seeing that an avenue of profitable expansion was being summarily closed off, were not so complaisant. Marshal Batitsky, the PVO commander, went so far as to publish objections to the ABM agreement, delivering gloomy warnings of the possible consequences for Soviet security.

Batitsky's forebodings about what the ABM treaty might mean for his own service were to a certain extent justified, since the PVO's share of the overall defense budget declined somewhat during the 1970s. By the CIA's calculations at least, the air defense forces were receiving about 15 percent of the budget at the beginning of the decade and not more than 12 percent at the end. The high command did, however, add a sweetener to soften the blow of the ABM cutback, since the production of antibomber interceptor fighters increased by as much as a third in the years immediately following 1972.

The results of the largesse distributed to the PVO over the years are certainly imposing in size. The whole air defense system comprises a network of 5,000 radar installations, 10,000 antiaircraft missile launchers, and 1,600 interceptor fighter planes. This array is controlled from a central headquarters and command center in Moscow, to which various regional command centers report.

The existence of this vast network has for many years provided both benefits and difficulties for the American bomber lobby. On the one hand, opponents of continued development of U.S. strategic nuclear bombers can and do point to the formidable appearance of the Soviet air defenses, suggesting that any attempt to penetrate these defenses will be a waste of money. This has been a favored argument for liberals, who find it convenient to show respect for this particular aspect of the Soviet threat, since such an argument offers the chance to attack Pentagon defense spending plans without appearing "soft" on Soviet military power.

Once the necessity of retaining long-range bombers as part of the U.S. strategic nuclear arsenal is accepted, however, the apparently formidable nature of Soviet air defenses becomes positively advantageous. Because of these defenses, previous bombers, such as the B-52, can be derided as obsolete, and their replacements, such as the B-1 and the Stealth, must of necessity be very sophisticated technologically and consequently enormously costly. As we shall see, the PVO, in fact, does not justify either of these arguments.

There is nothing to indicate that the PVO differs in any substantial degree from the other Soviet armed services as far as actual conditions for the men and officers are concerned. Former troops of national air defense give the same accounts of endemic drunkenness, wholesale theft of vital equipment, racism, and stereotyped training as other veterans. The route to higher rank for PVO officers lies through the familiar expedients of intrigue and collusion rather than the exercise of professional competence.

Viktor Belenko, who, as we recall, defected to Japan with his MiG-25, was an interceptor pilot with the PVO rather than a regular air force pilot. The Chuguyevka base, where he served and whose chaotic conditions he has described vividly, was a key element in the air defenses of Vladivostok, the most important naval base in the Soviet Far East. The émigré journalist Victor Sokolov was put to work on the construction of vital radars around Moscow during his military service, and yet there too the troops ruined equipment by cleaning it with gasoline instead of the precious alcohol or else stole anything that was movable and of value to sell on the black market. It was a senior PVO officer who gave Genady, the conscript from Leningrad posted to the far north, a token sentence for threatening an officer with a weapon in order to safeguard his own promotion.

Nor does the equipment of the air defense service appear to be any more reliable than, for example, tanks. The radars and missiles of the air defense forces suffer problems of reliability, just like the tanks and armored troop carriers of the ground forces. "The SAM is a bitch," a technician working on a captured sample at the White Sands Missile Range in New Mexico declares flatly. "It breaks down every hour." The long-range aircraft-spotting radar that Genady helped operate on the arctic island of Novaya Zemlya in 1973 and 1974 was out of action on one occasion for an entire month and could not be repaired until the necessary spare part was shipped from Murmansk. Pyotr, who served on a low-altitude SAM-3 battery in

Lithuania in the early 1970s, told me that his unit operated on a system of one month on, one month off, in order that there be time to properly service the complex equipment of the missile system.

The acid test of combat use has shown that the missiles that form the backbone of the PVO have severe limitations, but there is no indication that these are taken into account in the training of the crews. It is worth citing the record of the SAM-2, which, although no longer produced, is still the most widely deployed Soviet antiaircraft missile. First introduced in 1959, it scored a spectacular early success by shooting down Francis Gary Powers' U-2 spy plane in May 1960 (after several attempts). This forced the Americans to rely on satellites rather than aircraft for reconnoitering the Soviet Union, but the missile proved less successful at keeping enemy bombers out of the sky. Between 1965 and 1972 the North Vietnamese fired 9,158 USSR-supplied SAM-2s at U.S. Air Force and Navy planes. Out of this number, only 150 actually scored a hit, or 61 SAMs per American raider destroyed. By 1968 it was taking at least 200 SAMs to get a kill. Most of the U.S. planes in use over North Vietnam were relatively small and maneuverable fighter-bombers, as opposed to the big B-52s, which would be the PVO's main target over the Soviet Union. There was only a brief period when the big, slow, and unmaneuverable B-52s appeared over the North, during the Christmas bombing of Hanoi in 1972, and then the SAMs' kill rate was no better than 2 percent.

The SAM was ineffective because the intended victims quickly developed relatively simple countermeasures. The missile's guidance system depends on a radar on the ground that tracks both the target and the missile. This information is automatically fed into a computer, which then directs the missile by radio signals. The Americans found that if they maneuvered their planes in a quickly reversing turn, the guidance system could not redirect the missile quickly enough, and the missile would miss by 500 feet or more.

Despite the inability of SAMs to deal with maneuvering targets, there is no sign that Soviet SAM crews are trained to anticipate this problem. Although former radar and missile operators assert that they spent a good deal of time tracking planes as practice, these were invariably flying straight and level—planes landing at nearby airports are frequently used as targets. Nor were the operators given practice in dealing with electronic countermeasures, devices much favored by the Americans to confuse the tracking and guidance radars.

Opportunities for the crews of the 10,000 SAM launchers actually to fire their weapons in training are no less limited than those for U.S. antiaircraft troops. Very few American specialists get to fire their Hawk or Nike missiles more than once a year, and neither do their Soviet opposite numbers. Since a Soviet crewman serves for a maximum of two years, with the first six months spent in classroom training, this means that he leaves the service having fired his SAM just once, from the PVO firing range in the central desert of Kazakhstan. On this unique occasion, the target he shoots at, a radio-controlled drone, is flying a straight and level course, the optimal condition for a SAM intercept but not necessarily the most likely one.

The other striking arm of the PVO consists of the 2,500 interceptor fighters. There are no less than six different types in service, which must pose considerable problems for training and the provision of spare parts. Although these planes have different missions—the MiG-25, for example, is designed to shoot down (nonexistent) supersonic bombers flying at high altitude, while the Su-15 Flagon is meant to operate at low altitudes—they share some common characteristics. All were designed to operate more like a manned missile rather than a maneuvering combat plane. Their mission is to climb fast to intercept bombers, under the direction of ground controllers, who track both bomber and interceptors on their radars. The pilot has very little to do apart from steering himself as instructed, firing his missile, and returning to base. Almost all of the planes have very short ranges, which may be a disadvantage in a country the size of the Soviet Union. Belenko's base at Chuguyevka was 160 miles from Vladivostok, which meant that his MiG-25, which had a combat radius of 186 miles, could not afford to loiter over the city he was supposed to be defending before having to turn for home.

Empirical evidence on the shortcomings of the Soviet air defense system comes from the strange story of the lost Korean airliner. On April 20, 1978, a Korean Airlines Boeing 707 passenger plane, with 110 people on board, got lost on a flight from Paris to Alaska. Owing to a serious failure in the navigational equipment, the plane turned right somewhere over Greenland and flew deep into Soviet airspace.

It took one hour for the world's mightiest air defense system to intercept the intruder, at which point the plane was over the Murmansk area, headquarters of the Northern Fleet and the main base for Russia's missile submarines. Finally, an interceptor approached the airliner, which was flying straight and level at 35,000 feet, and started firing. The Koreans were frantically trying to communicate with their attacker, but they were broadcasting on the international emergency frequency, which Soviet interceptors are unable to pick up (reportedly because this makes it harder for them to defect). The burst of cannon fire damaged the airliner and it rapidly lost height. Displaying greater skill as a pilot than he had as a navigator, the captain managed to crash-land the plane on a frozen lake, where it remained for twelve hours before the Soviets managed to locate it.

The mere fact that the plane had been able to reach such a sensitive area unmolested was extremely embarrassing for the Soviets. The Pentagon has obliged its Soviet counterparts by keeping secret their recordings of intercepted air defense radio traffic during the incident. The recordings reportedly reveal an atmosphere of chaos augmented by mounting panic as the 707 flew steadily deeper into Russia. One exchange between the Murmansk air defense command and a fighter base concerned the whereabouts of an interceptor dispatched in pursuit of the Koreans. The base reported that the plane had not yet taken off because the pilot was drunk. Anxious to minimize publicity about the affair, the Soviet authorities released the passengers and crew after a very perfunctory interrogation.

The U.S. Air Force was no more ready to highlight the incident's implications—Soviet air defenses could perhaps be penetrated without extremely expensive and sophisticated aircraft. A senior but iconoclastic adviser to the Secretary of Defense made himself unpopular with the Air Force by suggesting that it replace the B-1 bomber canceled by President Carter the year before with a "B-707" and crew it with Koreans.

In a less well-known incident in February of 1978, a light plane from Finland was able to land outside Leningrad, tarry on the ground for a period of time, and take off again without any molestation from SAMs or fighter planes.

The 1978 affair was not, as it turned out, to be the last unauthorized appearance by Korean Airlines over Soviet territory. On September 1, 1983, for reasons that may forever remain obscure, a Korean Airlines 747 passenger jetliner with 169 people on board departed from its official route from Anchorage, Alaska, to Seoul and passed over Kamchatka peninsula and Sakhalin Island. Both of these places, just off the coast of Siberia, are suffused with sensitive military installations, guaranteeing an angry Soviet response to any intruder.

Just off Sakhalin, and less than a minute's flying time from the boundaries of Soviet airspace—and safety—the airliner was shot down by an Su-15 of the air defense forces. Everyone on board was killed.

This tragic incident, and the subsequent reaction by all concerned parties, reflected almost all the salient attributes of Soviet military power and the orthodox U.S. reaction to it. The air defense forces behaved with gross inefficiency, allowing the intruding aircraft to overfly highly secret bases on Kamchatka and Sakhalin, which include the main Pacific missile submarine base at Petropavlovsk on Kamchatka, the main landing area for ballistic missile tests, and much else besides. The Soviets, according to subsequent admissions by U.S. intelligence, were under the impression that the intruder was not a civilian jumbo jet but an American RC-135 electronic spy plane. Given that sincere belief, it seems a gross dereliction of duty on the local responsible officials' part to have allowed it to get as far as it did. Although the plane entered Soviet airspace off Kamchatka at 3:30 A.M. local time, after being within range of Soviet surveillance radars for some time before, it was not until 3:37 A.M. that interceptors were scrambled from airbases on Kamchatka. These failed to find the intruder in the pre-dawn darkness.

Nighttime interception is a difficult art at best, requiring great coordination and trust between the ground controllers and the pilots. The controllers must plot the trajectory of the target aircraft on their radars, and vector their own fighters to intercept. All the aircraft concerned are moving at high speeds, and the target may not necessarily be flying a straight and level course. The interceptor must be guided to a position where the pilot can actually see the target, which means a distance of no more than one or two miles. For positive identification of the aircraft type under pursuit the interceptor must get even closer—a quarter of a mile or less. The difficulties of the operation are compounded when the interceptors have an extremely limited flying time, which is a problem for all Soviet tactical planes for reasons discussed in Chapter 9.

It was not until the Korean airliner had crossed Kamchatka, flown out of Soviet airspace over the Sea of Okhotsk, back in over the Soviet island of Sakhalin, out over the sea, and was within a minute's flying time of escaping Soviet airspace altogether, that an Su-15 pilot finally brought it down.

As it turned out, of course, it would have been far better for the Soviets had they failed to find the plane, in which case the innocent civilian passengers of Korean Airlines Flight 007 would have survived and the Reagan Administration would have been denied a propaganda triumph.

However, had the Su-15 pilot failed to make his "kill," his commanders in the Far Eastern military district would have been in some trouble, because it was the sincere conviction of the local air defense apparatus that night that they were pursuing an intruding American RC-135 electronic intelligence plane.

In all fairness, it must be pointed out that the Soviets had every reason to suspect that the intruder was indeed an American military spy plane. As the white House reluctantly admitted a few days after the tragedy, there had indeed been an RC-135 in the area on the night of Flight 007's fateful journey—dispatched to monitor the final phases of a test of a new Soviet ICBM. But, according to President Reagan in a TV address to the nation, the spy plane was ordered to abandon its mission and return to base in Alaska when the Soviet missile test was canceled. It had, the President was at pains to observe, been on the ground for an hour when the airliner was shot down.

During the spy plane's patrol, however, which consisted of flying figure eight maneuvers off the Kamchatka coast, its route had converged with that of the errant airliner. Both the Soviets and the Americans agree that their routes actually crossed; but while the American authorities assert that the two planes were never closer than 75 miles, the Soviets insist that they actually flew alongside each other for about ten minutes before the military plane broke away. This convergence, which occurred at about 3:00 A.M. —half an hour before the airliner crossed into Soviet airspace—appears to have led the air defense radar trackers to misidentify the 747 as the RC-135, making an unprecedentedly bold espionage foray over Soviet territory.

It may be that Reagan and other administration spokesmen were not telling the whole truth about the U.S. military presence in the area that night, or indeed about the normal, provocative, pattern of the 135s' behavior off Kamchatka and Sakhalin. Two weeks after the incident, two former RC-135 crewmen published their own observations on the incident in the Denver *Post*. They asserted that there is *always* an RC-135—which is a modified Boeing 707 crammed with electronic equipment and a crew of 30—in the air off Kamchatka. Therefore, "We find the inference made by President Reagan that the Sakhalin-Kamchatka target area was abandoned by the RC-135 to be unbelievable and contrary to NSA policy." (The RC-135s, although flown by Air Force personnel, are under the control of the upersecret National Security Agency, NSA.)

Even more interestingly, the authors, T. Edward Eskelson and Tom Bernard, stated that "It has been our experience that on occasion NSA adjusts the orbits of RC-135s so that they intentionally will penetrate the airspace of a target nation to bring its air defense systems into alert. This allows NSA to analyze these fully activated systems for potential flaws and weaknesses." They go on to explain that the planes are able to protect themselves during these dubious excursions because they have the capability to monitor all the radar and radio transmissions of the Soviet air defense system, thus allowing them time to run for safety the moment these defenses become activated.

If this is what really goes on, it seems entirely unremarkable that the Soviet air defense commanders should have been so quick to assume that they had a hostile spy plane roaming about above some of their most sensitive defense installations. It also raises the question, posited by Bernard and Eskelson, as to why the RC-135, which would have been patrolling the area during the entire terminal phase of Flight 007, and which would have been monitoring the rapid escalation of frenzied activity of the Soviet defense network, made absolutely no attempt to warn somebody that a disaster was about to happen. It could certainly have done so, since these aircraft are plugged into a communications network powerful enough to put a message on the President's desk from any point on Earth.

That the Soviets did indeed think they were in pursuit of an RC-135 is beyond doubt. In a conversation monitored by a U.S. listening post—but not, unlike the conversation of the pilots who finally caught up with their quarry, publicized by the Administration—a Soviet radar operator informed Kamchatka air defense command that he had sighted an RC-135. When the airliner was passing over Sakhalin Island, antiaircraft missile batteries were put on alert to stop what was described as an "RC-135."

While it may be easy to understand how the radar operators misidentified the airliner, how could the interceptor pilots have done so when at least one of them actually had it within sight for several minutes? In the immediate aftermath of the incident, U.S. propaganda made much of the considerable differences both in size and shape between a

747 passenger jetliner and an RC-135. In discussing the "crime against humanity," President Reagan himself pointed to the distinctive hump above the cockpit of a 747 jetliner and declared: "There is no way a pilot could mistake this for anything other than a civilian jetliner."

Actually, as previously noted, it is exceedingly difficult to tell one aircraft from another at night, since the observer has no point of reference for determining relative size. In addition, and unfortunately for all concerned, the Soviet pilots were apparently flying below the 747, so the distinctive hump would have been obscured from their view. From that vantage point there is little to distinguish a 707 (on which the RC-135 is based) from a 747. There remains the question of the passenger plane's navigation lights, which should have served to indicate that it was not a military plane. In the course of his unprecedented press conference on the incident, Marshal Ogarkov stated adamantly that the plane was not showing lights of any kind. This claim is apparently belied by the clear statement of the Soviet pilot who said, according to a transcript later released by the Americans, "The A.N.O [air navigation lights] are burning. The [strobe] light is flashing." Perhaps by that point the pursuers were so caught up in the chase, especially as the target was on the point of escaping, that they simply did not pause to reflect on the oddity of a military plane displaying civilian navigation lights.

Within a few hours of the destruction of the airliner, the Soviets had to accept the horrible fact that they had killed 269 civilians and, as a practical matter, handed the U.S. a priceless propaganda opportunity. Their defense was to insist stoutly that even if the intruder had not been an RC-135, it had nonetheless been engaged in an espionage mission. Neither they nor anyone else were able to produce any definitive proof that this was the case. Nevertheless, there remain many unexplained aspects of the fateful Flight 007.

How was it that the plane was off course? By all accounts, it carried the very latest in navigational equipment, including a triply-redundant inertial navigation system, radio location equipment (which would allow it to fix its position in relation to ground-based radio transmitters), and two radars which would throw the distinctive topography of Kamchatka and Sakhalin into sharp relief. It has been suggested that a misprogramming of the navigational computer was responsible for the plane's errant course. If the plane had indeed proceeded in a straight line while over Soviet territory, this story might have had some credence; but it did not. A map later issued by the Soviets shows that its route over Sakhalin followed a dogleg, turning west so as to pass over the southern tip of the island and then south again en route to Seoul. Indeed, this course change is confirmed by a statement (on the tapes released by the U.S. government) by the Soviet interceptor pilot, who reports the target turning on a course of 240 degrees a few minutes before it was shot down.

Four minutes before the two heat-seeking missiles slammed into his 747, the Korean pilot made one other maneuver that is difficult to explain if he was simply and innocently off course. The pursuing Su-15 pilot is recorded as reporting that "The target is decreasing speed." At that point the Su-15 was two kilometers behind the 747. Fifteen seconds later the interceptor reported that "I am going around it," so the Korean must have done the equivalent of slamming his brakes on—a standard evasive maneuver.

Whether or not the Korean plane was deliberately off course on some kind of espionage mission we may never know. It is certainly true that its takeoff was delayed for 40 minutes at Anchorage airport, which, coincidentally or not, meant that its subsequent journey was in alignment with an orbiting U.S. Ferret reconnaissance satellite. It is also true that the drastic navigational error that put it 300 miles off course is also hard to explain. Some subsequent reports suggested that it could not have been on an espionage mission because U.S. intelligence services could get all the intelligence they needed from satellites or high-flying spy planes such as the SR-71. This sounds plausible, given the general impression that satellites can produce legible pictures of newspaper headlines, but in fact there is much that a plane flying at 30,000 feet can discover that a higher-flying vehicle cannot. This is particularly true in the case of infrared photography—which can take pictures at night by capturing heat rather than light sources on the ground.

What is beyond a shadow of a doubt is that, whether intentionally or not, the terminal journey of Flight 007 resulted in a real intelligence bonanza for the Americans. "Tickling" electronic air defenses into operation so as to force the revelation of the location and capabilities of the enemy's radar network is an ongoing pursuit for both sides, and has been since the Cold War. Sometimes the other side fails to join in the game. In 1978, for example, the Americans mounted a major intelligence operation in the Sea of Okhotsk—the very area later made famous by the Korean airliner incident. After months of planning they sent in several reconnaissance aircraft and half a dozen ships, including destroyers, in the hope that the Soviets would switch on their radars. But in fact nothing happened—either the Russians surmised the Americans' intentions and refused to play the game or, equally likely, they failed to realize that the U.S. force was there in the first place. This was certainly not the case with the Korean airliner's flight. As it cruised serenely over Kamchatka the Soviet air defense network sprang into frantic activity—all of which was monitored by both the Ferret satellite overhead and any other electronic intelligence-gathering planes or ships that the U.S. had in the area.

Grudging admissions after the event from within U.S. intelligence circles that perhaps the downing of the airliner represented a blunder on the part of the Soviets rather than a crime were not reflected in any U.S. Administration statements. The official position on the affair, as expressed by U.N. Ambassador Jeane Kirkpatrick, was that "the Soviets decided to shoot down a civilian airliner, shot it down, murdered the 269 people on board, and lied about it." As always, the realities of the issue were ignored in favor of the preferred monolithic view of the Soviet Union—the fundamental precept that whatever the Soviets do, they do deliberately.

And, as always, the shortcomings in the Soviet air defense system, thrown into such stark relief by their performance in the early hours of September 1, had absolutely no effect on U.S. defense policy. President Reagan used the incident to plead for rapid passage of the 1984 defense budget through Congress, an exhortation which the legislature obediently followed. Certainly they gave short shrift to attempts to cut funding for the B-1 bomber, a program supposedly necessitated by the rapidly improving state of Soviet air defenses.

Unshakable faith in the formidable nature of the Soviets' antibomber defenses has helped ensure that projected U.S. strategic bombers become increasingly complex and expensive. Since the early 1960s these bombers have been designed to fly low so as to evade the Soviet radar stations—ground-based radars cannot pick up objects below a minimum height. If, however, the Russians were able to install a radar in a plane that could spot enemy intruders between it and the ground, low-flying planes would become that much more vulnerable

In August 1977, U.S. intelligence claimed that they had detected signs that the Russians were testing a MiG-25 Super Foxbat, which might be able to "look down" and spot low-flying bombers. The Carter Administration used this as justification for increased funding of a Stealth bomber, which would be, supposedly, almost invisible to radar. Radar signals reflect best off sharply defined shapes and surfaces, so the Stealth is being designed with rounded surfaces, as well as special coatings that will muffle and absorb the signals. Such techniques can make a plane more difficult for the most modern radars to detect. Paradoxically, they offer no such protection against cruder and more old-fashioned radars of a type deployed by the Soviets in great numbers.

Modern radars have been operating on progressively shorter wavelengths, since these allow the use of smaller antennas. It is precisely these short wavelength systems that the special coatings on the Stealth are designed to defeat. But the coatings cannot be made thick enough to have any effect on old-fashioned long-wavelength radars, like the Spoon Rest and Tall King, which the Soviets have kept in service because of the slower pace of their electronics development and a reluctance to scrap old equipment. Meanwhile, the utility of look-down radars of the type that generated the Stealth program remains extremely doubtful (see Chapter 9). Thus, the United States, to meet a threat that probably does not exist, spends millions on Stealth, with the result that the crude old Spoon Rests and Tall Kings have a new lease on life.

As a threat, the troops of national air defense have done yeoman service on behalf of the U.S.-manned bomber lobby. The Soviet space program gives every sign of doing as much or more for the U.S. military effort in space.

In the fall of 1982, the U.S. Air Force inaugurated a new satrapy called Space Command, destined to take responsibility for such heavenly activities as satellite surveillance, the monitoring and interception of enemy satellites, and the military missions of the Space Shuttle. The occasion was marked by an outpouring of publicity about the Soviet space threat, with both the trade press and general-interest magazines dutifully doing their bit to get the message across. The Soviets, it appeared, were outspending the United States in an "aggressive" manner in space, maintaining a semipermanently manned space station, developing a space shuttle, dispatching many more satellites into orbit, and practicing hard at destroying U.S. satellites with "killer satellites."

The lurking possibility of Soviet control of the heavens is a venerable theme in threat inflation. It was the early Soviet successes with Sputnik and manned space flight that ushered in an era of unprecedented prosperity for the U.S. aerospace industry. While the Soviets had been soundly beaten in the race to put a man on the moon, they had persisted, in a characteristically Soviet way, in their program of manned missions around the earth. The Americans abandoned their Skylab space station, but the Russians kept on operating their equivalent, the Soyuz. Despite the unremitting effort, however, Soviet spy-satellite technology has always lagged behind that of the Americans. While U.S. spy satellites remain in orbit for an average of about 150 days, their Soviet counterparts plunge back into the atmosphere after about 18 days. This fact alone explains why the Soviets found it necessary to launch 98 spacecraft missions in 1981, compared to 18 launched by the United States—which still gives the Soviets one-third less coverage than the United States.

Since 1976, the Russians have been testing an antisatellite weapon. Consisting of a satellite armed with explosives, it is designed to maneuver close to an enemy satellite and then explode. The program has not been notably successful, since more than half the tests have ended in failure; but it has had the predictable result of justifying costly U.S. programs to harden and otherwise defend the American satellites.

It is unlikely that the Soviet space threat will recede. Too great are the attractions to the U.S. Air Force of a field of military procurement that is enormously costly (Milstar, a single-satellite communications system of uncertain performance for use in a nuclear war, will cost at least $2.5 billion) and in which the technology is so secret and arcane that outsiders have little chance of finding out what is going on.

As a matter of fact, the whole gigantic effort on either side (the CIA reports $18 billion for the Soviets in 1981, the United States admits to almost $15 billion) is almost certainly entirely useless. As one seasoned defense observer puts it, "If space systems couldn't be destroyed the moment a war starts, their communication signals to and from the ground could easily be jammed. These are strictly peacetime systems."

Fourteen

Civil Defense

Compared to the enormous if pointless air defense system, Soviet efforts directed at protecting themselves after the nuclear warheads have landed and exploded are comparatively modest. The Ministry of Defense oversees a civil defense organization that in total employs about 100,000 people. This organization is charged with preparing measures to mitigate the effects of a nuclear attack on civil society by removing the population in and around likely targets to safer areas, by protecting vital installations, and by sheltering key personnel. This is an enormous task, but even by the most generous CIA estimates the organization's annual budget amounts to little more than $2 billion a year. Since the estimates are derived by the traditional method of costing the program's various components according to U.S. prices and pay scales, they are quite certainly an exaggeration. Many of the 100,000 civil defense workers, for example, are in fact conscripts, each subsisting on the equivalent of $6.50 a month rather than the U.S. basic rate of $573 a month.

The most visible product of the Soviet civil defense bureaucracy is handbooks, leaflets, propaganda posters—containing profuse instructions and information about both the likely effects of nuclear detonations and the best measures for avoiding them. The millions of Soviet schoolchildren who attend Pioneer camps (roughly equivalent to boy-scout camps) each summer are given a handbook containing useful hints, such as the standard time for putting on a cotton and gauze mask (2½ minutes), unpacking a 10-foot by 12-foot "trench shelter" (3 minutes for a team of three), and decontaminating irradiated clothing with a soap and oil solvent (7 minutes). It also advises youthful readers that a nuclear blast wave takes 2 seconds to travel the first six-tenths of a mile, while those farther away will have "a few seconds" or more to seek shelter.

Publications such as these, which are readily available to Western researchers, can be and are taken as an ominous indication of Soviet readiness to fight and survive a nuclear war. General Daniel Graham (retired), a former head of the Defense Intelligence Agency, once outlined a scenario in which civil defense could be made to serve the interests of Soviet aggression: "The Soviets evacuate their cities and hunker down. Then they move against NATO or Yugoslavia or China or the Middle East with superior conventional forces. The United States is faced with the demand to stay out or risk a nuclear exchange in which 100 million Americans would die as opposed to 10 million Russians."

This kind of speculation depends on the customary assumption that every aspect of Soviet military policy and planning is merely a component of an overall, smoothly integrated, rational grand design being pursued with sagacious and ruthless determination by the men in the Kremlin.

Beyond this unshakable faith in the consistency and profundity of Soviet policy in general, a belief in the Soviet civil defense "threat" also relies on some exceedingly sanguine assumptions about nuclear war. The Defense Department official T. K. Jones, a major publicist for Soviet civil defense, excited some comment when he told an interviewer in 1982 that "with enough shovels" for the populace to dig personal shelters there was no reason why nuclear war should entail the destruction of a society. As pointed out in Chapter 12, any calculation about the effects of a nuclear war must be made in the absence of any information on which to base a conclusion. Nevertheless, simple common sense indicates that such measures as the Soviets have undertaken to protect themselves in the event of nuclear attack may be less than effective.

On paper, at least, the system will work in the following way. There are nine different warning signals of escalating urgency for the civilian population. When the ninth is broadcast, the evacuation and dispersal plans go into effect. Some groups of the population, namely, key workers and officials, will be dispersed in prespecified cars, trains, or buses to their allotted shelters outside the cities, from where, in the case of the workers at least, they can return to operate the vital factories once the attack has passed. The rest of the people are to be evacuated either on the remaining motorized transport or else on foot, walking in "orderly columns of 500 to 1,000" out into the countryside, where they are to build "expedient shelters" for their protection. These shelters are to be constructed out of simple materials, such as wooden planks, sheet metal, or bricks and cinder blocks, using simple tools, such as shovels.

At the same time, the country's industry will be protected against the anticipated nuclear blasts by the removal of flammable materials from industrial sites and the placing of hoods, canopies, earth, water, or sandbags over machinery. These measures, according to the 1974 Soviet civil defense handbook, are aimed at "increasing the . . . ability to continue production operations in wartime on a planned, normal basis, and to return quickly to production upon sustaining minor or moderate damage or when supply is disrupted."

The citizenry is constantly bombarded with leaflets and pamphlets, as well as classroom sessions and lectures, in preparation, supposedly, for the moment when the leaders decide that it is time to "hunker down." In view of this investment in time and money, it is not surprising that the official press frequently resounds with grandiose claims for the program's effectiveness. In January 1977, for example, General Aleksei Radzievsky boasted in the mass-circulation *Literaturnaya gazeta* (Literary Gazette) that "methods of protecting the population and the economy against attack" are "constantly being improved" and that Communist Party and Soviet government organizations at all levels are paying "unflagging attention to improving and developing civil defense." It is no less suprising that such claims are eagerly seized upon and touted abroad as evidence by such researchers as T. K. Jones or Dr. Leon Gouré of the University of Miami, who have made a career out of depicting the civil defense threat in the starkest terms.

The confidence exhibited by General Radzievsky stands in sharp contrast to what most Americans and Western Europeans feel to be the real state of their own countries' preparations for survival under nuclear attack—either non-existent or useless. There are of course extensive plans for the evacuation of the great American cities, plans which have been in existence since the early 1960s and which have been given great encouragement in both rhetoric and cash by the Reagan Administration. As a result, the United States is in an admirable position to resist the effects of a nuclear attack—on paper. There are "230 million identified shelter spaces," enough for every man, woman, and child, with space to spare. Relocation centers have been designated to which the inhabitants of large cities can flee, as well as the routes that the evacuees will use to get there. Plans have been laid for the postwar functioning of the banking and postal systems (checks can be drawn on incinerated banks but express mail service will be suspended). At the first alarm, the Declaration of Independence will be lowered in its case into a specially prepared nuclear blast-proof vault beneath the National Archives.

The timely securing of the Declaration in order to preserve it for postwar generations is the responsibility of the guard on duty. One of these guards told a reporter that he hoped that the first incoming Soviet missile would "fall right on my head," on the presumption that a postwar world would not be worth living in. The Reagan Administration's efforts to generate popular enthusiasm for civil defense instead of the prevailing pessimism show few signs of success. People appear to have the feeling that, whatever the schemes dreamt up by the bureaucrats that serve the U.S. civil defense apparatus, there is no way of mitigating the effects of thousands of nuclear explosions, each of which will be many times more powerful than the one that leveled Hiroshima.

It may be harder for people to treat the notion of a viable Soviet civil defense program with the same healthy cynicism, so accustomed are they to propaganda about the obedience of Soviet citizens and the efficiency of the Communist ruling apparatus. However, a brief glance at the actual mechanics of Soviet civil defense planning suggests that it may be no more realistic than the U.S. Federal Emergency Management Agency's hope of evacuating the island of Manhattan in 48 hours.

Soviet plans envisage the urban population moving out

of the danger areas in trains, in motor vehicles, or on foot. This immediately presents a host of practical difficulties. There are 2 million cars, 2 million trucks, and 200,000 buses for the entire USSR. Moreover, there are few roads in that vast and underdeveloped country, and no more than a third of these have hard surfaces. Railroads are the preferred method of long-distance transport in the Soviet Union, but most of the lines are single-track and most of the trains are loaded with freight at any given time. Moreover, it is unlikely that the trains would be in the right place at the right time to pick up millions of people and transport them out of danger.

Most of the population, including the halt and the lame, the aged and the toddlers, would have to evacuate themselves on foot and in those "orderly columns of 500 to 1,000." Even if these hordes were to move at an average speed of 1½ miles an hour, which is highly unlikely as far as the very young, old, and sick are concerned, they would still be no farther than 30 miles from their starting place at the end of a day and very much exposed to the effects of warheads exploding over their former homes. Muscovites who had managed to proceed even this far would still be caught in the capital's outer suburbs, while the roads ahead of them would be clogged by orderly columns of evacuating suburbanites.

Once the evacuees have walked a safe distance from likely target areas, or at least reached the limits of their endurance, they must proceed to the construction of their "expedient shelters." These are intended to be little more than reinforced holes in the ground, but even so, it is hard to understand how a people accustomed for the most part to living in apartment houses could be expected to find the requisite materials, much less carry them on their desperate forced marches away from the doomed cities. Should war come in the winter, when most of Russia is frozen solid, or in the fall, when continuous rains turn the countryside into a sea of mud, the operation appears still less feasible.

Assuming a hardy and resourceful Muscovite or other city dweller has managed to trot a safe distance from home and build the shelter on one of the "dry, firm-soil sites that do not flood when it rains" suggested by the handbook, he or she will still be faced with the problem of survival during and after the conclusion of hostilities. Evacuees are supposed to carry two weeks' supply of food with them, and since Soviet households are not normally equipped with well-stocked freezers, the inference is that ordinary people must stock up with the necessities between the sounding of the alarm and the beginning of the great trek.

Even the well-stocked and highly efficient U.S. retail food-distribution system would be put under a severe strain were millions of Americans suddenly and simultaneously to try and buy two weeks' worth of food. The Soviet food-distribution system is not very efficient at the best of times; housewives must stand in line for an hour or more every day just to buy what is needed for the morrow. Yet the Soviet civil defense organizers and their American proponents appear to assume as a matter of course that the two-week supply will suddenly materialize in the stores and that everyone will be able to get a fair share.

The protection of factories and the rest of the physical plant, such as bridges, airports, and so on, that ensure Russia's continued existence as a modern industrialized state, presents just as many problems as the care and feeding of the people. Were plant managers to follow the prescribed procedure for reinforcing their factories, the structures might possibly be capable of withstanding pressures from nuclear blasts up to 6 pounds per square inch. But a 100-kiloton warhead (not much of a blockbuster in strategic nuclear terms) landing 2 miles away would generate much higher pressures. To achieve even that modest level of protection is prohibitively difficult, as the normally upbeat authors of the 1975 handbook ruefully concede: "It is impossible to make buildings less vulnerable to a shock wave without radical structural changes that involve considerable technical difficulties and cost. . . . It is impossible to guarantee building survival in a damaged area even by somewhat increasing the strength of individual structures and their components."

With a large number of installations there is no point in even trying, and these are among the most vital ones. Pipelines, airports, railheads, marshaling yards, highway intersections, oil refineries, and a host of other major economic facilities cannot be covered with "canopies, earth, water or sandbags" and therefore must be left exposed to the thermonuclear blasts.

One way of providing some protection to Soviet industry against nuclear attack, or at least rendering its destruction more difficult, would be to disperse it over as wide an area as possible, a point that has not been lost on the civil defense planners. General Aleksandr T. Altunin, commander of the entire organization, has described industrial dispersion as a "decisive measure for ensuring the viability of the economy in wartime." Despite this, the Soviet economy is much more concentrated than that of the United States, entirely dependent on a very limited number of choke points, where basic industrial processes are carried out. Whatever General Altunin's views may be, there is no sign that this situation is changing; on the contrary, the economic planners are for the most part fostering growth in areas that are already heavily built up. Such a policy may make sense for a country with a heavily centralized economy and a comparatively underdeveloped transportation system, but it shows little regard for the exigencies of civil defense.

The economy cannot function, for example, without the chemical, steel, and electrical industries. Almost all the chemical plants in the Soviet Union are grouped in 25 cities. There are just 18 mills in the entire USSR that can deal with both iron and steel. The great industrial concentration of the Central and Volga regions, in which 60 million people live and work, relies for power on just five generating plants, two of which are nuclear power plants and are themselves located inside large cities.

Other key components of the Soviet economy are just as accessible to the American nuclear targeteers. The destruction of just 34 refineries would halt all gasoline production in the country. Eight bombs in the right place and the Russians would be without copper. The loss of the Kazakh city of Pavlodar would instantly deprive the Soviets of 65 percent of their aluminum production. Automobile factories, shipyards, food-processing plants, and other key facilities are no less vulnerable. The defense writer Fred Kaplan, who was one of the first to apply common sense to the alarmist fantasies of researchers like T. K. Jones and Leon Gouré, has pointed out that "It would take far fewer than a thousand warheads (less than 10 percent of the U.S. total) to knock out the crucial industries without which the Soviet Union could not maintain an advanced industrial society—much less a society able to execute and sustain the political threats for which Gouré, Jones and others presume they have a civil defense program in the first place."

Insulating any society against the anticipated consequences of a nuclear war, even in the most limited way, is almost certainly an insuperable task. Even the Soviet bureaucrats who make a living by pretending that it is possible do occasionally own up to the difficulties. General Altunin admitted in a "state of the program" message in 1976 that even though "our numerous [civil defense] activists can and should be trained," such training had frequently been less than satisfactory: "Many people assembled for such sessions and were led through the various points of a demonstration exercise, but the trainees did not receive what was most necessary. The practical portion was poorly organized and . . . stereotyped."

This kind of official pessimism merely reflects the widespread public apathy toward the whole effort, an attitude pungently expressed in the popular nickname for civil defense, which is *Grob*, an acronym derived from the Russian words for civil defense, *grazhdanskaya oborona*. *Grob* also happens to be the Russian word for "coffin." Émigrés recall that no one took the training exercises seriously and either successfully evaded them or treated them as an excuse for a day off work and a family picnic outing rather than a grim rehearsal for the holocaust. The Muscovites even tell this joke:

"What do you do in a case of nuclear attack?"

"Wrap yourself in a sheet and crawl slowly to the cemetery."

"Why slowly?"

"So as to avoid causing a panic."

In the face of well-documented derision from such critics as Kaplan and the evident indifference of the Soviet people, the program's protagonists, who subsist for the most part on the largesse of the U.S. Department of Defense, can only hew to their unshakable faith in the ability of the Soviet system to overcome all problems. Gouré declares defiantly in his book *War Survival and Soviet Strategy* that "the fact that [Communist] party and administrative officials undergo civil defense training in increasing numbers and that the party and administrative organs take an active part in supervising and supporting the program *ensures* that the program will essentially be carried out."

Note the touching faith of that "ensures," the same faith that renders threat assessors blind to the consequences of a drunken and half-trained conscript army, a high command riven with political intrigue, progressively less useful weapons systems, and a society more vulnerable than most even to a limited nuclear onslaught.

Active support and supervision by the Party and administrative organs does not, of course, ensure successful operation of the program by any manner of means. Beyond that, however, there is considerable evidence to suggest that these same bodies do not in fact take the whole business as seriously as is sometimes supposed. As noted above, industry is not being dispersed, and civil defense drills are undertaken only on a limited basis (after careful rehearsal, as is the way with Soviet exercises). There has been no attempt at the supreme test of evacuating a major city.

The U.S. Defense Intelligence Agency has claimed that on one occasion the Soviets did practice the evacuation of the work force of one industry from one (unnamed) city, although reliable authorities elsewhere in the intelligence community assert that the evidence for this is extremely dubious. Even if it were true, the evacuation of the workers from one industry from one city would be of little help in preparing for a mass migration into the countryside by the entire urban population of the USSR, any more than the testing of one or two rockets indicates an ability to launch a preemptive first strike.

Casting these doubts on the practicality of Soviet civil defense leaves one important question unanswered: since it is apparently impossible to protect a society against the consequences of a nuclear attack, why do the Soviets maintain an extensive apparatus on the pretense that it is possible? Former Defense Secretary Harold Brown once suggested that the Soviet leadership might itself be blind to the system's obvious shortcomings. The Soviet civil defense program, he told an interviewer in 1977, was worrying because through misplaced confidence in its potential, the Soviet leaders might "—mistakenly in my belief—arrive at the conclusion that they could survive as a functioning and powerful country after an all-out thermonuclear exchange." But this "madman" theory does not really gibe with what we know of the Soviet leadership: an aged and experienced body of men noted chiefly for their extreme caution and aversion to taking any kind of incalculable risk.

In truth, there is little need to grasp at such straws to explain Soviet civil defense efforts once it is realized that the Soviet program has little or nothing to do with actual warfare and everything to do with internal military politics, as is so often true with Soviet (or U.S.) military affairs.

Back in 1961 the Kremlin decided on a total overhaul of their civil defense apparatus, which until then had been organized under the aegis of the air defense forces on a local basis and had found practical expression in a rather desultory program of blast-shelter construction inside Soviet cities. While such shelters may have been the answer to the conventional bombs of the World War II German Luftwaffe, they were obviously not much of a barrier against the intercontinental nuclear bombers and missiles of the U.S. Air Force and Navy.

The same year the incoming Kennedy Administration in the United States embarked on a major military expansion, with considerable emphasis on a civil defense program. "Civil defense has become a direct reponsibility of all levels of government and the people," declared the young President.

The Kennedy rearmament program effectively sabotaged Khrushchev's efforts to curb the appetites of his own military, and it is from that year rather than the Cuban missile crisis of 1962 that the reversal of his planned cuts in military manpower, as well as the expansion in Soviet weapons procurement and modernization, can be dated. Civil defense was one of the areas that experience a major shake-up. Specifically, it was split off from the air defense organization and reorganized as a wholly separate service. It was now called Civil Defense of the USSR, with its commander, head of the Civil Defense Staff, reporting directly to the Council of Ministers, completely independently of the Ministry of Defense and the General Staff, a fact that was to be of crucial importance later on. Each of the 16 military districts was to have an assistant to the commander, a high-ranking position, who would deal directly with the civil defense organization headquarters in Moscow.

To head the Civil Defense of the USSR, Khrushchev called upon an old and trusted ally—Marshal Vasily I. Chuikov. Chuikov had commanded the heroic defense of Stalingrad during the most desperate period of the World War II battle, when the entire city was an inferno and the Soviet forces had been driven back to a tiny sliver of land on the banks of the Volga River. During this period, he had come into close contact with a political emissary from Moscow named Nikita Khrushchev, who was charged with reporting directly on events to Stalin.

Although Chuikov had hung on, the successful offensive against the Germans leading to their eventual encirclement and surrender had been carried out by commanders sent directly from Moscow, most notably Zhukov. Since Stalingrad turned out to be the most momentous battle and victory of the entire war, credit for the outcome long remained a bone of contention between the "southern" group, which included Chuikov, and the "Moscow" generals, particularly Zhukov.

Khrushchev found his closest military allies among the

"southerners," and when he came to power, their careers prospered accordingly. Still, in the early years of Khrushchev's ascendancy, it was Zhukov, the most famous of all Soviet wartime heroes, who was the new leader's most important military ally. Zhukov played a crucial role in helping defeat an attempted political coup against Khrushchev by the so-called "antiparty group" in 1957. After that, however, his position and power made him a positve political threat, and shortly afterward he was dismissed from his post of Minister of Defense and dispatched into comfortable oblivion. Upon his departure, the "southerners" came even more to the fore.

Chuikov already had an important job when he was tapped to run civil defense in 1961. He was commander in chief of the ground forces—the army—and he remained in this position while also assuming his new responsibilities. In 1964, however, he suffered a setback. An obscure intrigue within the military resulted in the abolition of the ground forces command and the absorption of its function into the General Staff. Chuikov was now left with one job—running civil defense—and he proceeded to make the most of it.

The old scheme had called merely for the population to stay put in the cities when the alarm was sounded. Chuikov and his new bureaucracy had something much more far-reaching in mind, which was to evacuate the entire population. For an ambitious bureaucracy, this policy had much to commend it, since it meant that in an emergency, the civil defense officials would actually control the entire transport system of the USSR. In peacetime, civil defense officers therefore would have to have an important say in the planning and disposition of road and rail networks. Since the transport system, even if totally controlled by civil defense, could not possibly shift the required numbers of people around, the bulk of the evacuees would have to move on foot in these orderly columns. That too had its attractions as an option, because the Khrushchev cutbacks of the late 1950s had left thousands of career army officers out of a job. As Richard Anderson puts it: "Soviet army officers may not know much, but one thing they do know about is marching columns of people around." Thus, many of the victims of Khrushchev's short-lived cost-cutting program found a haven in the growing civil defense empire.

Any burgeoning military program needs to be able to make its influence felt in the economy at large by buying things, and under Chuikov's plan that too was taken care of. While the roads and some of the railways were filled with evacuees, the key workers in the country's defense and basic industries would be shuttling back and forth between their blast- and radiation-proof concrete shelters and their workplaces. These shelters, of course, would require a huge investment in concrete alone, not to mention other materials.

This whole gigantic scheme, worthy of the man who had stopped Hitler's hordes on the Volga, was supposed to require a week to put into effect once the nuclear alert was given. And that was where the whole thing came unstuck, because in the mid-1960s the General Staff concluded that a week was far too long.

While the Soviet Union's intercontinental nuclear arsenal consisted of a limited number of sluggish and vulnerable bombers and even fewer and equally vulnerable missiles, which required 20 hours of preparation before they could be fired, the Kremlin's only option was to preempt. In other words, once it became apparent that a nuclear attack by the enemy was likely, the Russians would strike first. Such a scenario presupposed a lengthy warning period of escalating crisis, which gave plenty of time for Chuikov and his lieutenants to shuffle the people about.

But by the mid-1960s, things had begun to change. The strategic rocket forces were rapidly building up their fleet of ICBMs, and although the missiles were still liquid-fueled, to a certain extent they could be kept fueled up and ready for firing at short notice. At the same time, around 1964, the Soviets began emulating the American program of silo hardening. Previously, the ICBMs had stood out in the open, which meant that they could be destroyed by a nuclear blast several miles away. However, once the missiles were encased below ground in their silos, any enemy missile aimed at them would have to be very accurate indeed, which, in turn, meant that the Soviet missile force had a strong likelihood of surviving an initial American attack.

Military doctrine tends to evolve in response to demands from generals for an excuse to justify whatever they happen to be interested in spending money on, and the Soviet marshals and generals are no exception. Hardened missile silos and command centers cost a great deal of money, and so the military high command of the mid- and late 1960s increasingly favored the doctrine that nuclear war could come with little or no warning as a bolt from the blue.

The concept had political ramifications that were particularly attractive to Brezhnev during this period. In 1964, Brezhnev and Aleksei N. Kosygin had succeeded Khrushchev as equal partners at the apex of Soviet power. Brezhnev's cultivation of the "defense lobby" helped him nose out in front of his rival, but he was not by any means the sole undisputed leader in the way that Khrushchev, not to mention Stalin, had been. Now, if the supposition was to be that a nuclear attack could come at any time, necessitating an instant response, there was obviously an urgent need for a single authority empowered to make decisions on the spot, without the time-consuming formalities of consulting the rest of the collective leadership. And who better to fill such a role than L. Brezhnev?

Thus, the doctrine of instant war had powerful backers in the military and in the Kremlin, but there was one snag. Marshal Chuikov, the hero of Stalingrad, commanded a large bureaucracy, which was preparing to move the whole country around if and when war threatened, and the prosperity of his entire organization depended on the assumption that there would be at least a week's warning before the missiles actually started to fly.

In 1967 the official announcement of a new Western war scenario gave the military high command further cause for irritation over the obstacle posed by Chuikov and his schemes. That year, NATO officially promulgated the doctrine of "flexible response," which held that a war between East and West did not have to be nuclear, at least not to begin with. Instead, there might be a period in which both sides could engage just their conventional forces, without resorting to the more drastic options of nuclear strike and counterstrike. This idea was highly welcome to the Soviet commanders, particularly the commanders of the ground forces (which got back their separate command apparatus in 1967, though Chuikov himself was not rehired as commander in chief). The possibility of a lengthy land battle in Central Europe obviously demanded a strengthened and more lavishly equipped army.

The fly in the ointment was again Chuikov and his organization. If a conventional war were to start in Europe, or anywhere else for that matter, the likelihood would be that before too long things would escalate to the point of a nuclear exchange. Therefore, after the first shots were fired along the Elbe, the Civil Defense of the USSR would swing into action, taking over the railways and clogging up the roads with evacuees. Meanwhile, the General Staff was planning to use the same roads and railways at the same time for their protracted conventional war, moving troops and supplies up to the front, mobilizing reservists (whom Chuikov would be busily evacuating), and so forth.

If the civil defense organization had simply been a division of the Ministry of Defense, organized by the General Staff, things would have been far simpler. The civil defense doctrine could simply have been rewritten in order to chime in with the favored military scenarios. But Civil Defense of the USSR was a totally independent entity, completely separate from the General Staff and Ministry of Defense, and its steadfast adherence to the inevitability of a week-long warning period posed an implied criticism of all the bolt-from-the-blue conventional-warfare-phase scenarios.

Even if civil defense had been separate but under the command of someone of lesser stature, things could probably have been straightened out without too much fuss. It is a measure of Marshal Chuikov's prestige and prowess as a bureaucratic warrior that he was able to hold on as long as he did. As might be expected, the battle was all but invisible to the public eye, but we can see a strong Chuikovite offensive coming in 1968–70, when Chuikov himself, his chief of staff, and the chief of his political directorate all simultaneously published books defending their own theory of civil defense—evacuation, dispersal, and so on. That their political power base was small can be gauged from the fact that the only place their side could get a book published that specifically attacked the whole notion of surprise attack was in the obscure Kirghiz Republic, authored by the local head of civil defense.

While the battle was going on, both the military and the civil defense plans were simultaneously in effect. This meant that had war come during this period, which lasted about four years, both organizations would have laid claim to the same transport facilities. That such a potentially chaotic situation could have been allowed to endure for so long is a fair indication of how seriously the military chieftains of the Soviet Union treat the reality of war, as opposed to the lucrative business of preparing for it.

Finally, in 1972, the General Staff stormed the enemy ramparts. Chuikov was sent into what turned out to be permanent retirement (he died in 1982), and Civil Defense of the USSR was absorbed into the Ministry of Defense. To take charge of the newly tamed organization, the marshals appointed the fifty-one-year-old General Altunin. The comparative obscurity of the new civil defense commander compared with his illustrious predecessor provides a neat example of the diminished fortunes of the organization. Altunin had served for two years as chief of cadres on the General Staff between 1970 and 1972. Prior to that, he had occupied the lowly position of commander of the North Caucasus Military District, a far less prestigious position than the command of one of the important districts, such as Moscow, Leningrad, Kiev, or the Far East. As Richard Anderson remarks, "They replace a hero Marshal of the Soviet Union with the Commander of the North Caucasus Military District, and we are supposed to believe that civil defense is being upgraded in the USSR?"

The consequent changes for civil defense planning that followed the eclipse of Chuikov were both subtle and crucial. The military now had total control of the apparatus, which meant that any evacuee who got in the way of a troop movement would get short shrift. The first priority was to denude civil defense of its lock on the country's transportation network. Accordingly, instead of urban civilians being evacuated by truck or train, they were henceforth to move out on foot in those "orderly columns" of 500 to 1,000. More broadly, the emphasis was shifted from evacuation to the shelter program for the dispersed workers. A construction program for these radiation- and blast-proof shelters was to be instituted, and when that was completed, a permanent shelter program for the non-essential evacuees.

Impressive as such a program might look on paper, it has yet to find concrete expression. Even the first stage, the shelters for the key workers, is very far from completion.

The denouement of General Yershov's career—pensioned off as chief of staff of civil defense troops with modest perquisites—provides further and poignant evidence of the lowly status of civil defense within the Soviet military bureaucracy.

Meanwhile, Altunin is left to issue his homilies on the need for improved training, while the U.S. Federal Emergency Management Agency is left to profit to the tune of a $4 billion civil defense program authorized by Congress in 1982. In view of this, there is a bizarre irony to the hope expressed by the Republican Congressman Donald Mitchell in 1982: "Let's give the American people a civil defense system as good as the Soviets'."

Part V

The Sea Power
of the State

Fifteen

The Navy

One of the admirals most popular in the U.S. Navy is named Sergei Georgiyevich Gorshkov. He is held up as a shining example of what a resourceful naval leader can achieve in the face of determined budget cutters elsewhere in the military establishment and the civilian administration. "He sure knows how to get a budget through," Admiral Harry D. Train, Jr., commander of the U.S. Mediterranean fleet, told the New York *Times* in a typically admiring comment. Captain John Moore, who as editor of *Jane's Fighting Ships* has chronicled the rise of the Soviet navy, invariably refers to Gorshkov as "that great man."

The commander in chief of the Soviet navy has earned these plaudits not because he has distinguished himself in warfare on the high seas. With the exception of the British commander of the Falklands expedition, no admiral of any navy has had a chance to do that since 1945. Nor has

Gorshkov introduced new concepts of ship fighting or naval deployment, revolutionizing war at sea the way the German World War II general Guderian did land combat. What he has done is to build a very large fleet of surface vessels and submarines that can be construed as a paradigm of the "balanced fleet" espoused by Western admirals. The considerable differences that still remain in the size and capabilities of the Soviet fleet as compared with its potential adversaries can be, and are, easily glossed over and obfuscated by the maritime threat assessors.

The building of large fleets is nothing new for the Russians. It has been an ongoing tradition since Peter the Great moved his capital from Moscow to the new Baltic city of St. Petersburg at the beginning of the eighteenth century. And yet, despite all the shipbuilding activity, the tsars and their Soviet successors have rarely had much to show for their endeavors. It is true that Tsar Peter's new fleet, built and commanded by foreigners, did score a victory against the Swedes in 1714 and that in the late eighteenth and early nineteenth centuries the fleet proved useful in seizing control of the Black Sea from the Turks, a gain which was immediately reversed upon the appearance of the British and French fleets during the Crimean War.

By 1904, the Russian navy was the fourth largest in the world, which did not save it from total defeat at the hands of the Japanese at the Battle of Tsushima in May 1905. Undaunted, the Russians set out to build another fleet, a process that remained uncompleted by the time World War I broke out. The navy played no significant part in that war, but the disaffection of the sailors moored off Petrograd (as St. Petersburg had been renamed) in 1917 helped set off the October Revolution.

The Soviet defense buildup of the 1930s included an enormous naval contingent. When the Germans invaded in June 1941, the Soviets had the largest submarine fleet in the world, as well as a very large force of surface vessels. More ships were in construction, and there were even plans to build aircraft carriers. None of the uncompleted vessels could be launched in the face of the German blockade, and those already afloat played a very insignificant part in the war despite attempts by Soviet naval historians to claim otherwise. Their role was sufficiently marginal for 400,000 sailors to be drafted to serve as foot soldiers in the vital land battles. Such maritime activities as did take place were confined to the estuaries and coastal inlets of the Black Sea under the command of Rear Admiral Gorshkov, who, in a fortuitous circumstance, found himself working with a political adviser to the Southern Front named Leonid Brezhnev.

Despite the poor showing of the wartime navy, the attractions of a powerful Soviet fleet remained undiminished both for Stalin and for the U.S. Navy, which in the absence of a Soviet threat would have found less reason with which to justify its own existence. In July 1945, Stalin ordered the construction of a fleet of powerful cruisers, destroyers, and submarines that would be "still stronger and more powerful." Accordingly, the Soviets embarked on a twenty-year program to build a force of 1,200 submarines, 200 destroyers, 36 cruisers, 4 battleships, and 4 aircraft carriers. The U.S. Navy sounded the alarm even before this armada had had a chance to leave the drawing boards. In 1946, Chester Nimitz, chief of Naval Operations, stated that the Soviets were preparing to "neutralize" Britain by blockade, bombardment, and invasion—something the Germans had not succeeded in doing—and were aiming to launch submarine raids against American coastal cities.

Stalin did indeed have invasion on his mind, but the invasion he was concerned about was of Russia by her former allies. The United States and Britain had recently shown that they could use the sea to move large land armies over vast distances and support their operations ashore. If these Western countries could penetrate the Baltic or Black Sea, they might be in a very good position to project forces into the heart of Russia, especially if they were able to use the great rivers that flow into the Black Sea.

The fleet that Stalin planned and spent a great deal of money on was therefore almost entirely defensive in nature. Both ships and submarines lacked the capability to spend long periods at sea or to travel far from friendly ports. The fleet was also old-fashioned. Stalin was always extremely interested in heavy artillery, which may have been the reason for his insistence on building large numbers of gun-carrying heavy cruisers of a type that had proved to have little relevance to the sea battles of World War II. The submarines, when they were not simply refurbished 1930s Soviet designs, were based on captured German U-boats.

However misguided were Stalin's ideas of the kind of navy that Russia required, his orders for the buildup certainly kept the shipyards busy. By the time of his death in 1953, the yards were delivering more than 40 major surface ships a year and upwards of 70 submarines. Then everything suddenly came to a halt.

Stalin's successors lacked his fascination for heavy guns, and they did not share his fears of a Western seaborne invasion of the USSR. The leaders, including Khrushchev, decided that Stalin's "balanced fleet" was of little relevance and embarked on a radical change of direction, cutting back the amount of tonnage produced annually by 60 percent and turning most of the shipyards over to the more benign task of building cargo and fishing ships. Henceforth, the navy would be confined to the auxiliary mission of defending the coasts against attack from American bombers launched from aircraft carriers, using short-range submarines and missiles fired from coastal patrol boats and shore-based aircraft.

The naval high command did not care for this policy in the least, since the admirals yearned for a "proper" oceangoing fleet along the lines of the U.S. and British navies. Admiral Kuznetsov, the commander in chief, was so outspoken in his opposition that he was fired. Khrushchev, always perceptive in his remarks about the military, thought that the admirals resented losing the big oceangoing ships because such ships were so well suited to the requirements of senior commanders. In his autobiography, he recalls that the government agreed to retain four cruisers in the fleet "as a concession to the military, which was in favor of these ships. Our naval commanders thought they were beautiful and liked to show them off to foreigners. An officer likes to hear all the young sailors greet his command with a loud cheer. That always makes a big impression."

It was against this background that Gorshkov was summoned from the Black Sea Fleet in 1956, at the age of 45, to command the navy. He seemed ready enough to endorse the policy against which his predecessor had fought and accept the idea of a downgraded navy. Khrushchev recalls approvingly how Gorshkov easily conceded that one of the surviving Soviet cruisers was completely vulnerable: "We could sink it to the bottom in no time," he told his master, "either with our air-to-surface missiles or with our submarines. And if it got past our defenses at sea, we would sink it with our coastal installations or PT boats."

Such a concession by a service chief to a politician about one of his own newly acquired weapons amounts almost to outright treachery to the service, but it did not take long for Gorshkov to demonstrate that he was a navy loyalist at heart. In 1962, only six years after the sacking of Kuznetsov, Khrushchev had to go to the Zhdanov Shipyard in Leningrad to attend the launching of a new 6,000-ton cruiser! True, Khrushchev managed to throw in a snide remark about the new ship, the first of the Kynda class, being a "floating coffin," but the signs were unmistakable that once again the Soviet navy had slipped the leash and was heading for the open oceans and a balanced fleet.

Gorshkov's ally in the turnabout had been the American threat, more specifically the threat of longer-range carrier-borne bombers and the appearance of the new Polaris-missile-launching submarines. The limited coastal fleet envisaged in the policy shake-up of the mid-1950s had been justified on the basis of the menace of nuclear-weapons-carrying planes of limited range. Then in 1957–58, Gorshkov was able to point out that the range of these planes had increased and that he therefore needed longer-range vessels to deal with them. Thus, the November class submarine (a U.S. intelligence designation), the Soviet Union's first nuclear-powered submarine, was pushed into the anticarrier role when it became operational in 1959. At the same time, the imminent appearance of the Polaris boats, the first of which entered U.S. service in 1960, provided justification for longer-range surface ships specializing in antisubmarine work, such as the helicopter-carrying cruisers *Moskva* and *Leningrad*. Both of these were "laid down" at the beginning of the early 1960s and launched in 1967 and 1968, respectively.

The defense of the Soviet Union against enemy nuclear-missile-launching submarines might seem to be an eminently rational policy, certainly sensible enough for Gorshkov to have persuaded his superiors that it should be attempted. Yet on closer examination, this mission, which dominated Soviet naval procurement policy through the 1960s and early 1970s, appears increasingly less rational and more in keeping with the attitude that has provided the USSR with a vast and fundamentally pointless air defense system.

As described in Chapter 13, the air defense forces have invested heavily in an antiaircraft system that guards the skies against high-flying enemy bombers. There is little prospect that the Soviet Union will be attacked by high-flying bombers, since present plans by the U.S. Strategic Air Command call for low-level penetration of enemy airspace. The Soviet Union has no defense against low-flying bombers, but on the principle of "better something than nothing," they keep the air defense service going anyhow.

So it is with the navy. It is almost an impossible task to track nuclear-missile submarines, which move very quietly and slowly in random patterns in the ocean depths. Apart from chance encounters, this has never been successfully accomplished (despite navy claims) to this day by either the U.S. or the Soviet navy. The Americans have gone to the lengths of laying down SOSUS arrays, which are miles and miles of listening devices laid on the ocean floor and linked to shore by cable. This system may have a certain utility in peacetime, but it would be a slender reed on which to depend in war, since underwater cables are not that difficult to discover and cut, a fact the Germans found out at the beginning of World War I, when the British cut all German overseas underwater communications lines.

Antisubmarine warfance (or ASW, as it is commonly called) is, in fact, a far less understood art than is commonly supposed. It is true that the U-boat menace was effectively overcome by the British and the Americans by the end of the Battle of the Atlantic during World War II, but the true reasons for this success were very carefully obscured for thirty years. The Allies let it be known after the war that they had defeated the German submarines by the clever use of radar to spot submarines on the surface, sonar listening devices to detect them while submerged, and operations research, the technique of analyzing a submarine's probable course through examination of previous behavior patterns. This claim proved to be of great assistance to the radar, sonar, and operations-research industries, but it was not the determining factor in the defeat of the U-boats. What the British and Americans were concerned about was obscuring the role of Ultra, the code-breaking effort that had enabled them to listen in on all the German naval headquarters' communications with the submarine fleet. Fortuitously, the German naval commander Admiral Karl Doenitz believed in exercising tight control over his far-flung forces. Thus, the airwaves were full of priceless information about the exact location of the U-boats, which made their interception and detection a comparatively simple matter. Neither the Soviets nor the Americans can count on being so successful in cracking naval or other codes during a future war, and therefore it is more than likely that missile-carrying submarines will be able to go about their business unmolested by enemy antisubmarine forces.

Reality, however, rarely interferes with a military procurement program, and therefore Admiral Gorshkov has had little problem in extracting permission to build up a fleet in pursuit of an entirely unattainable objective.

The objectives of the fleet that Gorshkov built up after the Khrushchev reforms were and still remain primarily defensive—the suppression of the American missile submarine fleet and the protection of the Soviet missile boats. However, truly imperial and well-funded navies tend to have more ambitious roles. The imperative becomes sea control rather than limited defensive objectives. Such was the self-appointed role of the Royal Navy in the days of British maritime domination and is the fundamental purpose of the U.S. Navy today. In the early 1970s, Gorshkov made it clear that he envisaged nothing less for *his* navy. Hitherto, he had enjoyed remarkable success in persuading the supreme Soviet military and political leadership of the necessity and practicality of giving the navy a vital role in a strategic nuclear exchange. Nevertheless, he still had to play second fiddle to the ground and strategic rocket forces, which dominated military decision making and thus had overall control of assigning the navy its missions.

By the early 1970s, Gorshkov felt bold enough to challenge this dominance. The medium he chose was the naval journal *Morskoy sbornik* (Naval Collection). Starting in 1972, this magazine published a series of 11 articles over Gorshkov's by-line with the general title "Navies in Peace and War." The basic theme of the series was the importance to the Soviet Union of a strong fleet and the contention that naval matters were too important to be decided by soldiers. Navies, the articles argued by selective citation of historical examples, were increasingly important in influencing the outcome of wars of all kinds, as well as important as instruments of state policy in peacetime. If a country wanted to be a great power, it had to have a powerful fleet. By these criteria, in Gorshkov's opinion, the Soviet Union did not have the right kind of fleet. It did not have enough surface ships, and those it did have were too specialized. Overall, the navy was hampered by being oriented toward a specific and defensive mission. If the Soviet Union was to use sea power as a great power should, then it would have to build a proper fleet, something it could easily afford to do.

The soldiers seem to have recognized this for the interservice power play it was, and they fought back. One of the weapons they used was their overall control of military censorship, which they used to hold up publications of *Morskoy sbornik* halfway through the series. Marshal Grechko, who was Minister of Defense at the time, exercised his prerogative and advanced into the pages of *Morskoy sbornik* itself to publish a sharp rebuttal to the Gorshkov thesis. While acknowledging the need for a navy, he discussed its role purely as a wartime force for use both in delivering submarine-launched nuclear missiles at the enemy's home territory and in defending the Soviet Union itself, *not* as a tool for projecting Soviet policies worldwide in peace or war. In discussing a huge naval exercise held by Gorshkov the year before, Grechko made no mention of the surface ships that had taken part and that had constituted the largest component of the exercise.

Despite this formidable opposition, Gorshkov's bureaucratic agility carried the day for the navy. In May 1974, Grechko hauled down his colors with an article that acknowledged that the "historic function of the Soviet armed forces is not merely restricted to . . . defending the homeland and other socialist states," the notion that Gorshkov had explicitly attacked, but that, on the contrary, it had now been "expanded and enriched with new content," meaning that there was indeed a necessity for worldwide power projection, which could be carried out only by a navy endowed with a large fleet of surface ships.

Under the terms of the interservice cease-fire, Gorshkov did pay passing lip service to the notion that the primary mission of the navy was to assist in the overall nuclear-war plan. However, the emphasis of his articles, which were subsequently expanded and published in the book *Sea Power of the State*, is on promoting the notion of a traditional naval role—sea control—made possible by the acquisition of a balanced fleet.

The precise reasons for Gorshkov's victory are obscure. General Samuel Wilson, who served as a military attaché in the U.S. Embassy in Moscow in the early 1970s before becoming director of the Defense Intelligence Agency, once asked this rhetorical question: have the Soviets built up a big navy "in response to be able to meet certain foreign policy objectives, or did they build it just because they wanted a big navy that they could be proud of? I suspect, irrational as this may sound, that there was a considerable impulse deriving from the latter, and now that they have it they are seeking ways and means to use it. That may sound a little silly, but I really believe that that has to be considered. There is no question that it has been expensive."

Thus by the mid-1970s, the Soviet navy had fought its way back, under Gorshkov's inspired leadership, from the dark days of the Khrushchev cuts and was now freed from the shackles of army domination and relegation to a subordinate and specific mission. It could now portray itself as a proper fleet, just like the British and American navies of past and present. This renaissance found budgetary expression in the introduction of new and larger general-purpose surface ships, such as the 23,000-ton *Kirov* nuclear-powered cruiser. This ship is designed for long-range operations and, in a touch that would certainly have aroused cynical comment from Khrushchev, includes extensive quarters for an admiral and his staff.

Despite the addition of these and other imposing-looking vessels, the Soviets still have a long way to go before their fleet can equal the "balance" of the yardstick by which such things are measured: the U.S. Navy. Aircraft carriers, for example, which form the backbone of the American surface fleet, have yet to appear on the Soviet side. The U.S. threat assessors have been most generous in referring to the 37,000-ton Kiev class ships as aircraft carriers, even though they are nothing of the kind. These ships, the first of which appeared in 1976, carry helicopters and a number of small vertical takeoff fighters—Yak-36 Forgers. In common with other vertical takeoff aircraft, these planes use so much fuel in taking off and landing that they can spend very little time actually in the air going about their business; in fact, the longest that a Forger has ever been observed to spend in the air is 16 minutes.

The appearance of a true aircraft carrier comparable to the American behemoths, capable of catapulting conventional fighters and bombers off its decks and recovering them again, has been eagerly anticipated by Gorshkov's admirers in the U.S. and other Western navies. So far, none has actually appeared, but by 1982 there were reliable reports that the Soviets had indeed laid the keel of a 60,000-ton carrier, to be launched in the late 1980s. Along with the carrier itself will come the aircraft, the first fighters the Soviet navy will have had since the air force took over its land-based contingent in 1959. Of necessity, the carrier will have to be accompanied by the whole paraphernalia of a carrier task force—escorting air defense ships, anti-submarine warfare ships, fuel tankers, supply ships, and so on. This kind of effort is fearfully expensive (upwards of $17 billion for a U.S. carrier task force) and, as we shall see, of dubious utility in peace or war. Nevertheless, when the Soviet carrier finally joins the fleet, Gorshkov will have reached the apogee of naval fashion.

"The Soviet Navy," declares Gorshkov, "has been transformed into an important strategic force, into a force capable of opposing aggression from the sea and of accomplishing major operational and strategic missions on the World Ocean. . . . Its relative weight within the composition of the armed forces is continually increasing."

The American naval chieftains see no reason to quarrel with this assessment. Chief of Naval Operations Admiral Thomas B. Hayward informed the Congress in 1979 that "in the past 15 years the Soviet Navy has steadily grown from a coastal defense force into a blue water navy powerful enough to challenge the U.S. Navy in most major ocean areas of the world." To Hayward, the appropriate U.S. response seemed no less self-evident: "For the U.S. Navy to remain second to none, logic drives us to the clear conclusion that we must allocate sufficient resources for shipbuilding in the defense budget."

Aside from admirals' rhetoric, the potency of the Soviet fleet is less easy to determine. Once again there is the problem of calculating its actual size, although the threat assessors find no reason for equivocation here. *Understanding Soviet Naval Developments*, published by the office of the chief of Naval Operations, states that "in terms of ships the U.S. Navy is clearly outnumbered by the Soviet Navy, by a ratio of 3 to 1." The claim is buttressed by an imposing array of figures, which show the Soviets as having a total active fleet of 1,764 vessels, as opposed to 462 for the Americans. These totals include all classes of ships, from aircraft carriers to small patrol boats. Even when the smaller craft are excluded, the Soviets are still shown as having a terrific lead in every area except aircraft carriers, although even here the little Kiev class ships are considered comparable to the 13 great 80,000- and 90,000-ton U.S. carriers. In other kinds of surface warships, the Soviets are supposed to be ahead by 269 to 178, while their submarines outnumber those of the U.S. Navy by 362 to 120.

In one sense, these figures are far more solid than estimates of the numbers of tanks, artillery pieces, or armored troop carriers in the Soviet arsenal. Unlike land weapons, ships are easy to count; they can easily be photographed on the slipway by a satellite or high-flying reconnaissance plane, and they can be examined and identified at even closer range whenever they leave Soviet territorial waters. Nevertheless, the Soviet fleet of major surface vessels is considerably smaller than the U.S. Navy figures would have us suppose.

The inflation of the figures is possible because there is no dictionary definition of "major surface vessel." The U.S. Navy has chosen to define such a ship as anything more than 1,000 tons. This may seem a reasonable unit of measurement, except that it has the effect of augmenting the size of the Soviet surface fleet by about 100 ships. Quite simply, the Soviets have a large number of coastal craft that weigh just over 1,000 tons, such as the Riga class frigates. The United States has nothing between its smallest frigate, the Bronstein class, weighing 2,300 tons, and tiny patrol boats of 100 or 200 tons.

Not only does this kind of statistical sleight of hand have a significant effect on what we mean by the size of the Soviet navy, it can also be used to distort Soviet ship-building rates. In 1970, for example, the Russians began building a light corvette generically known as the Grisha class, each ship estimated to weigh just under 1,000 tons. Production of the Grisha corvettes continued at a fairly steady rate, between four and six a year throughout the 1970s. In 1976, however, these ships suddenly took on more formidable proportions in the eyes of the U.S. Navy, although their captains and crews may not have noticed any sudden increase in their combat capability. That year, the Americans decided that the weight of a Grisha corvette was in fact just over 1,000 tons, which is why U.S. intelligence graphs depicting Soviet major-surface-ship construction show a sudden upturn that year.

The Soviet submarine fleet presents a more awkward problem for the U.S. Navy. On the one hand, the large size of Gorshkov's underwater fleet, 362 as compared to an American total of 120, provides a useful statistic in depicting the ominous dimensions of the threat. On the other hand, more than half of these Soviet submarines are driven by diesel-electric engines, as opposed to nuclear engines. The U.S. Navy regards such nonnuclear boats as so hopelessly old-fashioned that it has refused to build any for more than twenty years, and by the beginning of the 1980s was getting rid of the few it had left from the prenuclear age. Thus, it is far harder to find warnings of the Soviet numerical lead in submarines from senior U.S. Navy officials than reference to the Soviet surface fleet. Suggestions that the United States might try to close the gap by building diesel-electric submarines, each of which can be built for about a quarter of the price of a nuclear vessel, have not yet been received favorably by the admirals.

The relevance of all these numbers is fundamentally affected by the facts of nature, which not even Admiral Gorshkov can do anything about. Although the Soviet Union has the world's longest coastline, it has very few ports. Most of the coast is blocked by ice for all or part of the year. Despite the fact that the site of Leningrad was chosen by Peter the Great because it gave Russia access to the open ocean, the port is sometimes choked by up to 3 feet of ice, and all the important Soviet naval bases need constant work by icebreakers to stay open during the winter. Only the Black Sea offers the Soviet navy warm and permanently ice-free ports.

Geography restricts the Soviet fleet as much as the weather. To get to the open seas ships must pass through narrow channels bounded by territory in the hands of U.S. allies. The Soviet Northern Fleet's route to the Atlantic skirts the northern coast of Norway; the Baltic Fleet has to sail through the 40-mile-wide Kattegat between Denmark and Sweden; and the Black Sea ships have to pass under the bridge linking the two halves of Istanbul at the Bosporus in order to reach the Mediterranean and run the gauntlet of the straits of Gibraltar in order to move out into the Atlantic. In the Soviet Far East, the main naval base at Vladivostok is hemmed in the Sea of Japan, where the 110-mile-wide Korea Strait between South Korea and Japan is the widest exit. Only the remote outpost of Petropavlovsk-Kamchatskiy on the eastern coast of the Kamchatka peninsula, which is completely without land routes to civilization, has easy access to an open ocean.

The vast distances that separate the limited and mostly constricted Soviet marine outposts deny the Soviets the possibility of concentration and place them at a severe disadvantage compared to the U.S. Navy. "The United States," admits John Collins of the Library of Congress, "is twice blessed with sheltered ports on ice-free coasts that open on the world's largest oceans and, in turn, on every continent. Power can shift easily in response to requirements. Most forces from European waters, for example, could reinforce the Far East with relative impunity, passing through the Panama Canal (as long as it is secure) to weight whatever effort takes priority. No other nation enjoys such freedom and flexibility." Certainly not the Soviets, whose geographic problems mean that the Northern, Baltic, Black Sea, and Pacific Fleets, into which the navy is divided, must operate on their own, without much prospect of mutual reinforcement. The most shattering defeat in Russian naval history—the Russo-Japanese War of 1904–05—serves as a reminder of this fact. The Imperial Japanese Navy was first able to eliminate the tsarist Pacific Fleet, and when the hurriedly dispatched Baltic Fleet arrived after a four-month voyage halfway around the world, the Japanese sank that too.

Therefore, no matter how large the Soviet fleet may be made to appear when compared with the total U.S. naval forces, the four Soviet fleet commanders know that locally they are each significantly outnumbered by the combined forces of the United States and its allies. In the seas around Northern Europe, NATO can deploy 409 ships and submarines against the Warsaw Pact's 309, excluding the ballistic-missile submarines on either side on the assumption that they would not take active part in battles between the fleets at sea. In the Mediterranean, the gap is equally large—144 to 118—added to which is the fact that most of the Soviet submarines assigned to that area must come all the way from the Northern Fleet bases near Murmansk because of limitations on their rights of passage through the Bosporus.

In the Far East the Soviets just outnumber the United States when it comes to numbers alone, 159 to 142, but the Soviets are not facing just the American Pacific Fleet. The Japanese, notwithstanding American admonitions about their lackadaisical defense effort, have built up a modern and potent navy, which includes 48 destroyers and frigates and 14 submarines. The Chinese, who are also possible opponents, have 83 submarines, which is one less than the Soviet total for the area, 27 destroyers and frigates, and an enormous number of small torpedo-carrying boats and other coastal craft.

Superiority in numbers does not in itself determine the outcome of a battle, as the Soviet navy should well understand in the light of the debacle of 1941. It is only worth enumerating the various components of the Soviet navy and those of its likely opponents because of the casual way these figures are treated by American officials anxious to make a case for a further increase in the size of the U.S. Navy. In a 1982 interview with *International Defense Review*, John F. Lehman, the Reagan Administration's Navy Secretary, invoked a "permanent, blue-water, offensive Soviet fleet of more than 100 modern combatants in the Pacific." The appearance of this force "in the last five years" represented, in Lehman's view, a direct threat to the northwestern United States. "Thus the expansion of our navy to the 15 battle groups (that is, 15 aircraft carriers plus attendant escorts) is essential." Factors that may well occupy the attention of the Soviet Pacific Fleet commander, Admiral V. P. Maslov, such as the Japanese and Chinese navies or the protection of the 35 ballistic-missile-firing submarines in his area, went unmentioned.

Qualitative evaluations of the Soviet fleet are less popular with U.S. Navy policymakers than simplified numerical comparisons. Although limitations on the threat are acknowledged, they are underplayed and, in addition, are sometimes self-serving. In 1977, for example, the U.S. Navy's director of intelligence remarked on the Navy's "lack [of] a meaningful sea-based tactical-air capability. [Its] strike and reconnaissance bombers are vulnerable to attack beyond the range of land-based Soviet fighters." Such caveats must be read in the light of the U.S. Navy's own unshakable faith in the primacy of the large aircraft carrier, a faith that is all the more bitterly defended as it comes under attack from sceptics within the U.S. defense community.

More importantly, the U.S. Navy officially concedes that "the Soviets' open ocean ASW [antisubmarine warfare capability] is low." This is really an astounding admission, in view of the fact that so much of Admiral Gorshkov's vaunted fleet is primarily equipped to hunt for submarines. In a comparatively thin section of *Understanding Soviet Naval Developments* entitled "Limitations," the authors declare, "Most modern Soviet surface combatants, a significant segment of their submarine force, and many of the combat aircraft of their navy are dedicated primarily to hunting Western submarines. Fortunately, their capability to find them does not appear to be improving much."

A close look at the operations of Gorshkov's navy does indeed reveal the same traits as in the other Soviet military services. Stated briefly, the ships are ill-suited for anything other than short operations, and the sailors who man them are deficient both in training and morale.

The most obvious and glaring example of the technological backwardness is to be found in the Soviet strategic-missile-firing submarines. The Soviets led the world in the arming of submarines with nuclear weapons, but this was through necessity rather than choice. Although they successfully tested an atom bomb in 1949, they had not managed, as we have seen, to build a bomber capable of getting it to the continental United States. The best they could do was to construct nuclear-armed torpedoes, in the hope that a submarine might be able to get close enough to fire one into an important harbor such as New York City or Norfolk, Virginia. They then experimented with submarine-launched nuclear cruise missiles, essentially pilotless airplanes of minimal accuracy and a range of about 300 miles. Finally, they progressed to longer-range ballistic missiles, which could be fired from underwater; however, these, which were first introduced in the early 1960s, were not and still are not comparable to the U.S. Polaris-missile boats introduced at the same time.

Polaris boats were originally meant to be armed with the liquid-fueled Jupiter missile. This approach was abandoned in favor of the solid-fueled Polaris as soon as it became feasible to build a solid-fueled rocket. Liquid-fueled rockets were simply too unstable for use on a submarine, given the tendency of the fuel to corrode its containers and to explode at unpredictable moments. To this day, the most modern U.S. Naval submarine-launched ballistic missiles lack the liquid engine incorporated in the upper stage of the land-based rockets, simply because it is considered too dangerous for use at sea.

The backward state of Soviet rocket technology allowed no such concern for safety in the early 1960s, and twenty years later the situation remains unchanged. As with the land-based force, the Soviets have made repeated attempts to develop a solid-fueled naval missile. In 1978 they even armed a submarine with such a weapon, the SS-N-17, which was duly hailed by U.S. observers as having "increased range" and "greater accuracy." Hardly had these endorsements gone to press, however, when the 12 operational SS-N-17s were withdrawn, never to be seen again. In the early 1980s the Soviets are trying again, with the SS-N-20 Typhoon missile, which so far has displayed an unwelcome tendency to explode in flight.

The perils of a Soviet missile submariner's life are not confined to his cargo of missiles. Most of the Soviet missile boats are nuclear-powered, as are 98 of the nonstrategic attack submarines. Nuclear-powered vessels in the U.S. Navy have always been constructed so as to minimize the crews' exposure to radiation, and as a result, accidents have been extremely rare. If the Soviets have been similarly concerned, the results have not been as successful. When Admiral Hyman G. Rickover, the father of the U.S. nuclear navy, was invited on a goodwill visit to the nuclear-powered icebreaker *Lenin*, he discovered that his half-hour tour had exposed him to more radioactivity than half a lifetime on American nuclear-powered boats. According to Navy Secretary Lehman, there have been a number of fatal accidents with Soviet naval nuclear power plants. Old sailors' homes in Russia have hairless inmates, presumably because they have been exposed to too much radioactivity while serving on the nuclear ships and submarines of the Northern and Pacific Fleets. Sailors of the Baltic Fleet, which contains no nuclear vessels, make the same point in a ghoulish joke that goes like this:

"How do you tell a man is from the Northern Fleet?"

"Because he glows in the dark."

These problems with both the submarines and missiles may account for the fact that only about 9 of the Soviet Union's 84 missile-carrying submarines are at sea at any one time. In contrast, the United States manages to keep half its missile-carrying vessels permanently out on patrol, which means that the United States has more submarines in use, even though its force of 36 such vessels is little more than half the size of the Soviet force. To achieve this, the Americans try to have two crews for every strategic submarine, so that they can alternate sea and shore duty. Keeping enough men with the necessary training and skill to endure the tedium of long months of underwater duty, cut off from all contact with the world, is by no means easy, and, in order to maintain the patrol rate, crewmen are being pressed to spend more and more time at sea. The Soviets reportedly find it difficult to find enough men of the required skill and willingness to risk premature baldness or worse to allot more than one crew per boat.

This inability or unwillingness to keep a large part of the force out at sea may account for the Soviet development of long-range submarine missiles, such as the SS-N-18, which can reach the United States even if launched from a submarine in or near its home port. If this is really the reason for the added range of these missiles, it is most illogical, since the whole point of a missile-carrying submarine is that it should be able to lurk beneath the surface without the enemy knowing its whereabouts until it commences firing. If the missiles are to be fired without the submarine leaving harbor, it would be just as useful and much cheaper to launch them from concrete silos like the ordinary fixed-base ICBMs of the strategic rocket forces.

Despite the extra problems associated with liquid-fueled missiles and nuclear reactors, the missile boats are not really so very different in their inactivity from the rest of the fleet. The Soviet fleet does not move about very much, spending most of its time tied up in port or resting at anchor out at sea. Thus, although the Soviets keep a large number of ships in the Mediterranean at all times, only one out of five will actually be under weigh. The rest are simply sitting at anchor at one of a number of gathering points, either at the entrance to the Aegean Sea or off the coast of North Africa.

Even when they do move about, Soviet ships are careful lest they be subjected to undue strain. Whereas the U.S. Navy habitually cruises at a minimum of 15 knots, even the most modern Soviet vessels seldom exceed 12 knots, and many prefer to proceed at an even slower pace. Sometimes they go to the lengths of taking each other under tow, either because unreliable propulsion machinery has broken down or with the aim of reducing wear and tear on the delicate propulsion systems.

One might imagine that these habits should not matter very much. The amount of fuel burned is very much reduced, and it would seem that the ships can always get up steam and put on a spurt whenever they have to. In reality, it means that the Soviet navy, for all Gorshkov's energy and reforms, is no different from the tank divisions that keep their weapons moldering in mothballs for most of the year or the frontal-aviation units that sit on the ground while their pilots' skills atrophy. Gorshkov's apologists like to point to his comments about the "battle of the first salvo," implying that the far-sighted admiral has deduced that since the war will be over almost as soon as it has begun, there is no need to prepare for anything more extensive or strenuous. This notion has a superficial logic to it, until one reflects that it is hardly wise to design a ship that can keep up a high level of operations only for a limited period before beginning to fall apart.

Like their tanks and aircraft, Soviet ships cannot be repaired except at an extensive and well-equipped base. With the possible exception of some of the newer and bigger surface ships, Soviet vessels are designed in such a way that it is very difficult to get at and repair various items of machinery that may break down unless the ship is in dock. Captain James Kehoe, a leading U.S. expert on Soviet ship design, writing in the June 1982 *International Defense Review*, states that they have "much more tightly packed propulsion-machinery plants and much less space for access, both in terms of passageways and space around equipment, as well as less space for workshops, storerooms and offices. These types of space are provided on American ships to enhance the crew's ability to maintain equipment at sea and hence sustain operations in locations like the Indian Ocean."

Kehoe once directed a team from the Naval Sea Systems Command in a paper experiment. The team members took the design of an up-to-date American frigate, the *Oliver Hazard Perry*, and "Sovietized" it, redesigning the warship as it might look if it had been planned and built in a Soviet shipyard to carry the same array of weapons at the same speed and range as the U.S. original. They therefore severely lowered the headroom below decks for the crew, allotted minimum space for maintenance, and crammed most of the weapons and electronic systems above rather than below deck, as would be the American practice.

The result was a ship three-quarters the size of the original and 16 percent smaller in tonnage. The vessel would also supposedly have been 35 percent cheaper to build, because it was smaller and required simpler construction techniques. Kehoe later noted that this smaller and less expensive ship, even if theoretically equipped with actual weapons built to American standards, would be both noisier and less resistant to damage. It would be "less capable of sustained operations, because it would have less accessibility to equipment, fewer workshops and storerooms, and less equipment redundancy." It would not handle heavy seas as well as the larger American frigate. "Essentially it would be a less capable anti-submarine warfare ship."

The catch, of course, is that real Soviet ships do not

carry American weapons; in fact, most of them are comparatively lightly armed, although they certainly do not look that way. "Graceful yet purposeful in appearance," as *Understanding Soviet Naval Developments* admiringly puts it, the decks and masts of their warships positively bristle with missile launchers and electronic antennas. By comparison, the decks of American ships look bare and spartan. The reason for this is quite simply that the Russians are showing all they have got, perhaps reflecting Sasha Dorman's dictum that for the military, "it is more important that a thing look good than that it be good." Once they have fired all those impressive-looking missiles stored on or just beneath the deck launchers—all highly vulnerable to even a strafing attack by enemy aircraft—they have shot their bolt. The American decks look empty, not because the ships are unarmed, but because the various weapons systems are stored out of sight.

Such armaments as the Soviets do have consist almost entirely of missiles guided to their targets by radar. For the shorter-range weapons, like the SS-N-2 Styx, the missile's radar simply homes in on the radar pulses reflected from the target ship. For longer-range weapons, such as the SS-N-3 Shaddock, the missile needs navigational assistance until within radar range, midcourse guidance as it is called, from another ship or aircraft, which can correct the missile's path and guide it toward the enemy. Unlike modern Western antiship missiles, such as the American Harpoon or the Anglo-French Exocet, which achieved instant fame in the Falkland Islands war, these Soviet missiles do not skim along just above the surface, which would make them harder for the target ship to detect. Instead they follow a parabolic course, cruising in at a height no lower than several hundred feet—some much higher—before gracefully and very visibly descending toward the intended victim.

While much is known about the combat capabilities of Soviet fighter planes or tanks, little is known about the actual combat performance of Soviet naval weapons. In fact, until the 1982 war between Britain and Argentina, there had been almost no examples of combat at sea in which theories of naval warfare evolved since 1945 could be tested. This is why the sinking of the Israeli destroyer *Eilath* in October 1967 by the Egyptians using two Soviet-supplied Styx SS-N-2 missiles had an enormous effect on military thinking both about warfare in general and Soviet naval weaponry in particular. The Egyptian navy at the time was respectfully reviewed by naval professionals as being "balanced" with the correct quotas of small, medium, and large surface ships.

In the 1973 Yom Kippur War, the Egyptians set out to repeat their *Eilath* success, but the 50 or more Styx missiles they fired scored not a single hit. The reason was that the Israelis had adapted to it by scrapping their few large destroyers and rebuilding their navy entirely around small, fast, and highly maneuverable patrol boats. In addition, these fast boats were equipped to fire large amounts of chaff, strips of aluminum foil that reflect back and clutter up the missile's radar receiver. This was not a new invention, having been discovered more or less simultaneously by the British and Germans during World War II, although both sides withheld its use for a while in case the other should discover the secret. The Israelis, however, exploited it to maximum effectiveness and, along with their small and quick-moving boats, were able to render the "balanced" Egyptian fleet obsolete.

By inference, these new tactics had also made the Soviet fleet obsolete, since its antiship armament consists almost entirely of radar-guided missiles no harder to defeat than the Styx. It can be argued, of course, that the Israelis have found the answer only to a particular situation in which enemy forces are attacking close to the defenders' home shore and that the fast boats would lack the range and seaworthiness for engagements out in the open oceans. This argument provides a neat excuse for the U.S. Navy to retain its "balanced" fleet of large oceangoing surface ships, but it also assumes as a matter of course that navies will continue to exercise the traditional function of sea control, attempting to dominate the waters far from their own territory and close to that of the enemy. In point of fact, the Saar 5 class of Israeli vessels, which have a displacement of 850 tons and a top speed of 40 knots or more, are big enough to go on such long-range missions as the British Falklands expedition—although the men on board would not have had a comfortable time in the mountainous seas of the South Atlantic.

Oceangoing admirals have therefore opted for a different solution to the threat of the antiship missile. The new tactics do not follow Israeli lines but involve complex and expensive hardware. The British fleet that sailed off into the South Atlantic to do battle with the Argentines was equipped with a profusion of electronic gadgetry to jam the radars of antiship missiles and with antimissile missiles to shoot them down. Nevertheless, three of the fleet's ships were hit by Exocets, a fact that immediately provoked a torrent of debate among experts, both professional and amateur, about the continued viability of oceangoing ships. The official response of the U.S. Navy was to see the British losses as further proof of the necessity for large aircraft carriers that can carry aircraft capable of spotting and intercepting the missile launchers before they can fire and the necessity for vastly expensive antimissile ships festooned with highly complex and vulnerable radar systems with which to track and intercept the incoming projectiles. Still more fancifully, considerable effort is being invested in shipborne laser beam systems of dubious practicality, again with the object of fending off salvos of Soviet antiship missiles.

In this welter of debate and billion-dollar research and development contracts, little thought has been given to more passive and simpler answers to the radar missile threat. Thomas Amlie, former technical director of the U.S. Naval Weapons Center, is one person who has done so, and he points out a number of reasons why the large surface ships of today are vulnerable. First, they all continuously emit a barrage of radar and radio signals, which makes it comparatively easy for the enemy to determine the ships' whereabouts; that indeed was how the Argentines were able to locate the ill-fated *Sheffield* in the middle of the South Atlantic wastes. Second, radar missiles home in on the target ship because it presents an outstanding radar image, alone in the middle of the sea. Amlie proposes that if the radar missile could be provided with an echo larger than that of the target ship, it would head for that and leave the ship unharmed. Such a device is easy to construct; called an off-board decoy transponder, it can be towed on a raft behind a ship at a safe distance, amplifying and reflecting back the attacking missiles' radar pulses and luring the firepower of the enemy fleet away from its targets large and small. "The U.S. Navy did carry out tests at one time on this kind of system in a half-hearted way," says one U.S. weapons expert. "It worked like gangbusters. But an individual model need cost no more than $20,000, which is maybe why there is no interest."

A considerable portion of the U.S. Naval budget is devoted to procuring the means for fending off the rather motley force of 400 or so Soviet land-based missile-carrying bombers under naval command. This should not be surprising, for until the long-awaited Soviet carrier appears, there will be little else to justify the existence of the F-14 fighter and its 100-mile-range Phoenix missile or of the enormous aircraft carriers that are needed to carry them. The bulk of Soviet naval aviation consists of extremely aged TU-16 Badger bombers, while the naval version of the more modern Backfire is being produced at the parsimonious rate of 15 a year at most. There are, of course, the vertical takeoff Yak-36 Forgers based on the four Kiev class "carriers," but it is hard to dress these up as much of a threat to anybody. When I suggested to a group of U.S. Navy fighter pilots from the Naval Fighter Weapons School at the Miramar air base in California that the Forgers might indeed pose a threat, the response was a burst of derisive laughter. Since these particular men were tactics instructors, extensively drilled in Soviet air-combat capabilities, their assessment of the Forger, with its 16-minute flight limit, speaks for itself. In public, however, the Navy takes care to leave taxpayers in no doubt as to the menace to U.S. carriers from Soviet aircraft.

There is less eagerness on the part of the U.S. Navy to draw attention to the carriers' vulnerability to submarines. How else can one explain the Navy's decision to censor a report on the NATO exercise Ocean Venture '81? The report in question was written by Lieutenant Commander Dean Knuth, who had umpired the war game and was responsible for deciding who would have won if the two sides had actually been firing at each other. Unfortunately for the Navy, Commander Knuth had concluded that the two aircraft carriers taking part would have been speedily sent to the bottom by the very small force of "enemy" submarines.

Admiral Rickover, the creator of the nuclear-powered submarine, declared when he was finally retired from the service in 1982 that the entire U.S. carrier force would last "about two days" if war broke out. "Operating against a carrier is too easy," reports Commander John Byron, an active-duty submarine officer in the U.S. Navy. "The carrier's ASW protection often resembles Swiss cheese."

This being the case, the huge Soviet submarine force might just wreak havoc upon the U.S. surface fleet, so long as it is able to make its way out of port into the open ocean. Apart from its numbers, more than half the Soviet submarine force could have an advantage generated purely by the U.S. Navy's affection for nuclear submarines. As Commander Byron puts it: "Within a few years, we will have decommissioned our last diesel-electric submarine. When that happens, two things will likely occur: our ASW skill against diesel submarines will evaporate; and our evaluation of the threat posed by diesel submarines will lose the reality that exercise results provide. Work against nuclear submarines leaves unexercised the ASW needed to counter the diesel boat. In addition to the Soviet diesel submarine fleet, which is still building such boats, there is the potential threat posed by the diesel submarines of some 30 other nations."

Diesel-electric boats are called thus because they use diesel engines when moving on the surface. Since diesels require a constant supply of air to function, such boats switch over to battery-powered electric motors when they submerge. The diesel-electric U-boats that sank so many Allied ships during World War II could only stay underwater for a few hours at a time because their batteries had a limited life before needing recharging on the surface. Since 1945, battery design—neglected in the United States—has moved far ahead in other countries. The most modern diesel-electric boats can now stay underwater for up to 150 hours. Once they have overcome the problem of short-lived batteries, diesel-electric submarines present some significant advantages over the more "advanced" nuclear-powered boats: they are much cheaper to build, they do not require a crew of very highly trained nuclear engineers, and, most important of all, they are very quiet.

Submarines are detected when they are underwater by the noise they make, which is why submariners under attack in World War II movies talk in whispers. The engine is the main source of noise, and this is the problem with nuclear-powered boats. A nuclear reactor must have a flow of coolant water pumping around the core at all times, even when the submarine itself is not moving. This provides an unceasing and dangerous degree of noise. A submarine moving on battery power will be less noisy anyway, and it can become totally silent by switching off its engine entirely, something the nuclear boat cannot do. The difference is so great that European submariners operating the latest West German diesel-electric boats report that their greatest worry on NATO exercises is being run into by U.S. nuclear submarines unaware of their presence.

The Soviet diesel-electric fleet is not as quiet as the latest models coming out of the West German yards. But its boats are considerably quieter than the nuclear submarines produced in the United States with the specific purpose of hunting them down. The balance is redressed, however, by the tremendous racket kicked up by Soviet nuclear submarines, a fact to which U.S. naval officials feel obliged to draw attention. "In comparison with U.S. submarines," *Understanding Soviet Naval Developments* delicately observes, "the Soviets still lag in . . . submarine quieting techniques." That is putting it mildly; when the Soviet Alpha class submarine was undergoing sea trials in the Norwegian Sea in the spring of 1980, the U.S. Navy was able to hear it from Bermuda.

"People go on about how big these new Oscar and Alpha class Soviet attack submarines are," a U.S. submarine officer remarked to me, "but I can't really see what they are talking about. A submarine's size should be measured in decibels not in feet, and if a boat is moving fast and deep it is effectively blind, deaf and noisy. She can't see what's going on because she can't use her periscope, and at speed she's making so much noise she can't listen for the other guy."

In addition to building faster and bigger boats, the Soviets have taken one other step that detracts from their numerical advantage in submarines over the U.S. Navy. Torpedoes are still the submarine's most effective weapon, a simple weapon relatively immune to countermeasures. But the focus of Soviet submarine armament is on longer-range missiles that are of the same type as that used on the surface ships and that are just as vulnerable to an enemy with the imagination to employ effective countermeasures.

A navy that comes equipped with noisy submarines, ships that break down after a few days of intensive operations, and a limited supply of easily neutralized missiles will have problems in wartime. However, admirals like to see another role for their fleets apart from actual combat; once upon a time it was called gunboat diplomacy, although nowadays it is more often demurely referred to as showing the flag.

Since the aim of showing the flag is to impress the natives rather than fight them, the mission requires ships rather different from those that are likely to be most useful in combat. Khrushchev, who had little use for this kind of self-advertisement, understood the difference well. After deriding the admirals for their affection for elegant cruisers in his autobiography, he gives his views on submarines: "A submarine doesn't make much of an impression. There aren't many people on board, and the craft itself looks like a floating metal cigar. But a submarine is still the supreme naval weapon nowadays, and I'm proud of the role I played in reassessing the direction in which our navy was going and introducing submarines as the basis of our sea power."

As we have seen, Khrushchev was outmaneuvered by the wily Gorshkov, who has succeeded in reinstituting big, expensive, and vulnerable surface ships in his navy. Although there is little reason to suppose that behemoths like the nuclear-powered cruiser *Kirov* or the slightly older Kara class cruisers, which were launched during the 1970s, would survive any longer than the American aircraft carriers in a (submarine torpedo) shooting war, they are certainly as impressive to look at. Even their vulnerabilities are an asset in this regard, since to the uninitiated, all the missiles and electronic equipment laid out for display on deck indicate a massive destructive capability. In just the same way, a 90,000-ton Nimitz class aircraft carrier, its deck carpeted with jet planes, is an omnipotent-looking symbol of the might of the United States and its Navy, whatever Cassandras like Rickover, Knuth, and Byron may say.

There might be some point to the vast expense of these peacetime ships if they really did help "secure state interests in peacetime," as the Russians put it. There is, however, no firm evidence from modern times that such ships do have much influence one way or another. As soon as the American diplomats in Tehran were taken hostage in 1979, for example, the U.S.S. *Nimitz* was dispatched in great haste to the scene. Thereupon, it cruised up and down at great expense outside the entrance to the Persian Gulf for months and months, having no effect whatsoever on the behavior either of the Iranian government or the crowd at the U.S. Embassy. Its sole contribution was to serve as a launching pad for the disastrously ill-managed and tragic rescue attempt. The presence of these carriers and their huge escort task forces should at least help protect the U.S. Navy's own ships, but when the Israelis spent 6 leisurely hours executing their bombing and strafing attacks on the U.S.S. *Liberty* off the coast of Egypt in June 1967, the mighty Sixth Fleet was unable or unwilling to come to its aid.

The Soviet fleet has not been inactive as far as naval diplomacy is concerned. The Arab-Israeli wars of 1967 and 1973, the Jordanian crisis of 1970, and the Indo-Pakistani war of 1971 have all elicited a surge of Soviet naval activity in the region, paralleling similar activity by the U.S. fleets. The most careful postmortems by scholarly experts have failed to find the slightest evidence that the presence of the naval contingents influenced the course of events. In 1972, when the American fleet was busily dispatching bombers to pulverize the capital city and major port of Russia's Vietnamese ally, hitting several Soviet merchant ships and killing a Soviet seaman in the process, the appearance of a Soviet naval task force in the area had no discernible effect on American actions.

An indication of how hard it is to find any evidence that the navy has helped the Soviets "secure state interests in peacetime" is the fact that the most frequently quoted example is the case of Ghana and the Soviet fishing boats. The story, as usually retailed, relates that when the Ghanians seized and interned two Soviet trawlers and their crews in October 1968, the Soviet government ordered a task force made up of two missile boats and a submarine to make a show of force off the Ghanian coast. Supposedly chastened and intimidated by the appearance of this seaborne mailed fist, the Ghanians backed off and released the crews. Admiral Elmo R. Zumwalt, the chief of U.S. Naval Operations at the time, later hailed the incident as a sign "that the USSR was ready, willing and able to protect its interests in parts of the world hitherto inaccessible to it." Such a modest triumph over so puny a foe would in any case hardly justify such grandiose claims, but as a matter of fact, the Soviet navy did not really emerge from the episode with even this minimal amount of credit. True, the trawlers and most of the crew were allowed to leave not long after the arrival of the Soviet warships; but the senior officers were kept behind bars until more than two weeks after the task force had steamed away.

Inconvenient realities are rarely allowed to cloud the judgment of military commanders when high policy is being decided upon. Thus, the Soviet navy will continue to grow ever more balanced with bigger and more splendid ships, so that admirals can cruise up and down off the shores of other Ghanas, perhaps in concert with American admirals on their spacious aircraft carriers. If they sail to no purpose, they will at least sail in comfort.

There is nothing novel about the habits and aspirations of Gorshkov's navy. Before World War I, Grand Admiral Alfred von Tirpitz took the lead in persuading the German Kaiser and the German people that Germany deserved to have a fleet as large and glorious as the Royal Navy. Alfred Vagts, the historian of militarism, has pointed out the consequences:

At a time when Britain possessed, with the means already at hand, an overwhelming preponderance at sea against any imaginable enemy, the British navy was far from satisfied; for the sake of modernity and technical perfection it called for dreadnoughts. But among the forces at sea as on land the tradition of convenience . . . extended its sway. This made the British seamen cling to the dreadnought with its ample deck space and cubic footage permitting comfortable cabins for the commanding officer in preference to the dirty hole of a submarine. If Tirpitz [the commander of the German Navy] had not been such an imperious person, imitative rather than creative, he might have furthered the undersea ship instead of slavishly adopting the British dreadnought; in that case he might conceivably have contributed to the security, instead of to the ruin, of his country.

It is a point on which Sergei Gorshkov might care to ponder as, sometime in the late 1980s, he watches the first

Soviet aircraft carrier slide into the warm waters of the Black Sea.

While the commanders of the Soviet blue-water navy may go to sea comfortably ensconced in their commodious cabins, the ordinary sailors are not so lucky. The life of an ordinary conscript who is sent to sea is no less rigorous than that of his contemporaries assigned to one of the other four services. But while the latter face a maximum of two years in uniform, the sailors, along with youngsters drafted into the naval section of the KGB border troops, must serve for three years. Their pay is the same—3.50 rubles a month (about $6.50), although they do get an extra ruble for sea duty. They get no more time off than the men in the army—twenty days' leave in the three years if they are lucky. Even when a ship goes into dock for an over-haul, a time when an American crew would be sent on leave, the crew has to stay on board in order to help with the repair work. The quarters are cramped and spartan, and on the older ships men sometimes have to sleep on the "warm-bunk" system, in which the same bunk is shared by sailors serving different watch duties.

The modern navy's penchant for showing the flag has given the sailors a privilege unique among Soviet ser-vicemen. Sailors are allowed to visit foreign countries, even, on one or two occasions, the United States. These visits are very different, however, from the shore liberty of an American or European sailor. Far from being allowed to roam the host port getting drunk and looking for girls, the men are allowed ashore only under close escort and with minimal foreign currency to spend. Such visits are the exception rather than the rule; even when Soviet ships are in harbor for months on end, as they used to be during the days when they had basing rights in Egypt, the crew stays cooped up on board night and day. Apart from films and a heavy diet of political lectures, it has little opportunity for recreation. Drink, apart from some unsavory substitutes, is hard to come by, but the miseries of the caste system, in which older men bully the youngsters, are reproduced in full measure.

One aspect of army life is missing: there is very little racial tension, because almost no non-Slavs are accepted for naval service. For this there are two reasons. Navies everywhere tend to be rather more elitist and snobbish than the land-bound services. It is a measure of Admiral Rickover's bureaucratic skill and strength of character that he managed to prosper despite the not so latent anti-Semitism of the U.S. Navy. More importantly, any modern warship is a highly complex mechanism, requiring a reasonably well-educated crew to run it; at the very least, they must all speak and understand the same language.

For these reasons, the crews on Soviet ships tend to be Slavs rather than members of the minority nationalities. But even though the manpower pool for Soviet naval recruits has a higher than average level of education and despite the improved training allowed by a three-year term of service, tasks requiring anything more than the simplest level of expertise still have to be done by officers. This lack of technical skill among the men makes it easier to understand why Soviet ships are so difficult to maintain away from their home ports, where specialized crews can do the job. As one intelligence specialist put it to me: "Given the quality of Soviet seamen, [the Soviets] would be foolish to try."

In order to make sure that the officers at least can operate the ships' systems, they are given an intensive five-year training course specializing in a particular subject before they are ever allowed near any kind of operational duty. Thus, future engineering officers will concentrate on engineering to the exclusion of other more general topics; the same goes for weapons specialists, navigators, and so forth.

The atmosphere in the officers' mess is clannish, as well as elitist. This can have its attractive side. An émigré officer, one of the rare Jews to advance to a relatively senior rank, who maintained to me that a naval lieutenant was the intellectual equivalent of an army colonel, also recalled how his professional friends refused to shun him after he applied for permission to emigrate, "as would certainly have happened had I been in the army." This clannishness is intensified by the growing tradition of "naval families," in which each succeeding generation follows its fathers into the service.

Nonetheless, the similarities between the navy and the rest of the Soviet military outweigh the differences. There is the same degree of rigid centralization, with individual ships' commanders and officers allowed little or no freedom of maneuver and initiative. As we can see from the downfall of Admiral Yegorov, chief of staff of the entire navy, following the embarrassing grounding of a Whiskey class submarine off the Swedish coast, the vertical stroke operates just as ruthlessly, with consequent encouragement of the habits of collusion and cover-up.

As in the other services, training is geared toward meeting the norm rather than simulating actual combat conditions. In 1975, Gorshkov deployed hundreds of ships in an enormous exercise spanning several oceans called Okean '75, the size and scope of which attracted much favorable comment in the West. However, it was apparent that the whole affair had an atmosphere of artificiality about it. Ships that were about to be attacked by "enemy" forces made no attempt to escape. They passively awaited their fate, thus making the attacker's job as easy as possible. This raises echoes of Operation Dnieper or the tank exercise that was ruined by snow. The target ships knew that the plan called for them to be attacked and sunk at a particular time and place. To attempt to maneuver out of harm's way or otherwise confuse their attackers would have interfered with the plan, so they did not do so.

Much of our knowledge of what really goes on in the Soviet navy and in the rest of the military is derived from an accumulation of tiny scraps of evidence: an émigré's tale, a curious article in the military press, or the behavior of ships during exercises. It is rare that a dramatic incident lights up the scene to confirm so much of what had been previously suspected. Belenko's flight to Japan was one of these, as was the shambles of the Czech and Polish mobilizations, Brezhnev's purge of the ground forces' high command in the winter of 1980–81, and the poor initial showing of the Afghan invasion force. The mutiny on board the destroyer *Storozhevoi* in the early morning hours of November 8, 1975, was another such illustrative episode.

To most people, especially the naval high command, Captain (third class) Sablin was just about the most unlikely person imaginable to lead a mutiny. It would have been more understandable if he had been a fanatic nationalist from one of the minority republics, like the three Lithuanian officers of the Baltic fleet shot in 1969 for spreading separatist agitation, or simply venal like KGB Major Aleksei Myagkov, who, with intent to profit, had defected to West Berlin in 1973 with a briefcase full of classified information.

Sablin did not fit any of these categories. He was a political officer, a commissar, charged with watching over the ideological purity of officers as they went about their tasks aboard the destroyer. It seems that he had been an outstanding member of the Communist Party's Pioneer and Komsomol youth organizations before entering the navy.

Nothing in his record indicated that there might be trouble ahead.

Had his superiors been watching and thinking with greater insight, they might have suspected that there was something wrong. The warning signs were there, precisely because Sablin *was* such a committed ideologue. He took his job seriously, in contrast to so many other political officers, who regarded their occupation with the same weary cynicism as the men whom they lectured on Lenin and the leadership role of the vanguard of the working class in the struggle against imperialism and reaction. The men liked and respected him, perhaps because he took a sincere interest in their well-being and morale, arranging compassionate home leave in cases of domestic crisis. This was a big favor, since most sailors have almost no chance of seeing their families during the entire three-year hitch.

The chief political officer for the Baltic Fleet, to which the *Storozhevoi* was assigned, might be excused for not exhibiting alarm when one of his officers showed exceptional enthusiasm for his job. But he should have borne it in mind when deciding how to handle the fallout from the disobliging article about the ship that appeared in *Krasnaya zvezda* on December 9, 1974. After all, if Sablin was prepared to tip off the press about the state of morale on the ship, who could tell what else he might do?

Storozhevoi did not emerge with credit from the piece. The author naturally couched his conclusions in the delicate code prescribed for such articles, which is to say he did not state in so many words that the ship's morale had fallen to rock bottom, that the officers were slacking off, that the crew was openly disaffected, and that as a result, the ship's battleworthiness was decling fast. The article's conclusion was simply that "the ship's Communists," meaning the officers, should "strive harder on the moral ethical front." But the message was there for all political and politically conscious officers to see.

Sablin had taken a very serious step in bypassing the chain of command and taking his complaints straight to the press. After all, it was not as if they were talking about one of the old rust buckets built just after the war, dangerous to sail much beyond sight of the coast. The *Storozhevoi* was a Krivak class destroyer, one of the most modern in the Soviet navy. Marshal Grechko himself, the Minister of Defense and a ranking member of the Politburo, had honored the ship by taking a short cruise on board only two years before. Sablin was doing no one any good, including himself, by going around complaining that things were in a bad way. Still, he was personally convinced that once the high command had realized what was going on, it would soon set things to rights.

He was wrong. Nothing at all happened except that Sablin earned the ire of his brother and senior officers for washing the ship's dirty linen in public. The system had simply covered up. Deeply disillusioned, the dedicated Communist began swinging in the opposite direction. The system in which he had believed had let him down, and so he began planning a most drastic method of escape. We do not know why or how other members of the crew became enlisted in the conspiracy. It may have been because of the general misery of life on ship or perhaps some particular incident, like the rotten meat that sparked the famous 1905 mutiny on board the tsarist battleship *Potemkin*.

In the early hours of November 8, 1975, the *Storozhevoi* was moored in the naval section of Riga harbor, which lies in the Irbe Strait off the Baltic Sea. Most of the officers were in town, celebrating the 58th anniversary of the 1917 October Revolution. Apart from Sablin, only the officers of the watch were on board. It was an easy matter for him to direct those members of the crew he had enlisted in the conspiracy to subdue and lock the officers up before they could raise the alarm. So it was not until the ship had slipped its moorings and was well out of the harbor that anyone on shore woke up to the fact that the *Storozhevoi* was putting to sea without authorization. Even though there was no reply to the puzzled radio inquiries as to what was going on, there was as yet nothing to indicate that the men had mutinied and were heading for the Swedish island of Gotland, 250 miles away.

With a top speed of 31 knots, the *Storozhevoi* might have had a chance to reach friendly waters before the end of the long northern winter night. But the mutineers had a crippling and ultimately fatal problem. Apart from Sablin, so far as is known, the rest of the officers were locked up or ashore, and since only the officers were trained to carry out skilled tasks, the men could not operate the ship effectively on their own and therefore were unable to get up more than half-speed.

In an effort to find out what was going on, Riga headquarters sent out planes to search for the missing destroyer. The planes picked up the vessel as it steamed out of the sound into the open sea. Panic-stricken, Riga headquarters radioed Moscow. In their excitement they communicated not in code but in clear Russian. Moscow ordered Riga to send out a task force and bring back the errant destroyer at any cost.

The matter was so serious that the air force had to be brought in. About ten planes, half of them TU-95 Bears specially equipped for reconnaissance from Soviet naval aviation and half of them air force fighter-bombers, were dispatched in pursuit, as well as another Krivak destroyer from Riga. Around 8:00 A.M., they caught up with the *Storozhevoi* and signaled it to stop. The ship plowed on, still at half-speed. Moscow ordered the posse of planes to open fire, which they did, managing to hit the wrong ship—the pursuing destroyer—in the process.

The mutineers did not fire back. Even if the ship had been carrying more than its exiguous peacetime supply of ammunition, they would not have been able to use it. Ironically, the Soviet navy was able to reap a benefit from one of its deficiencies, since only the officers were skilled enough to operate the weapons systems. Finally, under heavy bombardment, the *Storozhevoi* slowed and stopped, still 100 miles away from Swedish waters. A boarding party came over the side and retook command.

After that day, the *Storozhevoi* officially ceased to exist, being renamed and posted to another fleet. Because he had just been posted to Moscow, even though he had not yet taken up his new duties, Admiral Vladimir V. Mikhaylin, the commander of the Baltic Fleet up to that point, was able to argue successfully that he had not been in any way responsible. He was thus spared the vertical stroke, which fell instead on his deputy, Vice Admiral Kudel'kin, who was demoted and posted to the Pacific Fleet. Sablin was shot.

The following August, the new deputy commander of the Baltic Fleet, Vice Admiral Sidorov, took a small flotilla on a visit to Copenhagen. Asked about the mutiny during a press conference he replied stiffly: "Mutiny on a Soviet naval ship in the Baltic—unthinkable. It must be a hoax played by organs established for this purpose which pursue their thwarting aims in the West."

U.S. intelligence was no more ready to draw attention to the incident. It suited no one's preferred picture of the might and efficiency of the Soviet navy.

Part VI

Threat Inflation

Sixteen

The Consequences of
Threat Inflation

In the summer of 1982, Syrian and Israeli forces, using the wares of their respective superpower suppliers, clashed once again in and above the fields and towns of Lebanon. It was an unequal battle. Within a few days, the Israeli air force claimed to have shot down as many as 85 Syrian MiGs, half of which were up-to-date MiG-23s, without loss to themselves. At the same time, 19 SAM-6 antiaircraft missile batteries were also put out of action, and once again the Israelis reported no casualties. Soviet-built tanks fared no better, with several hundred being knocked out by the Israeli army, including about a dozen modern T-72s.

This carnage earned Soviet weapons their worse press since the defecting Belenko's arrival with his MiG-25 in 1976. It seemed for a moment that their reputation, and by extension the specter of the Soviet threat, might have suffered an irreparable blow. The issue was a difficult one for the U.S. military chiefs to face, and they responded in three ways.

First, they misinterpreted the actual events of the war so as to indicate that it was the much-criticized U.S. emphasis on complex and expensive high-technology weaponry that had ensured Israel's stunning victory. United Press International reported that "Pentagon officials view Israel's aerial performance as supporting the arguments of those who advocate developing high-technology weapons as opposed to the buy-them-cheap-and-simple school of thought." Among the contributing factors, according to Pentagon reports quoted in the U.S. press, were E-2C Hawkeye flying radar planes, used by the Israelis to track Syrian warplanes from the moment they took off, as well as Sparrow radar-guided missiles, used to shoot the planes down at extreme range.

Such interpretations were a combination of mendacity and wishful thinking. Reports from Israeli military sources indicate that stories about the Hawkeye radar plane were deliberate Israeli disinformation, broadcast to cover up the Israelis' more straightforward stratagem of listening in on radio conversations between the garrulous Syrian pilots and their ground controllers. "The Hawkeye hasn't been too popular with pilots since the time four F-15s, which were relying on it to warn them of approaching Syrians, got caught by surprise and almost shot down," one source reported. Claims that the Sparrow missile had played a key role were equally untrue, since the Israeli air force fighters credit it, at best, 15 percent of the kills. Meanwhile, it was suggested that the elimination of the T-72 tanks could be ascribed only to some sort of secret "supersmart" weapon, a notion discounted by one Israeli general questioned on the subject, who cited the twenty-year-old 105-mm tank cannon as the nemesis of the Soviet supertanks.

The distortion of the events of a war in order to conform with Pentagon prejudices is a long-established tradition. "That's a very interesting war," said General Motti Hod, the Israeli air force commander, after reading an official Pentagon account of the 1973 war, "but it's not the war we fought."

The second element in the U.S. military's reaction to the humiliation of Soviet arms was to denigrate the performance of the Syrian pilots and soldiers, implying that things would have been very different if there had been Russians at the controls. There was more truth in this: Syrian air force pilots are selected as much for their loyalty to the regime as for their combat skills, while the Israelis are, by common agreement, the best trained and most experienced pilots in the world. On the other hand, there is little to indicate that the Russians have done that much better; the Syrian tactics that proved so disastrous were Russian tactics. A pilot from a Third World air force reported after a tour as an instructor with the Syrian air force that Syrian pilots were "really hopeless at tactics, even worse than their Soviet instructors, and they were pretty bad." An incident during the "war of attrition" between Israel and Egypt that followed the 1967 war gave bloody confirmation of the lack of quality of Soviet combat pilots. The Soviets had sent MiG-21s complete with their regular pilots to help defend Egypt against Israeli bombing raids. On July 30, 1970, the Israelis shot four of them down, an event that reportedly caused some satisfaction among Egyptian pilots, who were irked by Russian slurs on their competence.

Finally, the Pentagon took solace in the imminent appearance of improved Soviet aircraft. It had to be conceded that the U.S. F-15s and F-16s had totally outclassed the MiG-23s, which *Air Force Magazine* had singled out three years before as "the aircraft [that] epitomizes the USSR's formidable aerospace strength, growing at an alarming rate." But, claimed the U.S. Air Force, the latest Soviet planes would present a far more formidable threat.

In case anyone should miss the point, a senior U.S. Air Force general summoned reporters to a breakfast briefing on August 4, 1982. The *Wall Street Journal* dutifully reported,

Newly acquired intelligence data about the war in Lebanon show that American weapons and tactics as employed by Israel can easily overpower current Soviet jets and missiles, a top Air Force officer said.

However, General Wilbur L. Creech, commander of the Tactical Air Command, said other recent intelligence data show that the Soviets have developed four new fighter planes that are far more capable than any used by Syria in the war or the standard jets currently flown by the Russian air force.

Gen. Creech asserted that if Congress reduces the new Air Force budget, the U.S. could find it tougher to cope with the latest Soviet fighters, two of which have already been deployed by the Soviet air force in small numbers.

The general's remarks and indeed the overall manner in which the Pentagon chose to portray the Lebanese war provide a perfect case study in threat inflation, which can be summed up as: "the inferiority of Soviet weapons to American high technology has been vividly and undeniably demonstrated in combat. Our success shows that we have made absolutely the right decisions all along—but don't let anyone consider that as an excuse for cutting the defense budget, because the Soviets are drawing ahead again." The only missing element was the otherwise standard observation that the technological superiority of U.S. equipment is offset by the Soviets' vast advantage in numbers.

There was, however, another and unusual aspect to the

debate over the war. The humiliation of Soviet equipment had been so dramatic that the Soviets themselves felt o-bliged to comment. The official Soviet news agency TASS declared in an indignant dispatch that "according to numer-ous comments of the participants in battles, Soviet tanks, infantry combat vehicles, antitank guided missiles and artillery have demonstrated well their efficiency." In tacit concurrence with the American suggestion that the blame should be put on Arab soldiers rather than Soviet weapons, the article remarked snidely that the arms given to the Arabs "are those which were in the hands of the Vietnam-ese and which defeated the American war machine."

It is very rare for the Russians to discuss the quality of their weapons in public. They can usually rely on the Americans to do it for them, but this may not be an entirely fortuitous process.

This book has emphasized the difference between the Soviet armed forces as they really are and as they are portrayed by the U.S. military bureaucracy and its allies abroad. The difference can be accounted for by a deliberate and continuous inflation of the threat by the American military. This has resulted in the emergence of a "war economy" in the United States, with wide sections of the community directly dependent on a high rate of defense spending, as well as on an ongoing atmosphere of fear, fear of the Soviets and of universal nuclear immolation.

At various times the Russians have pointed out that U.S. estimates of their own military strength are much exaggerated. When the Chairman of the Joint Chiefs, General Nathan F. Twining, visited the USSR with a high-ranking delegation in 1956, he was told by Defense Minister Zhukov that "I think you have the reports too high in estimating our strength." The remark was dis-missed by the Americans as an egregious piece of disin-formation, and they returned home with the conviction, as one of them wrote later, that "there could no longer be any doubt in our minds that the Soviets were rapidly reaching the point where they could successfully challenge our technological superiority." Twenty-five years later, with the Soviets still supposedly gaining rapidly on U.S. technological superiority, *Whence the Threat to Peace,* issued by the Ministry of Defense in Moscow, dismissed the Pentagon's *Soviet Military Power* as "tendentiously selected and deliberately distorted information about the Armed Forces of the USSR."

Both Zhukov and his successors were of course absolutely correct. Estimates of Soviet strength have always been deliberately distorted and exaggerated. But Soviet complaints, although well justified, are disingenuous. There is abundant evidence to indicate that the Soviets themselves have deliberately fostered and encouraged the prevailing fantasies of the U.S. military.

Some instances of this program of Soviet disinformation are well known. At the 1955 air show, held at Tushino just outside Moscow, the U.S. air attaché was alarmed to note the large numbers of Bison bombers circling overhead. As a result, U.S. intelligence revised its projections of Soviet bomber strength upward, and CIA director Allen W. Dulles solemnly reported later that "every indication pointed to [the Soviets'] having adopted [the Bison] as a major element of their offensive strength and to an intention to produce these planes more or less as fast as they could." Thus the bomber gap was born.

In fact, the Soviets had had their limited force of Bisons (the plane that Khrushchev said "did not meet our requirements") fly over the Tushino airfield and then, out of sight of the reviewing stand and the watching air attaché, circle around to make another pass. In terms of effect, it was the most successful air show ever.

The deception was not revealed until the U.S. Air Force

had lost interest in the bomber gap in favor of the even more threatening (and equally fictitious) missile gap. Once again, the Russians, particularly Khrushchev, went out of their way to provide evidence to fuel U.S. alarmism. In 1959, when the Soviets had no operational ICBMs, Khrushchev told a conference of journalists that Russia had "such a stock of rockets, such an amount of atomic and hydrogen warheads, that if they attack us we could wipe our potential enemies off the face of the earth." In the same speech, he boasted that a single plant had produced "250 rockets" in a single year. These claims were entirely false.

Circling bombers and Khrushchev's bombast were not isolated incidents. The Soviet disinformation effort has been far more extensive. The skill and cunning with which Soviet intelligence chiefs have managed to infiltrate their agents into Western intelligence agencies have been extensively chronicled. Two of their most successful coups have been the insertion of Harold ("Kim") Philby and Heinz Felfe into positions near the very top of the British M16 and the West German espionage organizations, respectively.

Although the treachery of these men has been lamented at length, one obvious consequence of their activities has not been fully explored. Since Philby and Felfe were in a position to inform the Russians about the identities of spies in Eastern Europe, the Russians could, in turn, apprehend these people and, if they were not imprisoned or executed, use them to transmit information to the West that had been tailored to reflect what the Soviets wanted the West to believe. What the NATO powers believed during the heyday of Philby (1940s and early 1950s) and Felfe (mid- and late 1950s) was that the Soviet armed forces in Eastern Europe were strong enough to pose a threat of invasion into West Germany, and reports from the heavily compromised intelligence agencies helped form the basis for this assessment. Felfe was particularly important in this respect, because the West German intelligence organization run by Reinhard Gehlen for which Felfe worked was probably the most important conduit of information about Eastern Europe for the CIA. By the late 1950s, it was reportedly supplying 70 percent of all NATO operational intelligence.

To be sure, an accurate report on, for example, Soviet ammunition stocks in East Germany during the late 1950s and early 1960s—which were too low for more than a few days' fighting—would not in any event have found much credence at NATO headquarters. Nevertheless, the Soviets would have been able to make sure that very few such threat-deflating items were allowed to leak through and to ensure that their strength continued to be overestimated.

From the late 1950s on, the classic cloak and dagger type of espionage, in which the Gehlen organization specialized, was gradually replaced by newer and more esoteric methods of intelligence collection. However, satellites can be fooled just as human operatives can, as the bizarre story of the rubber submarine makes clear.

In the early 1970s, the photointerpreters who pore over the endless reams of satellite pictures taken from above the USSR noted that a new ballistic-missile submarine had joined the Soviet Northern Fleet at Polyarnyi, near Murmansk. Its appearance was duly recorded for insertion in the updated assessments of enemy forces. Not long afterward, there was a severe storm in the Barents Sea, which raised heavy seas and effectively blocked out all satellite surveillance for a number of days. When the next batch of photographs finally arrived, the analysts saw that something very curious had happened to the new submarine: it had bent in half, which is something that real submarines made of metal do not do.

The construction and display of fake weapons may be standard Soviet operation procedure. Grigory, an ebullient engineer now living in upper Manhattan, spent his military service serving with the air defense antiaircraft missile troops on the island of Saaremaa opposite the port of Riga, past which Sablin and his mutineers sailed on the fateful voyage of the *Storozhevoi*. Grigory's story of his military career is much like that of any other former conscript— bad food, corrupt officers, and so on—except that the weapons for which he was responsible were made of wood. They were full-scale models of SAM-2s and SAM-3s and certainly posed no danger to any marauding American bomber that may have come along. "They looked very good, there was a special workshop for making them, and then my unit had to set them up with the proper kinds of housing and camouflage all around," he recalls. There were indeed a large number of real missiles also on the island, but as far as Grigory can recall—he served in 1973–74—these real missiles were outnumbered by the fake ones.

This kind of deception can have a tactical purpose— to confuse the enemy about the actual location of one's forces so that he can be surprised when the real missiles or other weapons are brought unexpectedly into action. However, on a strategic level, the Soviet disinformation effort over the past thirty years has not been concealing a real and hidden strength but the fact that that strength has not been there.

After World War II, the Soviet Union was totally shattered. Millions were dead, and the economy was in ruins. The lifeline of lend-lease supplies from the United States, which had helped sustain the Soviets through the war, was cut off as soon as the Germans surrendered. The United States, on the other hand, emerged from the war with an economy that had actually grown and prospered; casualties had been minimal, and the country now had a monopoly on what appeared to be the most powerful weapon ever devised. Even after the Soviet Union had developed its own atom bomb, it remained in a position of gross military inferiority, having no means of delivering it to the enemy's homeland. By every yardstick of military comparison, apart from nuclear weapons, the Soviets are still outnumbered by the combined forces of the United States, China, the European members of NATO, Sweden, and Japan, all of which the Soviets must reckon with as potential opponents. In the nuclear category, where numerical comparisons are in any case meaningless, they enjoy no more than a rough equilibrium. Small wonder then that they should have consistently worked to have their enemies exaggerate their strength.

There has been at least one confirmation from an authoritative Soviet source that this kind of deception has long been a conscious instrument of policy. Colonel V. M. Kulish is a military historian and strategic theorist who has been close to the center of Soviet military policy-making for many years. In 1971, while on a visit to Washington, D.C., he informed a dinner party, which included officials connected with the Defense Department, that America's greatest strategic error since World War II had been to "consistently overestimate our capabilities."

However successful the Soviet Union may have been in persuading its enemies to consistently exaggerate its strength, the Soviet people have paid a heavy price. At the same time, the American military, encouraged in its presumption that the threat is large and growing larger, has been able to secure the enthusiastic support of the American people in sinking more and more of the country's wealth into an already bloated military establishment. The price paid by the American people must be measured in more than economic terms, although these are onerous enough. The effectiveness of U.S. defense forces has been steadily declining, and it has been doing so as a direct result of a willful misperception of the Soviet threat.

The salient feature of this threat has always been numbers. Churchill told his audience at MIT in 1949 that the numberless hordes of the Mongols had returned again to menace the West. The U.S. Joint Chiefs of Staff stubbornly maintained for years on end that 25 underequipped NATO divisions were faced with 175 Soviet divisions. The current Soviet numerical superiority in tanks, aircraft, ships, and men is alleged to be as large as ever and growing.

As we have seen, these bean counts are and always have been fallacious. So hallowed by tradition are they, however, that no contrary information is ever allowed to disturb the familiar picture. In a 1982 report issued by the superhawkish Committee on the Present Danger, many of whose founding members were hired for high positions in the Reagan Administration, there is a casual reference to the Soviet production of "6,000 tanks a year." But in an accompanying chart, reproduced from a Defense Intelligence Agency's submission to Congress, Soviet tank production is listed at 3,000 a year. Thus do the distinguished and influential gentlemen of the committee assess the intricacies of the strategic balance. Their report was called *Has America Become Number Two?*, to which the answer was a predictable affirmative.

The response to the unquestioned "fact" of Soviet numerical superiority has been to rely on American technological ingenuity to redress the imbalance. If we cannot build as many planes or tanks or ships as the Russians, we will instead build planes and tanks and ships that can destroy several of the enemy at once. "Our technology is what will save us," former Defense

Secretary Harold Brown informed the Congress in 1979.

This policy has been disastrous. These "force-multiplier" weapons are inherently very expensive. In order to secure Congressional and Administration approval for their construction, the military services almost invariably understate their projected cost. As the programs proceed and the real costs become apparent, the size of the programs are cut back, thus helping make numerical shortfalls a self-fulfilling prophecy. Meanwhile, the complex high technology incorporated in these weapons that has been responsible for driving up costs in the first place turns out, as often as not, to be almost entirely useless.

For example, the U.S. Air Force originally planned to buy 250 copies of the C-5A, an enormous transport plane that was to have a number of "advanced" features, such as the ability to "kneel" close to the ground for easier cargo loading, as well as the ability to use grass fields close to the battlefield. When, amid scandalous circumstances, it was revealed that the bill was going to be at least $2 billion more than advertised, the Congress cut the program to 81 planes. The operational C-5As find it almost impossible to rise from a kneeling position, and so far from landing on grass fields the plane is restricted to a limited number of very large airports.

The same fate was to befall the F-111 fighter-bomber. Originally projected as a 2,000-plane program, it was taken out of production after a disastrous trial in Vietnam and after 563 had been built at a price five times the original estimates. The Phoenix missiles carried on the U.S. Navy's F-14 fighter are so expensive that operational pilots rarely get to fire more than one a year for training purposes, and they have never been fired in sequences of six—the capability that is supposed to justify the aircraft's cost.

The most widely publicized area of Soviet numerical

superiority is in tanks, usually denoted as 50,000 in the Soviet arsenal to about 10,000 in U.S. hands. The U.S. Army's reponse has been to order 7,000 models of the new M-1 tank. This would not bring numerical equality with the Russians, but the new tank is equipped with a variety of state-of-the-art features, including a gas-turbine engine, that are supposed to enable it to take on the Soviet armored hordes on a more equal basis. Once again, at the time of this writing, history appears to be repeating itself. Production, originally projected to reach 1,080 a year, is limping along at half that amount, while the price tag has climbed from a Congressionally mandated figure of $500,000 per tank to at least $2.8 million a copy. The tanks that have been built display a sorry catalog of failures, including an inability to keep the gun aligned with the sights, a basic flaw indeed.

The inevitable consequences of U.S. weapons design and procurement policies have long been pointed out by Cassandras within the Defense Department. In 1981 the journalist James Fallows drew them to the attention of a wider public in his book *National Defense*. After a long interval Dr. William Perry issued a reply. Perry epitomizes the high-technology force-multiplier school of thought. After building an electronics company that rose to prosperity on Pentagon contracts, he was appointed director of Defense Research and Engineering by President Carter. This is an immensely powerful position, whose incumbent has a decisive say over the kinds of weapons that the United States will buy. Perry was an unequivocal supporter of complex high-technology systems of the kind that had come under withering attack in Fallows' book. Perry's riposte, which appeared in 1982 in the journal *International Security*, was bluntly entitled "Fallows' Fallacies."

In magisterial tones Perry explained that the policies of which he had been such a vociferous advocate were mandated by the particular scope and shape of the Soviet threat. The root of the problem, he explained, was that the Soviets could afford to spend twice as much as the United States on buying weapons; this is because, while more than half of the Pentagon budget was committed to manpower costs (paying the wages), the Soviets need devote no more than a quarter of their defense expenditure to manpower (all those underpaid conscripts). Because of this imbalance, as Perry sees it, the United States can never afford to buy as many weapons as the Russians. That being so, the only answer is to build "quality" weapons to offset Soviet advantages in "quantity." The situation is, however, becoming more critical because the Soviets, while maintaining their rates of production, are now producing weapons that compare in complexity, cost, and performance with the most sophisticated U.S. systems. Needless to say, these new systems are providing more bang for both the buck and the ruble or, as Perry puts it: "Performance of military significance has increased proportionally to the cost increase."

Perry's riposte to Fallows is a useful document because it throws many of the most common falsehoods and misperceptions about the Soviet threat and our proper response to it into stark relief. For example, there is simply no evidence to support Perry's claim that the Soviets can afford to spend twice as much on buying weapons as the United States because their overall manpower costs are so much lower. Even the published CIA estimates reveal that the United States spends "about one fourth" of its budget on supporting its active, rather than retired, military personnel, while the Soviets spend 30 percent. Furthermore, since estimates of Soviet weapons spending are based on premises that are highly dubious (see Chapter 5), it is dangerous, to say the least, to base momentous policy decisions on them.

Most important, the assumption that more complicated and expensive weapons are proportionally more effective both for the Soviets and the United States is contradicted by the evidence. The new U.S. M-1 tank costs three times as much as the M-60 it will replace. Since it also breaks down twice as often, the Army will have far fewer tanks available for combat than it would have if it spent the same amount of money on M-60s. The M-1 will have a third less range than the M-60, carry one-third less ammunition, be more vulnerable from the rear, require slightly more time to load its less reliable gun, and be many times more vulnerable to heat-seeking missiles attracted by the exhaust from its jet engine.

Procurement of the M-1 has been justified by the threat of the Soviet T-72. But the T-72 compares unfavorably with the M-60 it has supposedly rendered obsolete. It has a third less range, breaks down 50 to 75 percent more often, has thinner armor on the sides, top, bottom, and rear, carries a third fewer rounds of ammunition, has an automatic gun loader that is highly dangerous to its users, and is easily destroyed by the M-60's cannon, as seen in Lebanon.

The same pattern recurs when one compares "quality" fighters like the MiG-23 or the F-15 with cheaper but supposedly less effective alternatives like the MiG-21 or the F-16. In these and other cases, the payoff for the added costs proves illusory or, more usually, negative.

Paradoxically, the policies advocated by Perry and the military-industrial establishment he represents have in the end helped weaken Soviet military effectiveness, although he would hardly concede the point. Soviet adherence to the military fashions set in America has ensured that the Soviets too are following policies that steadily diminish the actual combat performance of their forces. As weapons grow more expensive, the Soviets must also buy fewer of them (MiG-23 production is one-third less than that of the MiG-21). As they grow more complex, they are ready for action far less of the time and are less deadly to an opponent when they are in working order.

The baneful influence of Perry's way of thinking on Soviet military policymakers helps us understand the curious fact discussed in Chapter 5—there is far less to the Soviet "build-up" than is commonly believed. The overall production of weapons, such as tanks, artillery, ships, submarines, and fighter planes, has either stayed level or actually declined since the 1960s. The weapons being built today are indeed more complex and costly than yesterday's models, a trend that the U.S. military establishment equates with increased effectiveness. Since the evidence points in the opposite direction, it would seem that the implications of the continued high rate of Soviet defense spending are economic rather than military.

Given the way the Soviet military machine (and its American counterpart) operates these days, it is possible to predict with some confidence what will happen in the early years of Chernenko's leadership.

First, the Soviet defense budget will continue to grow— probably at an increased rate. Chernenko, after all, owes his position in large part to military support, and the defense establishment will expect a commensurate budgetary payoff.

Second, far from increasing Soviet strength, this boost in funding will almost certainly cause the size and capabilities of Soviet forces to diminish. Unless current trends are totally reversed, any added largesse will be invested in expensive research and development programs. These will bring forth considerably more complex and "sophisticated" weapons systems. Because these planes, tanks, ships, and other systems will be more expensive than their predecessors, they will be produced in fewer numbers, which is exactly what is happening in the United States as a result of the Reagan defense budgets. The increased complexity of the new Soviet weapons will almost certainly ensure their diminished effectiveness as instruments of war.

President Charles de Gaulle of France once wrote that for the military officer "armed power is something essential and, as it were, sacred. . . . Consequently nothing seems to him to be more necessary or more urgent than to accumulate the means to make victory more certain." This might serve as an apt description of the motivations that drive the defense bureaucracies of both the United States and the Soviet Union, except, as we have seen, so many of their activities do *not* make victory more certain. The reason is that military bureaucracies have far more than the straightforward pursuit of victory on their minds. The distinction has been best summed up by the historian Alfred Vagts. In the introduction to *History of Militarism*, he wrote:

Every war is fought, every army is maintained in a military way and in a militaristic way. The distinction is fundamental and fateful. The military way is marked by a primary concentration of men and materials on winning specific objectives of power with the utmost efficiency, that is, with the least expenditure of blood and treasure. It is limited in scope, confined to one function, and scientific in its essential qualities.

Militarism, on the other hand, presents a vast array of customs, interests, prestige, actions and thought associated with armies and wars and yet transcending true military purposes. Indeed militarism is so constituted that it may hamper and defeat the purposes of the military way. Its influence is unlimited in scope. It may permeate all society and become dominant over all industry and arts. Rejecting the scientific character of the military way, militarism displays the qualities of caste and cult, authority and belief.

The core of Vagts's history deals with the French and German armies, in the period leading up to World War I, a period in which militarism permeated the societies of France and Germany like a cancer, actively promoted by military leaders as a way of increasing the influence and prosperity of their caste.

When war finally erupted in 1914, it rapidly became clear that the General Staffs had almost entirely misunderstood the business at which they were supposedly so expert and in preparation for which they had long extorted enormous sums from their fellow citizens. For example, the German General Staff had totally failed to take account of the fact that their entire supplies of nitrate, vital to the manufacture of ammunition, came from distant Chile via a route that could be and was immediately blockaded by the British Royal Navy. Only the fortuitous genius of the German chemists enabled Germany to make synthetic nitrates and carry on the fighting. The French, meanwhile, were also in some embarrassment at the beginning of the war, for their supplies of phenol, a key chemical ingredient of explosives, came from Germany itself. These awkward facts, so crucial in a real war, had not disturbed the peacetime equanimity of the generals, even as they thundered on about the necessity of preparing for war. As Vagts puts it, "The military of all countries, nominally engaged in attending to the security of their respective nations, were forced . . . into increasingly bureaucratic procedures, full of the inertia and formalism of officialdom, except in the always lively pursuit of their immediate and specific interests as a peacetime concern."

The military leaders, having fostered militarism in society at large in order to further their peacetime objectives, became its prisoners. The populace swallowed their message of an ominous and growing threat and propelled them in 1914 into a war, which was all the more long and bloody because of the generals' incompetence.

Today we see militarism in the ascendant both in the Soviet Union and in the United States. To a generation that has been taught to fear a growing Soviet threat it may be comforting to learn how Soviet militarism has come to hamper and defeat "the military way" in that country. But while the Soviet generals, like those of the United States, may be more interested in governing soldiers in peacetime rather than in deploying them in battle, in buying weapons rather than in using them, the events of 1914 show how helpless they are to control the monster they create. Only by understanding the true motivations and actions of the military bureaucrats, both in the East and at home, can we hope to frustrate them, and thus avoid a denouement more terrible and final than 1914.

Notes

Part I: Perceptions

1: The View from Lenin's Tomb

Dusko Doder: Washington *Post*, November 8, 1981.

42.6 percent: The Administration prefers a lower figure of 26 percent (quoted by Ronald Reagan in TV address October 22, 1982). My higher figure has been calculated by the Council on Economic Priorities. It is based on the total "defense functions" within the federal budget for FY 1983. It includes not only the straightforward Pentagon budget but also other defense-related expenditures, such as military-related federal debt interest payments, the military activities of NASA, part of the coast guard expenditures, military-related expenditures on the merchant marine, and so on.

Nasser: Mohammed Heikal, *The Sphinx and the Commissar* (London: Collins, 1978), p. 27.

Children guarding war memorials: This is a personal observation of Professor David Holloway of the University of Edinburgh, a noted authority on Soviet military policy and a frequent visitor to the Soviet Union. This is not the only example of the increase in militarism in Soviet society during the last decade. Harrison Salisbury has pointed out to me the growing torrent of lurid war fiction during the 1970s. In the Khrushchev years, by contrast, war toys were not on sale in the stores.

Trucks with two sets of plates: David C. Isby, *Weapons and Tactics of the Soviet Army* (London: Jane's Publishing, 1981), p. 17.

3,500 defense-related plants: Figure given in statement by Major General Richard X. Larkin, director of the Defense Intelligence Agency, to the Joint Economic Committee, Subcommittee on International Trade, Finance, and Security Economics, July 8, 1981.

Factory 13: John Barron, *MiG Pilot* (New York: Reader's Digest Press, 1980), p. 50.

Numbers of Soviet weapons divisions: U.S. Department of Defense, *Soviet Military Power* (Washington, D.C.: Government Printing Office, 1981). The relative balance is, of course, open to many interpretations, but the numbers are cited here in this way to show the official Pentagon perception of Soviet military strength.

Soviet weapons production: *Ibid.*

M-1, Trident submarine: *Defense Week*, August 9, 1982.

Milshtein: *CBS Reports*, *The Defense of the United States*, part 5: "The Russians," June 18, 1981. Soviet spokesmen do not deliver off-the-cuff statements in interviews with the Western media, so it is safe to assume that Milshtein's sentiments as expressed were cleared at the highest levels.

"cannot read the road signs": For an amusing example of this actually occurring, see p. 258.

Different railroad gauges: The Russians are reported to have laid two broad-gauge lines across Poland for the supply of their troops in East Germany. Isby, *op. cit.*, p. 17.

Rumanian refusal to take part in joint Warsaw Pact exercises: Christopher Jones, "Soviet Military Doctrine and Warsaw Pact Exercises," in *Soviet Military Thinking*, ed. Derek Leebaert (London: George Allen & Unwin, 1982).

Ustinov in Hungary: Statement made by Major General Harold Aaron, director of the Defense Intelligence Agency. U.S. Congress, Joint Economic Committee, *Allocation of Resources in the Soviet Union and China* (subcommittee hearings), 1978, p. 172 (hereafter JEC, *Resource Allocations*, 19–).

"The armies of the Warsaw Pact": *The Threat to Europe* (Moscow: Progress Publishers, 1981), p. 12.

"Faced in the West": *Ibid*.

"each submarine carrying enough warheads": There are only 18 Soviet cities with a population of a million or more, while there are 271 with a population of 100,000 or more (John M. Collins, *U.S./Soviet Military Balance* [New York: McGraw-Hill, 1980], p. 132). Thus, it would take only two of the relatively obsolescent Poseidon submarines, each of which carries 16 missiles with 10 warheads per missile, to incinerate all of the latter category of Soviet cities. However, there might be problems in getting a satisfactory spread of the individual warheads.

"exact copy of the IBM 360": Emmanuel Bobrov, "Applied Computer Science in the USSR, A Personal Account," Harvard Russian Research Center paper, 1737 Cambridge Street, Mass. 02138.

"as of today": *Commentary*, July 1977.

"The United States of America": Ministry of Defense of the USSR, *Whence the Threat to Peace* (Moscow: Military Publishing House, 1982), p. 12.

FM-287: Quoted in Fred Kaplan, "Soviet and American Intentions," *The Atlantic*, July 1982.

"Concept of operations of U.S. strategic offensive forces": *Whence the Threat to Peace*, p. 61.

"an approximate military balance has arisen": *Ibid.*, p. 63.

"for more than three decades": *Ibid.*, p. 77.

"almost twice the combat capabilities of the M-60": *Ibid.*, p. 39.

"the C-5A Galaxy military transport plane": *Ibid.*, p. 46.

"action radius of 740 kilometers": *Ibid*.

Inferiority of the M-1 to the M-60: The literature on the failings of the M-1 is extensive. See, for example, "M1 Tank's Problems Persist, Report Says," Boston *Globe*, September 20, 1982, "Worst Enemy of the Army's New M1 Tank May Have Been Itself, U.S. Testing Shows," *Wall Street Journal*, September 20, 1982; and "M1 Tank Still Troubled by Breakdowns, Group Says," Washington *Post*, September 20, 1982. The U.S. Army replied to these and many similar stories that subsequently appeared with indignant denials but its case is weakened by the fact that the press reports were based on the Army's own tests of the troubled vehicle.

C-5A limitations: *Airlifter Comparisons*, Boeing Corp. research paper D6-33551-025-2R, January 1982. While Boeing had an interest in denigrating the performance of the C-5 by comparison with its own 747 at the time this paper was prepared, the data quoted here were derived from internal U.S. Air Force studies and checked by Boeing's own aerodynamicists.

F-18 range: U.S. Navy Optevor Operational Test Results for F-18, 1982. (The figure is for combat radius without auxiliary tanks.)

T-64 tank production: This is a subject of intense discussion and argument, albeit within a limited circle. *Soviet Military Power* gives a figure of 500 for T-64s produced in 1980. However, these 500 tanks are supposed to have been produced at Kharkov, which because of its persistent cloud cover, is an extremely difficult location on which to gather satellite reconnaissance information. According to intelligence analysts, 500 is the figure the agencies ascribe for any production number for which they have little or no information. The former Soviet tank officer who pseudonymously authored *The Liberators* (London: Hamish Hamilton, 1981) states flatly that the T-64 was taken out of production because of its poor performance.

"while small by comparison": *Soviet Military Power*, p. 49.

U.S. shipbuilding: information drawn from Christopher Wright, "Developing Maritime Force Structure Options for the U.S. Defense Program," M. Sc. thesis, MIT, 1976.

Declining Soviet tank production: Gerald Halbert, "World Tank Production," *Armor Magazine*, March–April 1981.

Soviet arms exports: *Defense Week*, February 7, 1983.

The RAF's plans for war with France: H. R. Allen, *Who Won the Battle of Britain?* (London: Arthur Barker, 1974), p. 104.

The U.S. Navy's plans for war with Britain: Stephen Roskill, *Naval Policy Between the Wars*, Vol. I (London: Collins, 1968).

The MiG-25 and the B-70: Barron, *op. cit.*, p. 180.

"finest interceptor in the world": *Ibid.*, p. 9.

"that we might have to reappraise": *Ibid.*

The busy life of the Backfire: Defense Secretary Harold Brown, in his FY 1981 Defense Posture Statement, spoke of the Backfire as an important component of the "major modernization of their theater [meaning medium range] nuclear forces" (p. 6). He also reflected gloomily that "with the appearance of the Backfire in increasing numbers, Soviet naval aviation could come to be a bigger threat to our sea lanes of communication and naval forces than Soviet submarines" (p. 9). *Soviet Military Power* lays particular emphasis on the menace of the Backfire as a strategic bomber (p. 61).

Herbert York statements: PBS-TV documentary *The Red Army*, May 6, 1981.

2: Looking at the Soviets

Cyrus R. Vance and the taxi driver: Interview with the author, October 1982.

Intelligence and the caliber of the T-72 cannon: Jack Anderson's column (written by Ron McRae), as published in the Washington *Post*, November 24, 1981.

"The T-80 tank": *Soviet Military Power*, p. 71.

Exchange between Stratton and Maloney: U.S. House of Representatives, Armed Services Committee, *Department of Defense Authorization for FY 1983* (hearings), part 3, March 1982, p. 557. At the time of the hearings, Maloney was director of weapons systems in the Office of the Army's deputy chief of staff for Research, Development, and Acquisition.

Calculation of Soviet missile production: Necessarily anonymous intelligence source.

Missing North Vietnamese Party newspaper: Frank Snepp, *Decent Interval* (New York: Vintage Books, 1978), p. 137.

Burning of 40 tons of excess material: James Bamford, *The Puzzle Palace* (Boston: Houghton Mifflin, 1982), p. 65.

"The Soviet Union and its colonial satellites": Speech delivered at Wake Island, October 17, 1950.

"The key point to understand": *Soviet Military Power*, p. 16.

"If you believe": Personal communication.

"A lot of people think": PBS-TV documentary *The Red Army*, May 6, 1981.

"Since I've joined the army": *Ibid.*

Soviet Jewish emigration to the United States: According to the New York–based Hebrew Immigration Aid Society (HIAS), 261,000 Soviet Jews emigrated in the 1970s. The rate varied during the decade, rising to more than 30,000 in 1973 and then falling to just over 10,000 in 1975, in the wake of the Jackson-Vanik amendment, a piece of legislation purportedly intended to force the Soviet authorities to allow more Jews to emigrate by linking such permissions to the granting of favorable trade terms by the United States. After 1975 the numbers rose again, peaking at 50,000 in 1979 before going into a precipitous decline. By 1982, the number of Jews emigrating had become infinitesimal. Over the years, the number of emigrants choosing to go to the United States rather than Israel rose steadily, from 20 percent in 1974 to 80 percent in 1981.

Rarity of preemigration defectors: Victor Marchetti and John D. Marks, *The CIA and the Cult of Intelligence* (New York: Dell, 1974), p. 285.

"Despite the fact that": Foreword by Colonel Robert Bartos to Richard A. Gabriel, *The New Red Legions, A Survey Data Source Book* (Westport, Conn.: Greenwood Press, 1980). At the time Bartos wrote his foreword, he was chief of the Intelligence Division in the Office of the Assistant Chief of Staff for Intelligence, U.S. Army.

Part II: People

3: The Unfortunates

Organization of the Soviet draft system: My own observations on how the system works are buttressed in this book by the comprehensive researches of S. Enders Wimbush and Alexei Alexiev, which are summarized in their report *The Ethnic Factor in the Soviet Armed Forces*, Rand Corp. paper R-278/1, March 1982.

Genady: Personal interview.

Bribing the draft board: Wimbush and Alexiev, *op. cit.*, p. 10.

"Sometimes they would simply fly": *Ibid.*

Living space of Soviet soldiers: Richard A. Gabriel, *The New Red Legions: An Attitudinal Portrait of the Soviet Soldier* (Westport, Conn.: Greenwood Press, 1980), p. 77.

"there is a giant toilet shortage": *Ibid.*, p. 68.

Dried fish every night for two years: Isby, *op. cit.*, p. 66.

"The whole year round": Personal interview.

"When we were given meat": Interview carried out under the auspices of the Defense Department. Quoted in a press release from the office of Congressman Les Aspin, May 3, 1982.

Weight gain of Soviet and Western youths, and diet-related illnesses: Gabriel, *op. cit.*, pp. 51–52.

Theft from the state: Konstantin Simes, *USSR, the Corrupt Society* (New York: Simon & Schuster, 1982), p. 50; Hedrick Smith, *The Russians* (New York: Times Books, 1976), p. 110.

"Fur-lined winter helmets": Personal interview with the author.

"It's simply not true": Interview carried out under the auspices of the Defense Department. Quoted in a press release from the office of Congressman Les Aspin, May 3, 1982.

"in a state of drunkenness: *Krasnaya zvezda*, November 1, 1974.

"It was so ingenious": Personal interview.

"Drink, and how to get hold of it": Personal interview.

"Except for a television set": Barron, *op. cit.*, p. 97.

Deicing fluid, boot polish, cologne: PBS-TV documentary *The Red Army*, May 6, 1981.

"All of them were badly poisoned": Personal interview.

Victor Sokolov: Personal interview.

"The Preobrazhensky regiment": Excerpt from Antonov-Ovseenko's *Notes on the Civil War*; quoted by Bertram Wolfe in the introduction to John Reed, *Ten Days That Shook the World* (New York: Vintage Books, 1960).

"dependence on alcohol in the Soviet armed forces": PBS-TV documentary *The Red Army*, May 6, 1981.

U.S. Navy plane crashes caused by alcohol: "Navy Links Plane Crashes to Pilots with Hangovers," Washington *Post*, September 18, 1981.

World War II Soviet units overrun because of drunkenness: See, for example, Colonel Albert Seton, *The Battle for Moscow* (New York: Playboy Press, 1980), p. 224. A German general named Kübler is reporting to Hitler's adjutant on the desperate situation of the German army in front of Moscow in December 1941: "17 Infantry Division was at that moment holding an eight mile frontage with a divisional strength of 1,400 men, of whom 900 were fighting as infantry. The division would never have been able to break up the attack launched against it that day, said Kübler, had not the attackers been completely drunk. . . . Admittedly 40 Corps had just retaken the locality of Meshkovsk, but in case the High Command might snatch at this straw, Kübler stressed to Schmundt that Meshkovsk had been defended by Red Army troops who lay in a senseless drunken stupor."

"the time for the Americans to attack": PBS-TV documentary *The Red Army*, May 6, 1981.

Eastern Ukrainian NCOs: Wimbush and Alexiev, *op. cit.*, p. 21.

"About 75 percent of the noncommissioned officers": Personal interview.

"You always find them": Personal interview.

"You and I, reader": Kyril Podrabinek, *The Unfortunates.* Eng. trans. in "Russia," No. 3, 1981. Published by Foundation for Soviet Studies, Silver Spring, Md.

Vicious hazing not unique to Soviet Army: See, for example, "Sailors at Norfolk Tell Hill Probe of Beatings, Handcuffs, Verbal Abuses," Washington *Post*, September 30, 1981.

Blame for collapse of U.S. Army in Vietnam: Richard A. Gabriel and Paul L. Savage, *Crisis in Command* (New York: Hill and Wang, 1978).

"My God": Cincinnatus, *Self-Destruction: The Disintegration and Decay of the United States Army During the Vietnam Era* (New York: Norton, 1981), p. 162.

Political work on submarines: *Krasnaya zvezda*, June 10, 1972; quoted in Herbert Goldhammer, *The Soviet Soldier* (New York: Crane Russak, 1975), p. 245.

"low level of civic development": Susan Curran and Dimitry Ponomareff, *Managing the Ethnic Factor in the Russian and Soviet Armed Forces: An Historical Overview*, Rand Corp. paper R-2640/1, 1982, p. 6.

Central Asian rebellion against conscription: *Ibid.*, p. 8.

1938 law on the draft: Helene Carrere d'Encausse, *Decline of an Empire* (New York: Harper Colophon Books, 1981), pp. 158–59.

National units and their defection to the Germans: Curran and Ponomareff, *op. cit.*, p. 34.

1967 law on the draft: d'Encausse, *op. cit.*, p. 160.

"Our army is a special one": *Ibid.*

"there are several reasons": Wimbush and Alexiev, *op. cit.*, p. 13.

920,000 construction and railroad troops: An estimate of the strength of the construction and railroad troops can be made from the information developed by the Rand researchers. They learned that 80 percent of the conscripts serving in the combat arms are of Slavic origin, while 80 percent of the conscripts in the labor units are non-Slavs. It is known that the combat arms require about 1.5 million conscripts every year; 750,000 of those eligible for conscription are non-Slavic minorities, and 90 percent of these are drafted. This gives a figure of 675,000 non-Slavs who are drafted every year. Since 20 percent of the combat troops are non-Slavs, this means that 300,000 non-Slavs go into combat units every year (20 percent of 1.5 million). This leaves 375,000 non-Slavs drafted into the construction troops and railroad troops every year. Since they serve for two years, this means that there are $2 \times 375,000$ non-Slavs serving in the labor units at any one time—750,000. These make up 90 percent of the conscripts in the labor units. The other 10 percent are criminals, those judged mentally or physically unsuitable for combat training, and political undesirables. So altogether we have about 835,000 construction and railroad conscripts. We know that a further 10 percent are officers and a few career NCOs, so the total number of men in the noncombat arms is about 920,000.

Calculations developed in the Office of Congressman Les Aspin, for press release June 24, 1982.

"From the beginning": Wimbush and Alexiev, *op. cit.*, p. 40.

"The soldiers who come": Personal interview.

"Ivashenko stole a Kazakh soldier's girlfriend": Interview conducted under the auspices of the Defense Department.

Aleksandr Makushechev: Quoted in Les Aspin, "The Russian Soldier," New York *Times*, June 8, 1982.

"One of my acquaintances": Personal interview conducted under the auspices of the Defense Department.

"If Soviet officers can't trust": Press release from the office of Congressman Les Aspin, April 14, 1982.

Wartime Red Army feats of valor: Both German and Russian observers of the savage fighting that characterized the Eastern Front throughout the war paid tribute to the incredible courage and determination of the Soviet soldier. The incident of the wounded tank crewman waiting to strike one last blow is related in James Lucas, *War on the Eastern Front* (New York: Stein and Day, 1980), p. 52. "The turret of a Soviet tank, which it was believed had been destroyed during the fighting round the citadel at Brest Litovsk, began to swing and align its gun on a divisional headquarters set up in the grounds of the citadel. When the machine was finally disabled three of the crew were found to be in an advanced state of decomposition and the fourth man, although badly wounded, had held on without food or water, medical aid or support and in the stench of the decaying bodies of his comrades for more than a week. He had obeyed the instruction to strike one last blow for his country." Lucas also quotes a general of the Waffen SS, Max Simon, "The Russian infantryman, however, always defends himself to the last gasp . . . even crews in burning tanks kept up fire as long as there was breath in their bodies. Wounded or unconscious men reached for their weapons as soon as they regained consciousness."

4: Politics and the Professional Warriors

Officers paid 20 times more than privates: Gabriel, *op. cit.*, p. 86.

The Soviet general who expected to be driven by an officer: "Soviet Officers Said to Admire American Army," New York *Times*, December 19, 1977.

Officers crewing the *Sverdlovsk*: Personal interview with former Soviet naval officer.

"To build up only one division": Viktor Suvorov [pseud.], *The Liberators* (London: Hamish Hamilton, 1981), pp. 67–68.

Relative social prestige of officers in the Soviet Union: Zev Katz, "Sociology in the Soviet Union," *Problems of Communism*, May–June 1971, p. 37.

"by the perquisites": Harriet Fast Scott, "The Military Profession in the USSR," *Air Force Magazine*, March 1976.

Belenko in Salsk and Chuguyevka: Barron, *op. cit.*, pp. 84, 94.

"I tell you": James Fallows, *National Defense* (New York: Random House, 1981), p. 110.

Unity of command and the vertical stroke: According to the *Officers' Handbook* (Moscow, 1971 [translated and published in the U.S. under the auspices of the U.S. Air Force], p. 9), the officer in charge "is the absolute master of the forces entrusted to him; who bears full responsibility for all aspects of the life and activities of the unit, subunit, ship, formation, or establishment, for the state of the combat and political training of its personnel, its fighting efficiency and combat readiness."

"Major V. Bosoi found out": *Krasnaya zvezda*, August 1, 1976.

The vertical stroke and Admiral Yegorov: "Soviet Admiral Lost Job After Grounding," Boston *Globe*, December 12, 1981, p. 3.

"These men . . . know how": *Soviet Military Power*.

"the military is an administrative arm": William Odom, "The Party Connection," *Problems of Communism*, September–October 1973, p. 25.

"primary concentration of men and materials": Alfred Vagts, *A History of Militarism* (New York: Meridian Books, 1959), p. 13.

"Crustacean bureaucrats": Personal communication.

U.S. Navy suppressing bad news about aircraft carriers: "Navy Puts Secret Stamp on Criticism of Carriers' Survivability," Washington *Post*, May 4, 1982.

Edward Lozansky: The personal details of Ivan Yershov's history recounted in this chapter are based on a series of interviews with Edward Lozansky. Once Yershov had achieved the rank of general, both his postings and those of his high-ranking friends can be checked with the offical Soviet records of promotions and postings. These are conveniently summarized in the CIA's annual *Directory of USSR Ministry of Defense and Armed Forces Officials*.

Yershov's houses in Kiev: An even more impressive account of the luxurious accommodations enjoyed by the Kiev high command is provided in Suvorov, *op. cit.*, pp. 25–41.

The American officers' ethics class: Fallows, *op. cit.*, p. 12.

"wanted it known at the Pentagon": Lucian Truscott IV, "Mr. T and Colonel Haig," *Village Voice*, May 17, 1973. Quoted in Roger Morris, *Haig: The General's Progress* (New York: Playboy Press, 1982), p. 92.

"The key point to understand": *Soviet Military Power*.

Zakharov: Raymond L. Garthoff, *Soviet Military Policy* (New York: Praeger, 1966), p. 60. Zakharov had been Malinovsky's chief of staff at the Second Ukrainian Front in 1944–45 and during the brief Manchurian campaign in August 1945. The Egyptian journalist Mohammed Heikal has recorded that Zakharov bore a striking resemblance to the film director John Huston.

Gromyko's speech in 1969: John Newhouse, *Cold Dawn* (New York: Holt, Rinehart & Winston, 1973), p. 163.

Dispute between Brezhnev and the generals: For Brezhnev's side, see *Pravda*, October 26, 1973, January 31, 1974, March 16, 1974, and June 15, 1974. The generals spoke up in *Pravda*, January 9, 1974 (Grechko's speech that was cut) and February 23, 1974, *Krasnaya zvezda*, March 19, 1974, and *Pravda*, June 5, 1974. Kulikov's historical article appeared in *Pravda*, November 13, 1974. See also comments by Marshal P. F. Batitsky, commander of the air defense forces, who warned in his service journal *Vestnik PVO strany* (Journal of the National Air Defense Service), November 11, 1974, that "powerful and influential forces [in the West]" would "try to frustrate the implementation of agreements" between the USSR and the West.

Vance's March 1977 mission to Moscow: Strobe Talbott, *Endgame* (New York: Harper Colophon Books, 1980), pp. 37–67.

Brezhnev's coup: For a full account of this affair, see Richard D. Anderson, "Soviet Decision Making and Poland," *Problems of Communism*, March–April, 1982. The account provided here is based on Anderson's brilliant dissection of the story.

U.S. intelligence reports for Soviet intervention plans: The reports were distributed to the press on a background basis—see, for example, New York *Times*, October 27, 1980: "officials said that Soviet forces along the border with Poland had conducted maneuvers and that armored equipment had been fueled and kept more ready for operations than usual."

"Differences of opinion": *Pravda*, November 17, 1980.

"War with Poland is forced upon us": *Krasnaya zvezda*, November 16, 1980. The author was Dmitri D. Lelyushenko, a retired general of World War II fame.

"Fawning on foreign authorities": *Krasnaya zvezda*, November 27, 1980. Brezhnev had just met with Senator Charles Percy, who was due to become chairman of the Senate Foreign Relations Committee. Percy had warned Brezhnev that any invasion of Poland would remove any hope of arms negotiations with the incoming Reagan Administration.

Mobilization turned into shambles: Washington *Post*, February 13, 1981; *Financial Times*, February 13, 1981.

"One interpretation of Politburo decisions": Anderson, *op. cit.*, note, p. 32.

"We know well": Speech of Yuri Andropov to Communist Party Central Committee before his election as Party leader. Reprinted New York *Times*, November 13, 1982.

"the backing": Dusko Doder, "Andropov Seeks to Quickly and Tightly Consolidate Rule." Washington *Post*, November 21, 1982.

"we were getting": Personal interview.

"foreign nations": Richard D. Anderson, "Politics of the Soviet Defense Burden." Unpublished paper, August 1980.

5: The Weapons Makers

"It gave off an air of sorcery": Tom Wolfe, *The Right Stuff* (New York: Farrar, Straus & Giroux, 1979), p. 71.

Korolev: James Oberg, *Red Star in Orbit* (New York: Random House, 1981), pp. 16–38, *passim*.

Kurchatov and the Soviet bomb: David Holloway, "Entering the Nuclear Arms Race: The Soviet Decision to Build the Atomic Bomb," working paper No. 9, Woodrow Wilson Center, Washington, D.C., 1979; Peter Pringle and James Spigelman, *The Nuclear Barons* (New York: Holt, Rinehart & Winston, 1981), pp. 57–70.

Swedish television team in Moscow: New York *Times*, December 15, 1981. p. 9.

4 and 7 million people in defense work: David Holloway, "The Soviet Defense Industry," in *Defense Industries*, ed. Leitenberg (London: Croome, Helm, 1983). For the lower figure, Holloway cites a calculation by Seymour Melman, professor of industrial engineering at New York's Columbia University, in his paper for the UN Center for Disarmament, "Barriers to Conversion from Military to Civilian Industry," April 1980. The higher figure comes from "Regional Employment Trends in the USSR," in *Soviet Economy in a Time of Change*, Joint Economic Committee, 1979, p. 604.

135 plants: Statement by Major General Richard X. Larkin, director of the Defense Intelligence Agency, JEC, *Resource Allocations*, 1981, p. 83.

Styling change in military uniforms: Suvorov, *op. cit.*, p. 193.

The Ministry of General Machinery: Mikhail Agursky, "The Soviet Military Industrial Complex," Jerusalem Papers on Peace Problems no. 31 (Jerusalem: The Magnes Press, 1980).

Voyenpredy: JEC, *Resource Allocations*, 1977, p. 25. Discussing Soviet defense production, Sayre Stevens, then deputy of the CIA for intelligence, told the subcommittee that "the approach that the Soviets are using is essentially one of brute force. It is an inefficient method that relies on producing a high output of goods and then simply rejecting a good deal of what is produced. This is really the only feasible course of action given the labor intensive approach which they take to their weapons production. They depend on what we call the Voyenpred system and on a system of fines for faulty production to ensure quality control for military hardware. The Voyenpreds are military representatives who are located at the plants who monitor weapons production in all its phases. They have three major functions: To prevent production bottlenecks by being expeditors for the necessary material inputs; to police pricing of military products and finally, to ensure that products sold to the military meet all the quality standards required."

Agursky states that in the major plants the *voyenpredy* may be generals (*op. cit.*, p. 10).

"50 percent": This is a common figure given for the spending gap; see, for example, statement by Caspar Weinberger, New York *Times*, March 5, 1981.

Defense costs do not equate to military effectiveness: JEC, *Resource Allocations*, 1976, p. 19. George Bush, then director of the CIA and later Vice President of the United States, made that very point: "While there is *some* relationship between dollar costs and military capabilities, the dollar cost estimates can *not* [Bush's emphasis] be used to draw inferences about relative military effectiveness." The Army claimed in 1972 that the cost of the M-1 tank would be $507,000 each in 1972 dollars. In 1982 it reached $2.8 million. There had been inflation in the meantime, but not that much.

17 billion rubles: JEC, *Resource Allocations*, 1980, p. 43. Taking the official valuation of 1.50 rubles to the dollar, this would give the Soviets a defense budget of about $26 billion, which seems a little on the low side.

CIA change of mind in 1975 about Soviet defense industry efficiency: JEC, *Resource Allocations*, 1976, p. 20. Statement by George Bush, director of the CIA: "As a result of an intensive collection and analytical effort over the past several years, we have acquired a great deal of new information on the ruble prices of Soviet military equipment. This new data has changed markedly our appreciation of the ruble costs of Soviet military programs. . . . The new estimates for 1975 are about twice the previous intelligence estimate of defense spending in that year. About 90 percent of the increase in the estimate is accounted for by our new understanding of Soviet prices and costs."

The following year, Sayre Stevens gave more explanations of why the Soviet defense budget had suddenly gone up (JEC, *Resource Allocations*, 1977, pp. 17–18): "As you will recall, the ruble estimate we presented last year was substantially higher than our previous estimates. The reasons for this change and its significance have been widely misunderstood. We raised our estimate because we discovered that in the past we had underestimated the prices of Soviet defense goods. . . . The increase in our ruble estimates did not represent a change in our estimate of Soviet defense activities or Soviet military capabilities. . . . The Soviets are far less efficient at producing defense goods than we had previously estimated them to be."

This change of heart did not occur before the spending gap had begun to affect U.S. defense budgets. Defense Secretary James R. Schlesinger, for example, cited increased Soviet defense spending in support of his FY 1976 budget.

CIA reluctance to accept hard data on Soviet budget: Intelligence sources. John Prados, *The Soviet Estimate* (New York: The Dial Press, 1982), p.

247, reports that the "real" Soviet defense budget as approved by the Kremlin was 58 billion rubles.

Soviet defense industry in the 1930s: David Holloway, "The Soviet Defense Industry," *op. cit.*; Holloway quotes M. V. Zakharov, *Voenno-istoricheskii zhurnal* (Military Historical Journal), no. 2, 1971, p. 7.

Soviet military research and development in the 1930s: One experimental long-range bomber actually made a nonstop 7,000 mile flight from Moscow to Vancouver in 1937. The spade mortar consisted of a spade (for digging trenches) with a hollow handle that doubled as the mortar barrel, with the spade providing the base. Stalin was extremely taken with the idea and only abandoned it after several tests and accidents. The T-40 amphibious tank had just gone into production when war broke out (following the earlier amphibious T-37 and T-38). There being less demand for such technological frivolities in wartime, production was abruptly terminated.

Soviet wartime production: In 1942 the USSR produced 25,430 aircraft, while Nazi Germany built 14,700. In the same year, the Soviets built 24,668 tanks, while the Germans turned out 4,278.

Khrushchev's January 1960 speech: *Pravda*, January 15, 1960. Khrushchev's cuts included the premature retirement of 250,000 officers, an initiative that did not endear Khrushchev to the officer corps.

Arms reduction reversed: Despite the common presumption that the major change in Soviet military policy occurred as a result of Russia's "humiliation" in the Cuban missile crisis of 1962, scholarly analysis indicates that in fact the basic turnaround took place in 1961, prompted in the first instance by the Kennedy rearmament program in the United States, and in the second, by the Berlin crisis of that year. These events enabled the military to force Khrushchev to change course. See Michael MccGwire, "Soviet Military Requirements," in Joint Economic Committee, *Soviet Military/Economic Relationships* (Washington, D.C.: Government Printing Office, 1983).

Tank production: Gerald Halbert, "World Tank Production," *Armor*, March–April 1981, p. 45. Figures for 1980–82 from statement by Major General James Williams, director of the Defense Intelligence Agency, JEC, *Resource Allocations*, 1982, pp. 17–19.

Fighter production: JEC, *Resource Allocations*, 1982. See also David Holloway, "Soviet Defense Industry," unpublished paper; Holloway quotes

M. V. Zakharov, *Voenno-istoricheskii zhurnal* (Military Historical Journal), no. 2, 1971, p. 7.

Soviet weapons increasingly going for export: JEC, *Resource Allocations*, 1982.

Shortfall of T-72s to Warsaw Pact: International Institute for Strategic Studies, *Strategic Survey*, London, 1981.

Foxtrot submarines made solely for export: Office of Chief of Naval Operations, U.S. Department of the Navy, *Understanding Soviet Naval Developments*, 4th ed. (Washington, D.C.: Government Printing Office, 1981). The figures suggest that in the case of armored vehicles and combat planes, exports are running at nearly 45 percent of production.

Soviets obliged to find hard currency: Central Intelligence Agency, *Communist Aid Activities in Non-Communist Less Developed Countries*, National Foreign Assessment Center, ER 80–10318U, October 1980.

Ustinov hurrying to New Delhi to seel MiG-27: "India Chooses French Jet Over a Soviet Plane," New York *Times*, April 18, 1982. The Indians, however, did agree to manufacture some MiG-27s themselves under license.

"We are not afraid of coercion": A. S. Yakovlev, *Aims of a Lifetime* (Moscow, 1966); translated by U.S. Air Force, National Technical Information Service no. AD 674316. Yakovlev recounts that Stalin made his chilling observation "with a smile," but Stalin's sense of humor had its grim side.

"What would have happened": Pringle and Spigelman, *op. cit.*, p. 63.

Soviet fighter competitions of the 1950s: Richard D. Ward, "Soviet Practice in Designing and Procuring Aircraft," *Astronautics and Aeronautics*, September 1981.

"We have the fine MiG 15": Yakovlev, *op. cit.*

"A direct result": Harold Brown, in his FY 1981 Department of Defense Report, pointed out, "There currently are eight classes of manned interceptors deployed, which suggests that the Soviets may have a standardization problem of their own" (p. 76).

"They have . . . a license to exist": Personal communication.

Current directors of Soviet design bureaus: Personal communication from Richard Ward.

Yangel's infiltration of German V-2 program: Oberg, *op. cit.*, p. 45.

Cholomei anecdote: Personal communication with former associate of the designer.

"A dog of a missile": Talbott, *op. cit.*, p. 134.

"a certain sign": *Aerospace Daily*, December 10, 1982, p. 210.

"Don't worry about it, Art": A. Ernest Fitzgerald, *The High Priests of Waste* (New York: Norton, 1972), p. 116.

Agursky, Kovalev, machine tools, and the SS-18: Agursky, *op. cit.*; personal interviews with Agursky in Jerusalem by Leslie Cockburn.

Life inside the Soviet military research and development sector: Agursky, *op. cit.*; personal interviews with Agursky conducted by Leslie Cockburn. Also interview with Mark Kushment of the Harvard Russian Research Center, who has been conducting interviews with émigrés who have worked in military research and development. As one part of his survey, Kushment asked a number of these émigrés, "Is the quality of military R&D higher than that found in civilian institutes?" Ninety percent answered "yes"—it was indeed better because of better quality personnel, more funds, etc. He then asked, "In your own particular laboratory or institute, was the quality of military work higher than civilian?" To this question, 90 percent answered "no"—in their own direct experience the military work was inferior to the civilian. It seems that misconceptions about Soviet defense are not confined to the United States.

Inman and Carey: *Aviation Week and Space Technology*, February 8, 1982, p. 10.

14 percent of all the doctorates: Agursky, *op. cit.*

Medvedev and the secret job: The classified research job offered to Medvedev was actually the investigation of the radiobiological effects of the great Urals nuclear disaster of December 1957. See Andrew Cockburn, "The Nuclear Disaster They Didn't Want To Tell You About," *Esquire*, April 1978.

"In research and development": JEC, *Resource Allocations*, 1976, p. 55.

"The Russians are a wonderful threat": Interview on BBC *Horizon*, "The Race to Ruin," November 9, 1981.

Chrysler getting M-1 contract in 1976: ABC, *20/20*, "Tank off the Tracks." Interview with former Secretary of Defense Donald Rumsfeld, January 20, 1980.

"like trying to pull Excalibur": *Defense Week*, May 17, 1982. Interview with former Assistant Secretary of the Navy James Wolsey.

"If you stop and think": Address to the Manhattan Institute, published in *Manhattan Report*, April 1982.

Part III: Hordes, Tanks, and Other Weapons

6: The Hordes

"It's difficult for me to think that": Presidential Press Conference, October 1, 1981.

"I must not conceal from you": Winston Churchill, *Complete Speeches 1897–1963* (London: Chelsea House, 1974), vol. VII, p. 50.

"Those in the West": Speech delivered to International Club before Georgetown University's Center for International Affairs. Text reprinted in New York *Times*, April 7, 1982.

"In the case of the Soviet Union": Edgar M. Bottome, *The Balance of Terror: A Guide to the Arms Race* (Boston: Beacon Press, 1971), pp. 4–5. Quoted in Matthew A. Evangelista, "Threats Misperceived— Soviet Military Capabilities and Objectives in the Early Postwar Period 1945–53," Unpublished Harvard B.A. thesis. This work effectively punctures the durable myth of Soviet conventional superiority in the postwar years. As the references will show, much of the early part of this chapter is drawn from it. Evangelista has published an updated version of his conclusions in *International Security*, vol. 7, no. 3, Winter 1982.

"We are going to have to fight": Ladislas Farago, *Patton: Ordeal and Triumph* (New York: Ivan Obolensky, 1964), p. 806.

"It has been estimated recently": Hal D. Steward, "The Russian Army Today: An Estimatorial," *Armored Cavalry Journal*, September–October 1947.

No Soviet accurate record of troop numbers: Cornelius Ryan, *The Last Battle* (New York: Simon & Schuster, 1966), p. 347.

2.8 million: figure taken from Khrushchev's speech published in *Pravda*, January 15, 1960.

Half a million Russian troops in occupation zones: Figure drawn from Evangelista, *op. cit.*

Russians seizing baths: Milovan Djilas, *Conversations with Stalin* (New York: Harcourt, Brace & World, 1962), p. 164.

"of poor quality": L. C. Manners-Smith, "The Soviet Army in Occupation: The Second Phase," in B. H. Liddell-Hart, *The Soviet Army*, p. 160. Quoted in Evangelista, *op. cit.*

Lend-lease supplies: Despite the lend-lease supply of Studebaker trucks, the Red Army employed 1 million horses in 1945.

New York *Times* assessment: "World Military Assessment," New York *Times*, May 12, 1947, p. 14.

Omar N. Bradley: Bradley's revelation occurred in the course of a speech to the American Forestry Association (not, perhaps, the most public of forums), October 12, 1949. The speech is reprinted as Appendix 3 in Louis B. Ely, *The Red Army Today* (Military Service Publishing, 1949), p. 227.

Emmanuel Shinwell: Shinwell gave his figure in the course of a Parliamentary speech. Quoted in *Times* (London), July 27, 1950.

Churchill and the Mongol hordes: Actually Churchill, not untypically, was misrepresenting history, as well as contemporary events. The Mongols of Genghis Khan did not constitute a horde; in fact, they were almost invariably outnumbered by their opponents in battle. Their victories were due to superior tactics, training, and organization. See James Chambers, *The Devil's Horsemen* (New York: Atheneum, 1979).

"As the perceived size of the Soviet force": Alain Enthoven and K. Wayne Smith, *How Much Is Enough* (New York: Harper Colophon Books, 1971), p. 119.

Relevant combat troops of the Soviet armed forces: Figures derived from a press release from the office of Congressmen Les Aspin, May 24, 1982. For the basis of the 920,000 figure for construction and railroad troops, see p. 468.

Strength of individual Soviet divisions: The number of divisions in the ground forces varies slightly according to the source. *Soviet Military Power* pegs it at 180 plus. *Military Balance*, published by London's International Institute for Strategic Studies, goes even higher and puts the number at 187. John M. Collins, the authoritative senior specialist in national defense at the Congressional Research Service, lists the number at 173 in *U.S./Soviet Military Balance, CRS Report No. 81–233 S*. David Isby, in his excellent and exhaustive *Weapons and Tactics of the Soviet Army* settles on 177 plus. As is explained later, a large proportion of these divisions are inactive. Others, such as one of the eight airborne divisions, are purely training establishments. The precise overall number therefore is not of great relevance.

"When I went out": Edward L. Warner, *The Military in Contemporary Soviet Politics: An Institutional Analysis* (New York: Praeger, 1977), p. 146.

"Our military doctrine": N. Ya. Sushko and S. A. Tyushkevish, eds., *Marksizm-Leninism o voyne i armii*, 4th ed. (Moscow: 1965), p. 244.

"Other kinds of weapons": Quoted in Harriet Fast Scott and William F. Scott, *The Armed Forces of the USSR* (Boulder, Colo.: Westview Press, 1979), p. 54.

Hungary in 1956: Veljko Micunovic, *Moscow Diary* (New York: Doubleday, 1980), p. 154.

Czechoslovakia in 1968: Jiri Valenta, *Soviet Intervention in Czechoslovakia, 1968* (Baltimore: Johns Hopkins University Press, 1979), p. 108 ff. Valenta points out that the Soviet high command was by no means united in their determination to intervene; the ground forces were the most in favor, while the strategic rocket forces were uninterested.

Most effective type of combat soldier: James Dunnigan, *How to Make War* (New York: William Morrow, 1982), p. 19.

"Comforting old myths": Enthoven and Smith, *op. cit.*, p. 164.

7: Mobilizing the Hordes

Castrated divisions: Suvorov, *op. cit.*, p. 140.

"It is no secret": *Krasnaya zvezda*, August 22, 1968. Quoted in Valenta, *op. cit.*, p. 112.

"After receiving its 'battle technology'": Suvorov, *op. cit.*, p. 142.

Chaos in the invasion: Leo Heiman, "Soviet Invasion Weaknesses," *Military Review*, August 1969.

"As they left Czechoslovakia": Surovov, *op. cit.*, p. 198.

Afghan mobilization: S. Enders Wimbush and Alex Alexiev, *Soviet Central Asian Soldiers in Afghanistan*, Rand Corp. paper N-1634-NA,

1981. Prepared for the director of Net Assessment, Office of the Secretary of Defense.

Polish mobilization: "Soviets Reportedly Deactivate Reservists Near Polish Border," Washington *Post*, February 13, 1981, p. A33. The correspondent, Kevin Klose, cited Soviet sources in reporting that "discipline among the reservists, who were said to have been told only that they were being called for retraining, was a major problem from the beginning. These sources alleged that the reservists, with family and friends nearby, melted away from their duties in numbers so large that punishment became impossible. They cited persistent insubordination, low morale and poor performance as major problems. These were said to have been major factors leading to the order to disband. Even the deactivation, they said, was marked by confusion. One unit, they asserted, was assembled and moved three times in the last three days before being released from duty. The call-up frustrated factory and plant managers who lost parts of their work force, adding to the general unhappiness and confusion, the sources said."

"drunkenness, abuse of rank": *Krasnaya zvezda*, January 16, 1981.

"Very reliable sources": Personal communication.

Ogarkov: N. Ogarkov, "Safeguarding Peaceful Labor," *Kommunist*, no. 101, July 1981, pp. 80–91.

"While it is possible": JEC, *Resource Allocations*, 1981, p. 163.

"The Soviets can mobilize": Speech to Defense Preparedness Association, May 19, 1982.

5.5 million men mobilized in eight days in 1941: H. F. Scott and W. F. Scott, *op. cit.*, p. 322.

8: Tanks and Other Armor

Spinal and kidney injuries: Isby, *op. cit.*, p. 93.

Loading a T-62 gun: There is a popular misconception in the U.S. Army that T-62 loaders must be left-handed, but this is not so.

"rugged, well constructed": H. F. Scott and W. F. Scott, *op. cit.*, pp. 297–98.

T-62 manual: The handbook in question was for the use of platoon commanders, not for individual crews. Individual crews are not thought capable of looking after the maintenance of their vehicles beyond a very basic level.

M-60 overhaul rates: Information supplied by Continental Teledyne, the manufacturer of the M-60 engine. Confirmed by U.S. Army sources.

Truck overhaul rates: Confirmed by the Detroit Diesel Division of the General Motors Truck Division.

Czechs rebuilding engines: Isby, *op. cit.*, p. 84.

T-34 development and production: Steven Zaloga, *T-34 in Action* (Carrollton, Texas: Squadron/Signal Publications, 1981); Steven Zaloga and James Grandsen, *The T-34 Tank* (London: Osprey Publishing, 1980).

French aircraft engine: There has been dispute over the conceptual ancestry of the T-34 engine, but it seems clear that it was indeed an adaptation of the Hispano-Suiza Y-12 aircraft engine.

Radios in the T-34: Zaloga, *op. cit.* Radios did become a standard feature in all T-34s beginning with the model 43.

T-34s captured in the Korean War: The analysis was carried out by a team from the Chrysler Corporation, then the main U.S. tank manufacturer.

Horsepower of Soviet tanks: Steven Zaloga, *Modern Soviet Armor* (Englewood Cliffs, N.J.: Prentice-Hall, 1979).

"the heavier weights": JEC, *Resource Allocations*, 1978, p. 96.

"the engine itself was not only bad": Suvorov, *op. cit.*, pp. 75–76.

T-72 horsepower: Article in Soviet military journal, *Znamenosets* (Standard Bearer), by Colonel V. Knyazkov; reported and paraphrased in newsletter *International Defense, DMS Intelligence*, DMS, Inc., Greenwich, Conn., August 17, 1981.

Automatic loader on T-64, T-72: Isby, *op. cit.*, p. 104.

"this is how the Red Army Chorus": *Ibid.*

"from the very first look": Suvorov, *op. cit.*, p. 75.

Comparison of effectiveness of U.S. and Soviet tank guns: Zaloga, *Modern Soviet Armor*, p. 20.

U.S. Army assessment of the superiority of T-72: *Defense Daily*, July 1, 1982, p. 5.

Indian army's refusal to buy many T-72s: *International Defense Review*, vol. 14, no. 4, 1981, p. 383.

U.S. Army's plan to change to 120-mm German gun: The agreement on the German gun was the result of a byzantine series of negotiations between the Pentagon and the Federal Republic of Germany's Ministry of Defense. The Americans had originally promised the Germans that the Leopard 2 tank would be allowed to compete against the M-1 for the U.S. Army contract, a *quid pro quo* for German agreement to accept the introduction of the AWACS radar plane into NATO (paid for by the Germans). However, the conditions imposed by the U.S. Army in the tank competition led the Germans to conclude, not without reason, that the outcome was fixed. Agreement to buy the German 120-mm gun at some future date was thus a sop to soothe German sensibilities.

Deficiencies of M-1 tank: It is difficult to present any conclusive data on the M-1's performance problems, since each new set of figures tends to reveal that the situation is even worse than had been previously supposed. Durability tests in the fall of 1982 had to be suspended when all five of the M-1s taking part broke down (New York *Times* editorial, October 22, 1982).

"a combined arms team": JEC, *Resource Allocations*, 1978, p. 177.

U.S. Army substitutes American engine in BTR: The engine used is the Dodge T-245 from the old ¾-ton M-37 truck.

"This is probably the best": JEC, *Resource Allocations*, 1978, p. 177.

Bradley fighting vehicles: John Fialka, "The Bradley Fighting Vehicle," *Washington Monthly*, April 1982, p. 22.

SAM-6 losses in 1982: In all fairness it must be admitted that the deficiencies of the SAM-6 system were compounded by the incompetence of their Syrian handlers. In the words of one non-Israeli Middle Eastern military expert who was in close touch with the situation during the 1982 war, "Everything the Syrians could do wrong they did."

SAM-7 performance: Isby, *op. cit.*, p. 264; also internal Israeli military sources.

U.S. measures to neutralize SAM-7: Isby, *op. cit.*, p. 266.

Relative effectiveness of guns and missiles in downing planes in North Vietnam: James Hansen, "The Development of Soviet Tactical Air Defense," *International Defense Review*, vol. 14, no. 5, 1981, p. 531.

"craps out entirely": "Military Failed to Put Missile to a Real Test," Washington *Post*, February 24, 1982.

Shilka going off of its own accord: Isby, *op. cit.*, p. 238.

"Soviet equipment tends to be simplistic": JEC, *Resource Allocations*, 1977, p. 61.

Resistance of the U.S. Army to the M-16: The horrific story of how the Army Material Command set out to sabotage the privately developed M-16, with lethal consequences for the American soldiers in Vietnam, is trenchantly described in Fallows, *op. cit.*, pp. 77–95.

Success of the RPG-7 in the 1973 war: Isby, *op. cit.*, p. 139.

"the Viper suffers": C. T. Hanson, "The Viper: Too Little, Too Light," *Washington Monthly*, April 1982, p. 30.

9: The Air Force—Keeping Up with the Joneses

"Because of this Soviet modernization program": *Aviation Week and Space Technology*, June 7, 1982.

The American nuclear-powered bomber: *Aviation Week and Space Technology*, December 8, 1958.

Relative performance of the A-6 and the A-26 in Vietnam: Pierre M. Sprey, *Impact of Avionics on Tactical Air Effectiveness*, staff study prepared for the Office of the Assistant Secretary of Defense for Systems Analysis, 1968; declassified 1974.

Effectiveness of the Sparrow missile in Vietnam: Jeff Ethell, *F-15 Eagle* (London: Ian Allen, 1981), p. 100. In actual numbers, the Sparrow (AIM-7) achieved 55 kills out of 589 scoring attempts; 65 percent of the Sparrows malfunctioned because of launch, guidance, or fusing failures.

Defense Facts of Life: Spinney had been a colonel in the Air Force before becoming a civilian analyst in the Pentagon Office of Plans, Analysis, and Evaluation. For almost two years before the study was released for public scrutiny by the Pentagon he had been delivering his study in the form of a briefing to Pentagon officials with the requisite security clearances, although high-ranking officials, it seemed, were less than interested in the defense facts of life. The study was released, over Pentagon objections, at the behest of the powerful Senator Sam Nunn.

Development of the F-16: Fallows, *op. cit.*, pp. 95–106.

Sturmovik: In all, 40,000 Sturmoviks (IL-2s) were built during the war.

MiG-21s in Vietnam: In the latter half of 1966, the exchange ratio was in favor of the North Vietnamese. Overall, from 1965 to 1968, the first stage of the air war, the Americans lost 48 planes in air combat, while the North Vietnamese lost 110, a ratio that was unacceptably bad for the Americans. Between 1970 and 1973, the ratio improved to 12.5 to 1 in favor of the Americans, mainly owing to improved training.

Smoking F-4s: A "smokeless" fighter is visible to the naked eye no farther than about 4 miles. The black plumes behind the F-4s made them visible from about 20 miles, and, of course, identified them to any interested North Vietnamese as an enemy.

Tactical Air Command's infatuation with nuclear bombs: See Robert F. Coulam, *Illusions of Choice* (Princeton, N.J.: Princeton University Press, 1977).

"American equipment and Israeli pilots": "The Latest Wars: What They Have Told the Generals," Washington *Post*, June 17, 1982.

"The MiG-21s we flew against": Personal communication.

"I would put": PBS-TV documentary *The Red Army*, May 6, 1981.

"Key people in the Pentagon": Fitzgerald, *op. cit.*, p. 132.

"the inherent problems": *Ibid.*, p. 133.

"the fact that the avionic systems": *International Defense Review*, vol. 14, no. 6, 1981, p. 717. The article makes it very clear how much the design of the Fencer followed that of the F-111. However, it understates the wing loading on the Fencer and overstates its thrust-to-weight ratio.

F-111's bombing record: Sprey, *op. cit.*

"our planes can track": Personal communication.

"with Doppler, laser, . . . systems": *Aviation Week and Space Technology*, June 7, 1982.

"AA-9 air-to-air missile": *Ibid.*

Falcon: Fallows, *op. cit.*, p. 55.

"if their developers": Fitzgerald, *op. cit.*, p. 25.

exact copy of 1950s model: The model in question was the AIM-9-B. The latest model in service as of 1982 is the AIM-9-L. The Soviets also reportedly obtained a set of blueprints from a military attaché from a neutral country attached to the Pentagon.

Combat radii of F-111 and Su-24: Both sets of figures are based on the assumption that the plane will use its afterburners at some point in the mission.

Combat radius of MiG-25: According to Barron's *MiG Pilot*, Belenko made this very point in trying to convince his U.S. interrogators of the MiG-25's limitations. Nonetheless, *Soviet Military Power*, published in 1981, was still stoutly insisting (p. 34) that the MiG-25 had a radius of 900 km (558 miles).

Overhaul of the Mig-21 engine every 300 hours: Interview with General George Ezzat in *Aviation Week and Space Technology*, December 21, 1981. It should be noted that General Ezzat, and the article as a whole, is keen to emphasize the virtues of the MiG-21.

Burn and maintenance data for J-85 engines: These figures are based on the experience of the F-5s in the Top Gun program at the Naval Fighter School at Miramar, Calif. Since these planes are "worked" far harder than any others in the services (apart from their counterparts in the Air Force Aggressor program), their frequency of engine overhaul is higher than most.

Stalin's astonishment: Yakovlev, *op. cit.* "What sort of a fool would sell his own secrets?" declared Stalin when the Rolls Royce deal was suggested to him.

Su-7s and Su-17s: Hosni Mubarak, then head of the Egyptian air force, was the official who delivered the verdict on the Su-17. See Lieutenant General Saad El Shazly, "The Crossing of the Suez," *Mideast Research*, 1980, p. 158. For a useful roundup of the Su-7's attributes, or lack of them, see "Whale of a Fighter," *Air International*, September 1982, which draws on the experience of the Indian air force with the plane. Although the author does his best to be complimentary, he acknowledges that the Su-7 has an extremely limited range (and this is by comparison with the MiG-21!), extremely limited visibility from the forward cockpit, which makes life hard for any pilot trying to see what is happening on the ground, and a very limited payload and requires 6 or 7 seconds from switching on for the afterburner to ignite.

Treaty of Key West: For an excellent summation of the career of the helicopter in the U.S. Army, see Greg Easterbrook, *Washington Monthly*, September 1981, an article that drew a predictably outraged response from the U.S. Army.

Soviet helicopters too dangerous for Khrushchev: *Khrushchev Remembers* (New York: Penguin Books, 1977), vol. 2, p. 68.

Soviet helicopters have 40 percent less power: Isby, *op. cit.*, p. 317.

"We are not afraid": New York *Times*, January 12, 1982, p. 2.

"nemesis of the *mujahedin*": *Time*, October 26, 1981.

"significantly high": *Aviation Week and Space Technology*, February 2, 1982.

Vulnerabilities of Hind in Afghanistan: Jim Coyne, *Soldier of Fortune*, December 1982.

Hind attack on Pakistani border post: David C. Isby, "Afghanistan: The Unending Struggle," in *Jane's 1982 Ground Forces Annual* (London: Macdonald & Jane's, 1982).

Egyptian use of helicopters in the 1973 war: Isby, *Weapons and Tactics of the Soviet Army*, pp. 325–26.

The British and the F-111: In 1968 the press was referring to the F-111 as "McNamara's flying Edsels," a reference to the disastrous motor car of that name introduced by the Ford Motor Company under Edsel Ford's stewardship.

Crossman and the F-111: *Diaries of a Cabinet Minister*, vol. 2 (London: Hamish Hamilton, 1976), p. 647.

10: Organizing the Troops for War

"Whereas the supply discipline": S. L. A. Marshall, *The Soldier's Load and the Mobility of a Nation* (Quantico, Va.: Marine Corps Association, 1980), pp. 85–86.

"with the help of an empty oil can": *Ibid.*

Soviet advances in World War II: The most notorious example of the Red Army's cumbersome "tail" is the delay that occurred after Soviet troops reached the Oder in January 1945. Marshal Chuikov, who commanded the foremost forces over the bridgehead, afterward complained in his book *The Fall of Berlin* (London: MacGibbon & Kee, 1967), that "if Supreme Command . . . had organised supply properly and had been able to get the necessary amounts of ammunition, fuel and stores up to the Oder," the Russians could have continued their advance and taken Berlin in February 1945 rather than at the end of April.

Chuikov also makes the point that, because of the predilection of commanders like Marshal Zhukov, his immediate superior, for immense superiority of forces in an assault and an overwhelming barrage of artillery, the supply train was more cumbersome than necessary. It is certainly true that the final assault on Berlin commenced with a barrage from 40,000 guns, most of which was entirely wasted because the Germans had withdrawn from the fortifications under bombardment the night before.

That being said, it is true that the Soviets did draw significant advantages from the ability of their troops to survive with a minimum of *personal* supplies. A story retailed by Marshall, based on German sources, of a Soviet regiment that was cut off and surrounded in a forest near the Volkhov River in the winter of 1941 and that survived on a ratio of frozen bread, leaves, and pine needles is only one of many such that attest to the ordinary Soviet soldier's amazing feats of endurance during World War II. Whether the modern Soviet conscript, brought up to a far higher standard of living than his grandfather, would stand up to similar conditions with such fortitude is open to doubt.

"increasing weapons complexity": Spinney, *op. cit.*

Complexity of the MiG-23 in relation to the MiG-21: Even before the CIA had detailed information on the MiG-23, it was estimated that "the MiG 23 will require about twice as much effort to maintain as the MiG 21" (JEC, *Resource Allocations*, 1975, p. 53).

Soviet conscripts who have never driven a car before joining army: This is one of the jobs that DOSAAF is meant to take care of, but a Soviet military journal reported in 1972 that conscripts who had qualified as drivers under the DOSAAF program, and who had received additional instruction in the army, were easily unsettled by the "high speed" narrow streets and other demanding circumstances of East German roads (*Starshina Serzhant*, June 1972).

"While the education": Isby, *Weapons and Tactics of the Soviet Army*, p. 63. This section also contains a useful discussion of the Soviet system of centralized maintenance.

"the higher effectiveness": From Harold Brown's FY 1982 Consolidated Guidance Memorandum on Tactical Air Cost, Complexity, and Readiness, issued February 8, 1980. Leaked to and quoted by *Armed Forces Journal*, May 1980, p. 29.

3,000 exported planes and 2,725 unaccounted-for planes: No Su-24 has been exported and only several dozen MiG-25s; MiG-23 exports did not start until 1976. Some of the excess production can be accounted for by late-model MiG-21 variants, perhaps as many (to be generous) as 750 or so. The authoritative U.S. estimate quoted is that appearing in John M. Collins's Congressional Research Service report, which is based on Defense Intelligence Agency information. It is probably an accurate figure, since aircraft can only be stationed at airfields, which are fixed and therefore relatively easy to count with reasonable precision.

"for every one plane": Personal interview.

"the political reliability": U.S. Department of Defense, *Annual Report for FY 1982*, p. 74.

Tank numbers: Sources include NATO, *Force Comparisons*; Collins, *U.S./Soviet Military Balance*, Congressional Research Service, 1981; International Institute for Strategic Studies, *Military Balance 1981–82*; and "NATO Seeks to Match Soviet Conventional Forces," New York *Times*, September 19, 1982, p. 4. The IISS estimates another 20,000 tanks in the western USSR. If this is correct, these tanks would be reserved for Category 2 and 3 divisions, for reservists, with consequent fallibilities discussed above. David Isby, however, provides an interesting breakdown of Soviet force inventories (drawing from Defense Intelligence Agency data) as of early 1978. This lists the number of all Soviet tanks, ancient and modern, in the western military districts as 9,376. Even the most generous estimates of Soviet tank production since then do not quite make up the discrepancy, allowing for the export production and natural wear and tear of tanks already in the inventory. Suvorov, after all, states that once a tank has run for 750 hours it is junked. The NATO specialist quoted by the New York *Times* made no reference to tanks in the western Soviet Union but stated that 20,000 were "in storage."

It should always be borne in mind that tank counting is a very inexact science. Satellites cannot see inside tank sheds, so the bean counters must perforce calculate the number of tanks a shed could hold and then multiply that by the number of sheds that show up on the photographs without any guarantee that the sheds are full.

Worn-down Soviet tanks in 1941: Zaloga, *Modern Soviet Armor*, p. 28.

Preventive maintenance: The alternative is called requirement centered maintenance and was pioneered by the U.S. airline industry. The U.S. military, as unconcerned as its Soviet counterpart with economy and the efficient use of resources, is also addicted to preventive maintenance, although the higher level of technical skill among the personnel involved means that the results are not quite so deleterious.

Superior performance of Guard pilots: See *The Economist*, May 1, 1982, p. 31. The best exposition of what the U.S. National Guard system contributes to U.S. military strength as a whole is to be found in *Vista 1999*, a report issued by the Guard in 1982.

DOSAAF: Wimbush and Alexiev report that DOSAAF is quite active in large Russian cities (as opposed to other parts of the USSR). It does offer courses in exciting activities, such as parachute jumping, scuba diving, and radio operation and repair. These courses do provide a significant training base for youths who are inducted into the comparatively small and elite airborne units and signals specialties. However, these glamorous courses tend to be open only for youths with "special educational qualifications, unblemished records, or family connections." Others simply think of DOSAAF as another official propaganda agency that exacts dues from its members and, except for the lucky few, offers little more than uninspiring political lectures in return.

   Outside Russia itself (i.e., in other parts of the USSR), the Rand researchers concluded, "DOSAAF does not operate as widely and does not offer as rich a menu of activities. . . . In some parts of the Soviet borderlands, particularly in Central Asia and the Caucasus, no DOSAAF organizations exist." When they do, "preinduction youth from the southern and eastern borderlands generally are limited to driver's training and truck operation, if anything."

T-64 crews training on T-62s: Isby, *Weapons and Tactics of the Soviet Army*, p. 75.

"Our attaché was out in a green jeep": JEC, *Resource Allocations*, 1978, p. 266.

"The Soviets rely on junior officers": JEC, *Resource Allocations*, 1975, p. 126. Graham was at that time director of the Defense Intelligence Agency.

"We knew that firing range": Personal interview.

Sasha's admiration for officer directing affairs: As befits the heavily centralized Soviet military, coordination between troops on the ground and aerial units that are supposedly supporting them comes at a far higher level than is customary in the U.S. forces—battalion or, more likely, division. Alongside this, however, there is a system by which frontal-aviation teams stay up near the front line, operating from modified armored personnel carriers. Unfortunately, such units are few and far between, a fact attested to both by the émigrés and by observers of the Afghan fighting.

Underwater tanks: Getting tanks to behave like submarines seems to be an idea that appeals to the military mind. In 1940 the Germans seriously considered sending specially adapted tanks across the English channel on the bottom which would emerge dripping under the White Cliffs of Dover. The story of how the tank armies crossed the Dnieper in 1967 has been circulating in Western intelligence circles for some time. Viktor Suvorov gives a hilarious account of the episode on pages 69 and 70 of his book.

Generals Pavlov, Konstantinov, and Nosov on unimaginitive pilots: Pavlov, *Kraznaya zvezda*, April 8, 1976; Konstantinov, *ibid.*, March 13, 1977; Nosov, *ibid.*, April 27, 1976. All quoted in Joshua Epstein, "On Conventional Deterrence In Europe: Questions Of Soviet Confidence," *Orbis*, Spring 1982.

"Soviet pilots receive only half": *Defense Week*, July 13, 1981.

Exercises for Israeli trainee commanders: S.L.A. Marshall, *Sinai Victory* (New York: Morrow, 1967), p. 249.

"we are not training our troops": Colonel V. Golubovich, "From the Experience of Operational-Tactical Training of Reserve Armies," *Voenno-istoricheskii zhurnal* (Military Historical Journal), September 1979, pp. 37–38. Marshal of the Soviet Union G. K. Zhukov sent a directive to the leadership of the General Apparatus of the People's Commissariat of Defense and to the General Staff on October 21, 1944, criticizing deficiencies in training the troops in the technique of conducting close combat. "By a survey of Red Army men and sergeants it has been established that they were taught to attack only loudly crying 'hurrah' and were not taught at all the technique of the offensive or the combat use of terrain," Zhukov wrote. The directive made reference to the weak knowledge of combining the movement of infantry with artillery, mortars, and tanks in direct support, to the inability of commanders of companies and battalions to evaluate the terrain and to use it in attack and defense.

"The rigidity of Russian attacks": General Von Mellenthin, *Panzer Battles* (New York: Ballantine Books, 1971) p. 223.

"The Russian is a unique type": Balck's sapient observations appear in a series of interviews conducted by Pierre M. Sprey on behalf of Battelle Columbus Laboratories, Tactical Technology Center, Columbus, Ohio, and published by them in 1980 (ref. no. FY7615-78-05106).

"The nice neat charts": Isby, *Weapons and Tactics of the Soviet Army*, p. 169 ff.

"There are obvious disadvantages": *Soviet Army Operations*, U.S. Army Intelligence and Threat Analysis Center, 1978 (ref. no. IAG-13-U-78, p. 4).

Soviets learning lessons of Afghanistan: Philip Jacobson, "The Red Army Finally Gets a Chance to Test Its Stuff," Washington *Post*, February 13, 1983.

British photographer in Afghan ambush: David Isby, "Afghanistan 1982– the War Continues," *International Defense Review*, Vol. 15, No. 11, 1982.

Syrians on the Golan: Sunday Times Insight Team, *Yom Kippur* (London: Andre Deutsch, 1974).

"continuously halted": Anthony H. Cordesman, "Lessons of the Iran-Iraq War: Tactics, Technology, and Training," *Armed Forces Journal International*, June 1982, p. 68 ff.

"Regardless of the recent Soviet emphasis": *Ibid.*

Meremsky on daring thrusts: *Voyennyi vestnik* (Military Bulletin), no. 1976; translated in William Scott and Harriet Scott, *Soviet Military Doctrine* (Boulder, Colo.: Westview Press, 1982). "Daring thrusts" owe their recent popularity in assessments of the Soviet threat to the work of Phillip Karber of the BDM Corp. (a large Washington consultancy firm, with many lucrative U.S. Army contracts). The September 1982 edition of *International Defense Review* carried an article by Christopher Donnelly, "The Soviet Operational Manoeuvre Group—A New Challenge for NATO," which is likely to be equally or more influential in military academic circles.

Donnelly argues that rather than pushing out battalion- or regiment-sized groups to operate behind the enemy's front, the modern Soviet doctrine is to use far larger forces—at least a division—for the purpose. One advantage of this from the Soviet point of view would be that there is a greater chance of the senior commanders in charge of these larger formations displaying the qualities of initiative so conspicuously absent in their juniors. However, as David Isby points out, revolutions in Soviet tactical doctrine tend on closer examination to turn out to be a fairly venerable concept worked over.

"If the government and party apparatus": Zhores Medvedev and Roy Medvedev, "Nuclear Samizdat," *The Nation*, January 16, 1982.

Khudenko's experiment in agriculture: Hedrick Smith, *The Russians* (New York: Times Books, 1976), pp. 262–63.

"On what does the effectiveness . . . depend": *Krasnaya zvezda*, June 2, 1971.

"These qualities are *compulsory*": *Krasnaya zvezda*, March 24, 1972.

"You see, our every good beginning": *Aviatsiya i kosmonavtika* (Aviation and Astronautics), no. 11, 1962, p. 56. Quoted in Epstein, *op. cit.* Kutakhov was air commander of the Odessa Military District at the time.

11: What the Red Army Is Supposed to Do

"A second wave": "Surprise Attack Could Make Nuclear Weapons Useless," *Times* (London), March 15, 1976.

The Third World War: Composed by General Sir John Hackett, former commander of the NATO Northern Army Group, and others (London: Sidgewick & Jackson, 1978).

"of broadly comparable performance": *Ibid*.

"The offensive is the basic form": From V. G. Reznichenko, *Tactics*. Reznichenko was for many years head of the department of tactics at the Frunze Military Academy.

Rates of advance of different armored formations: These figures are taken from Jeff Record, *Sizing Up the Soviet Army* (Washington, D.C.: Brookings Institution, 1975), p. 44.

Force of short-term conscripts: Some are shorter than others. Defense Secretary Harold Brown pointed out in his FY 1981 Report to the Congress that "about 20 percent of the enlisted personnel (in the Soviet forces in Germany) are recruits who are rotated every six months into the divisions. Some of these personnel have not completed their basic training when they joined the divisions" (p. 102).

"the impression gained": R. O. Welander, J. J. Herzog, and F. D. Kennedy, Jr., *The Soviet Navy Declaratory Doctrine for Theater Nuclear Warfare*, a report prepared for the director of the Defense Nuclear Agency, 1977. Quoted in Epstein, *op. cit.*, p. 79.

"The high command know": Personal communication.

Suggestions for modern line of concrete fortifications: See, for example, John Keegan, "Soviet Blitzkrieg: Who Wins?," *Harper's*, May 1982. Keegan asserts that "the Maginot line was never breached," although Von Mellenthin recalls that "the Maginot defenses were breached in a few hours by a normal infantry attack, without any tank support whatsoever" in Lorraine by units of the First Army, in which he was then a divisional chief of staff (*Panzer Battles*, pp. 26–27).

"Who are you trying to guard against?": Quoted in Adrian Hill, "Could Napoleon's Army Win Today?," *Royal United Services Institute Journal*, March 1977.

Manpower comparisons between NATO and the Warsaw Pact: International Institute for Strategic Studies, *Military Balance 1981–82*, p. 112. The "paradox" is cogently discussed by Steven L. Canby, "Military Reform and the Art of War: Military Superiority Worldwide at FY 82 Budget Levels" (paper presented at Woodrow Wilson Center, Smithsonian Institution, Washington, D.C., June 7, 1982).

"When I see": Interview conducted on behalf of the Defense Department, November 1979, and published by Battelle Columbus Laboratories, Tactical Technology Center, Columbus, Ohio.

B-52 mutiny: Jeff Ethell and Joe Christy, *B-52 Stratofortress* (New York: Charles Scribner's Sons, 1981).

Twice as many men needed to maintain the M-1 as the M-60: 85 M-60 battalions require 45,650, while 85 M-1 battalions require an additional 42,000 maintenance personnel, a figure cited by Pierre M. Sprey in an address delivered to the XXth West Point Senior Conference, June 1982.

Cutting out excess fat: No one is, of course, in favor of *not* cutting out excess fat—the disagreement arises over what constitutes fat. The notion that senior military men find especially disagreeable is that fat cutting and reorganization could vastly enhance U.S. and NATO combat potential *without* raising the budget.

Part IV: Weapons of Mass Destruction

12: Missiles and Bombers

"Whatever [the Soviets] claim": Attempts at public relations such as this letter underline the alarming point that Weinberger actually believes what he is saying. Passages quoted here taken from Los Angeles *Times*, August 25, 1982.

"We used to believe": "The Man Not Worried by the Bomb," Washington *Post*, April 11, 1982, p. B1.

Tighe's perceptions: JEC, *Resource Allocations*, 1979, p. 129.

KGB and nuclear warheads: Desmond Ball, "Can Nuclear War Be Controlled," Adelphi Paper no. 169, International Institute for Strategic Studies, 1981, p. 45. Further information from intelligence sources.

Numbers of Soviet strategic warheads: Figures drawn from fact sheet compiled by Center for Defense Information, Washington, D.C., January 1983. The warhead totals (based on the valid proviso that not all MIRV-capable missiles are in fact MIRVed) breaks down thus:

ICBMs	5,158
SLBMs	1,842
Long-Range Bombers	290
Total	7,290
(If bombs carried on Backfires included)	
Total	7,490

If all MIRV-capable missiles were to carry their full complement of warheads, then the ICBM total increases to 5,540 and the SLBM total to 1,900.

Cold launch: A cold-launched or pop-up missile leaves behind an intact silo, thus in theory allowing the Soviets to reload another missile, a fact that excites the darkest suspicions of Defense Secretary Caspar Weinberger. The former U.S. Air Force deputy chief of staff, Kelly Burke, poured cold water on this idea, however, telling a Congressional hearing in 1982: "I don't think we have had hard intelligence as to how long they expect it to take them [to release] but I think on the order of two or three days at a minimum. If that area has been struck by nuclear weapons, then it might not be possible to get them in at all." Hearings, House Appropriations for FY 1983, part 4, p. 551. There is in any case considerable misconception about the true purpose and nature of cold-launched missiles. These missiles are kept encased in a close-fitting metal tube inside the silo. This tube serves the purpose of providing additional hardening for the missile against nearby explosions as well as making it easier to transport and assemble the weapon. When the missile is "popped" out of the tube and silo, however, the latter still suffers considerable damage. First of all, the heavy silo lid must be blown off, with consequent damage. The hot gases propelling the missile itself on the first stage of its journey themselves wreak considerable damage to the inside of the silo. Thus any silo that has cold-launched a missile needs considerable repairs before it can be used again. The quickest that the Soviets have ever been observed to reload a silo after a test launch is three months, although the process normally takes twice that time. An intensive investigation by the CIA in the late 1970s failed to produce any evidence whatsoever that the Soviets were planning to reload and refire their ICBM silos during hostilities.

"This plane failed to satisfy": *Khrushchev Remembers*, vol. 2, pp. 70–71.

Korolev and the SS-6: Oberg, *op. cit.*, p. 36.

"both sides": "Survey Finds 3-to-1 Backing for A-Freeze," Washington *Post*, April 27, 1982.

"pacifists, politicians, and fools": Harry H. Semmes, *Portrait of Patton* (New York: Appleton, 1955), p. 75.

"as long as the U.S.": *Air Force Magazine*, May 1979, p. 26. Quoted in *Misguided Expenditure*, Council on Economic Priorities, 1981, p. 22.

The Soviet counterforce first-strike plan for striking at America's silos: This bizarre notion has an equally bizarre history: it was originally a scheme dreamt up at the Rand Corporation in the early 1950s as an *American* strategy for striking at *Soviet* nuclear bases. In the late 1950s, Hermann Kahn, who had participated in the original discussions, "mirror-imaged" the concept as a possible Soviet strategy, and the idea was developed by a Rand group called the Strategic Objectives Committee, whose deliberations were based on the assumption that habits of thought in the Kremlin are more or less identical to those of Rand Corporation senior analysts, which is not necessarily the case.

In the mid-1970s the notion was dusted off and given a new lease on life by Paul Nitze, initially in "Assuming Strategic Stability in an Era of Detente," *Foreign Affairs*, 1976, No. 2, and more explicitly a year later in "Deterring Our Deterrent," *Foreign Policy*, Winter 1976. For this and more blackly humorous history, see Fred Kaplan, *Wizards of Armageddon* (New York: Simon & Schuster, 1982).

"The prelude": Richard L. Garwin, "Civil Preparedness and Limited Nuclear War," *Hearings Before the Joint Committee on Defense Production*, April 28, 1976, p. 55.

"In that sense"; "Would you care": "Soviet Has Edge, U.S. General Says," New York *Times*, May 12, 1982.

"Demonstration by the Soviet Union": *Aviation Week and Space Technology*, June 28, 1982.

Soviets launch SS-11, SS-20, SS-N-8, and other missiles: *Aerospace Daily*, June 22, 1982, and New York *Times*, June 20, 1982.

"Their accuracy stinks": Jonathan Marshall, "Missiles That Fizzle," *Inquiry* magazine, March 1983.

Failed U.S. operational silo tests of 1960s: Kansas City *Times*, June 4, 1982.

70 percent alert rate for Soviet ICBMs: Washington *Post*, "Debut of Soviet Missiles Could Color U.S., NATO Politics," June 26, 1980.

"It's dangerous": CBS, *60 Minutes*, November 8, 1981.

"There is always": Personal communication.

"This was the first Soviet attempt": JEC, *Resource Allocations*, 1977, p. 88.

"has been flight-tested": U.S. Department of Defense, *Annual Report for FY 1981*, p. 81.

"crumbling in their silos": Robert Birman and John Baker, *Soviet Strategic Forces* (Washington, D.C.: Brookings Institution, 1982), p. 102.

political furor: The best summation of the political background to the Schmidt request for the introduction of new medium-range missiles is Fred M. Kaplan, "Warring Over New Missiles for NATO," *New York Times Magazine*, December 9, 1979.

The press and the SS-20: Misprint of CIA report reproduced in Jack Anderson's column, April 1, 1982.

"huge, wheeled vehicles": Evans and Novak column, April 5, 1982. Original CIA figure from CIA sources.

"two kilotons apart": CBS News, "The Nuclear Battlefield," June 18, 1981.

SS-20 accuracy and yield: International Institute for Strategic Studies, *Military Balance 1982–3* (London: I.I.S.S. Publications, 1982).

"After observing seven tests": Washington*Post*, January 18, 1982.

Failure of 1982 test of solid ICBM: "New Soviet Missile Failed in First Flight, Officials Say," Washington *Post*, December 4, 1982.

"Whoever thinks that the Soviets": Personal communication.

Soviet missile accuracy and the argument over the SS-9: The best roundup of this whole controversy appears in an article by Les Aspin, "Debate Over U.S. Strategic Forces: A Mixed Record," *Strategic Review*, Summer 1980. For the strange episode of the Soviet official who told the U.S. delegation at the Moscow summit that they were *underestimating* Soviet missile accuracy, see Lawrence Freedman, *"U.S. Intelligence and the Soviet Strategic Threat"* (London: Macmillan, 1977), p. 173.

"The Mod 2 had serious problems": Testimony before the House Armed Services Committee, Subcommittee on Research and Development, Hearings for FY 1980, part 3, p. 129.

Are our missiles now vulnerable to the Soviets?: Harold Brown officially unveiled Presidential Directive PD 59 in a speech at the Naval War College on August 20, 1980. In it he declared, "In the future, Soviet military programs could, at least potentially, threaten the survivability of each component of our strategic forces [meaning missiles, bombers, and submarines]. For our ICBMs, that potential has been realized, or close to it. The Soviets are now deploying thousands of ICBM warheads accurate enough to threaten our fixed Minuteman silos."

In the press conference of March 31, 1982, President Reagan announced that the Soviets had "a margin of superiority" in strategic nuclear weapons. On April 14, 1982, Caspar Weinberger told reporters on Capitol Hill, "We have a lot of warheads. But you have to look at total capability, and the Soviet missiles are now much more accurate than ours, much more accurate than they used to be" and "there is a degree of superiority and strategic edge on the Soviet side that is necessarily a matter of great concern" (New York *Times*, April 15, 1982).

Two days later, Weinberger trimmed his sails slightly. He told the American Defense Preparedness Association that "the Soviets have *begun to build* an edge of superiority." Washington *Post* reporter George Wilson, reporting this speech, also quoted "Pentagon officials" as saying that Weinberger had "overstated Soviet capabilities when he said on Wednesday that 'Soviet missiles are now more accurate than ours.' When queried, the officials said that no intercontinental ballistic missile that the Soviet Union has deployed is as accurate as the latest U.S. Minuteman II missile now on the line" (Washington *Post*, April 17, 1982).

The latest Minuteman III on the line is equipped with the Mark 12A warhead, which is guided by the NS 20 guidance system. This is deemed officially of being capable of delivering "accuracies" of 600 feet.

Team B and missile accuracy: Prados, *op. cit.*, pp. 251–52.

Intelligence and Soviet strategic weapons: Aspin, *op. cit.*

Missile accuracy and the bias factor: This subject, which is of the highest importance, has not received as much attention as it deserves. Discussion may have been inhibited by the attendant technical complexities, as well as the thick veil of secrecy that the missile establishment traditionally uses to obscure the actual evidence for their grandiose claims of "silo-killing accuracy." See Andrew Cockburn and Alexander Cockburn, "The Myth of Missile Accuracy," *New York Review of Books*, November 20, 1980; Paul Mann, "Panel Reexamines ICBM vulnerability," *Aviation Week*, July 13, 1981, p. 141; editorial by Arthur Metcalfe, *Strategic Review*, Summer 1981; General Robert T. Marsh, "Missile Accuracy— We DO Know," *Strategic Review*, Spring 1982, and rebuttal by Professor J. Edward Anderson of the University of Minnesota in the same issue; Desmond Ball, "Can Nuclear War Be Controlled?," Adelphi Papers no. 169, International Institute for Strategic Studies, p. 13. For throw weight, see Fred M. Kaplan, "Missile Envy," *New Republic*, Ocrober 11, 1982.

"The precision that one encounters": Testimony before the Senate Foreign Relations Committee, April 30, 1982.

Amoretta M. Hoeber: See, for example, *Soviet Strategy for Nuclear War* (Stanford, Calif.: Hoover Institution Press, 1979).

McNamara and Brown on winning nuclear wars: McNamara's 1962 speech, delivered to NATO defense ministers in Athens, was originally top secret. Brown's remarks appear in his FY 1981 report to the Congress.

Both are quoted in Fred Kaplan, "Russian and American Intentions," *The Atlantic*, July 1982.

"U.S. defense policies": New York *Times*, June 17, 1982, p. A 25.

"prevailing with pride": *Ibid*.

"Mass nuclear missile strikes": Translated in U.S. Air Force, *Soviet Military Thought Series*, no. 9 (Washington, D.C.: Government Printing Office, 1974), p. 217.

"the U.S. Army must be prepared": Quoted in Fred Kaplan, "Russians and American Intentions".

"There is profound error": "The Philosophical Heritage of V. I. Lenin and Problems of Contemporary War (A Soviet View)"; translated in U.S. Air Force *Soviet Military Thought Series*, no. 5 (Washington, D.C.: Government Printing Office, 1974), p. 17.

"It is a dangerous madness": Quoted in "Soviet Military Power: Questions and Answers," *The Defense Monitor*, vol. 1, no. 1, 1982.

"In our days": *International Affairs*, no. 5, May 1965. Talensky was no nonentity. He was the former editor of *Voennaya mysl'* (Military Thought), a high-level military theoretical journal that is confidential; that is, it is not officially released to the West like much other Soviet military literature. His remarks quoted here, and the vehement response, are cited in Raymond Garthoff, "Mutual Deterrence and Strategic Arms Limitation in Soviet Policy," *International Security*, Summer 1978.

"We consider that strategic air warfare": Norman Moss, *Men Who Play God* (London: Penguin Books, 1970), p. 124.

The rationale for the U.S. MIRV: Fred Kaplan, *Wizards of Armageddon*.

The cost of Soviet ICBMs in the 1970s: National Foreign Assessment Center, *Soviet and U.S. Defense Activities, 1971–80: A Dollar Cost Comparison* (Washington D.C.: Central Intelligence Agency, 1981), p. 5.

"The Russians today": Personal communication.

The Soviet nuclear cannon: Isby, *Weapons and Tactics of the Soviet Army*, p. 194.

Rotmistrov: See particularly Rotmistrov's *Time and Tanks*; translated in excerpt in U.S. Air Force, *Selected Soviet Military Writings* (Washington, D.C.: Government Printing Office, 1976), p. 251.

"units and subunits": Speech by Grechko to the All-Army Conference of Young Officers, November 1969. Quoted in H. F. Scott and W. F. Scott, *The Armed Forces of the USSR*, p. 55.

"More than in any Western Army": Philip Karber, *The Tactical Revolution in Soviet Military Doctrine*, BDM Corp., McLean, Va., 1977, p. 1.

"Statements in these Soviet volumes": Milton Leitenberg, "Background Information on Tactical Nuclear Weapons [Primarily in the European Context]," in Stockholm International Peace Research Institute, *Tactical Nuclear Weapons: European Perspectives* (London: Taylor and Francis, 1978), p. 88.

Frogs in the 1973 war: Isby, *Weapons and Tactics of the Soviet Army*, p. 212.

"Tactical nuclear warfare": "Tactical Nuclear Warfare and NATO: Viable Strategy or Dead End?" *Nato's Fifteen Nations*, June 1976.

Development of chemical weapons by Germans: Joseph Borkin, *The Crime and Punishment of I. G. Farben* (New York: Free Press, 1978). pp. 16-17. Gas warfare, of course, had been thought of before; indeed, the civilized nations of the world had gone to the lengths of solemnly outlawing it at the Hague Convention in 1907.

Declining lethality of chemical agents against protected troops: Conclusion of researches by Matthew Meselsen and Julian Perry-Robinson of MIT and the University of Sussex, respectively. They are the two most eminent authorities in this field.

U.S. Army war game and shocked hausfraus: ABC, *20/20*, 1980.

Use of chemicals in Afghanistan, Abyssinia, Yemen: Robert Harris and Jeremy Paxman, *A Higher Form of Killing* (New York: Hill and Wang, 1982), pp. 43-44, 49-50, 234-35.

"this fact alone"; differing methods of classifying chemical weapons: Christopher Donnelly, "Winning the NBC War, Soviet Army Theory and Practice," *International Defense Review*, No. 8, 1981.

Half-hourly dose of cold water: To assist this cooling "mechanism," the soldier will be wearing a cotton surcoat, rather as the crusaders adopted the practice of wearing cotton surcoats over their armor under the blazing sun of Palestine.

"This could be used to clear": Personal communication.

Senator Tower: Personal interview, March 1981.

13: Air Defense

Downgrading of U.S. air defense force: Needless to say, the decision was not taken on rational grounds alone. The interceptor lobby inside the U.S. Air Force got greedy, progressing from the relatively simple F-102 to the vastly more complex and expensive F-106. It finally came unstuck with the YF-12, which was to be an interceptor version of the SR-71 spy plane. The projected cost of this program appeared so threatening to other and more powerful factions within the Air Force that it was canceled, and the North American Air Defense Command went into a long period of decline.

Intelligence predictions about protection of major Soviet cities: For useful data, see Les Aspin, "Debate Over U. S. Strategic Forces: A Mixed Record," *Strategic Review*, Summer 1980.

Soviet boasts: Prados, *op. cit.*, pp. 155–56.

"Upon nearing the Soviet warhead": William J. Broad, "Nuclear Pulses" and "Nuclear Pulse: Awakening to the Chaos Factor," *Science*, May 29, 1981, pp. 1009–1012.

Cut in air defense share of budget: *Soviet Armed Forces Review Annual*, section on PVO by David Jones, 1980, p. 87.

"The SAM is a bitch": *Times* (London), December 20, 1981.

SAM-2 in Vietnam: Isby, *Weapons and Tactics of the Soviet Army*, p. 247. For a good account of the B-52's encounters with SAM-2s, see Ethell and Christy, *op. cit.*

Lost Korean airliner: *Flight International*, April 1978.

Lost Finns: Washington *Post*, "Soviet Dissident Group Names 2 to Challenge Official Candidates," February 2, 1979. The story reported how a dissident, Lyudmilla Agapova, had tried to fly out of the USSR in the Finnish plane but had missed the rendezvous.

14: Civil Defense

Handbook for Pioneer-camp schoolchildren: "Russians, Too, Joke Sadly on Atom War Survival," New York *Times*, June 11, 1982.

"The Soviets evacuate their cities": U.S. Senate, Foreign Relations Committee, *United States/Soviet Strategic Options* (Washington, D.C.: Government Printing Office, 1977), p. 163. Quoted in Fred Kaplan, *Dubious Specter* (Institute for Policy Studies, 1980), p. 33.

"with enough shovels": Interview of T. K. Jones by Robert Scheer in *Los Angeles Times*, January 16, 1982. The phrase was later adopted by Scheer as the title of his book on the deranged attitude of Reaganist officials to nuclear war.

1974 Soviet civil defense handbook: Translated at Oak Ridge for Energy Research and Development Association and Defense Civil Preparedness Agency ("increasing the . . . ability" quote appears on p. 107, U.S. version).

General Radzievsky: Quoted in Leon Gouré, "Another Interpretation," *Bulletin of the Atomic Scientists*, April 1978, p. 48. Gouré's article is in answer to two lengthy articles by Fred M. Kaplan in that and the preceding issue of the *Bulletin*. All critical examinations of the efficacy of the Soviet civil defense system tend to draw on Kaplan's studies, including this one. This is hardly surprising, since once the fundamental question is posed—"How do you shelter an urban population and economy from nuclear attack, especially one as concentrated as in the USSR?"— there is not much more to be said, despite the expostulations of Messrs. Gouré, Jones, and Altunin.

Civil defense, express mail, and the Declaration of Independence: Ed Zuckerman, "How Would the U.S. Survive a Nuclear War?," *Esquire*, March 1982, p. 37.

"fall right on my head": *Ibid.*

48-hour evacuation of New York: Federal Emergency Management Agency.

"Orderly columns": Leon Gouré, *War Survival in Soviet Strategy* (Miami: University of Miami, 1976). Quoted in Fred M. Kaplan, "Civil Defense," *Bulletin of the Atomic Scientists*, March 1978.

Digging shelters when the ground is frozen: This question has indeed engaged the attention of T. K. Jones. In *With Enough Shovels* (New York: Random House, 1982), Robert Scheer describes an evening *chez* Jones in which Jones demonstrated with an imaginary shovel beside his dining-room table how it would be perfectly feasible to carry out the operation. The precise mechanics remain unclear, however, nor is it apparent if Mr. Jones has ever attempted to actually dig a personal shelter with a real shovel in a piece of really frozen ground.

"It is impossible to make buildings": Fred M. Kaplan, "Civil Defense."

"decisive measures": Quoted in Gouré, *War Survival in Soviet Strategy*, p. 140.

"it would take far fewer": Fred M. Kaplan, "Civil Defense," *Bulletin of the Atomic Scientists*, April 1978. Economic information from same source.

"state of the program" message: "The Main Direction," *Voyennye znaniia* (Military Sciences), October 1976.

"the fact that . . . officials": Gouré, *War Survival in Soviet Strategy*.

Defense Intelligence Agency claim about evacuation of a Soviet city: Statement by Lieutenant General Tighe, director of the Defense Intelligence Agency, JEC, *Resource Allocations*, 1979, p. 113.

"mistakenly, in my belief": "Could Russia Blunder into Nuclear War? Interview with Harold Brown, Secretary of Defense," *U.S. News & World Report*, September 5, 1977.

Pre-1961 Soviet civil defense: Before 1961 it was known as *Mestnaya protivovozdushnaya oborona*, or MPVO (local antiair defenses).

"Civil defense has become": U.S. Office of Emergency Planning, *The National Plan for Emergency Preparedness* (Washington, D.C.: Government Printing Office, 1964).

"Southern" group and "Moscow" generals: Raymond Garthoff, *Soviet Military Policy* (New York: Praeger, 1966), p. 46 ff.

Books from the Civil Defense organization attacking the proposed change in doctrine: Chuikov's book was called *Civil Defense in a Missile Nuclear War* (Moscow: Atomizdat, 1968). Colonel-General V. A. Beliavsky, the chief of staff of the Civil Defense of the USSR, published *Civil Defense— A Concern of the Entire People* (Moscow: Atomizdat, 1968). The chief political officer of Civil Defense of the USSR, O. B. Tolstikov, published *The CPSU on the Necessity of Perfecting Civil Defense* (Moscow: Atomizdat, 1969). V. A. Pomortsev, their lonely ally in far off Kirghiztan, published *Materials on Civil Defense* (Frunze: 1970). Beliavsky stated that "To build shelters for the entire population of the country requires enormous means and many years of intense effort. This is not yet within the capability of any, even the most highly developed, state. That is why, along with the construction of shelters, great attention is paid in many countries to the prior dispersal of the population, limiting its concentration in large industrial centers, and to the carrying out of measures for the *timely evacuation* of the population before the enemy delivers his nuclear strike."

Some researchers, such as Gouré, have deduced from the fact that Altunin was made a Deputy Minister of Defense that civil defense had been upgraded in status. But this misses the point that prior to October 1972, civil defense had not been part of the Ministry of Defense, but a separate organization. The changing position of civil defense can be charted through the annual yearbooks of the Soviet Encyclopaedia. The 1972 year book does not list civil defense as one of the branches of the armed forces (such as ground forces, strategic rocket forces, etc.) The 1973 year book listed civil defense as a branch of the armed forces alongside the ground forces and rocket troops. The 1974 year book lists the branches as being strategic rocket forces, air defense forces, air force, navy, and ground forces. Civil defense is listed under the heading of "and also," along with the "troops of the rear" and other support organizations. Thus it settled down as a component of the overall military organization run by the Ministry of Defense, but of lower status than the front line forces.

"Let's give the American people": Rep. Donald Mitchell, "In Defense of Civil Defense," Washington *Post*, April 28, 1982.

Part V: The Sea Power of the State

15: The Navy

U.S. Navy's admiration for Gorshkov: For example, Rear Admiral Sumner Shapiro has stated, "The Soviet Navy of today and the foreseeable future is the dream of Admiral of the Fleet of the Soviet Union, Sergei Gorshkov, for nearly 25 years its commander-in-chief and architect. He has savored that rare pleasure in history of planning and then seeing through to completion a massive and successful national undertaking." Quoted in Office of the Chief of Naval Operations, U.S. Department of the Navy, *Understanding Soviet Naval Developments*, 4th ed. (Washington, D.C.: Government Printing Office, 1981), p. 79.

"He sure knows how": Washington *Post*, July 27, 1982, p. 2, 2.

July 1945 naval buildup plan: Michael MccGwire, "Soviet Military Requirements."*loc. cit.*

Nimitz: Memorandum from Nimitz, "Discussion of Recent Activities of the Soviet Union," July 23, 1946. Quoted in Daniel Yergin, *Shattered Peace* (Boston: Houghton Mifflin, 1977), p. 242.

Stalin's concern about possible invasion: Michael MccGwire, "The Rationale for the Development of Soviet Seapower," *Proceedings of the U.S. Naval Institute*, May 1980.

Early postwar submarines: The German models that served as inspiration were of the XXI and XXIII classes. The Soviet Z and W classes that were based on them did not begin to appear until 1951. Before then, every submarine in the Soviet navy was based on 1930s designs.

40 surface ships and 70 submarines: Chris Wright, "Developing Maritime Force Structure Options for the U.S. Defense Program," M.Sc. thesis, MIT, 1976.

Khrushchev cutback: MccGwire, "The Rationale for the Development of Soviet Seapower," *loc. cit.*

"as a concession": *Khrushchev Remembers*, vol. 2, p. 64.

The evolution of Soviet naval strategy as a response to U.S. initiatives: The pioneer of this analysis is Michael MccGwire of the Brookings Institution. See "Naval Power and Soviet Global Policy," *International Security*, Spring 1979. See also the more voluminous studies by MccGwire and others in *Soviet Naval Developments* (1973), *Soviet Naval Policy* (1975) and *Soviet Naval Influence* (1977), all published by Praeger.

Code breaking and the defeat of the U-boats: The clearest description of this, the salient element in the Battle of the Atlantic, is to be found in Patrick Beesley, *Very Special Intelligence* (London: Hamish Hamilton, 1977). German U-boats were required to report their locations twice a day. It is hard to see what operational purpose was served by such a system, apart from giving Admiral Doenitz, the German submarine commander, something to do.

Gorshkov's series in *Morskoy sbornik*: For a succinct summary of the Gorshkov series see MccGwire, "Soviet Naval Doctrine and Strategy," in *Soviet Military Thinking*, pp. 135–46. Grechko's articles mentioned here appeared in *Morskoy sbornik* (Naval Collection), July 1971, and *Voprosy istori KPSS* (Problems of the History of the CPSU), May 1974.

Perhaps predictably, MccGwire's charting of the disputes with the Soviet high command over the role of the navy is anathema to U.S. hawks, since it disturbs their preferred image of a monolithic Soviet control structure. The Scotts, for example, in *The Armed Forces of the USSR*, state briskly, "A number of Western analysts considered that the Soviet admiral's views represented one side of an ongoing debate within the Soviet defense structure and were not necessarily statements of approved Soviet policy. . . . It is highly improbable that the ongoing debate theory has any validity; Gorshkov's writings are expressions of top Party policies, which the Soviet leadership wished to be made known" (p. 58).

"in response to be able to meet": JEC, *Resource Allocations*, 1976, p. 107.

Kirov cruiser: For a good comprehensive description of this ship, "reminiscent of the battleships and battlecruisers of the past," see Kehoe and Brower, *International Defense Review*, no. 2, 1981.

16-minute Forger: *Defense Week*, September 22, 1980.

"the Soviet Navy . . . has been transformed": Quoted in *Understanding Soviet Naval Developments*.

"In the past 15 years": Military Posture Statement, FY 1980

"The United States . . . is twice blessed": Collins, *U.S./Soviet Military Balance*, p. 240.

"permanent, blue-water, offensive Soviet fleet": *International Defense Review*, no. 5, 1982.

"lack [of] a meaningful . . . capability": Quoted in Norman Polmar, *Soviet Naval Developments*, 1979, p. 22.

"Most modern Soviet surface combatants": *Understanding Soviet Naval Developments*, p. 26.

Nuclear-armed torpedoes: Michael MccGwire, "Soviet Military Requirements," *loc. cit.*

Exploding Typhoon: "Soviets Believed to Have Problems with New Typhoon Missile," Washington *Post*, January 8, 1982. Information from cognizant officials indicates that at the time of going to press little had changed.

Lehman and hairless nuclear submariners: "Soviet A-Submarine Fatalities Reported," Washington *Post*, March 17, 1982.

Nine of 84 Soviet missile subs at sea: Ball, *op. cit.*, p. 45. Seven of these submarines are in the Atlantic, two in the Pacific.

One out of five Soviet ships under weigh: Bradford Dismukes and James McConnell, *Soviet Naval Diplomacy* (Elmsford, N.Y.: Pergamon Press, 1979), p. 47.

Towing ships and reduced speed: *Understanding Soviet Naval Developments*, p. 20.

"battle of the first salvo": See, for example, Polmar, *op. cit.*, p. 23.

"much more tightly packed": *International Defense Review*, no. 6, 1982.

"less capable of sustained operation": *Ibid*.

"Essentially it would be": *Ibid*.

"Graceful yet purposeful": *Understanding Soviet Naval Developments*, p. 22.

The Styx missile and the Israeli navy: Yeshayu Ben-Porat *et al.*, *Kippur*, (Tel Aviv: Special Edition Publishers, 1974), pp. 270–74.

Amlie and off-board reflectors: The British did go halfway toward adopting this solution in the Falkland Islands war. They deployed helicopters near their fleet, with reflectors suspended underneath. On the approach of an Exocet, the helicopter would climb abruptly, leaving the missile (which has an altitude limiter) to pass harmlessly underneath. The drawbacks of this method are, firstly, that keeping a helicopter aloft whenever the ship is in danger can be expensive and unreliable business, and secondly, even though the method may decoy the missile away from one target, once decoyed it will proceed to look for another—which was how the British container ship *Atlantic Conveyor* was hit in the Falklands war.

Commander Knuth and the aircraft carriers: "Article Critical of Carriers Stamped 'Secret' by Navy," Washington *Post*, May 4, 1982.

Rickover: Rickover delivered this Parthian shot at the carrier admirals against whom he had battled for so long in his valedictory testimony before the Joint Economic Committee in January 1982.

"Operating against a carrier": Commander John Byron, "The Victim's View of ASW," *Proceedings of the U.S. Naval Institute*, April 1982.

"Within a few years": *Ibid*.

Noisy Alpha: *Newsweek*, February 9, 1981, p. 58.

"People go on about how big": Personal communication.

"A submarine doesn't make much of an impression": *Khrushchev Remembers*, vol. 2, p. 65.

U.S.S. *Liberty*: For a full account of the deliberate and bloody attack on the *Liberty*, see James Ennes, *Assault on the Liberty* (New York: Random House, 1981).

The Ghanian incident: Stephen S. Kaplan, *Diplomacy of Power* (Washington, D.C.: Brookings Institution, 1981), pp. 520–38.

"At a time when Britain possessed": Vagts, *op. cit.*, p. 373.

Ships passively awaited fate in naval exercises: Dismukes and McConnell, *op. cit.* p. 51.

Execution of the Lithuanian officers in 1969: Intelligence source.

Captain Sablin and the *Storozhevoi* mutiny: The documentary sources which I have used, supplemented by information from cognizant intelligence officials, include *Krasnaya zvezda*, December 24, 1974, which carried the report by regular correspondent Captain I. Lysenko on his visit to the *Storozhevoi* (probably in November 1974). Here is an example of the type of goings on on the ship that so shocked Lysenko:

"In an interval, I was told of the following episode. A sailor once returned from the guard room. He had only taken a couple of steps along the deck when he heard 'Hey fellows, Petrov's come back home.' And a minute later the 'fellows' were hugging this man, who had broken discipline. And do you know who you could see among them? Outstanding sailors, class-rated specialists; i.e., men esteemed in the collective. They know how to attain complex norms and carry out accurate missile firings. Everybody can see this and value their worth. But the fact is that these same comrades have fallen down on the ethical front.

"It is true that the sailor who had slipped behind in his service should have had the attention of the collective. But how? Clapping him on the shoulder doesn't help. He was returning from being under arrest. And, having arrived on deck, he should have said to his colleagues, 'Comrades, I stand guilty before you. But I ask you to trust. . . .' And then to show by diligent service he was not trusted in vain. But if the (battery) commander and communists (ship's officers) don't create such circumstances in the battery, then even the strictest rebuke loses half its force."

This may not seem like the snappiest form of journalism, but in the context of *Krasnaya zvezda*'s customary circumlocutions, it was a stinging rebuke of the "communists."

The rest of the article is in a similiar vein. We also learn from it of Grechko's earlier visit to the ship. Sablin is mentioned, but his position as the ship's political officer is mentioned in another *Krasnaya zvezda* article, December 18, 1974.

Chronicle of Current Events, the underground Soviet dissident journal, gave an account of the mutiny in an issue that reached Western correspondents in Moscow in early February 1977. The article said that Sablin had been the leader.

The German press agency DPA reported some bare details of the *Storozhevoi*'s attempted escape in a dispatch with a Stockholm dateline of May 5, 1976.

Bernard Nossiter of the Washington *Post* drew on high-level Swedish military sources for an account of the pursuit of the mutineers (June 6, 1976).

"Mutiny on a Soviet ship": Quoted in *Berlinske Tidende* (Copenhagen), August 11, 1976.

Part VI: Threat Inflation

16: The Consequences of Threat Inflation

"Pentagon officials view": UPI dispatch, as carried in the St. Louis *Post-Dispatch*, June 13, 1982, p. 7A.

"That's a very interesting war": Personal interview with Leslie Cockburn.

Egyptian satisfaction at Israeli air combat victory over Soviets: This was reported by none other than Hosni Mubarak, then commander of the Egyptian air force and later President, when he met with Israeli air force officers, including Motti Hod, after Sadat's visit to Jerusalem.

"the aircraft [that] epitomizes": *Air Force Magazine*, March 1979, p. 5.

"Newly acquired intelligence data": "U.S. Arms Used in Lebanon War Outstrip Soviets," *Wall Street Journal*, August 5, 1982, p. 7. The *Journal*, it should be noted, was not the only paper to pass on the thoughts of Creech. It is worth mentioning one other threat inflationary device much favored in times of crisis, that is, when Soviet weapons are seen to be putting up a poor performance such as in Lebanon. That is the suggestion that the weapons in question are merely "export versions," far inferior in quality to those in the hands of domestic Soviet forces. This tactic was reportedly employed by certain elements in the U.S. Army after the T-72 debacle in Lebanon, implying that the Nizhny Tagil tank plant has an annex in which skilled workers attack completed T-72s that are destined for export with crowbars and hacksaws in order to degrade their performance to a level suitable for operational use by the Syrians or whoever. It should be noted that the analyses of the T-72 in this book are based on evidence emanating from inside the Soviet Union itself, such as a cutaway drawing published in the military journal *Znamenosets* (Standard Bearer).

"according to numerous comments": "Moscow Defends Quality of Arms It Sells to Arabs," New York *Times*, July 2, 1982, p. A5.

"I think you have the reports": Prados, *op. cit.*, p. 45. The author of the remark about "Soviet technological superiority" was General Tom Power.

"tendentiously selected": *Whence the Threat to Peace*, p. 3.

"Every indication pointed to"; Prados, *op. cit.*, p. 43.

"Such a stock of rockets": Prados, *op. cit.*, p. 111.

Heinz Felfe: The best account of the Gehlen organization and Felfe's treachery is E. H. Cookridge, *Spy of the Century* (New York: Random House, 1972).

Soviet ammunition stocks in East Germany: John Erickson, "Soviet Military Capabilities in Europe," *Journal of the Royal United Services Institute for Defense Studies*, vol. 120, no. 3, March 1975.

"They look very good": Personal interview.

"consistently overestimate our capabilities": Fallows, *op. cit.*, p. 75.

"6,000 tanks a year": *Has America Become Number Two?*, Committee on the Present Danger, Washington, D.C., June 1982, p. 13 (the 6,000 figure) and p. 14 (the Defense Intelligence Agency chart).

C-5A cost overruns and cutback of production run: Fitzgerald, *op. cit.*, *passim*.

F-111 and F-14: Tom Gervasi, *Arsenal of Democracy II* (New York: Grove Press, 1981), p. 90.

Original price of M-1: Figure cited in the U.S. Army "fact sheet" on M-1.

Inability to aim the gun: "M-1 Tank Critics Get More Ammo," Chicago *Sun-Times*, September 20, 1982. The reporter's information was derived from the army's own OT 111 test reports.

Perry's riposte: William Perry, "Fallows Fallacies," *International Security*, Spring 1982.

"Performance of military significance": *Ibid.*,

Proportions of defense budget spent by U.S. and Russia on personnel: Perry is particularly fond of this point. In the *International Security* article he puts it this way: "The United States spends more than half of its defense budget on manpower while the Soviets—with twice the manpower—spend only a fourth of theirs on manpower. As a result, they can devote half of their budget to equipment procurement while we devote less than a quarter of ours to equipment. This leads us then to a 'reality' of overriding importance—that even with equal defense budgets, the Soviets can—and do—spend twice as much on equipment procurement as the United States. This fundamental and overwhelming advantage . . . "

To employ Dr. Perry's own blunt mode of delivery: this is rubbish. For a start, the United States does *not* spend over half its military budget on manpower. If one adds up the figures given for outlays on military personnel, retired pay, and housing usefully provided at the back of the Defense Posture Statement delivered annually by the Secretary of Defense, the amounts of FY 1983 come to, respectively, $47.9 billion, $16.5 billion, and $2.8 billion. Added together and calculated as a percentage of the total obligated budget for FY 1983, they come to 26 percent. This continues a trend that should make Dr. Perry very happy, since the amount expended on personnel as a proportion of the budget is going down. For FY 1982 it was 28.2 percent, while for FY 1981 it was 29.8 percent. The CIA paper *Soviet and U.S. Defense Activities, 1971–80: A Dollar Cost Comparison* states: "U.S. personnel costs are about one-fourth of total U.S. outlays (when civilians and retirees are included the share is over 50%); Soviet estimated dollar personnel costs are about one-third of the estimated total cost."

One-fourth for the United States, one-third for the Soviets. Where then does Dr. Perry find the U.S. spending "more than half its defense budget on manpower, while the Soviets . . . spend only a third of theirs on manpower?" The answer must lie with those civilians. Now it is true that the U.S. Defense Department employs just over 1 million personnel (many of them highly paid), plus a further 2 million or so directly employed in military industry. But any valid comparisons with Soviet defense costs should also include the costs of Soviet civilians employed in their defense sector. This is also a large number, perhaps a million working directly for the ministry of defense, plus further millions working in their defense industries. The trouble is no one knows how many, possibly not even the Soviets themselves. Estimates (quoted in Chapter 5) vary between 4 and 7 million. So the only even vaguely reliable figure we can work with is the active manpower cost comparison. If one does want to start factoring in civilian costs on *both* sides, then the considerable, but indeterminate, costs for the Soviets must also be included.

There is one further caveat. The CIA comparison (one-quarter for the U.S., one-third for the Soviets) is a dollar equivalent, meaning that the Soviet manpower costs are calculated on U.S. pay scales (that is, Soviet conscripts are ascribed a salary of $573 a month instead of the $6.50 they actually earn). This obviously has the effect of inflating Soviet personnel costs when calculated in dollar terms. However, the alternative method is to calculate a *ruble* equivalent, that is, to calculate the cost of the U.S. defense budget if the whole U.S. defense effort were to be produced in the Soviet Union. In that case, the Soviet personnel costs, since they would be calculated at the true ruble pay scales (3.50 rubles a month for conscripts), would come down. But since the U.S. personnel costs would also be calculated at Soviet rates, the proportions would stay about the same.

Inferiority of complex and costly weapons compared with their predecessors: These facts were brought out in a somewhat sulphurous encounter between Dr. Perry and defense analyst Pierre M. Sprey at the XXth West Point Senior Conference in June 1982. Sprey had actually taken the trouble to examine the combat effectiveness and reliability of the weapons mentioned here, as well as others. He also pointed out, unkindly in the view of many of those present, that Dr. Perry's thesis so grandly outlined in the Fallows review, Congressional testimony, and the paper that Perry delivered to the conference was riddled with basic factual errors. For example, Perry's claim that the Soviets spend twice as much on procurement as the United States is contradicted even by the CIA's figures, which show the Soviets spending 1.6 as much on procurement as the United States. Perry also claimed that complex modern Soviet weapons cost the same as U.S. weapons, a statement contradicted by his own FY 1982 statement to the Congress, in which he stated that, in dollar terms, in 1980 U.S. tactical aircraft on the average cost 2.67 times as much as such Soviet aircraft, while average U.S. land-force equipment cost 2.1 times as much as similar Soviet equipment.

Sprey's formal paper for the conference was entitled "The Case for More Effective, Less Expensive Weapon Systems: What 'Quality Versus

Quantity' Issue?" His rebuttal of Perry's paper came in the form of an oral lecture with slides and was called "Dr. Perry's Case for 'Quality.'"

More expensive weapons being produced in fewer numbers: For a trenchant analysis of how the Reagan "build-up" is actually leading to a decline in the American force structure, see George Kuhn, "Defense," in *Agenda '83*, Washington, D.C., The Heritage Foundation, 1982.

"Every war is fought": Vagts, *op. cit.*, p. 13.

The German General Staff and nitrates: Borkin, *The Crime and Punishment of I. G. Farben*, pp. 14–15. It should be noted that the General Staff, unsure that the chemists of I. G. Farben would be able to come to their rescue in time, dispatched a fleet to capture the Falkland Islands, which would thus enable them to break the British blockade of the supply route from Chile. The British took measures to stop them—which were ultimately successful—but without having the slightest idea why the Germans should be so interested in the sea route from Chile.

The French and phenol: Vagts, *op. cit.*, p. 352.

"The military of all countries": *Ibid.*, p. 375.

Index

517

About the Author

ANDREW COCKBURN was born in 1947 and grew up in Ireland. He was educated at Trinity College, Glenalmond in Scotland and at Worcester College, Oxford. A contributing editor of *Defense Week*, he has specialized in defense issues for the last nine years, both for newspapers and magazines and for British and American documentary television programs. *The Red Army*, which he produced for PBS, won the George Foster Peabody Prize for documentary television in 1982. Mr. Cockburn lives in New York with his wife and daughter.